Advance Praise

Just as the dynamics of capitalism shuts down opportunities for labour organizing, it can also open up new possibilities. In this important book Ashok Kumar traces the history and geographical spread of the garment industry, how retailers have secured ever more power that has led to the restructuring of the global production chain and increased the structural power of the most exploited workers. Exemplary engaged research that challenges the fatalism accompanying neoliberalism.

Michael Burawoy, University of California, Berkeley

With surgical precision, Ashok Kumar opens up key sites in global supply chains to rigorous investigation and offers urgent insights about how sweatshops work, and how they might work differently. Powerful and profoundly illuminating, this book is a must-read for all those concerned with labour and its movements, and supply chain capitalism and its alternatives.

Deborah Cowen, University of Toronto

A major theoretical and empirical contribution to our understanding of the evolving state of contemporary global industrial capitalism.

David Harvey, City University of New York

The sweatshop economy is pervasive in today's global capitalism. Ashok Kumar charts its evolution, shows how market power is becoming concentrated, and also charts the rise of worker resistance which exploits vulnerabilities in the new production systems.

Richard Hyman, London School of Economics and Political Science

Unlike many a book on capitalism and labour, Ashok Kumar not only goes global, but also, most significantly, moves into the innards of the most labour-intensive sectors. Thus, beyond the familiar narratives of exploitation, he proposes a theory of monopsony power in global value chains which brings together the inner logics of capital and the collective power of workers in analysing the evolution of the sweatshop.

Saskia Sassen, Columbia University

Monopsony Capitalism

Monopsony Capitalism explores the combination of capital's changing composition and labour's subjective agency to examine whether the waning days of the 'sweatshop' have indeed begun. Focused on the garment and footwear sectors – which epitomize the leading edges in the advance of globalization and the spread of vertically disintegrated value chains – the book introduces a universal logic that governs competition and reshapes the chain. Simply put, deregulation produces high degrees of monopsony power, increasing the value share for the lead firm. This intensifies competition, exerts downward pressure, and winnows the number of suppliers able to compete. The result is supplier-end consolidation. Consolidation increases the surviving suppliers' share of value, which expands access to finance, facilitates self-investment, and raises entry barriers. In 2005, the *regulatory* regime that had once enforced a degree of spatial inflexibility finally dwindled to nothing with the phase-out of the Multi-Fibre Agreement (MFA). The subsequent emergence of *market* spatial inflexibility, which gives labour new openings, occurs with free, unrestricted flows between supplier and buyer.

This book analyses workers' collective action at various sites of production primarily in China, India, Honduras, and United States, and secondarily in Vietnam, Cambodia, Bangladesh, and Indonesia. It observes how this internal logic plays out for labour who are testing the limits of the social order, stretching it until the seams show, and making it possible for bosses to come to the proverbial table, hat in hand, to hash out agreements with those who assemble their goods. By examining the most valorized parts of underdeveloped sectors, one can see where capital is going and how it is getting there. The findings contribute to ongoing strategies to bolster workers' bargaining power in sectors plagued by poverty, powerlessness, and perilous workplaces. Indeed, with these changes in global capitalism and a capable labour movement, there's hope yet that workers may close the gap.

Ashok Kumar is Lecturer in International Political Economy at the School of Business, Economics and Informatics at Birkbeck, University of London.

Development Trajectories in Global Value Chains

A feature of the current phase of globalization is the outsourcing of production tasks and services across borders, and the increasing organization of production and trade through global value chains (GVCs), global commodity chains (GCCs), and global production networks (GPNs). With a large and growing literature on GVCs, GCCs, and GPNs, this series is distinguished by its focus on the implications of these new production systems for economic, social, and regional development.

This series publishes a wide range of theoretical, methodological, and empirical works, both research monographs and edited volumes, dealing with crucial issues of transformation in the global economy. How do GVCs change the ways in which lead and supplier firms shape regional and international economies? How do they affect local and regional development trajectories, and what implications do they have for workers and their communities? How is the organization of value chains changing and how are these emerging forms contested as more traditional structures of North–South trade complemented and transformed by emerging South–South lead firms, investments, and trading links? How does the large-scale entry of women into value-chain production impact on gender relations? What opportunities and limits do GVCs create for economic and social upgrading and innovation? In what ways are GVCs changing the nature of work and the role of labor in the global economy? And how might the increasing focus on logistics management, financialization, or social standards and compliance portend important developments in the structure of regional economies?

This series includes contributions from all disciplines and interdisciplinary fields and approaches related to GVC analysis, including GCCs and GPNs, and is particularly focused on theoretically innovative and informed works that are grounded in the empirics of development related to these approaches. Through their focus on changing organizational forms, governance systems, and production relations, volumes in this series contribute to on-going conversations about theories of development and development policy in the contemporary era of globalization.

Series editors

Stephanie Barrientos is Professor of Global Development at the Global Development Institute, University of Manchester.

Gary Gereffi is Professor of Sociology and Director of the Global Value Chains Center, Duke University.

Dev Nathan is Visiting Professor at the Institute for Human Development, New Delhi, and Visiting Research Fellow at the Global Value Chains Center, Duke University.

John Pickles is Earl N. Phillips Distinguished Professor of International Studies at the University of North Carolina, Chapel Hill.

Titles in the Series

1. Labour in Global Value Chains in Asia
   Edited by *Dev Nathan, Meenu Tewari and Sandip Sarkar*
2. The Sweatshop Regime: Laboring Bodies, Exploitation and Garments
   Made in India
   Alessandra Mezzadri
3. The Intangible Economy: How Services Shape Global Production and Consumption
   Edited by *Deborah K. Elms, Arian Hassani and Patrick Low*
4. Making Cars in the New India: Industry, Precarity and Informality
   Tom Barnes
5. Development with Global Value Chains: Upgrading and Innovation in Asia
   Edited by *Dev Nathan, Meenu Tewari and Sandip Sarkar*
6. Global Value Chains and Development: Redefining the Contours of 21st Century Capitalism
   Gary Gereffi
7. Gender and Work in Global Value Chains: Capturing the Gains?
   Stephanie Barrientos

Monopsony Capitalism
Power and Production in the Twilight of the Sweatshop Age

Ashok Kumar

CAMBRIDGE UNIVERSITY PRESS

CAMBRIDGE
UNIVERSITY PRESS

University Printing House, Cambridge CB2 8BS, United Kingdom

One Liberty Plaza, 20th Floor, New York, NY 10006, USA

477 Williamstown Road, Port Melbourne, vic 3207, Australia

314 to 321, 3rd Floor, Plot No.3, Splendor Forum, Jasola District Centre, New Delhi 110025, India

79 Anson Road, #06–04/06, Singapore 079906

Cambridge University Press is part of the University of Cambridge.

It furthers the University's mission by disseminating knowledge in the pursuit of education, learning and research at the highest international levels of excellence.

www.cambridge.org
Information on this title: www.cambridge.org/9781108731973

© Ashok Kumar 2020

This publication is in copyright. Subject to statutory exception and to the provisions of relevant collective licensing agreements, no reproduction of any part may take place without the written permission of Cambridge University Press.

First published 2020

Printed in India by Shree Maitrey Printech Pvt. Ltd., Noida

A catalogue record for this publication is available from the British Library

ISBN 978-1-108-73197-3 Paperback

Cambridge University Press has no responsibility for the persistence or accuracy of URLs for external or third-party internet websites referred to in this publication, and does not guarantee that any content on such websites is, or will remain, accurate or appropriate.

To Amma & Appaji for everything

Contents

List of Figures	*xiii*
Acknowledgements	*xv*
Introduction: The Enduring Age of the Sweatshop	1

PAST

1 The Bottleneck	17
2 The Global Sweatshop	52

PRESENT

3 China: A Strike at a Giant Footwear Producer	89
4 India: A Warehouse Workers' Struggle at a 'Full-Package' Denim Firm	120
5 Honduras: A Transnational Campaign at a Cotton Commodity Producer	144

FUTURE

6 Cartels of Capital	173
7 Labour's Power in the Chain	205
Conclusion: The Twilight of the Sweatshop Age?	229
Bibliography	237
Index	267

Figures

I.1	Rana Plaza	3
1.1	Sourcing Price of $2 for basic men T-shirt – retail price $15	21
2.1	Price-settlement committee assesses in order to determine price, ultimately settled between jobber, contractor, and union (est. 1950s)	61
2.2	Striking dressmakers take a break in a diner, 1955	65
3.1	Striking workers at Yue Yuen Facility, Dongguan, China, 23 April 2014	105
3.2	Workers at Pou Yuen in Ho Chi Minh City gather for talks	108
4.1	Garment workers on wildcat strike, 2016, Bangalore	132
5.1	A union sign attached to a sewing machine at JND reads, 'We demand fair wages.' 2 April 2013	159
5.2	JDH union leaders Moises Montoya and Norma Chavarria at University of Minnesota, 13 February 2011	166

Acknowledgements

This book, like many, distils years of conversations and experiences, but also the input of contacts, translations, co-authorship, commenters, as well as the wise counsel of friends. Though I think it offers an original framework for understanding the logic of global capitalism and the role of worker power, I cannot say that any of the ideas advanced originates with me.

I am indebted to comrades who taught me early the value of internationalism which helped shape this book. A short and by no means exhaustive list would include the following: Joel Feingold, for countless late-night debates – always offering precise and practical comments for my writing (like for the title of this book). Charlie Hoyt for sharpening my early commitment to trade union democracy. Jack Mahoney, whose collaboration helped form Latin American contacts and my initial analysis. Indeed, some of the interviews in Chapter 5 can also be found in our paper in *Journal of Labor and Society* (see Kumar and Mahoney 2014). Thanks to Liana Dalton for connecting me to trade unionists in Cambodia and Turkey. To Teresa Cheng for connecting me to activists in China (and the minor feats of redirecting my PhD research and first piquing my interest in the global, rather than just domestic, dimensions of labour). A large debt is owed to the insights of Jeff Hermanson, whom I frequently bounced ideas off while conceiving this book.

Jane Wills, Amy Horton, Adrian Smith, Louis Hartnoll, Maia Pal, Alberto Toscano, Nicholas Simcik-Arese, Liam Campling, and Philippa Williams provided invaluable advice in the early stages of the proposal. A primitive version of Chapters 3 and 4 were part of my PhD thesis and were read by my supervisors at Oxford, Linda McDowell and Craig Jeffrey, and my viva assessors, Danny Dorling and Kevin Ward. These chapters were read later by Eli Friedman, Hannah Schling, Dalia Gebrial, Eric Hoyt, and Lukas Slothuus as well as by members of Queen Mary University's Centre for Labour and Global Production. I benefited immensely from their commentary. Earlier versions of these chapters were published in *Competition and Change* and *Global Networks* (Kumar 2019a, 2019b), respectively. My more recent collaborations with Giorgos Galanis, as well as our brilliant PhD student, Takis Iliopoulos, have contributed to some of the theories detailed in the later chapters.

A special gratitude is reserved for my friends and comrades Leila Cass-Darweish, Becka Hudson, Rosa Gilbert, David Broder, Sai Englert, Annie Teriba, Matt Hall, Maev McDaid, Ben Rose, Emir Nader, Carl Williams, Donald Spann, Henry Lodge, Aberon Truneh, Dan Cunix, Shriya Blon, Amber Sethi, Matt Mellen, Romi Revola, Dan Oldfield, Emily Fu, Philip Proudfoot, Natasha Jones, Sebastian Budgen, Olivia Herbert, Sophie Carapetian, Elif Sarican, Nathan Gayle, Carl Williams, Donald Spann, Chi Chi Shi, Matt Cole, John Merrick, Bethan Bowett-Jones, Henry Lodge, and Rob Knox who have contributed in various ways to my thinking and supported me along the way. I am particularly grateful to my brother Chetan whose political commitment to justice and equality continues to inspire. A special shout-out is owed to my frequent writing partner, Alex Gawenda, whose editorial acumen has always enhanced my work. Thanks also to John Kelly for his guidance and mentorship at Birkbeck.

Thanks to the issue editors, anonymous peer reviewers, as well as the gentle reassurances of my editor at CUP, Anwesha Rana, who, despite my obviously annoying delays, allowed me to proceed at my own pace. I am grateful to the Fulbright committee for funding my initial research on Sri Lanka's garment workers and to the generous funding by the Leverhulme Trust as well as Birkbeck University of London, which offered me the time and space to write this. Finally, to the many workers and organizers who sat down with me, gave me their time, and told me their stories.

Introduction

The Enduring Age of the Sweatshop

> It is not the consciousness of men that determines their existence, but on the contrary, their social existence that determines their consciousness.
> – Karl Marx

On 23 April 2013, a national strike or *hartal*, called by the official opposition to Bangladesh's ruling Awami League, was in its third day and traffic in Dhaka was lighter than usual. Factory owners were under pressure to get their employees back to work. Only a few weeks earlier, the Bangladesh Garment Manufacturers and Exporters Association had reported that the combined cost of recent *hartal*s was estimated at $500 million. Workers were scarce throughout the area's industrial corridors, but could still be found in Rana Plaza, a towering structure that loomed over the Dhaka-Aricha Highway. There, 20 miles from Dhaka in the town of Savar Upsala, on the main artery connecting the city to its garment districts in the suburbs, some five thousand workers worked on eight cramped floors, making clothes for Walmart, Primark, Mango, Benetton, and other Western brands.

Like a Bollywood villain, the man who owned the place could be seen driving around the town on his motorcycle, 'as untouchable as a mafia don', accompanied by several paid heavies.[1] His name was Sohel Rana and he had acquired the land for his five-factory complex – which he humbly named after himself – through threats and intimidation, obtained building permits through bribes and graft, and constructed its top floors with no regard to government regulations. His position as Secretary of the local student chapter of the Awami League had enabled him to exercise control over local strikes and use them as bargaining chips. Rumours about guns and drug smuggling on the side had long been circulated.

The sound of an explosion echoed through Sohel Rana's third floor. Terrified workers ran outside and were told by supervisors to leave early. An engineer,

---

[1] This quote, the estimated $500 million cost of the *hartal*s, and the quote later from Sohel Rana are sourced from Yardley's (2013) *New York Times* profile.

Abdur Razzak, was called in to inspect the deep cracks that now appeared in the concrete pillars and walls. He warned that the building was structurally unsound, declaring it 'vulnerable'. But Rana would not accept this verdict. As reporters arrived on the scene, he gestured at the damage, explaining, 'This is not a crack … the plaster on the wall is broken, nothing more. It is not a problem.' A lone journalist, Nazmul Huda, later snuck inside to carry out his own investigation, but was chased away by Rana's men after recording only a few minutes of the film. The story was broadcast on the local news that evening.

Factory owners were under constant pressure to produce more for less – and quicker. Those who could somehow keep apace would be rewarded with big contracts. Those who could not, would go under. A transnational competition was underway, turning local regulations into hindrances, and productivity a religion. In these circumstances, where other variables were effectively controlled by the absence of capital reserves at the point of production, survival came down to what could be wrung from workers at the least expense.

However, Rana Plaza was running again the next morning. Word of the incident had spread around the neighbouring slums, the *basti*s, and many had stayed home out of fear. Others gathered outside the factory but refused to enter until their safety had been guaranteed. At Rana's instructions, supervisors ordered workers to their stations or face penalties. Jason Motlagh (2014) profiled one of the garment workers, employed by the Ether Tex factory:

> Upon the fifth story, amid Ether Tex's sprawling rows of electric sewing machines and fluorescent lights, the mood was charged with anxious chatter over how bad the cracks really were. Paki and her coworkers approached a supervisor to voice their worries but were reminded of a fast-approaching shipment deadline for an important Western client: If they protested any further, he told them, they would lose a month's wages.

At 9 a.m., an hour after the workers were made to enter on pain of lost wages, the Rana Plaza complex collapsed. Of the 3,100, mostly women, workers employed on that day at the site, 1,129 perished and many more were injured. It marked the deadliest structural failure in modern human history.

This was not an isolated case. The previous November, a fire raged through Dhaka's Tarzeen Fashion Factory killing 112 and injuring 200. Tarzeen had been producing clothes for Walmart, Sears, and Disney. The last four months of that year, 2012, were particularly deadly. There were three other factory fires in three different countries that, including the Tarzeen disaster, took nearly 500 lives, concluding what was by then the deadliest year in history for sweatshop workers. Just four months later, Rana Plaza broke all records.

Figure I.1 Rana Plaza

Source: Taslima Akhter.

First as tragedy

Unionization in 'sweatshops' is a Sisyphean task. Workers – decomposed and dispensable – organize on their own intuitively and with great difficulty, given the circumstances. But when they demand recognition as unions or take strike action, the factory owners retaliate – often viciously. Even if workers succeed in outlasting the owners, the now-unionized factories come under threat from their buyers (Nike, Adidas, GAP, and so on) who are liable to 'cut-and-run' to the next factory, where labour is still unorganized and, therefore, much cheaper. Time and again across the Third World,[2] from Central America to Africa, from Pakistan to the Philippines, attempts by workers to organize have been crushed in much the same manner by a hyper-mobile 'globalized' capital.

This paradigm of hyper-mobile capital is marked by a retreat of the state as the realm of workplace conflict resolution. Thus, the struggle for rights and

---

[2] I use the terms 'Third World', 'Global South', and 'emerging economies' interchangeably. 'Third World' was used to describe a project rather than a place during anti-colonial struggles (Prashad 2007), but its use is increasingly marginal. Frequently, the term 'emerging markets' is preferred in the pages of the *Financial Times* or within MBA programmes.

higher wages only accentuates injustices. As one of the leading edges in the advance of globalization and the spread of vertically disintegrated supply chains (those giving buyers their pick of suppliers), garment and footwear epitomize this tension.[3] It has been the central problem of trade unions and their global anti-sweatshop allies. While there has been a fundamental geographical shift over the last century, the dynamics of workplace struggle feel frozen in time – an enduring age of the sweatshop. Workers – women, mostly – bent over sewing machines, producing clothes for the better-off in London, New York, Paris, and, in its latest stage, for the entrepôt cities of Bangalore, Bangkok, and Guangzhou. Any attempt to organize on the shop floor faces stiff and often violent resistance from management, Pinkertons, and police, followed by capital flight in quick succession.

The Rana Plaza tragedy is often compared to the smaller 1911 Triangle Shirtwaist Factory fire that killed 146 in New York City. The same macroeconomic dynamics which created the Triangle Shirtwaist disaster – now a solemn milestone discussed in American history textbooks – still hold sway, but on a global scale. Like Rana, the Triangle Shirtwaist Factory was located in the top floors of a complex well known for its dangers. The factory was run by strongmen in a city rife with corruption, employing almost exclusively young women. In the decades leading up to the Triangle Shirtwaist disaster, New York City's garment district had become a locus for domestic apparel production. As tales of shopfloor crowding and long hours in the district's lower east side factories gradually made their way into the press, the term 'sweatshop' entered the public American lexicon.

Englishman Charles Kingsley first defined the sweatshop in 1849 in a pamphlet entitled *Politics of the People*. The 'sweated system,' he wrote, 'is a surviving remnant of the industrial system which preceded the factory system, when industry was chiefly conducted on the piece-price plan, in small shops or the homes of the workers.' In short, the sweatshop was defined by the factories' outsourced position in the value chain. As economist John R. Commons explained in 1901, 'In the factory system the workmen are congregated where they can be seen by the factory inspectors and where they can organise or develop a common understanding. In the sweating system they are isolated and unknown.' By the turn of the twentieth century, sweatshop had become synonymous with the garment sectors.

---

[3] Within this book, 'garment sector' includes footwear, except when explicitly stated otherwise or in reference to the Multi-Fibre Agreement (MFA) which does not include footwear. This is addressed comprehensively in Chapter 3.

However, an increase in union density in the 1930s witnessed declining sweatshop conditions in the sectors. From the 1940s through the 1960s, a confluence of factors served to open the door for the relocation of factories from the Northeast, which were free of so-called right-to-work laws (let us call these states 'right to organize') to right-to-work states in the South, as well as Southern California.[4] These included the Northeast labour shortage concomitant with World War II, large government contracts for military uniforms, the success of union collective bargaining of 'jobbers' agreements' increasing the union density of the International Ladies' Garments Workers Union (ILGWU), and the passage of the anti-union Taft-Hartley Act (1947). As the ILGWU continued expending resources, 'chas[ing] the runaways', unions' bargaining power had begun to wane and the quality of contracts declined.[5] By the late 1960s, the sweatshop had returned – typified in the garment sector – with US brands outsourcing to Global South factories – first to Mexico, then to Central America, and finally across China and the rest of Asia.

Power within the garment sector turns on a twin axis: that on which workers and factory owners are balanced and which connects disaggregated producers – that is, factory owners – to buyers. Low barriers to entry for production have thrown small firms into larger and larger bidding wars for contracts with a relatively static number of retailers and brands. This created enormous incentives to drive down costs in production (Anner, Bair, and Blasi 2012), keeping margins thin and making for a production environment of low-value firms, with small factories and unsophisticated technology (Dicken 2007). The most elastic variables are labour cost and labour intensity. These value chains are therefore 'buyer-driven' (Gereffi 1994, 2002), since they develop according to the demands of brands and retailers. Organizing labour within this structure, for better pay and working conditions, can only lead to order-loss, as prices go up and buyers disappear. It creates a 'race to the bottom', where failure to maintain labour discipline becomes an existential threat for producers (Ross 2004).

This has created a geo-economy of supply chains determined by retailers as well as brand-name merchandisers who, by selecting manufacturers globally, accumulate enormous profits and power away from those who produce the goods. By exploiting geographic differentiation in costs, a large reserve army of labour, and the restructuring of state regulation, capital has been able to construct tighter

---

[4] Harvey (2014) claims that by the 1960s, labour unions were pushing for the centralization of workers' rights which led big capital to ensure the ongoing decentralization through 'states" rights.

[5] Phone interview, Jeff Hermanson, 12 August 2013.

and tighter complex supply chains and has succeeded in transforming the global apparel industry into one of the most horizontally internationalist and vertically outsourced areas of production in the world. This has left manufacturing firms under the constant threat of brands/retailers ending orders which in turn puts constant downward pressure on workers.

The history of the impact of Global North activism on Global South garment labourers is complex and contradictory. In a major victory, pressure by unions in the Global North produced the international MFA in 1974, establishing 30-year import quotas for garments and textiles produced in the Global South. However, it would only ever be a stopgap, targeting one factor in a larger process. The cheaper labour costs of the unorganized Global South continued to lure the major players, who were able to manage transnational empires much more effectively through advances in telecommunication and transportation. Ultimately, the MFA did little to stay the collapse of the garment industry in the Global North. From 1990 to 2004, the US sector contracted by as much as 60 per cent (Moran 2010). As footwear tariffs and others were relaxed over the years, the MFA, particular to garments and textiles, remained one of the few checks on this process. But even when restrained, value nonetheless accrued to buyers sitting at the top of the chain, widening the power gap separating them from workers.

Since previous efforts by established American and European garment unions to stem the globalization of their work rested on protectionist measures, such as the MFA – which proved ineffective, and mere speedbumps in the process – links were eventually made with their burgeoning counterparts in the Global South. Once an understanding of the broader, macroeconomic dynamics in which both parties were caught up was established, new ideas could emerge.

Enter the anti-sweatshop movement of the late 1990s. Traditionally, most labour strategies in the garment and footwear sectors were sited on the shop floor. However, the above-mentioned difficulties – of setting workers at a spatio-political remove from the real centres of power (transnational brands and retailers) – forced innovation. It was from this crucible that the campaign for 'ethical consumption' – sited in the Global North – was born. It was hoped that raising awareness of sweatshop horrors among Global North shoppers would force brands into more ethical sourcing habits – and to swallow the costs.

US-based labour union UNITE HERE (the modern, multi-sectoral incarnation of the ILGWU that now goes by the name of Workers United) made its last successful stand in organizing thousands of workers at over 30 Guess Jeans cut and sew shops in Los Angeles Basin. The company immediately responded by relocating its production to Tehuacan, Mexico. UNITE leaders, however, refused to allow UNITE organizers to 'follow the work' and organize the Tehuacan workers.[6]

This precipitated a campaign to target consumers, fighting for hearts and minds where compliance was not enforced by market mechanisms. Linking up with the 'global justice movement', it began building activist networks on campuses, trade unions, and urban centres – bringing international attention to millions of garment workers in the Global South. Soon 'sweatshop' was a household term, shrouded in ignominy. Clothing tags now tell a story of sweat and misery exacted from workers in far-flung corners of the world. But even as the anti-sweatshop movement joined other activist groups in the early 2000s to form a broad front against neoliberal capitalism (first forged at the 'Battle of Seattle' in 1999), its capacity to affect the shop floor remained infinitesimal since the basic constitution of the industry had not been altered. Shopper-shaming damaged reputations but not sales (the low prices proved too attractive and there were few alternatives). Over time, a sense of resignation took hold among labour activists; after so much work, barely a dent had been made. As Jeff Ballinger (2009: 23) observed, it seemed like 'nearly twenty years of anti-sweatshop activism [had] come to naught'.

In spite of the apparent success in 'raising awareness' of how the industry's sausage was made, little was done (nor could be done) to alter its basic structure and shield it from market forces. And so as globalization rolled on, bringing new environs into capital's sweep and expanding the market floor without enlarging its apex, competition – and thus exploitation – intensified apace. Soon buyers were able to shuttle capital not only from town to town and village to village but also from country to country and continent to continent, expanding their operations and fleeing even rumours of organized labour or regulation with newfound ease. More and more small sellers (producers) were thrown into competition to accommodate the same handful of large buyers (brands/retailers), who exercised enormous power over the production process. Attempts at the time, like that of UNITE HERE, to place simultaneous pressure at the top and the bottom of the value chain, and ally consumers with workers in production, only achieved what was possible without addressing the larger questions of globalization – that is, small Pyrrhic victories – but would lay the groundwork for the later changes of

---

[6] Ironically, a few years later, the Tehuacan workers rebelled against their employers, then producing for Gap, and many of the factories were closed as the brands relocated production to China.

the organic composition of capital and those struggling against or within it that form the subject of this book.[7]

The organizers from the Bangalore-based Garment and Textile Workers' Union (GATWU), with whom I was working, were pushing the same rock up the same hill, in every city and village. For this project, I was reunited with Pratibha and Jayram, key GATWU organizers, whom I had met some 10 years before, as an undergrad, while conducting my first bout of labour research. They and their cohorts were flitting about Karnataka, building union chapters and offering assistance where conflicts had broken out with management.

The union used a 'hot shop' organizing model, following the trail of labour unrest from case to case, factory to factory, establishing and strengthening union footholds. There was never a shortage of workplace conflicts, and the four to five full-time organizers were always busy. In a month, I visited Mysore, where workers were trying to stop a planned closure; Kolar, where new factories had appeared when the gold mines closed; and Ramnagara, a warehouse town outside of Bangalore.

I hear you speak Kannada

It was early evening in Mysore when I received a call from an unknown number. The South Asia field representative of the Workers' Rights Consortium (WRC) was on the phone.

> Workers' and their family members have been attacked. A worker is now in the hospital. We're going to initiate an investigation immediately and we are in need of an interpreter – I hear you speak Kannada.

The town of Ramnagara lies 30 miles southwest of Bangalore on the Mysore–Bangalore highway. It is famous for its silk production and has the highest concentration of silk cocoons in Asia. Recently, its location has acquired strategic importance for the circulation of production in and out of the state of Karnataka. The warehouse under WRC investigation was owned by Arvind Mills and was located at a critical geographic node, with finished products packaged and made ready for distribution across India and the Middle East.

---

[7] Of course, it is not as simple as that. Workers' strategies are moulded through victories and failures. Indeed, had UNITE provided resources and persevered, it might have established strong unions in Central America; and that could have demonstrated the viability of a strategy of international solidarity organizing which might have been extended to Asia in time.

I was already familiar with the case before I was asked to come down and interpret for the investigation. I had visited the city with GAWTU's Jayram a number of times and knew that workers at the warehouse had been organizing, incurring the violent wrath of management. I interviewed the worker who was attacked that day and accompanied him to the local police station where he attempted to file a report. As he talked to the officers inside, co-workers and sympathizers gathered outside. The factory's management was called to the site and after several hours the Chief of Police went outside and addressed the crowd. 'Go back to your homes and leave this trade union business,' he said. 'The union will offer you nothing. Look what it did to the factories in Bangalore, they are all packing and leaving. Is that what you want for us?' As we left, a number of young men, who I later learned were hired by the factory management, approached us and began making threats of violence – I pulled out my audio and clicked *record*. The next day I sent the audio to international campaigners. The following day I received a call from the WRC.

We arrived at the warehouse to find that Arvind management and a representative from Phillips Van Heusen (PVH), the world's largest shirt and neckwear conglomerate, were already waiting. The investigation began from the bottom. First, we interviewed workers chosen by management, then we interviewed management and security guards, and, finally, near the end of the day, we spoke with Arvind's Executive Vice-President.

As I translated, I tried to situate the conversations within the theories I had been taught. Garment and footwear brands pulled the strings, and factory owners were their helpless accomplices. Workers on the shop floor were grist for the mill, with no bargaining power. These were the bald facts. By the day's end, this orthodoxy would start to unravel.

Rather than prosecute an adversarial case on behalf of the worker (as a response to consumer pressures to avert reputational damage), the PVH representative seemed to be on the side of the Arvind executive, defending his points and conceding her own, wherever they conflicted. It quickly became clear that there was another layer in the power dynamics at play. The Arvind executive did not feel obliged to give an inch to PVH, throwing his weight around like a bull in the proverbial china shop of accepted global value chain (GVC) theory – secure in PVH's ongoing business.

What I witnessed came into direct conflict with foundational truths in the study of clothing value chains. It was understood that global brands in garment and footwear resort primarily to what Harvey (2006) calls a 'spatial fix' rather than a technological or organizational fix, which was central to the historic growth strategy of global brands and retailers. These various 'fixes' represent the intrinsic mechanism by capital to overcome its inherent crisis tendency. The garment value chain relies on the unequal power dynamic of many suppliers and few buyers – *monopsony*. The result is a low level of surplus value capture at the production phase of the supply chain, which ensures chronically low capital investment in industrial upgrading.

In short, the long-established rules of the game are as follows: fragmentation and low capital investment in garment and footwear value chains had created low barriers to entry, resulting in bidding wars between thousands of smaller firms from around the world (or a high degree of monopsony power [DMP]). These chains were 'buyer-driven' (Gereffi 1994a) insofar as brands and retailers commanded them. Global brands/retailers rewarded firms with the lowest labour costs, resulting in persistent downward pressure on workers. Within this dynamic, worker action or organization resulted in order-loss, and so the global race to the bottom entailed labour discipline. This structure of the garment and footwear value chain drew value to the top of the supply chain, to global brands/retailers, further curtailing the structural power of labour. Finding themselves thrown out of work by Pyrrhic victories over factory owners, and too isolated to pressure international brands, workers appealed often to 'anti-sweatshop' allies in the Global North to increase sourcing prices to manufacturers and make them more responsible for labour rights. Thus, the spatial and political distanciation between areas of value creation and value capture left workers without a means of direct resistance, which the Global North–based anti-sweatshop movement attempted to ameliorate, specifically by endeavouring to relocate the site of struggle from the sphere of production to the sphere of consumption.

On the ride back to Bangalore, after day one of the Arvind investigation, I told myself that this had been an anomaly or had involved a personal relationship I was unaware of. But when I asked the WRC investigator his thoughts, he told me that this was not an isolated phenomenon but rather one that he had been seeing with increasing frequency. I would soon discover that large and growing production firms with increasingly brazen executives were not even unique to India. Rather, they were part of a global process, tracing its roots to the liberalization of trade and more specifically the 2005 end of the global quota system: MFA.

In this book, I propose a dynamic *universal* logic to global value chains in which DMP is reflected in the bargaining power of workers. This logic is based on the underlying forces of competition, in which value chains everywhere are subject to similar laws of motion, and workers everywhere are driven by a common set of interests and aspirations, albeit with diverse strategies of resistance shaped by any number of contingent factors (that is, cultural mores, state labour regimes, and so on).

My application of this logic to the contemporary garment sector is as follows: In accordance with existing theories, as we moved into the post-MFA era of the mid/late 2000s, trade liberalization resulted in a high DMP for buyers in garment GVCs. This resulted in a high share of value being captured by increasingly oligopolistic buyers. The drive by buyers to maximize profits and the high DMP amongst suppliers resulted in a falling source price offered by buyers, increasing the downward pressure on suppliers. Under these conditions, fewer and fewer suppliers were able to compete. The result was the weakening of globalized competition and falling DMP. An almost endless pool of small garment firms across the globe began to steadily disappear, absorbed into larger rivals or forced to merge. In place of the numerous small firms grew the now-ascendant megaproducers in the most valorized sections of the sector, concentrated in a handful of labour-rich countries. Meanwhile, large retailer/brand oligopolies have come to simultaneously benefit from growing profits brought on by economies of scale and integration while becoming gradually dependent on increasingly oligopolistic outsourced manufacturers. What emerges is an increasingly calcified *symbiosis* – locking-in global buyers with global suppliers – intensifying the integration of supplier-end capital; horizontally, as factories grow larger; and vertically, from factory to warehousing, logistics to retail. Increased access to finance is reinvested into labour-saving technology, catalysing the erecting of insurmountable barriers to entry, which steel-reinforces the producers' market position. Greater value capture at the bottom of the global supply chain closes the historical and geographical gap between spaces of value capture and value creation.

The emergence of large oligopolistic producers changes who is in the driver's seat of sectoral GVC governance, altering the power relations for all the actors within it. Under the period of embedded liberalism (end of World War II to the 1970s), a higher degree of regulatory spatial inflexibility contributed to greater bargaining power for workers. As that regime ended and capital became more spatially flexible, workers' bargaining fell with it. Now, as DMP falls, the degree of spatial flexibility falls with it. In response, workers' bargaining power steadily grows. Indeed, these changes in the value chain do not necessarily result in higher wages and benefits for workers on the shop floor, but, in totality, *increase the possibilities* for workers to bargain with their – now value-laden and increasingly powerful – direct employers.

All work exploits (but some more than most)

This book is neither about grand narratives regarding the end of capitalism or the rise of China nor is it a compendium of the well-documented suffering endured by garment workers nearly everywhere. But rather, as its banner suggests, it introduces a theory of global value chains as shaped through DMP to map the future of what are called sweatshops. While the sweatshop is mostly an affective definition, by journalistic and literary convention, it evokes a scene of intense labour in cramped quarters, and the stench of the eponymous fluid. But to trade unionists, a sweatshop might be any workplace without a form of collective bargaining. In the West, sweatshops are something far away, whose faint outline, of exploited labour and passive misery – much of it of children's – can be seen in the Third World provenance listed on clothing tags. However, child labour and many other conditions of these stereotypes have successfully been abolished in export-oriented production (though it is of course impossible to determine their *absolute* extinction). Meanwhile, many other forms of highly exploitive labour – domestic work, farm labour, and service work – endure, untrammelled. This book looks at the sector most associated with the sweatshop. So, the title is an observation of a tendency but also a question – pursued through in-depth cases and analysis of broader trends.

I begin answering this question by looking at the sector itself and the history of the sweatshop within it, then proceed to describe its modern phase in the globalized age. Reactions to this new, transnational economic epoch have been mixed. Some are giddy at the prospect of a new global working class and insist every Third World labour campaign signals either the emergence of a Polanyian 'double movement' or the expanding army of what Marx termed 'capitalism's gravedigger'. Others despair at the concomitant destruction of First World unions, and the introduction of the Third World to the immiseration that unions were conceived to mitigate. And others still are ambivalent, holding their breath while anticipating the dialectical synthesis.

I take what we know about these sectors and build on that knowledge by situating them within a historical and geographic context. This deployment of various lenses should be viewed as a form of triangulation – an approach that holds that an object is best viewed from different vantage points. In this respect, I begin in Chapter 1 by outlining the basic contours of the garment and footwear sectors, how the sectors have been theorized, and how our understanding of the sector is now changing. Chapter 2 examines how the historical antagonisms within the sector inform current strategies and the ways this contributed to the vertically disintegrated structure we see today. These chapters set the stage for three empirical chapters. Chapters 4–6 are three case studies that represent the most valorized sections in the sector and reveal clues for changes across the labour-intensive GVCs: beginning with a mass strike in China at the largest footwear producer in the world, followed by a worker's struggle at a warehouse of a 'full-package' denim manufacturer in south India, and finally, a transnational campaign at a vertically integrated commodity producer in Honduras. These cases have been chosen because the aim is to understand the political economy of industrial capitalism through the struggle of workers. Indicatively, the higher valorizability of these goods is an early signifier for the entire sector – and industrial capitalism more generally. The production of shoes (Chapter 3), jeans (Chapter 4), and underwear (Chapter 5) is more susceptible to technological investment because the products are sold year-round (not seasonal) and are less fashion-sensitive. Due to a number of regulatory, structural, geographic and historic factors, these areas of production operate as 'starters' within the sector. As such, they hint at what to expect from the sector at large – from shirts to shorts to sweaters and socks. Finally, Chapters 7 and 8 analyse the logics of DMP as outlined earlier, how these changes within the sector are reflected in the bargaining power of workers, and the tensions between the subjective agency of workers and the material conditions of exploitation.

The book combines the details of a case study with a more generalizable analysis.[8] This design aims to reconcile the tension between the specificity of place and the generalizability of theory. As Doreen Massey (1984: 70) argues, 'The challenge is to construct an approach which is neither detailed description and empiricism nor a "mechanistic Marxist" insensitivity. It is possible both to recognise specificity and to situate it within the grander historical movements of capitalist societies.' It is the assertion of the book that the rise of value chain consolidation and of the large vertically consolidating supplier are transforming the power relations between brands and their suppliers and between workers and their employers.

There can be little doubt about the importance of this new phase. The low-investment, low-capitalization garment and footwear sectors are 'starter' industries for export-oriented countries, meaning they are the first to come and the first to go. Asia and Latin America's early export-led growth could be predicted through an analysis of these sectors. The sector is a canary in the coal mine, a barometer, or stress test for industrial capitalism. Accordingly, changes in the most valorized sections in these sectors have the potential to reveal changes in the global political economy.

The primary structural advantage enjoyed by capital over labour is a unitary interest in accumulating more capital, which gives it direction and a simple premise to organize around. Organizing labour, however, is usually a more

---

[8] The methodology deployed for each case is briefly outlined in the notes at the top of each chapter. The research approach borrows from geographic action research, which stems from a particular strand of radical geography and feminist research (McDowell 1992). To rephrase Marx, radical geographers resolved to not only observe and interpret the world but also change it. By emphasizing praxis – the fusing of practice with theory – the research aims to be rigorous and relevant.

coalition affair, whose tentpoles can be abstract ideas, like freedom or equality. Karl Marx and Friedrich Engels (1848) argued that global capital would generate a global proletariat that would ultimately be its undoing. That is, 'What the bourgeoisie (capital's collective agents) therefore produces, above all, are its own grave-diggers.' While it is widely accepted that capitalism creates a class of workers, much evidence around the world suggests the workers pursue individual rather than collective interests. The challenges seem so great that workers will often choose self-protection, given how workplaces are structured to isolate and atomize. In other words, perhaps collective worker action is the exception under capitalism. Maybe capital's structural advantages in certain sectors, like garment and footwear, have effectively resolved the dialectical struggle in favour of capitalists. It would explain the largely frustrated efforts of labour in the last 30 years (AFL-CIO 2013; Ballinger 2009; Chibber 2011; Greven 2008; ILO 2000). Do certain economic configurations immunize capital against worker power?

A decade ago, Ronaldo Munck (2008, 220) optimistically asked, 'But what if the labour movement is entering a new cycle of activism and militancy, precisely through the contestation of neoliberal globalisation? Is it inconceivable that a global contest between labour and capital might now emerge as Marx predicted?' This age-old idea of a dialectical backlash and a new – now global – proletariat rising against a new regime of exploitation sheds light on emerging fronts in the garment industry struggle, especially since the financial crisis of 2007–2008.

By attacking it from this angle, I hope to upturn some of the prevailing orthodoxy on the subject and help open new frontiers in labour strategy. Without understanding capital dispersion in the context of class struggle, and the short-term imperatives of capital, it devolves into a vague series of flows and shifting patterns, like meteorology. But in this framework it acquires sense, and one can trace its developments from Midtown Manhattan to South China through to South Asia, and begin to see a larger picture.

The intention is not to reanimate old debates of the academy or advocate for this or that line of technocratic reform, but to analyse the political economy of industrial capitalism as a living thing, an unfolding struggle between capital and labour, whose twists and turns are marked by strategic innovations, in resistance and domination. The aim is to inform the strategies of workers in this context, to not only better resist but also to anticipate the snares set by the system and go on the offensive.

PAST

1

The Bottleneck

In September 2000, as activists laid siege to the International Monetary Fund and World Bank summit in Prague, South African Finance Minister Trevor Manual pondered the relevance of protesting against a system that felt so inevitable, 'I know what they are against but have no sense of what they are for' (Kingsnorth 2012). The anti-sweatshop movement was in full swing; it was part of anti-capitalist social movements at the end of the twentieth and the beginning of the twenty-first century that became known as the 'global justice movement' under the banner 'Another World Is Possible'.

Unlike the perceived indecisiveness of much of the anti-capitalist movement at the time, the anti-sweatshop movement remained steadfast in its demands. Issues such as liveable wages, independent worker organization, and collective bargaining remained at the forefront. The problem was not that workers and activists did not know what to fight for – it was how to get it. Achieving these fundamental rights becomes a seemingly insurmountable hurdle under conditions of globalized hypermobile capital. In the garment and footwear sectors, structural barriers, such as vertical disintegration, subcontracted manufacturing, just-in-time production practices, and end of the 2005 MFA, were said to have compounded the difficulties of establishing workers' rights. This final prediction, which informed a decade of strategy by workers and activists in responding to the state, transnational capital, and domestic firms, would prove to be wrong.

Dynamics of the global garment sector

Between 1995 and 2013, the number of workers at the jobs related to global value chains increased from 296 million to 453 million, with much of this increase occurring before the 2008 financial crisis, demonstrating the profound ways in which GVCs were transforming the global labour market (ILO 2015). Most occurred in Global South countries, directed for Global

North consumption Among these, clothing is one of the world's largest and oldest export industries.

The economic geography of the garment industry has been determined principally by retailers as well as brand-name merchandizers, or 'buyers', who, through their ability to select suppliers from around the world, concentrate enormous profits and power away from those who produce the goods (Gereffi 1994, 1999). The functionally and geographically disintegrated garment industry is one of the most exploitative, labour-intensive, and feminized sectors in the world economy (Hale and Wills 2011). Fluctuations in purchasing patterns, seasonality, and fickle 'fast-fashion' trends require high-volume production and quick turnarounds to accommodate just-in-time orders (Brooks 2007). Accordingly, for the past century, garment production has been the link of the clothing value chain that brands and retailers have sought most to outsource, using high rates of fluidity to reduce liabilities of investment (Collins 2009).

By limiting the investment to bulk purchasing contracts, brand companies have been able to maximize profits by throwing factory owners, who have thinner profit margins, into bidding wars. The pressure of this competition is then transferred onto workers, who must work longer hours for less compensation and in conditions that get progressively worse. Factory floor workers are soon left without the wiggle room in negotiations with their direct employers; they become virtually powerless to form trade unions, obtain liveable wages, or improve workplace conditions (Collins 2009; Hale and Wills 2011). These structural limitations on labour agency and organization in the garment sector have inspired alternative attempts to establish workers' rights such as through the WTO and bilateral trade agreements, corporate codes of conduct, and auditing – which have either fallen far below a basic threshold of success (that is, liveable wages, collective bargaining agreements, trade union density, workplace safety, and so on) or have simply failed outright (Brooks 2007; Seidman 2009; Kumar 2015). Indeed, despite numerous initiatives, real wages continued to fall in the global garment sector (WRC 2013a), as union density contracted (Maree 2009) and official collective bargaining remained absent in the sector (Esbenshade 2004). And as recent preventable disasters, or 'industrial accidents' – some of the worst in history – attest, workplace safety is still a significant problem (Manik and Yardley 2013).

Although labour conditions have fluctuated, the structure of the garment and footwear value chain has remained relatively constant through the past century. The reconfiguration of technology and production has seen many transnational corporations (TNCs) abandon their in-house manufacturing capacity in favour of subcontracted supply chains. This phenomenon is most evident in global apparel, which, as Hale and Wills (2011: 5) describe, is 'the most globalised industry in the world', where major brands tend to keep only the marketing, branding, and design functions in-house.[1] By exploiting geographic differentiation in costs, surplus labour, and state policy, TNCs have constructed complex supply chains and succeeded in transforming the global apparel industry into one of the most horizontally internationalist and vertically subcontracted areas of production in the world (Ho, Powell, and Volpp 1996; Hale and Shaw 2001; Raworth and Coryndon 2004; Hale and Wills 2011; Rodriguez-Garavito 2005; Brooks 2007; Tewari 2008; Carty 2010).

The literature on subcontracting recognizes three primary motivations behind companies who choose to operate a vertically disintegrated chain of production: cost savings from input prices, supplier firm flexibility of output, and specialization (Mead 1984). These motivations are particularly acute within the garment and footwear sectors. It is both cost-effective and risk-averse for brands to handle seasonal surges, fluctuating orders, and constantly changing fashion trends by outsourcing production (Collins 2009). Cheaper input prices resulting from outsourced production allow for cost savings from raw materials and labour for lead firms. This was further exacerbated under conditions of globalization, when the buyers in the labour-intensive garment sector were able to capture the lion's share of value by outsourcing its production to the Global South. Fluctuations in outputs, because of seasonality, have always been a prime motivator in brands' decision to construct vertically disintegrated chains of production in the garment and footwear sectors.[2] An additional contributing factor to the erratic nature of garment production, as well as its labour-intensity, is the ephemerality of fashion trends, resulting in the constant alteration of patterns, designs, and cuts. Again, this is dependent on specialization.[3] These facts, alongside contributors such as low start-up costs, meant that outsourcing became central to the industry from the very early days of mass garment production.

The garment industry can be broadly divided into a few universally applicable segments or phases from production to consumption. It begins with the domain of producers of raw materials (such as cotton) which is then manufactured into

---

[1] There are exceptions, of course, such as in *haute couture* and some brands like Adidas have a handful of small directly owned shops, mostly to manufacture samples or highly specialized products. The other exception is on clothing commodity production, which is detailed in Chapter 5.
[2] High demand for jackets, for example, typically falls just before and during the winter season, with similar patterns in swimwear just before and during the summer.
[3] These dynamics are explained in greater detail in Chapter 5.

textiles or synthetic and natural fibres; those textiles are then dyed and finished; cut, assembled, and laundered; and finally, a finished product is distributed, marketed, and sold at retail shops (Bair and Gereffi 2001). Beginning at the sphere of production, which includes textile plants, garment production, export chains (including associated logistics and warehousing), and ending at the domain of consumption, such as retail stores, design, marketing, financing, and administering the process of production, distribution, and sales, these component parts that make up the production of the commodity are hidden from view at the point of consumption. As Marx (1911) observed early on, 'From the taste of wheat it is not possible to tell who produced it, a Russian serf, a French peasant or an English Capitalist' – even today, the label inside does not reveal who picked the cotton, or cut, sewed, and packaged the shirt.

While the former acts as the primary nodes of material production and consumption, the latter, largely 'affective' phases of the production process (Hardt and Negri 2001), gives brands the 'directing' power over the entire system. Firms involved in each part capture a different proportion of the value generated in the commodity chain. The garment plant phase is considered a 'lower order', or 'dead end', function, and is therefore subordinated under 'higher order' firms with access to propriety technology, brand reputation, and consumer relations. The majority of profits are captured by these higher order firms, while the lower orders, consisting of the labour-intensive cut-make-trim (CMT) phases, are too hard-pressed by competition to expand (Merk 2008).

In Figure 1.1, Graph A breaks down the proportion of the value distribution for a basic men's T-shirt which is produced as an assembly-only firm for retailing in the US at $15. This is from 2005, the year the MFA was phased out (much more on this will be discussed later). As can be seen, 75 per cent of the total value of the shirt is eaten up by the brand and the retailer, $2 goes towards the garment factory to absorb the full cost of the materials, labour, and overhead involved in producing the garment, and the final $1.75 goes towards transportation, taxes, and import costs.[4]

Graph B breaks down the $2 'sourcing price' to the garment manufacture (based on figures calculated from 2004 in Bangalore).[5] As can be seen, manufacturers accrue only 5 per cent of profits, and 15 per cent, or 30¢ (about 2 per cent of total cost), is shared among all the garment factory workers involved in the production of each shirt. The potential bargaining power of workers from low-margin assembly-only manufacturers, therefore, hovers around nil.

---

[4] Compiled from data in Vijayabhaskar (2002).
[5] Original data compiled by Mark Francoise in 2005 (data collected by request).

Figure 1.1 Sourcing Price of $2 for basic men T-shirt – retail price $15

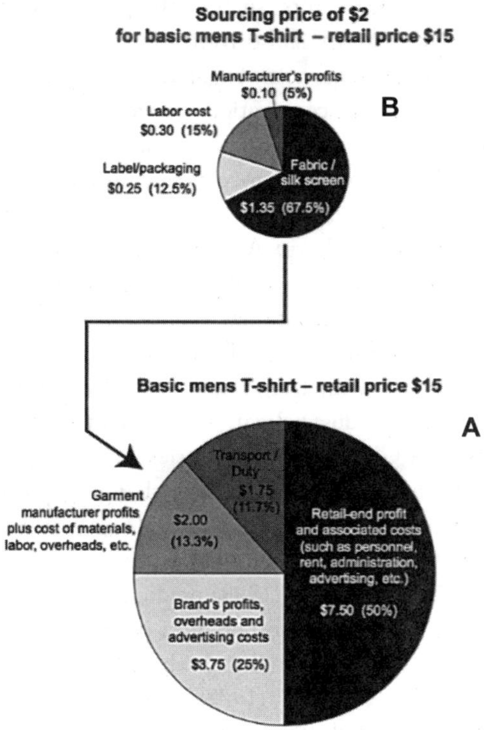

Sourcing price of $2 for basic mens T-shirt – retail price $15

B
- Manufacturer's profits $0.10 (5%)
- Labor cost $0.30 (15%)
- Label/packaging $0.25 (12.5%)
- Fabric / silk screen $1.35 (67.5%)

Basic mens T-shirt – retail price $15

A
- Garment manufacturer profits plus cost of materials, labor, overheads, etc. $2.00 (13.3%)
- Transport / Duty $1.75 (11.7%)
- Retail-end profit and associated costs (such as personnel, rent, administration, advertising, etc.) $7.50 (50%)
- Brand's profits, overheads and advertising costs $3.75 (25%)

Thus, the low-investment, low-capitalization garment and footwear production phase is usually the first to come and the first to go – having played a central role in Asia's early export-led growth.

Globalization and the state

Despite its contested use, there is a broad agreement that globalization led to intensified trade competitiveness, multi-nationalization of production, and integration of financial markets (Ohmae 1993; Hensman 2001; Harvey 2005; Kiely 2005; Munck 2008). With respect to its origins, Harvey (2005) identifies the late 1960s as the beginning of the current neoliberal permutation of globalization, and maintains that it was a method for capital to combat its crisis in profitability brought on by the antagonisms of the organized working class in the Global North.

Trade union membership in the Global North was historically the strongest in the manufacturing and public sectors, which fell alongside de-industrialization throughout the 1970s and 1980s. Subsequently, the remaining holdout of union members in the 'immobile' sectors, such as the public sector, contracted due to the combined effect of austerity and privatization. In many countries, the march towards a post-industrialized economy began decades ago; in the UK, for example, the total employment in public corporations between 1979 and 1991 fell by around 66 per cent from 2.1 million to 0.7 million (Losada 2010).

Buttressed by globalization, this process radically empowered TNCs, injecting capital into landscapes that were once peripheral to manufacturing capital. With unrestricted access to Asian, Latin American, and Central European markets, capital benefited from rapid urbanization and proletarianization, opening up greater opportunities for transnational brands, especially in labour-intensive manufacturing, to take full advantage of a seemingly limitless pool of labour. This period experienced a shift away from import-substitution industrialization (ISI) towards export-oriented industrialization (EOI) in the national development strategies of most large Global South countries.

From the beginning of this period, the changing power of the state was a primary point of contention for scholars. Indeed, as early as the turn of the twentieth century this globalization process was forecasted as part of the development of capitalism. Lenin (1999) predicted a deepening of nation–state rivalries, challenging Kautsky's vision of 'ultra-imperialism', in which competing nation-states would make way for the combined exploitation of the world by international capital. Robin Murray (1971), writing at the onset of the economic crisis of the 1970s, contended that the internationalization of capital weakened both the power of the state as well as that of the domestic bourgeoisie while simultaneously strengthening foreign capital and maintaining inter-state rivalries in a 'territorial dialectics of capital'. As Nicos Poulantzas (1978: 73) identifies, Murray's claims can only function by overlooking the domination of American capital and its internationalization that 'neither suppresses nor by-passes national states, either in the direction of a peaceful integration of capitals "above" the state level, or in the direction of their extinction by the American super-state'. By insisting that such domination is maintained by, and integrated within, national capitals and host states, it is possible to recognize that such states themselves become internationalized, not through the loss of their sovereignty but insofar as the dominated states internally articulate their relationship to the dominant ones. Over time, this process of globalized capital strengthens the hand of the state and the domestic bourgeoisie.[6]

---

[6] In this vein, Desai (2013) has observed a hardening of the materiality of nations in which the ongoing reconstitution of global capitalism is still primarily the result

The dominant view that activists came to respond to was that traditional states, with their state-bounded regulatory power (Crouch and Streek 1997: 173), were being challenged and undermined by globalization. Schmidt (2002: 13), speaking about the weakening of the regulatory power of the state, maintained that 'exogenous pressures caused by globalisation have increased in magnitude, speed and volatility [...] decreas[ing] national governments' ability to control their effects'.[7] There was also a tendency, particularly in reports produced by the World Bank or institutional third sector organizations, to assume this weakening of labour rights and environmental standards was a result of a lack of enforcement and mismanagement. However, it is necessary to stress that the cause of this race to the bottom is not simply an ineffective bureaucracy but a part of the deeper, more structural logic of capital.

Crucially, governments that take action against the interests of capital do so against the constant threat of capital flight and economic crisis. Sivanandan (2008: xiv) claims that not only are nation-states limited in their opposition to the interests of global capital but they also now operate as an appendage of global capital: 'The state in the global era is no longer, primarily, a nation state working on behalf of its people but a servitor of the global economy run by multinational corporations and the market. We have moved from the welfare state of late industrial capitalism to the market state of global capitalism, the market state is the vehicle of global capitalism.' Sivanandan's description of the state's role coheres with the experience of workers within the cases of this book – a dynamic that is particularly acute in the industrializing Global South. The process of globalization meant a downward pressure on labour standards and the erasure of barriers to imports that resulted in an unobstructed shift of production to countries with lower labour and environmental standards. Governments that

---

of the interactions between states. Desai argues that the state plays an increasingly stronger role in managing capitalism's crisis tendencies. Likewise, Gindin and Panitch (2013), expanding on Poulantzas and Wood (2005), regard the state as central to the making of 'globalization'. For Gindin and Panitch (2013: 1), states supply the infrastructure upon which global markets depend, while capital depends on states 'maintaining property rights, overseeing contracts, stabilizing currencies, reproducing class relations and containing crisis'. These lines of argumentation suggest that globalization has led to individual nation-states forgoing an element of their sovereignty and autonomy, while also managing the expansion of capital's terrains of profitability and mitigating capitalism's crisis tendencies.

[7] This view is supported by many others (Tilly 1995; Crouch and Wolfgang 1997; Haas et al. 2009), with Keohane and Nye (1972: 393) identifying a 'control gap' between the states' desire to regulate stocks and flows and their actual capacity to do so.

depress wages, working conditions, and institute policies that encourage (or force) labour migration into industrial areas are rewarded with higher outsourced production and foreign direct investment (FDI).[8]

While the debate over the changing state–capital relation continues – whether the state has ceased to be an institution capable of exerting significant influence or not – there remains broad agreement that a single state has little power over transnational capital (Teeple 1995; Cerny 1997; Evans 1997; Swank 1998; Yeung 1998; Arrighi 2000; Dunning 2000; Robinson 2001; Harris 2003). As states become more interdependent within globalized capital, economic phenomena must be analysed from multiple geographic points and assessed within the context of transnational capital.

As will be demonstrated, workers' collective actions at the firm level expose the underlying tensions between transnational capital and domestic capital. Indeed, the key variable that explains the high degree of exploitation within the export-oriented garment and footwear firms is the relationship between global buyers and producers in which states are key enablers. International competition operates in much the same way as national competition – with international competition favouring and intensifying low-end producers (Shaikh 2016). This has been demonstrated in a study by Anner, Bair, and Blasi (2012). The authors identified the top 20 countries producing apparel (by volume) for the US year-on-year from 1989 to 2010. They found countries that increased their share of garment exports to the US violated a greater number of core labour standards. In effect, lower wages, poorer conditions, and weaker union density were rewarded with larger contracts from transnational brands/retailers. It proved what most intuitively know – the resurgence of the sweatshop was not an anathema but fortified by the very system that professed to oppose it. Anner, Bair, and Blasi (2012) conclude that any solution to ending these immiserated conditions of work in the export-oriented garment sector must address the pricing dynamics between buyers and producers. While the authors place the onus on global buyers, the cases discussed in this volume demonstrate something different. That any prescription must consider the changing 'objective' material conditions – greater surpluses captured by manufacturing firms – alongside the subjective agency of

---

[8] Roy (2004: 28) describes this relationship as beyond the jurisdiction of sovereign governments, stating that 'radical change cannot and will not be negotiated by governments: it can only be enforced by people. By the public. A public that can link hands across national borders' (2004: 29). While the kind of internationalism that Roy calls for had not been seen in the labour movement for nearly a hundred years, in some senses, neoliberal globalization forced trade unionists and activists to look beyond their borders.

workers' collective actions against their now value-laden employers at the point of commodity production.

Despite an immense body of work on industrialization and the developmental state, the relationship between export processing and the state has remained undertheorized. Smith (2015) argues that the role of the state should not be relegated to policy functions but be analysed as a facilitator of capitalist accumulation. To Smith (2015), the state is central to the development process both within the firm and in the GVC. Indeed, the explosive growth of Asian firms is a consequence of the conscious interventions by the developmental state (Woo 1991; Kohli 2004), through market distortion (Amsden 1989), industrial policy shift from import-substitution industrialization (ISI) to export-oriented industrialization (EOI) (Stubbs 1999) with the state often taking the role of entrepreneur (Amsden 1989) or state-driven globalization through joint ventures (Huang 2003). Indeed, Chibber (2003) argues that ISI created virtual monopolies with no external competitors, which stunted technological investment considerably. Even in the present world order, the state continues to play a central role in the development of large capital-holding firms. For example, Ngai and Chan (2012: 385) maintain that the state facilitated mergers, acquisitions, and geographic expansion to help transform Apple supplier Foxconn into 'a monopoly capital firm [that] now dominates the global market'. Indeed, as is demonstrated in this volume, the forces of international competition required that supplier firms succeed in R&D in order to survive.

The economic geographer Henri Yeung (2014) maintains that inter-firm dynamics and the process of strategic coupling in East Asia command domestic firms that are gradually dis-embedding themselves from the developmental state and re-embedding themselves within different global production networks (GPNs). In the case of Yue Yuen (Chapter 3) and Arvind (Chapter 4), we find a hybrid form of mutually dependent embedded inter-firm relations that are also profoundly circumscribed by the developmental goals of the state.

As the empirical cases explore, states operate in the interests of transnational capital and/or the domestic bourgeoisies, albeit in uneven ways, with these forces at times coming into conflict. In Chapter 3, a confluence of actors including the central Chinese state, state-run media, local administration, and even the functionally state-run union operate independently from capital, even conceding ground to the striking workers of Guangdong, but ultimately to benefit capital. In Chapter 4, the police force in Ramnagara, India, and the district labour commissioner assist the factory management during the dispute, working openly in the interest of the factory owners against the workers. And in Chapter 5, the state does not intervene when the factory is closed in Honduras. It remains unresponsive to the workers' rights and the successes of the campaign happen not only despite the inaction of the state but also because of the inaction or weakness of the state.[9]

The evolution of governance typologies

Critical to understanding the power of workers within the garment sector is to make sense of GVCs, the genealogy of which began with the framework of global commodity chain (GCC) theory (Gereffi 1994; Bair and Gereffi 2001; Gibbon 2001). First coined in the 1970s by Hopkins and Wallerstein as part of world systems theory, they defined the 'commodity chain' as 'a network of labour and production processes whose end result is a finished commodity' (1994: 17). Within GCC literature, much of the attention is given to issues of governance, which while including elements of the buyer–producer power relation tends to eschew the employer–worker power relation at the production end. This is a particular problem in sectors characterized as 'buyer-driven', such as garments and footwear, because in the GCC framework labour at best is treated as subordinate within commodity and value chain analysis (Coe, Hess, and Dicken 2008; Selwyn 2013). As Smith et al. (2002: 47) stated, 'Insofar as "workers" are present in this literature, they appear as passive victims as capital seeks cheap labour.' New schools of thought gave rise to the GVC and GPN frameworks of analysis.[10]

Since the early 2000s, a large part of the GVC literature has attempted to build upon Gary Gereffi's (1994) original governance dichotomy: buyer-driven versus producer-driven. In producer-driven chains, value is captured primarily at the point of production because of high-barriers to entry, limited competition, and enhanced 'control over backward linkages with raw material and component suppliers, and forward linkages into distribution and retailing' (Gereffi 2002: 3). As he states, 'Producer-driven chains usually belong to international oligopolies. Buyer-driven commodity chains (that supply brands like Nike or retailers like Gap), by contrast, are characterised by highly competitive and

---

[9] The reaction by developing states towards workers' campaigns often results in negative consequences. In fact, there are innumerable examples of victories occurring because of the inaction of the state. For example, in Haiti, the most important labour victory was achieved during the coup d'état, when the government was not functional; and the same in Honduras (see Chapter 5). The disinterest of the state is generally a positive factor in workers' campaigns in the Global South since globalization.

[10] Bair (2009) argues that the GVC is a combination of the GCC with the neoclassical tradition of transaction cost economics. But these delineations are not strict. Milberg and Winkler (2013), for example, use GVC and GCC concepts interchangeably.

globally decentralised factory systems with low barriers to entry in production.' Gereffi's theory is based on the assumption that 'lead firms' in producer-driven chains typically belong to international oligopolies (for example, Ford, Airbus, Caterpillar, and so on). These large, often transnational, oligopolistic firms, with access to finance and increased self-finance (through the retention of profits), are capable of substantial technological enhancement. Increased investment in fixed capital simultaneously raises the firm's liability while helping it to be dominant in the value chain, exerting a great deal of influence on smaller and highly dependent subcontracted firms.[11] Through this structure, brands are able to outsource risk and narrow their focus to high-value-added activities, resulting in maximum profits and minimum capital investment and liability. Contained within Gereffi's 'buyer-driven' thesis here is the implicit premise that production and consumption are delinked – a fact exacerbated and spatialized under globalization. This 'buyer-driven' theory was extended to footwear, empirically, by Schmitz and Knorringa (2000: 3) who found 'big buyers [...] are the key players'. Fundamentally, in Gereffi's original formulation, production-end garment manufacturers remain largely passive victims, and as marketplace pressure mounts, affected workers are rendered increasingly powerless to resist it.

At the other end of the spectrum, we find 'buyer-driven' GVCs, which are in sectors that are low value, low technology, and vertically disintegrated. They are in garments and footwear alongside toys, furniture, and light electronics. These sectors maintain a high degree of 'fragmentation' (Arndt and Kierzkowski 2001) and a wide spatial spread. This extensive geography is an outgrowth of low barriers to entry at the producer-end since manufacturing costs are low with minimum capital investment, resulting in mostly small- and mid-size firms competing intensely at the various 'lower end' phases of the GVC.[12]

While Gereffi's category of 'producer-driven' resembled the Fordist model of production in capitalist modernity, the novelty was found in his introduction of

---

[11] Unlike direct investments, subcontracted or outsourced production is harder to measure, but Foster and McChesney (2012: 109) estimate that 'at least 40% of world trade is linked to outsourcing'.

[12] Notably, Henderson, Dicken, Hess, Coe, and Yeung (2002) develop a framework to include the development of 'strategic alliances' between firms ('relational rents') taking account of contextual conditions, technological and licensing agreements, and lead firm strategies to confront the contradiction of place and global flows. To Henderson et al. (2002), the GCC dualism relies too heavily on barriers to entry within particular sectors, treats the production and distribution process as linear, limits itself to existing chains, and lacks recognition of state and local policy in firm development.

the buyer-driven GVC (Gibbon, Bair, and Ponte 2008). A key intervention is the recognition that the relationship between buyer and producer in buyer-driven GVCs is not an equitable one, yet without a formal hierarchy. The question of power in the absence of formal hierarchy becomes a central driver in the GVC (Bair 2009). Many studies emerged that empirically supported the original binary, in which powerful actors dictated the size, capacity, and upgrading of outsourced manufacturers (Lee and Cason 1994; Knutsen 2004; Tokatli and Kizilgun 2004).

Among the most influential interventions in this debate is the work of Sturgeon (2001, 2002, 2003).[13] Sturgeon (2001) builds on the original framework of Gereffi by focusing on the degree of standardization of production and how this is reflected in the GVC. As Sturgeon (2001: 15) states, 'We need to link our terms not to firms, sectors, or places but to the specific bundles of activities that firms are engaged in.' To that end, he creates the following five types of value chain/production network 'actors', defined by their 'scope of activity': integrated, retailer, lead firm, turn-key supplier, and component supplier.

Integrated firms are a classically Fordist production process and maintain a high degree of vertical integration. Sturgeon's designation of *retailer* operates at the consumer end with its scope of activity including sales, marketing, packaging, and/or system integration and includes retailers such as Gap and Walmart. The *lead firms*, brand-name vertically disintegrated producers who drive the GVC, and *turn-key suppliers* are firms outsourced for core functions and can include large full-package suppliers. Finally, *component suppliers* are lower tier subcontractors often supplying secondary or periphery parts or services.

Sturgeon (2002, 2003) goes beyond simply the 'turn-key' supplier arguing for three distinct kinds of supplier firms. In addition to the turn-key, he adds commodity and captive suppliers. Again, this helps add an additional layer of clarity to a complex phenomenon. However, as with Sturgeon (2001), the focus here is based on the degree of standardization of production. Similarly, Humphrey and Schmitz (2000, 2002) and Palpacuer (2000) emphasize supplier firm 'competency' as the distinguishing characteristic between suppliers and the power dynamics therein.

As a response to the above-mentioned challenges to Gereffi's original types, Gereffi, Humphrey, and Sturgeon (2005: 79) generate a framework to capture the 'shifting governance structures' to move beyond the duality of the buyer- and producer-driven framework. In particular, they focus their attention on the 'possibilities for firms in developing countries to enhance their position in global

---

[13] For a summary of different types of critiques, see Gibbon, Bair, and Ponte (2008).

markets', and in theory, the research here is motivated by a similar purpose. Where we part ways is in what is proposed. Gereffi, Humphrey, and Sturgeon (2005) suggest a five-part typology to value-chain governance taking account of the evolving nature of GVCs and upgrading potential. By taking account of the degree of explicit coordination and increasing power asymmetry, these governance categories are understood in the following order: market, modular, relational, captive, and hierarchy.

Market GVCs have minimum costs, transactions are easily codified with simple product specifications, and both buyer and suppliers are able to switch partners with relative ease. *Modular*, similar to Sturgeon's (2002, 2003) 'turn-key', are value chains in which the supplier firm produces exclusively for lead firms with higher liability for the supplier firm. *Relational* value chains have a high degree of capability at the supplier-end contributing to a mutually dependent relationship. These value chains contain high asset specificity, are costly to switch, and are often predicated on factors such as spatial proximity, social groups, familial links, or reputation. In *captive* value chains, there is a clear asymmetrical (or dependent) relationship of power between small suppliers and large lead firms. In these GVCs, the lead firm maintains a large degree of control. *Hierarchical* value chains are vertically integrated, with a high degree of managerial and centralized control. In these value chains, the limits on finding suppliers force the lead firm to develop and manufacture in-house.

Furthermore, Gereffi, Humphrey, and Sturgeon (2005) attempt to go beyond the buyer/producer dichotomy by adding the complexity of transactions, codifiability of information, and capability of suppliers in determining value chain governance structures. The proposed logic outlined in this book owes much to the proposed typology, which explains the conditions of industrial upgrading and its effect on the GVC. This work builds on Galanis and Kumar (2018) by extending Gereffi, Humphrey, and Sturgeon (2005) in two directions. First, while the governance categories of Gereffi, Humphrey, and Sturgeon (2005) express a *discrete* spectrum of GVC governance characteristics, it is important to recognize the spectrum as continuous. Second, while the aim of Gereffi, Humphrey, and Sturgeon (2005) is to more accurately describe the characteristics of each of the categories, this book demonstrates that the focus should remain squarely on the forces that drive the change from one structure to another and to identify any long-run trend.

Both in Gereffi, Humphrey, and Sturgeon (2005) and in this book, power relations are framed as essential to understanding the changes in GVC structures. Each of these typologies corresponds to a 'spectrum' of power asymmetry distribution and explicit coordination between the actors of production, from low in the case of *market relationships* to high in the case of *hierarchical relationships*.

Notwithstanding the fact that the new typology introduced by Gereffi, Humphrey, and Sturgeon (2005) dominated the analysis of power relations and was viewed as an 'improvement' to the previous GCC dichotomy, the new framework remained static and too homogenizing with geographical, social, and institutional specificities unaccounted for. Mahutga (2012) highlights, in particular, the imprecise analysis of the coordinating role played by the lead firms in the creation of a value chain and the inability to predict the geographic distribution of governance linkages as the most important flaws in the proposed typology. The GPN literature, responding to this critique, added much-needed complexity by understanding global governance as a multifactorial and contingent process. A GPN is defined as 'the nexus of interconnected functions, operations and transactions through which a specific product or service is produced, distributed and consumed' (Coe, Hess, and Dicken 2008) performed by the firm and non-firm actors, such as regional, national, and international institutions, labour groups, and relevant stakeholders.

With these critiques in mind, a succeeding version of the GPN approach, GPN 2.0 (Yeung and Coe 2015), reframed the GPN–GVC approaches. Yeung and Coe (2015) highlight the 'structural competitive dynamics' and the 'actor-specific strategies' that shape and control production networks. Instead of the three determining factors (transactions complexity, information codifiability, and supply capabilities) found in Gereffi, Humphrey, and Sturgeon (2005), Yeung and Coe (2015) introduce three 'structural competitive dynamics', the optimization of the ratio between costs and production capabilities, and the market development and financial discipline, which generate, under uncertain and risky conditions, four distinct corporate 'strategies' (*intra-firm coordination, inter-firm control, inter-firm partnerships*, and *extra-firm bargaining*), which bear resemblance to governance structures.

I draw on the work by Mahutga (2012, 2014) who has argued that 'the original buyer/producer-driven governance scheme is a continuum running between the buyer and producer-driven ideal types' (Mahutga 2012: 9). Mahutga (2014) utilizes Gereffi's binary to highlight the significance of barriers to entry in determining the bargaining power of actors within the global supply chain. He makes the case that the relative supply of manufacturers and buyers in a given chain – similar to what I call degree of monopsony power (DMP) – is an indication of a manufacturer's barrier to entry and therefore their bargaining power. Supporting this claim empirically through cross-national data, Mahutga shows that a manufacturer's bargaining power is inversely related to the available alternatives. Simply put, for a manufacturer, fewer alternatives mean greater bargaining power, more alternatives mean less bargaining power, and vice versa for buyer firms. Critically, 'the main point of similarity across buyer/

producer-driven chains is that their structures reflect the most optimal location of activities, both inside and outside of the lead firm, *from the perspective of the lead firm*' (Mahutga 2012: 6, emphasis in original).

Workers in a bottleneck

As detailed earlier, transnational garment brands and retailers, through size and access to critical technologies, were able to exploit smaller globally dispersed supplier firms, and dominate the sector with ease, driving GVCs, and controlling location, output, investment, price, and employment. Through these 'bottlenecks', or economic monopsony, large retailers and brands circumscribed smaller players within the chain, limiting their ability to upgrade.

The attractiveness and vulnerability of the garment sector are entwined. Disintegrated production and low capital investment resulted in a low price of entry for new garment factories, which attracted global buyers (that is, brands and retailers) who quickly seized the reins, leaving the large and growing number of outsourcing suppliers/producers firms powerless within the GVC (Gereffi 1994). The phases of outsourcing, involving low-skill,[14] low-value, low-wage work, require the multiplying effects of intensification (more productive means of manufacture) and extension (higher output volumes) in order to create profits. Without the investment necessary to procure upgrades in machinery, build new factories, or acquire competing firms, they were left with thin profit margins, menaced by every fluctuation in the marketplace. This takeover was an instance of the 'spatial fix', wherein crisis of capitalism is transferred – geographically or compartmentally – to less developed markets. In the garment sector, the spatial fix has taken the form of the chronic relocation of manufacturing away from the advances in labour organization that have taken place since the turn of the twentieth century.

Thus, the spatial dynamics of the global garment sector harboured a tension that left workers and their direct employers geographically incapable of changing their conditions. This tension is located in the global separation between the space of value creation at the point of production (via the labour process) – and its realization – at the point of consumption (via its sale). Endemic to the garment sector, since its earliest days, is the disjuncture in power between producers and brands/retailers.

---

[14] Workplace 'skill' is a contested category and is shaped by gendered demarcations of labour (Kumar 2014a).

Most literature on the configuration and constitution of commodity chains and production networks conclude that labour is relatively powerless (Frenkel 2001). Studies that do incorporate labour dynamics, such as Selwyn (2008), Collins (2009), or Nielson and Pritchard (2008), focus on trade union power, labour unrest, and its impacts on commodity chain configuration with singular agriculture-based models. However, there remains more of a gap in the argumentation in the study of workers' power and its impact on complex commodity networks such as garment and footwear production. The research that does address workers' power does so as the recipient of capital's actions, not as active agents in shaping and remaking the global economy (Boston 1987; Blecher 2002; Esbenshade 2004). Thus, an insight into workers' power, organizational structure, and collective consciousness is essential to understand the trajectory of production and the drivers of value chains, to research the (re)configuration of regional and global commodity chains in light of the expiration of the MFA and to document successes or failures of new forms of resistance to exploitation.

Changes in GVC power dynamics can be understood by analysing the drivers of the value chain. As Bair (2009) and Gereffi (1994) position it, driveness is a crucial variable in determining the shape of GVCs – changes in GVC governance determine the bargaining power of workers (Riisgaard and Hammer 2011), but workers' actions also shape and circumscribe the actions of capital (Herod 2001). Although later developments in the theory, such as of global production network (GPN), were critical of GCC and sought to critique it from the standpoint of an expanded field of actors, it contributed valuable insights to understanding the process of value capture in commodity production. However, labour continued to be expressed as, at best, only responding to capital. As Coe and Hess (2013: 5) point out, with some notable exceptions (Cumbers, Nativel, and Routledge 2008; Rainnie, Herod, and McGrath-Champl 2011; Riisgaard and Hammer 2011), GPN literature has hitherto 'been largely silent on the issue of labour agency'. The volume *Putting Labour in Its Place* (Taylor, Newsome, and Rainnie 2013) does make significant headway towards shifting the terrain of debate over labour agency in GVCs. Taylor et al. attempt to place labour (and labour process theory) firmly in the centre of GVC analysis. However, despite their claims, it largely reproduces managerial capital-centric approaches since labour is still considered only a factor of production. As Andy Herod (1997: 2) points out, many Marxists and neoclassical economists have put the power within production squarely in the hands of capitalists themselves. To Herod, it is workers who actively shape economic landscapes, whereas to most Marxists, it is 'capital which acts, capital which produces landscapes in its continual search for profit'. Workers, on the other hand, are simply factors of capital, as 'variable capital, an aspect of capital itself'.

Indeed, the bargaining power of the workers is contingent on the power relationships within the value chain; in turn, power relations within the value chain are informed by the actions of workers. As Tokatli and Kizilgun (2004: 222) state, 'power relationships indeed play an important role in determining the upgrading opportunities of manufacturers. [...] Power, after all, is relational (the exercise of power by one party depends on the powerlessness of other parties in the network), power relationships are dynamic, and manufacturing firms are more than merely reflexes of the way that networks are organised'.

Silver (2003: 13) cites three factors for the increase in labour's market bargaining power:

(*a*) The possession of scarce skills that are demanded by employers.
(*b*) Low levels of general unemployment.
(*c*) Workers' ability to withdraw from the labour market entirely and survive on non-wage sources of income.

As is evidenced in later chapters, some of these phenomena at the sectoral and structural levels are contributing to the increased market bargaining power of garment and footwear workers in some of the world's labour-rich economies. Technological upgrading and the consequent 'skilling' of the shop floor combined with increased labour shortages in the industrial centres such as South China has resulted in increased market bargaining power. These changes have reverberating impact across the world with growing global market bargaining power in the sector. Increased social wages have also allowed workers to withdraw their labour power, with upgrading contributing to greater liability due to higher 'sunk costs'. As detailed later and in Chapters 6 and 7, at the macro – more global – level, labour agency is directly linked to increased power and relative surplus value of production-side firms within the GVC.

However, an analysis of production and power would be incomplete if it did not incorporate the dynamics of the other phases in the supply chain – including consumption – as well as the role of the state. Peter Dicken (2007: 4) describes global commodities as 'derived more and more from an increasingly complex geography of production, distribution and consumption'. In this, he recognizes the changing position of the state from one that is, at times, antagonistic to capital, to one that is integral to enforcing its will through its various appendages such as militarized borders, its laws, or the military. What we find throughout the world are coalitions of social movement actors at the phases of production, distribution, and consumption cobbling together one of the only means of combating the asymmetrical relationship between capital and labour in the new international division of labour.

The cases discussed in these pages reveal that the actions of workers, domestic manufacturers, and transnational capital are both antagonistic and symbiotic and therefore cannot be delinked from national labour relations regimes – countering value chain analysis that tends to downplay the role of the state. The thesis here argues that the growth of supplier-end firms into larger, integrated firms, throwing their weight into high-rent activities, affects not only the relationship between buyers and suppliers but also deepens their embeddedness, leading to greater upgrading on the shop floor, thus enhancing the bargaining power of workers to exact a larger share of value from their now value-laden direct employer. Ultimately, the combined development of rising costs, state interventions, commodity chain consolidation, and the extinction of small firms brings the struggle back to the point of production and the workers themselves.

A crisis in garment workers' rights

The crisis of unionization and workers' rights in labour-intensive sectors intensified during globalization.[15] It was in these sectors that real wages declined

---

[15] It is hard to know the exact number of garment workers worldwide. In 2005, the estimate was around 25 million in the formal sector in low- and middle-income countries (ILO 2005) and that number stood at 30 million when footwear and textile workers are included (ILO 2000). Hale and Wills (2011) put the number closer to 40 million and worth £190 billion with year-on-year growth. Today, this number may be lower due to firm consolidation and technological advancement or higher due to greater consumption levels worldwide. Another statistic that is difficult to obtain in the sector is the historical changes in union density and collective bargaining (see Ishikawa and Lawrence 2005). Global Union Federation IndustriALL, which represents many garment trade unions globally, puts their membership in the sector at 1.7 million as of 2007, and maintains that, at most, global union density in the sector is 12 per cent, but this estimate is difficult to substantiate due to widespread reporting inaccuracies. Even within industrial clusters, it is difficult to determine the exact number of workers or union density. Doug Miller (2008: 162) recounts an illustrative example from a particular industrial cluster in Bangalore to highlight the difficulty of verifying statistics within the sector. 'The total workforce is estimated at 600,000. The Garment Workers Union estimates its membership at 54,000 (9%); however, only 4,000 of its members actually pay membership dues [...] the Garment and Textile Workers' Union estimates its members at 1,200 with a presence in some 85 factories. Finally Communist-aligned All India Trade Union Congress is present in 10012 units, and the Centre of Indian Unions in some 12 factories, but they both have unspecified membership.' In 1995, the United Nations Industrial Development

(WRC 2013a), union membership fell to historically low levels, and only a few cases of collective bargaining agreements in export-oriented production were brought to bear (Miller 2008; Anderson, Hamilton, and Wills 2011; Mani 2011; Carswell and De Neve 2012). During this period, global garment and footwear industries became among the most profitable and exploitative of the modern industries (Ho, Powell, and Volpp 1996), and simultaneously a powerful force behind the rise of the informal sector and the proletarianization of large parts of the Global South (Hale and Wills 2011). Thus, despite progress made in improving workers' rights when production was located in the Global North, much of it was undone under neoliberal globalization, with TNCs able to accumulate greater levels of capital as a consequence. From the 1980s up until 2010, the garment sector witnessed a significant decline in the workers' rights benchmarks and an increase in violations of core labour standards (Anner, Bair, and Blasi 2012). Sexual harassment and extra-economic forms of exploitation compounded this even further in the feminized garment sector (Collins 2009).

Globalized garment production fuses retrograde manufacturing practices with some of the most innovative techniques of labour domination. One major change is the mechanization of just-in-time supply chains, which have advanced radically alongside developments in logistics harmonization – such as containerization – in the 1970s.[16] To reiterate and emphasize its centrality, the garment sector uses variable production: supply must meet ever-changing consumer demands. The

---

Organization estimated that 'more than two-thirds of the global labour force in the clothing industry is accounted for by women and the industry account for almost one-fifth of the total world female labour force in manufacturing'. As an example, within Bangladesh's garment sector women account for an estimated 85 per cent (Delahanty 2009). The garment sector straddles both 'formal' and 'informal' sectors, which contributes to the difficulty of verifying exact numbers of workers. Data on the informal garment sector is even harder to verify, though Miller (2008) suggests that there are the same number of workers in the informal garment sector worldwide as in the formal. 'Informalization' is a deliberate strategy to undermine workers' rights and regulate work-time to maximize profits, while also providing an important valve for women workers to enter and exit the labour market as needed (Kumar 2014a). This research is conducted entirely within the 'formal' garment sector. The export-oriented garment sector, especially for major brands, is conducted within registered large-scale factories. The dearth of accurate data reveals the asymmetry of research between labour-intensive and capital-intensive research as well as between work considered 'masculine' and that considered 'feminine'. It reveals a necessity for more qualitative and quantitative research in the area.

[16] See Cowen (2014), Toscano (2011), and Chua, Danyluck, Cowen and Khalili (2018) for more on logistics, 'containerization', and contestation.

industry has remained labour-intense, not lending itself to the automation found in other sectors (Bonacich 2001). Just as in the early twentieth century, brands have limited fixed capital investment in production, which decreases liability while increasing labour flexibility and capital mobility. A brand's profit margins are squeezed out through variable capital (that is, labour), while constant capital, mostly in low technology (that is, sewing machines) and raw materials (that is, cotton), remains largely unchanged (Bronfenbrenner 2007).[17]

The global sweatshops that emerged in the past four decades, like New York's garment sector before the 1930s, were marked by an absence of unions, poverty wages, and chronically dangerous workplace conditions (Ballinger 2009; WRC 2013a). The primary reason for this enhanced exploitation can be found in the mounting pressure on supplier factories to compete with one another in a race to the bottom to secure business from brands. Producing at the lowest costs entails constantly tightening the screws on workers, depressing wages, and worsening conditions, to allow production targets to climb steadily. Indeed, the evidence pointed to decreasing pay and workers' rights for garment workers in parallel with increasing profits and control of major apparel brands.

An abundance of methods have been utilized to confront the abysmal conditions workers face in the Global South. Approaches have spanned from 'fair trade' and global framework agreements (GFAs) to more voluntary codes of conduct and the inclusion of the 'social clause' in trade agreements.

By the late 2000s, there was a sense of acceptance among union activists that, despite some isolated successes, two decades of effort to establish workers' rights in the garment supply chain had accomplished little to impact conditions or dent capital's relentless maximization of production. Despite their efforts, traditional trade unions have faltered in establishing a foothold in outsourced manufacturing companies that, until recently, operated exclusively at the behest of the transnational brands they produced for. Garment sector capital is marked by its ability to shift, manoeuvre, and relocate production at the slightest advance by organized labour on the factory floor with few sunk costs. Various strategies have been employed to fight a system of localized workers within the borders of a guarded nation-state and the hypermobile global power of capital.

Garment trade unions of the Global North initially reacted to capital flight and deindustrialization with calls for protectionism, blaming so-called cheap

---

[17] The first functional sewing machine was created in 1830 by French Tailor Barthelemy Thimonnier, but French tailors, fearing the invention would result in the destruction of their trade, rioted and burned down Thimonnier's shop. By the mid-1830s, an American version was created and by the 1850s, Isaac Singer's creation helped his company become the dominant producer of sewing machines, even to this day.

workers in the South, and making little effort to develop links between the two spheres (Kabeer and Mahmud 2004; Brooks 2007). The 1990s, however, witnessed a rapid expansion of global capital and with it an eruption of anti-sweatshop solidarity campaigns specifically targeting major clothing TNCs. These campaigns proliferated as stories of cramped factory conditions and the overworked and underpaid women who toiled for long hours in the Global South began trickling up to the North.

The early 2000s experienced a wave of animated grassroots anti-capitalist protest on the heels of the historic convergence of environmental and labour activists ('teamsters and turtles') against the WTO meeting in Seattle in 1999 alongside the development of a global resistance to neoliberal globalization. An oppositional consensus began to take shape among workers and activists in both the hemispheres of the globe. Yet, despite widespread campaigning, the conditions of garment workers remained largely unchanged and each unionization effort resulted in major brands 'cutting and running' to another site of production.

Notwithstanding this, factory workers had been successful in a handful of cases in winning union recognition. Take the 2001 case at the Korean-owned Kukdong factory in Mexico – a factory that supplied collegiate apparel for the sports brands Nike and Reebok. Workers went on strike after their employer denied them the right to form a union and what ensued was a standoff between US student activists, who had direct contact with workers, and college administrators, who had direct contact with brand executives. In its conclusion, the dual tactic of worker action and consumer solidarity resulted in the reinstating of all the sacked workers, recognition of the union, and collective bargaining (Hermanson 2004). This multi-pronged campaign strategy ensured that action on the ground led by garment factory workers dovetailed with consumer-end action in the form of boycotts, ultimately building enough power to challenge transnational brands to change workplace practices. This strategy was successfully reproduced in Honduras at a Fruit of the Loom factory in the latter half of the decade (see Chapter 5).

Owing to the resurgence of sweatshops, the 1990s saw a surge in students and activists responding to expensive big-brand marketing by making demands on TNCs and turning logos into liabilities (Klein 2000). Transnational corporations in the garment sector responded to the flurry of anti-sweatshop activity in the Global North by immediately introducing 'codes of conduct'.[18] Codes of

---

[18] A survey of 48 top US apparel brands found that 37 provided detailed labour practice corporate codes of conduct. Nike, PVH, and Russell Athletic/Fruit of the Loom examined in Chapters 3,4, and 5, respectively, have long-standing codes of conduct: US Department of Labour (1995), *The Apparel Industry and Codes of Conduct*.

conduct were meant to inform consumers to choose products with higher ethical standards, sometimes including third-party monitoring of working conditions such as that undertaken by the Fair Labour Association (FLA) or the Workers' Rights Consortium (WRC). While many codes included language on forced and child labour, few, if any, initially included many of the rights enshrined in the International Labour Organization's (ILO) core conventions – this included collective bargaining or freedom of association rights (Sethi 2002). As time went by, other strategies were employed by those seeking to combat the increasingly downward spiral in workers' rights and proliferation of sweatshops. Independent consumer groups attempted to create a market in union-made clothing. For example, Ben Cohen, of Ben & Jerry's ice cream, attempted to produce and market union-made T-shirts with his company SWEATX – which failed both because of poor 'market penetration' and also because the costs of the facility ran the company into the ground (Ross 2006: 53). Later on, although the word 'union' continued to be avoided, many codes began to include 'freedom of association' provisions (Seidman 2009). Arguably, the avoidance of union-related terminology was a conscious effort on the part of brands to attempt to make unions and collective action appear old fashioned and irrelevant. Indeed, this is a part of neoliberal vernaculars, in which unions have been actively erased discursively and legislatively (Harvey 2005).

Today, the code of conduct model within a consumer choice regime continues to remain the strategy of many Global North 'anti-sweatshop' or 'fair trade' NGOs, yet codes of conduct originally proliferated as a direct result of trade union pressure (Murphy 2004; Hale and Wills 2011). There is a vast body of literature analysing the effectiveness of establishing workers' rights solely through consumer choice of the Global North (White and Montgomery 1980; Raiborn and Payne 1990; Compa and Hinchliffe-Darricarrere 1995; McCabe, Trevino, and Butterfield 1996; Liubicic 1998; Jenkins 2001; Kolk and van Tulder 2002; Miller 2004; Locke and Romis 2006). Some conclude that these codes have proven useful as leverage during a corporate campaign (Hale and Wills 2011); however, the voluntary nature of codes have made issues of enforceability nearly impossible (Compa and Hinchliffe-Darricarrere 1995; Liubicic 1998; Emmelhainz and Adams 1999; Lu 1999; Herrnstadt 2000; Hong 2000; Rodriguez-Garavito 2005) and still others claim that codes not only mirror but also reinforce 'neocolonial' development modes (Freidberg 2003; Hughes and Reimer 2004; Hughes 2006). Indeed, other 'top-down' initiatives in labour-intensive sectors – such as labour protections in trade agreements (Campling et al. 2016) or CSR initiatives (Mezzadri 2014) – have been found to be largely ineffective or the research framework to be flawed. While NGOs and TNCs tend to support codes of conduct (Compa,

Hinchliffe-Darricarrere 1995; Kolk and van Tulder 2002; Sethi 2002; Braun and Gearhart 2004; Compa 2004; Locke and Romis 2006), trade unions tend to call the expansion of trade union rights as the enforcement of workers' rights from the shop floor (Howse 1999; Gallin 2001; Taylor and Bain 2001). The varying perspectives on how to respond to and resolve worker exploitation in the garment industry reflect wider ideological and political differences: those who represent international aid organizations and TNCs have tended to either overtly or tacitly support codes of conduct, while trade unions have tended to support the creation and support of trade unions to enforce workers' rights.

Proponents of codes have pointed to an increase in wages in some countries as examples of their efficacy, but these results can often be attributed to other compounding variables. For example, the Harrison and Scorse (2010) study of the impact of anti-sweatshop activism on labour market outcomes in Indonesia found that wage increases were not on account of the highly publicized introduction of codes by major brands such as Nike, Adidas, and Reebok, but can be attributed to factory compliance with local minimum wage laws. Opponents to this position argue that codes of conduct are a convenient public relations tool for TNCs in order to prevent the involvement of trade unions in the battle over workers' rights (Frundt 2004; Roman 2004; Sum and Ngai 2005; Egels-Zandén and Hyllman 2006; Egels-Zandén 2009). Rohini Hensman (2001: 294) describes the flaws of the codes of conduct observed during a consultation in India in the late 1990s, with workers claiming that codes 'won't be much use', and that codes would only be effective when workers enforce them.

Alongside codes of conduct, market-based, consumer choice–driven certification programmes such as 'fair trade' have persisted. These are primarily based in the agricultural sector and have little relevance to industrial labour conditions. Seidman argues that certification programmes are a mere marketing technique to help establish 'premium' commodities in order to reassure ethically minded consumers. Citing the case of Rugmark in India, Seidman (2009) holds that certification schemes are corrupted by their inherent volunteerism (which proponents see as its strength) and the premise of consumers 'protecting' victimized workers. Volunteerism, Seidman further claims, entrenches corporate power, since many of the 'independent' third-party NGOs that oversee the certification programme are funded by those very TNCs they are tasked with holding to account.

Consumer-driven efforts in the context of the garment sector have been heavily criticized. Brooks (2007) argues that the language of consumer agency, where 'buying' remains central, privileges individual or institutional 'purchasing power' in the process. The hierarchy is further entrenched through the restrictive access to moneyed purchasing institutions, such as universities, with an inherent and increasingly restrictive access to a small group of elite students within the Global North with the time, wealth, and educational access to act.[19] Thus, under early globalization, those who toil in the production process remain increasingly alienated from their labour, and those who are not provided access to incomes with 'purchasing power' are excluded and deprived of agency within a consumer-driven protest regime. Agency outside of consumption paradigms is organized in ways that make it politically and culturally palatable in the economically developed North. In addition, Brooks (2007) argues that consumer-led transnational corporate campaigns depend on the patronage and sense of noblesse oblige of TNCs through regimes of conscientious consumption, which promulgate the primacy of brand names themselves.

After realizing the shortfall of a consumer choice–centred strategy, some NGOs shifted gears, lobbying to provide resources to state governments to enable them to enforce their own labour laws. Advocates of this strategy, such as Dani Rodrik (1997), look to the regulatory power of nation-states in order to combat the hegemony of capital. This too, by all available accounts, has not proved to be fruitful due to the changing relationship between global capital and the state (Hensman 2001). As argued earlier, global capitalism is constructed in such a way as to compel the states to consciously undermine their own laws to create the optimum environment for capital accumulation, or, in Marx and Engels' terms, to 'draw from under the feet of industry the national ground on which it stood', leaving the state an impotent mass (Marx and Engels 1848).

Thus, activists began looking to non-state actors and institutions to enforce workers' rights from above. To quote Tilly (1995: 4): 'Without authorities, no rights exist. However, the relevant authorities are by no means always sovereign states.' Unions, such as the International Confederation of Free Trade Unions (ICFTUs), proposed subverting the meta-national governance regimes (free trade and WTO agreements) that have accelerated the capacity of capital to globalize to include a minimal standard of workers to organize and collectively bargain (Dominelli and Hoogvelt 1996; Leary 1996; Breitenfellner 1997; Howse 1999; Compa 2001; Hensman 2001; Kucera 2001; Klett, Ferguson, and Douglas 2004). The demand for workers' rights through trade agreements and the supranational bodies of the GATT and WTO (commonly referred to as the 'social clause amendment') led to limited success (Fairbrother and

---

[19] For example, Chapters 2 and 5 reference a consumer-led campaign called the Designated Suppliers Program (DSP) that inadvertently vested power in Western consumers by making students and university administrators the monitors of workers' rights, which can also – in part – explain its failure.

Hammer 2005; Bartley and Smith 2008; Egels-Zandén 2009; Hensman 2001; Kumar 2015). One of the few trade provisions that included a degree of labour protections are the Maastricht Treaty in Europe, the North American Free Trade Agreement (NAFTA), and the North American Agreement on Labour Cooperation (NAALC). Compa (2001) and Wills (2002) argue that the success of the NAALC and Maastricht, respectively, depends entirely on the strength of the existing trade union organization. On WTO 'social clause', however, Jane Wills (2002: 681) states that

> while a majority would agree that there is a real need to regulate the actions of corporations and stop the 'race to the bottom', opinion is divided as to whether lobbying the WTO and using the ILO are the best way to achieve it. Indeed, as the WTO has led the process of neoliberal globalisation, it has little credibility as far as social and environmental standards are concerned.

As well as this method of enforcement, activists sought to enshrine labour rights through the ILO – whose preamble states: 'The failure of any nation to adopt humane conditions of labour is an obstacle in the way of other nations which desire to improve conditions in their own country.' In 1944, the ILO reaffirmed the commitment to freedom of association and the right of workers to organize and engage in collective bargaining; however, Harvey (2006b: 56) argues that the existence or strengthening of guidelines at the supranational level does little to affect rights on the ground.

> Even within the liberal conception as laid out in the UN Charter there are derivative rights such as [...] rights to organise unions and the like. Enforcing these rights would have posed a serious challenge to the hegemonic practices of neo-liberalism. Making these derivative rights primary and the primary rights of private property and profit rate derivative would entail a revolution in political-economic practices of great significance.

While organizations like the ILO exist ostensibly with the aim of improving workers' rights, operating within the confines of neoliberal globalization makes challenging the hurdle of the global race to the bottom almost insurmountable.

Workers' self-organization as human rights

The allocation of rights remains conflicted within international legal and governance regimes. Many scholars of business and human rights presuppose moral imperatives for capital or institutional applicability of universal declarations

(Hsien 2017). Take Hoffman and McNulty (2009: 114) who state that 'even under optimal conditions, good companies sometimes are susceptible to moral lapses'. Both the problem and the solution are understood as individualistic. Thus, the human rights literature is littered with moral, legal (Buhmann 2006), third sector (Outhwaite and Martin-Ortega 2017), or trade agreement (Compa 2001, 2004) solutions to human rights abuses. Absent from much of this literature is a recognition of the underlying logics of capital – competition and exploitation – and the agency of workers to collectively change their own conditions.

However, critiques of human rights are by no means a recent phenomenon. Marx (1867) famously wrote that 'between two rights' – that of the propertied classes and the working class – 'force decides'. This extends to the neoliberal context, as the rights of the dominant social process of capital accumulation through market exchange against the rights of workers for economic democracy and collective action. Despite the recognition of the utility of embracing some of the languages of human rights by social movements, Marxists have by-and-large rejected much of mainstream business and human rights approaches (O'Connell 2018). Much of the human rights literature avoids an analysis of history as one that is shaped through conflict. Marx applies this to the current mode of production, capitalism, as one that pits the rights of workers in direct conflict with the interest of capital. Marx continues, 'In the history of capitalist production, the determination of what is a working-day, presents itself as the result of a struggle, a struggle between collective capital, *i.e.*, the class of capitalists, and collective labour, *i.e.*, the working-class.'

Critically, the argument 'between two rights' by Marx is less a question of *ends* – certainly, the ILO core conventions' freedom of association, broadly understood as the right to a democratic trade union, is framed within the language of human rights – but a question of *means*. The right of a worker to form a union is a human right, but more importantly it is the means by which workers can collectively confront their employer to win concessions (that is, wages, benefits). As such, the reality of ensuring workers' rights under globalization, as demonstrated in the cases in this volume, lies somewhere in the middle of human rights and class antagonism – between the exercise of a universalist language versus the self-organization and internationalism of labour, respectively. Relying on the moral obligations of corporations, in lieu of an enforceable system of transnational regulation or the sheer dint of strength demonstrated by the workers' collective action, may not deliver sustained workers' rights under the current conditions.

Labour rights and human rights have historically 'run on tracks that are sometimes parallel and rarely meet' (Leary 1996: 22). Indeed, while human rights organizations focused on issues of political and civil rights (that is, political prisoners, torture, or free speech), the workplace remained the realm of trade unions and labour rights organizations (Leary 1996). Certainly, social movements around the world from housing, racial equality, or environmental justice, or where trade unions have had difficulty finding footing (immigrant workers, day labourers, and labour-intensive industries), have increasingly framed their struggles and demands, at least in part, through the language of human rights (O'Connell 2018).

Labour rights are playing a more prominent role within business and human rights literature but are still relying on the individual decisions of the proprietors of capital. For example, Buhmann and Wettstein (2017: 6) cite that the Rana Plaza collapse was caused by the 'economic decisions to produce under cheap conditions [and] the fact that those incidents were not rare but unfortunately common have called for critical assessments of decisions of certain firms'. Here, as with much of the business and human rights literature, the emphasis is the decision of a few firms. This 'bad apples' theory cannot coexist with a critique that understands this phenomenon rooted in competitive logics. As an instructive example of workers succeeding against their employers through such a more structural analysis, one need not look any further than the history of the garment sector.

Go back to 1911 and New York City's Triangle Shirtwaist Factory fire. Enter the ILGWU whose raison d'être was actualized through collective organization, action, and a demand which challenged the hierarchies of the clothing industry, triggering improved working conditions for decades. As such, it was workers – not the employers – who have eliminated US factory fires to date. Brand companies at the turn of the twentieth century maximized profits by creating bidding wars between factory owners. Factory owners, in order to stay competitive and survive, would increase downward pressures on the workers. Workers at the factory-floor end of this chain reaction were left with poverty wages, deteriorating workplace standards, and increasing incidences of factory fires and collapse.

From as early as the late nineteenth century, due to the vertical disintegration of the garment sector, workers sought to put pressure at both points of production and consumption (Collins 2009). The ILGWU leveraged buyers (brands and retailers) through secondary pickets and boycotts and relied on the language of both human rights and solidarity to win converts from outside the shop floor. It was precisely this tactic that was internationalized with the global garment sector (Seidman 2009). However, with its emphasis on individual business decisions (rather than capitalism itself), and business solutions (rather than workers' self-organization), much of the literature and language of business and human rights remains incongruent with the history of change in the garment sector, or indeed of workers under capitalism.

The rights of workers and the right to organize trade unions are well established in principles 3–6 of the UN Global Compact, the UN Guiding Principles on

Business and Human Rights as set out by the International Bill of Rights and the ILO's 1998 Declaration (ILO 1998; UN 2008, 2011). This is particularly the case in instances where formal trade union rights are limited, such as in South China or Vietnam, and the language of rights can help raise workers' consciousness to build autonomous organizing and strikes (Chan 2018). In different ways, workers in South China and in south India rely on the twin forces of rights and conflict in their struggles. As is evidenced in the cases studies – and in a similar vein to Lund-Thomsen and Lindgreen (2018) – as the value chain moves from a short-term *market-based* to a more cooperative *hierarchical* GVC (Gereffi, Humphrey, and Sturgeon 2005), the possibilities for workers to utilize ethical frameworks increases. Indeed, codes and other rights-based frameworks are tools that are only as powerful as the workers and activists who can enforce them.

As discussed in Chapter 2, just as the blueprint for the global race to the bottom in the garment sector began taking shape within the US, production started relocating from Manhattan's garment district, and so did new modes of countervailing power and solidarity. Indeed, links between workers are found in the earliest days of the industrial revolution (Featherstone 2012). Andrew Herod (1997) claims that such internationalist links began to form as a result of economic booms and crisis evident in the 1840s and 1850s and the utilization of foreign strike-breaking workers during periods of labour unrest, especially by British employers. He states that the first structures of internationalism among labour can be traced to 1844 and the British Owenites and Chartists, together with refugees from Germany, France, and Poland, of the London-based 'Democratic Friends of All Nations'. In the 1850s and 1860s, over a half-dozen international worker organizations were formed and trade unions in particular industries took shape. Herod (1997) argues that 'the formal transnationalisation of labour in many ways predates that of capital, at least with regard to the arrival on the world stage of the transnational corporation and the global assembly, two entities which are often seen as emblematic of globalisation'. In sum, these examples of early internationalism illustrate that cross-border worker solidarity predates the contemporary permutation of globalization and transnational capital. However, with the intensification of this globalizing process, worker internationalism becomes fundamental to the ability of workers to counter their conditions and increase their bargaining power.

A new era begins

Clearly, the global garment industry is in flux. The new world of 'fast fashion', requiring just-in-time production and minimal inventory, necessitated production-side upgrades that process retailer point-of-sale and logistics data, creating 'closer connections between the different stages of the production to retail chain' (Azmeh and Nadvi 2014: 708). Although the extraction of raw materials and textiles has a long history in Asia, modern export-oriented garment production did not begin in earnest until the 1980s and 1990s – and, here, the history of 'liberalized' industries elsewhere makes for an illuminating comparison.

What we find is that there have been significant changes in the global production and distribution of garments since the 2005 phase-out of the global quota arrangement MFA. The MFA, originally negotiated in 1974, was a compromise between the developed and developing nations in which rich (importing) countries agreed to establish textile and clothing quotas – quantitative ceilings – for each exporting country. The MFA meant that the sector became the most widely distributed industry in the world. Its phase out, and the near end of quotas in the sector, resulted in the restructuring of global investment in the industry, introducing massive volatility by concentrating production in a handful of countries ensuring significant industrial job growth in China, Vietnam, Bangladesh, and India (Majmudar 2008).[20] Ross (2014) sees these economic developments as a further entrenchment and expansion of capital across both the textile and clothing commodity chains, 'from the cotton fields to the retail rack'. The combination of the phase-out of the MFA and the intensification of the globalization process meant that apparel exports rose, prices fell, and production relocated to the above-mentioned labour-rich countries (Lopez-Acevedo and Robertson 2012). More options for buyers concentrated greater profits to the top, intensified downward pressure, and allowed the strongest supplier to survive. The result: higher concentrations of production in fewer countries and, in quick succession, vertical and horizontal growth in large domestic producers – consolidating production in the hands of fewer firms.

In Bair and Gereffi's (2001) study of the blue jeans industry of Torreon, Mexico, it was found that the 1994 introduction of the NAFTA gave rise to a similar phenomenon of production in the context of the US, Mexico, and Canada. Low-value manufacturing firms, *maquiladora* or *maquila* for short, quickly ascended the value chain. NAFTA allowed buyers, primarily within the US, to circumvent MFA restrictions enabling an uninhibited flow of goods and capital between regional garment buyers and producers. Bair and Gereffi (2001) point out that, in 1993, before NAFTA,

> the only link on the Mexico side was assembly; by 1996, textile production as well as the post-assembly stage of laundering and finishing, one of the

---

[20] The Asian bloc of China, Bangladesh, Indonesia, India, and Vietnam makes up 95 per cent of all garment imports to the US (Ross 2014).

first production processes liberalised under NAFTA, were added. In 2000, the full range of production activities was taking place in Torreon. The other links of the chain that have been transferred to Torreon mean that more backward linkages and value are being added in the region beyond the assembly activities that were dominant prior to the emergence of full-package networks.

Bair and Gereffi (2001) note that upgrading in Torreon occurred with a small number of first-tier manufacturers possessing the capacities and capital needed to coordinate full-package networks. Having already acquired familiarity with US retailers and brands through their experiences in *maquila* production, these manufacturers were able to develop direct links with those same firms – eliminating the middlemen and expanding vertically – achieving higher profits than they ever had with *maquila* orders.

The rise of the *maquila* industry in Mexico, which witnessed a new dynamism with the addition of new jobs and blossoming export business, also experienced the rapid consolidation of large garment manufacturers and the consequent closure of many small- and medium-sized firms. As in Italy during the 1970s and 1980s, Mexico of the 1990s and 2000s saw new networks in specialized garment manufacture lead to an economic upswing, and a subsequent rise in real wages (Bair and Gereffi 2001).[21]

In the examples of Yue Yuen (Chapter 3) and Arvind (Chapter 4), both firms cemented the vertical and horizontal organizational benefits of sectorally specialized geographic clusters found in Italy, Mexico, and South America in the preceding decades of the 1970s and 1980s. The firms mirrored the vertical-integration of industrial clusters in terms of capacity exchange and production transfer by absorbing the industrial geography and growing upstream in the supply chain. On the other hand, Fruit of the Loom (Chapter 5) became vertically integrated almost exclusively as an outgrowth of the product they produced and these early trade interventions in Central America.

Contrary to what many scholars predicted, the argument here is that the expiration of the MFA sparked a chain reaction that would ultimately lead to a growth in the bargaining power of garment sector workers. The specialization of production combined with the growth of a domestic market in the emerging economies permits sufficient capital accumulation for organizational and

---

[21] This boom was very short-lived, as competition from China ('the China price') and elsewhere combined with other factors saw real wages in Mexican manufacturing decline for the past 20 years.

technological expansion, allows large capital-holding firms to erect insurmountable barriers to entry for smaller capitals, and results in aggregated profits for those firms that survived. As outlined below and at length in Chapter 6, this trend is strongest in labour-rich regions of Asia, which have also witnessed the greatest concentration of post-MFA production. These dynamics are not static of course, and there is a likelihood of significant proletarianization in other regions not highlighted in-depth in this book (that is, Africa). While certainly there is some movement in capital towards these regions, at this stage it is still not substantial.

In Asia, the consolidation of capital contributed to time–space compression by increasing the speed, amplitude, efficiency, and reliability of goods from production to consumption. The rise of large multinational garment producers and their effect on the relationship between buyers and suppliers, workers and management is yet to be widely documented (notable exceptions include Appelbaum 2008; Merk 2008; Appelbaum 2009; Azmeh and Nadvi 2014; Gereffi 2014; Kumar 2019a, 2019b). Azmeh and Nadvi (2014: 709) argue that 'such firms could one day challenge the power of the global buyers they now serve, and potentially become global buyers in their own right. There remains a complete absence of [analysis on] how these changing dynamics may alter the position of workers vis-à-vis their direct employers'. Indeed, there remains a dearth of research on the large and growing specialized garment and footwear sectors, let alone the labour relations involved therein.

Large buyers are increasingly agreeing to longer-term, larger-volume relationships with a progressively smaller number of full-package producers, changing power relations within the value chain as well as workers' strategies. The decline of assembly-only-oriented garment capitals is part of a process outlined in greater detail in the chapters ahead.[22]

In the post-MFA period, specialized garment producers based in Asia have grown apace; Korea-based Yupoong Inc. has become the world's largest producer of hats, Datang is now responsible for more than a third of the world's sock output, Taiwan-based Nien Hsing has reached the summit of denim production,[23]

---

[22] Fold's (2002) 'bi-polar' supply chains are fundamentally asymmetrical since large cocoa buyers 'control' competition through source distribution while specialization within clothing production results in increasingly interdependent 'symbiosis' between buyers and producers.

[23] Nien Hsing has publicly made much of large investments in Lesotho in southern Africa. Since 2000, garments have become the tiny country's largest sector, with Nien Hsing becoming the largest employer. They produce for brands such as Levis, VF (Lee and Wrangler), and Children's Place. In 2018, Lesotho's trade unions succeeding

and Panarub, in Indonesia, is Adidas' exclusive cleats manufacturer. As Richard Appelbaum (2008: 70) notes, 'We are now entering an era in which a qualitatively higher degree of integration between production and distribution has begun to reshape the entire buyer-driven global commodity chain ... [which is] altering the relationship between "manufacturer" on the one hand and "retail buyer" on the other.' In addition, Milberg and Winker (2010) maintain that geographic consolidation, both horizontally and vertically, became even more pronounced in 'buyer-driven' value chains since the 2008 global financial crisis.

These changes at the point of commodity production are uneven since the ascendance of branded apparel firms is highly dependent on the developmental process (Jin, Kandagal, and Jung 2013). Take the South Asia region as a case in point. Large capital-holding garment manufacturers have spread across South Asia, exploiting uneven regional development. The late appearance of Indian firms on the international stage compared to other large emerging economies is a consequence of the widespread resistance of India's business elites to state policies of discipline or liberalization (Chibber 2003). However, while large firms have emerged in India and Sri Lanka, firms in Bangladesh and Pakistan remain comparatively small and limited. India's burgeoning consumer market and Sri Lanka's early entry into garment production explain the contrast in domestic firm maturation. In Sri Lanka, two firms are now pre-eminent: Mas Holdings and BrandX. Both are heavily invested internationally but Mas Holdings has a diverse portfolio, possessing factories in India and Bangladesh, real estate investments in the United Kingdom, holiday resorts and spice plantations, joint ventures in major garment brands, and a finance section that operates out of the Maldives. Gokaldas, in India, has nearly 40 large factories in Karnataka. Shahi has over 56 large factories. Celebrity Fashions has expanded beyond India to Bangladesh and has established sizeable domestic brands.

In Korea, there are about 20 firms that produce a significant proportion of the clothing destined for global markets. The biggest is Sae-A, which has 17 large factories in Vietnam, Indonesia, China, Guatemala, Nicaragua, and Haiti, producing for Walmart, Gap, JC Penney, Kohl's, and several other big retailers. Another is Youngone Group, with 28,000 workers in its factories in Bangladesh and about as many in Vietnam, producing for Nike, The North Face, Patagonia, and several other big brands. This diversified geographic sourcing is typical of the Korean and Taiwanese firms who shifted away from their native countries long

---

in winning a 62 per cent minimum wage increase after they called for a shutdown of the garment and textile industrial areas of Maseru, Maputsoe, and Nyenye (Barrie 2018).

ago because of a combination of high costs, in some cases politically motivated incentives, and in response to a very militant trade union movement led by the garment workers.[24]

The Chinese, Indian, and Bangladeshi companies are more oriented towards domestic production because of the size of the domestic market into which they hope to expand and the large reserve army of labour available at low cost. One of Asia's largest trouser manufacturers and dress shirt makers is Hong Kong–based TAL Group. TAL produces for the brand-retailers Banana Republic and J. Crew and claims that it makes one in every six dress shirts sold in the US. In 2007, TAL opened a large-scale trouser factory of 2,400 workers in Dongguan, China, with the expectation that they would remain there for at least two decades. However, citing increased wages, they announced its closure in 2015. TAL chief executive, Roger Lee, stated that the company was losing money since 2013 or 2014 and would move its production to its factory in Malaysia as well as expand to Vietnam (Chu 2015).

However, issues of upgrading, relocation, labour-intensity, and skill are complex and interdependent. Take the example of TAL cited above. While falling profits at TAL Groups trouser factory in Dongguan forced the firm to relocate to Malaysia and Vietnam, it continued to operate its dress shirt factory of 4,000 workers in China. The 'skill' involved in the production of dress shirts contributed to TAL's ability to corner the market, thereby allowing it the space to edge out competitors and continue its production at a profit in China. As a *Wall Street Journal* article aptly stated, 'The shirts can be more complicated – and therefore more profitable – to sew than pants, because the fabric is thinner and puckers more easily' (Chu 2015).

The appearance of new world production systems has forced trade unions, which traditionally focused efforts at national-level targets, to reach beyond their borders to coordinate, deepen, and expand transnational cooperation to pressure TNCs. While genuine internationalism has not been seen in the labour movement for nearly a hundred years, in some senses neoliberal globalization forced trade unionists and activists to look beyond their borders. As Stiglitz (2016: 7) argues, after the 1999 WTO protests in Seattle it became clear that 'globalisation had succeeded in unifying people from around the world – against globalisation'. It is not the case that a majority, or even a noticeable proportion, of workers and social movements are united against globalization – what is clear

---

[24] Jeff Hermanson (interview, 12 February 2019) was told by Kihak Sung, founder and owner of Youngone Group, that he was taken prisoner in his own factory in Korea for 30 days by the union. Sung's experience was not an exception.

is that production in labour-intensive sectors is radically transforming. However, while neoliberal globalization works to destroy old forms of organization, it also creates new ones in its wake. The old world is indeed dying, and a new world is struggling to be born.[25]

Chapters 6 and 7 delve deeper into the question of consolidation and labour agency, respectively. I expand on the idea of 'buyer–producer symbiosis' as a new formation of power between actors in the global supply chain. *Buyer–producer symbiosis* fills a lacuna in Gereffi (1994, 2002) and Gereffi, Humphrey, and Sturgeon (2005) by recognizing the growing symbiotic power relationship in garment and footwear between large transnational buyers and large *transnationlizing* producers. GVCs are not static, and just as 'the increase[ed] disaggregation of value chains [...] allowed new kinds of lead firms to capture value' (Pickles and Smith 2016: 25), so too the mergers, acquisitions, and consolidation of supplier-end capitals into large capital-holding firms allow new kinds of garment and footwear supplier firms to capture value. The introduction of 'symbiosis' is an observation of the power relationship, through an analysis *inter alia* of changes in structure, technology, and territoriality, as the consequence of the emergence of giant capitals on either side of the garment and footwear GVC.

Conceptually, these changes in the production process in labour-rich countries are changing the landscape of global production, informing the distribution and capture[26] of value across the chain. While the spatial fix played a prominent role in capitalist globalization, now, through an 'organizational fix', capital can invest in fixed capital, which hinders the spatial fix, while absorbing its crisis tendency. What emerged from capital's 'organizational fix' was a new large-scale monopolistic network with territorially embedded firms in the sector, resulting in supplier-end upgrading, raising insurmountable barriers to entry, and calling into question established orthodoxy. These economies of scale, a monopolistic 'strategic asset', has the effect of changing the monopsonistic relationship between global buyers and producers into a buyer–producer symbiosis, adding restraints to a historically footloose capital, and may help grind this 'race' to a halt in 'sweated' manufacturing entirely.[27]

---

[25] Quoted from Antonio Gramsci (1992).

[26] The utility of 'value capture' in this book is primarily at a conceptual level. For a more comprehensive analysis of the spatialized and contextualized conceptual understanding of value capture in production networks, see Pickles and Smith (2016).

[27] Monopoly capital, Baran and Sweezy (1969) argue, emerges in advanced capitalism typified by the giant corporation. Thus, the growth of these manufacturing firms should be understood within the larger development of global capitalism. Similar to Baran and Sweezy (1969), 'monopsony capital' is intended more as an analytical

Through an understanding of the generation, concentration, and distribution of value alongside the GVCs, this book analyses the shifting dynamics of capital and the world economy as a whole. By utilizing Gereffi's buyer- and producer-driven binary chain model for its explanatory power as it relates to workers' strategies by homing in on the changing materiality of production-end firms, it also attempts to move beyond the buyer/producer-driven dichotomy. In place of the earlier assembly-only CMT firms, which had integrated across the supply chain into higher value sectors, it is argued that the dominance of 'full-package' specialized garment and footwear producers is giving the relationship between 'producer' and global 'buyer' an increasingly symbiotic character, dramatically affecting power dynamics, and finally offering a new opportunity for every challenge it presents for workers' resistance and greater bargaining power in those sectors that have long defined the sweatshop.

---

device rather than a quantitative measure. While monopoly can best be understood as a horizontal relation, monopsony is a vertical one. Outlined in great detail in Chapter 6, I propose this theory to outline the meteoric rise of large outsourced firms with incredibly high competitive advantages, shifting power relations within the GVC and opening up new vistas for labour strategies. Indeed, theories of monopoly are not entirely new to the GCC/GPN/GVC tradition but intimately linked to its foundations. As Starosta (2010: 439) notes, 'It is remarkable that one of the founding works in the GCC paradigm by Gereffi, Korzeniewicz and Korzeniewicz (1994) explicitly situates the emerging approach broadly within the intellectual lineage of monopoly capital theory; or rather, in what the world-system approach shared with it.'

2

The Global Sweatshop

In 2005, the late Neil Kearney, then General Secretary of the International Textile, Garment, and Leather Workers' Federation (ITGLWF),[1] delivered a series of speeches under the banner 'Life beyond Codes'. Kearney drew attention to the losses the garment workers had experienced over the previous decade, during which real wages had fallen by 25 per cent and working hours had risen by 25 per cent to an average of 60 hours a week. He painted a 'pretty depressing picture' of the existing governance regimes (ITGLWF 2007). 'Ten years of corporate code of conduct application,' Kearney proclaimed, 'had brought little change to workplaces, with conditions often worse than they were a decade ago. [...] Now the time has come to be looking at "life beyond codes".' Neil Kearney's personal evolution, as a banker turned garment sector union leader, is not incongruent in a regime of 'social models' where structural antagonisms are blurred, and the emphasis is placed on class cooperation. Nonetheless, Kearney recognized the profound restructuring global capitalism had undergone since the late 1960s and the consequent need for labour to globalize its own strategies in response. For Kearney and the ITGLWF's case, this meant globalizing the 'social partnership model'.

As outlined in Chapter 1, contemporaneous with the rise of globalization, new initiatives emerged to counter the fragmentation of state-based trade unions and the increased fluidity of capital in an attempt to globalize workers' rights. Top-down initiatives, often face-saving measures for TNCs, included consumer-led campaigns driven by NGOs, in addition to efforts by supranational bodies such as the International Labour Organization (ILO) and World Bank. Global North garment trade unions responded to globalization with two different types of transnational countervailing strategies: the Global Union Federation (GUF)–initiated global framework agreements (GFAs) and the US-led anti-sweatshop strategies.

---

[1] In 2012, the ITGLWF merged with GUFs ICEM and IMF to form IndustriALL. IndustriALL is based in Geneva.

In Europe, capital and labour confrontation became a compromise and was bound up with a strong state regulatory apparatus. But in North America, more specifically the US but later also Canada, where regulations were comparatively weak, the International Ladies' Garment Workers' Union (ILGWU) was nonetheless successful and overcame many of the same hurdles that mark today's globalized epoch. Two irreconcilable garment worker trade union strategies grew out of Europe's partnerships versus US antagonistic models.

Both European and North American approaches to tackling globalization's consequences in the garment industry fell under the 'global governance' regime of the 1990s, but utilized very different tactics.[2] In Europe, unions reconfigured the International Trade Secretariats (ITSs) as GUFs; in the US, they pursued campaign strategies through an uneasy alliance with the anti-sweatshop movement. These strategies – and indeed their failures – were responding to structures that had been intact for a century, embedded into the structure of the garment and footwear sectors. Despite this, there was a time when garment workers' wages, union density, and collective bargaining matched their male counterparts in the auto sector. In the US, between the 1920s and 1960s, the ILGWU would combine a supply chain 'jobbers' agreement (JA)' demand and a clandestine organizing strategy to win enormous gains for workers.

The novelty of the US garment sector was that it has long been vertically disintegrated, and, not coincidentally, the federalist system of laws that governed the ebbs and flows of US domestic commerce across state borders bear comparison to the globalized garment industry in its infancy. Innovations by labour led to innovations by capital, which led to further innovations by labour, which led to further innovations by capital, and so on (Tronti 1966; Herod 1997; Silver 2003).[3]

---

[2] There is a vast and growing body of literature that has identified governance measures under different labels, among which are 'soft law' (Cini 2001), 'outsourced regulation' (O'Rourke 2003), 'privatised regulation' (AFL-CIO 2013), 'self-regulation' (Blackett 2000), 'stateless regulation' (Seidman 2007), 'auditing regime' (Kumar and Mahoney 2014), 'non-state driven governance' (Cashore 2002), and simply 'governance' (Levy and Prakash 2003; Hassel 2008).

[3] In the 1960s and 1970s, Italian autonomist Marxists began to develop a theory of capital and labour based on observing the car factories of Turin. Italian *operaismo* (or 'workerism') posits an internal history of capital in which the militancy of the industrial working class catalyses the valorization of capital. Similar ideas were applied to labour geography, primarily through the work of Andy Herod (1997). It was an alternative understanding of capitalist history. Rather than simply capitalists shaping capital, it was workers who helped shape and circumscribe capital. The contemporary structure, composition, and dynamics of labour and capital should

Labour's successful attempt to 'chase the work' to combat garment capital's internal 'race to the bottom' within the US and then across North America was prognostic for the sector's internationalization. The ILGWU's demand for a JA, while efficacious in winning gains for US and Canadian garment workers for a half century, never directly confronted the three-part structure of the sector – it merely worked around it.

Global apparel production resembles the jobber–contractor system of production that characterized the US domestic industry before the rise of offshoring of production in the second half of the twentieth century. The domestic outsourcing of American garment production began at the turn of the twentieth century in lower Manhattan. The outsourced system began as a means of ensuring union-free workplaces, low fixed costs, and therefore low liabilities in a highly volatile sector. By the late 1960s, the 'sweatshop' had returned almost exclusively to the garment and footwear sectors with US brands outsourcing to Global South factories – first to the Caribbean, then to Mexico, then to Central America, and finally across China and the rest of Asia.[4]

Unions have since had to confront the related problems of capital flight and a race to the bottom in labour costs. Over five decades, production moved from the unionized shops of lower Manhattan and Montreal to the non-union US Northeast, and then to the US South and West – which were historically hostile to efforts to organize labour – and from there to Puerto Rico. At the time, the ILGWU utilized a systematized and clandestine organizing method – which included wall-to-wall factory floor organizing, retail consumer boycotts, and industrial action to demand collective bargaining directly from brands such as Calvin Klein and Ralph Lauren, who were known as 'jobbers' because they outsourced – or 'jobbed out' – their production to their contractors, the direct employers. These direct brand–union agreements were called 'JAs'. Jobbers' agreements ensured workers received

---

be read with this in mind. Indeed, some of the strategies and demands deployed by workers then may have helped to cement the structure of today's transnational garment sector.

[4] Item 807 of the US Tariff Code permitted the assembly of US components in the Caribbean Basin, with tariffs paid only on the 'value-added', which was almost nothing because of low wages. US jobbers set up cutting shops in the Miami area, employing immigrant workers, and sent the cut parts to the free trade zones of the Dominican Republic for assembly. As was witnessed in the New York City Garment District in the late 1970s, this approach was also used in Mexico, with 'twin plants' on both sides of the border. Calvin Klein jeans, for example, were cut in El Paso, Texas, and sewn in Torreon. The bigger, definitive move to Mexico took place after the signing of NAFTA in 1994 (interview: Jeff Hermanson, 12 February 2019).

better pay and conditions, embedding the antagonism between labour and capital within a relatively combative system of industrial relations.

Meanwhile, in Europe, a diametrically opposite method developed under the aegis of social democratic states where labour and capital undertook 'social dialogue' to form 'social partnerships'.[5] Compared to its North American counterpart, European capital in the sector remained relatively fixed, vertically integrated, and *cooperative*. European trade unionists were still largely insulated from the hazards that accompany outsourcing and a wage race to the bottom. This 'social model' developed out of, and was the result of, the historic class conflict and social confrontation between labour and capital, and this 'class compromise' became institutionalized in the 1930s across much of Western Europe and led to enormous gains for workers and formed the basis for the welfare state (Wahl 2004: 2). Consequently, this process sidelined the trade union militants, de-politicizing the working class, and eased the antagonisms between workers and their employers (Hobsbawm 1995). The achievements of the social partnership model engendered a working-class ideology attracted to peaceful social dialogue, averse to confrontation, and 'deeply rooted in the national and European trade union bureaucracy' (Wahl 2004: 4). However, the class compromise was always a delicate arrangement predicated on capitalist growth within the West. Thus, this social partnership became increasingly untenable during the economic crisis of the 1970s and onwards as capital internationalized and class contradictions heightened.

Transnational collective bargaining?

When production began its migration to the Global South in the late 1960s, these two approaches, the European 'social model' – let us call it the 'inside model' – and the US 'outside model' (which opted to respond to workers' struggles at the factory-level through clandestine campaigns), were at loggerheads as both sought to expand the scope of their activities to meet the challenges of hypermobile capital. The European garment trade unions lacked the recent experience of US unions, who had already battled regionally decentralized capital and reactionary anti-unionism for decades – problems both sides of the Atlantic now faced. US unions, for their own part, were hesitant to advance beyond their own national

---

[5] 'Social dialogue' also known as social pact, social contract, class compromise, or consensus policy is 'the relatively stable power relations and peaceful cohabitation between labour and capital, which was dominant in the post-War period in particular in most of Western Europe' (Wahl 2004: 1).

borders. And because of these respective failings, globalized capital in the garment sector has so far succeeded in its objective of expansion – at the expense of labour.

Formal union bureaucracies launched various governance initiatives, namely GFAs. The GFAs be understood as 'institutional transnationalism' because they are led and instituted by the formal union bureaucracies, which may have a broad reach and support in local union efforts. These agreements often negotiated and signed within the headquarters of TNCs and GUFs, far away from the subcontracted sites of production, lack the participation of grassroots actors (local workers and local management alike) (McCallum 2013). On the other hand, some organizing campaigns may be considered as examples of 'participatory transnationalism', in which workers target factory owners and brands, and later ally with consumers to launch campaigns against brands and retailers, building power through the active participation of workers. Although the latter tactic has succeeded in isolated cases, it lacked the institutional scale to be more than short-lived victories.

Both US and European industrial relations should be understood as the regulation of work by the combination of three factors: state intervention, market forces, and collective bargaining (Hyman 2005). First coined by British Fabians Beatrice and Sydney Webb, 'collective bargaining' described the negotiations between trade unions and employers in the late nineteenth century. In Webbs' book *Industrial Democracy* (2010), the Collective Bargaining Agreement (CBA) was said to have revolutionized the operation of supply and demand, introducing new 'rule makers' and 'regulators' that enabled workers to 'ward off the evil effects of industrial competition' (Webb and Webb 2010: 867). They noted that the employer and the employee have opposing interests. Thus, 'a collective bargaining agreement [was], in an institutional form, the temporary outcome of a conflict situation' (Gallin 2008: 26). Furthermore, the Webbs found that the scope of collective bargaining was progressively enlarged, 'from the workshop to the whole town, and from the town to the whole industry' (Flanders 1968: 3), as workers made rational extensions of their victories. The CBAs served to consolidate the balance of power in society. Collective bargaining, and indeed industrial relations in most countries, first developed on local and occupational bases and did not expand to national institutional frameworks until much later (Hyman 2005). And it was quickly discovered that 'the greater the scale of the bargaining unit, the greater their advantage' (Flanders 1968: 3). More workers in the collective meant more power at the negotiating table – as long as workers were willing to take collective action. A similar conclusion can be drawn today at a transnational level as the fundamentals remain mostly unchanged. Despite the obvious trajectory of such an antagonism, decades of general strikes, factory occupations, and depression-era work stoppages had to transpire before the integration of a US regulatory apparatus, of which some sectors, such as garments, always remained largely outside.

Recent years have seen a growing body of literature on transnational workers' movements, many documenting instances of cross-border and transnational trade union solidarity (Bronfenbrenner 2007; Friedman 2009; Anner 2011). In spite of this, class struggle is still often portrayed as a sealed chapter in history following the deindustrialization of the Global North (Castells 1996). Even within labour studies, much of the focus remains confined to nation-states (Pasture 2002). Historically, however, working-class nationalism and internationalism have emerged simultaneously, with the trade union movement becoming nationally oriented over time (Hensman 2011). Trade union transnationalism often maintained its internationalist political rhetoric while gradually developing into a kind of trade union tourism or diplomacy in international bodies such as the ILO (Wahl 2004). Pasture (2002) claims that, while internationalism once played a significant role in the formation of socialist working-class identity, trade unions focused their energies only on winning social advances and transforming their local regimes into welfare states (Pasture 2002). From industrialization into the post–World War II era, capital controls and trade regulation ensured that the industry remained largely fixed within national boundaries, such that internationalism was not yet a necessity for Global North workers (Tilly 1995). Even in an era of globalized capital, trade unions in the North, instead of launching international campaigns, still often resort to protectionism by appealing to nationalist sympathies and allying themselves with domestic producers (Haworth and Ramsay 1988).

Charles Tilly (1995) has argued that globalization threatens the established labour rights by undermining the state's capacity to guarantee those rights. He claims that globalization has returned industrial relations to their state in the early nineteenth century and that the kind of industrialization that led to regulatory apparatuses, enshrining the collective rights of workers, has now come to an end. Tilly contends that the state operated as an arbiter between labour and capital, a history that is contested by Peter Evans (2010: 356) who claims that the state has rarely been a dependable ally of labour, stating:

> Such moments can be easily interpreted as consequences of labour mobilization rather than causes of successful contestation. The Tilly (1995) vision of the state as essential ally may be plausible for mid-twentieth century European social democracies, but state as ally to capital and implacable adversary to labour is the more familiar role in the Global South (and the United States). […] In short, equating neo-liberal globalisation with the loss of the state as ally is a dubious proposition.

Varieties of workers' association

The first efforts of the national unions to make global connections were confined to specific trades and industries. By the middle of the nineteenth century, there had been a proliferation of what were then called International Trade Secretariats (or ITSs, now Global Union Federations, or GUFs). These developed contemporary to, and often in consequence of, exacerbations of racial, geographic, and class divisions caused by imperialism. Attempts at global industrial relations in the garment sector grew out of the national traditions of the late twentieth century, namely Europe's 'inside model', the US's 'outside model', Japan's management-dominated 'company employment relations model', the state subordinated models of other East Asian trade unions (Deyo 1989), and some emerging garment unions in the Global South (that is, Philippines in the 1980s and 1990s) that espoused a militant, revolutionary model. Of these, the US- and Europe-based models became the primary transnational approaches to resisting globalization in the 1980s, 1990s, and 2000s.

Defining the European social 'dialogue', 'partnership', and social model (or here simply as 'inside model') precisely is difficult and heavily contested (Guest and Peccei 2001), but generally 'social dialogue/partnership' is meant to identify a relationship between employers and trade unions which ensures a 'cooperative set of relations within the firm' (Heery 2002: 21). This *inside model* matured in the highly developed system of social protection and extensive labour market regulation of the post–World War II era known as the 'golden age' of welfare capitalism in Western Europe (Esping-Andersen 1999). In Europe, the system was enshrined in the 1957 Treaty of Rome, before being repackaged and included in the 1993 Maastricht Treaty, and then modernized again in 2009's Lisbon Treaty. Despite this model being a nationally embedded system of industrial relations, Hyman (2005) highlights a few important underlying similarities across Western Europe. First, a regulated and a robust welfare state led to significant limits on the degree to which labour power could be commodified; second, CBAs had taken priority over the individual labour market contract; and last, the acceptance that labour necessitated representation, a premise from which it followed that labour should be a 'social partner', shaping the work life of a nation, from its individual firms to governmental policy. Social partnerships solidified the relationship of labour and capital, leading to unified demands upon the state that ensured job security, extensive training, flexible working hours, and broader social protections (Knell and Britain 1999). Unfortunately, the system also led to the protection of the immediate employment-centred interest of union members and deliberate insecurity for those less likely to be unionized (Heery

2002). Even within much of Europe, with a few exceptions (namely Germany), the inside model only lasted a few decades, and 'flexibilizing' this model was declared the objective of governments and political parties in parts of Europe at least since the 1980s.

Before the relocation of production to the Global South, the power imbalances in these 'partnerships' were already heavily tilted towards employers (Guest and Peccei 2001). Once deindustrialization began to set in, and the necessity for new tactics became clear, European trade unions merely adapted the already weakened social partnership model to a global stage. This grew out of a combination of habit, an entrenched bureaucracy, and fatalism. It failed to understand that the strength of labour grew out of collective action and the weakness of labour in the present did not necessarily symbolize an interminable decline in labour in terms of class consciousness but was merely 'synchronised with the rhythms of the capitalist economy' (Kelly 1998: 1) and was therefore spatially, temporally, and materially contingent.

Without the intercessory power of the state on their side, a lack of union density, and often weak client states in the Global South, these efforts of 'institutional transnationalism' largely proved fruitless. Despite some healthy diversity in the ranks – for example, the centralized French state began a centralized labour movement, while the decentralized Swiss state began a dispersed labour movement (Hanagan 2003) – this effort (first taken up by the ITGLWF, then taken up by IndustriALL) has mostly fallen flat.

Across the Atlantic, in the US, pluralistic state structures led to different, more economistic business unionism (Levi 2003) – though a few sectors were left out. Garment, and later agriculture and service work, remained largely excluded from new labour protections. While the mostly black, and later Latino, agricultural and service workers were subject to the prejudices embedded in the 1935 Wagner Act – a direct legacy of antebellum slavery – garment sector exemption was a function of its supply chain structure (Perea 2011). Antagonistic conditions limited trade unions in these sectors. What I call the *outside model* would emerge in conjunction with an increasingly deregulated US labour market. The outside model, which includes both hot shop tactics and strategic mapping, descends from, at least, the early twentieth century, with the 1905 strike movement and the subsequent repression in Russia leading to a clandestine approach and popularized throughout the world by the Communist International and in the US by the Communist Party USA (Patel 2013). Its formulation as the 'organizing model' would arrive much later.

Officially coined by the American Federation of Labor and Congress of Industrial Organizations (AFL-CIO) in 1988, the 'organizing model' distinguished itself from the 'servicing model' to 'help people by solving problems for them' by 'involv[ing] members in solutions' (AFL-CIO 1988: 6). It was conceived expressly to shift power and decision-making to the rank and file, and marked a shift in practice regarding recruitment, operations, and targets. In contrast, the traditional 'service model' emphasized the role of dedicated staff in the arbitration process and grievance procedures, charged solely with providing service, which effectively suppressed membership participation (Banks and Metzgar 1989). The 'organizing model' jump-started active recruitment, launching confrontational campaigns stressing strategic research and supply chain mapping, and encouraging membership leadership, while also building clandestine worker committees and establishing broader community support (Heery et al. 2000).

This model was a formalization of tactics and strategies deployed by the least institutionalized sectors and trade unions in twentieth-century US labour history. Rather than simply target immediate employers or the state, the organizing model focused its efforts on leveraging primary actors in the supply chain: jobbers in the 1930s garment sector (Anner, Bair, and Blasi 2012); retailers in the agricultural sector in the campaigns of the UFW in the 1960s (Shaw 2008); the clients contracting out cleaning services in the Service Employees International Union's (SEIU) 'Justice for Janitors' campaigns in the 1980s (Waldinger et al. 1996).

To understand 'participatory transnationalism', we must consider the historical traditions out of which it has grown. Different kinds of capitalism led to differences in how value chains were formed and the way civil society actors attempted to challenge and transform them (Bair and Palpacuer 2012). The US jobber–contractor system and the European social system engendered different forms of domestic industrial relations, a divide which has persisted since the earliest efforts to globalize garment labour strategies (Voss and Sherman 2000; Heery 2002).

As noted earlier, the JA within the US garment labour tradition is a reaction to domestic outsourcing in the garment sector, to capital's flight from state to state, in search of a higher return. Globalization has since exacerbated the challenges that capital mobility creates for workers, who must now collectivize if they are to have a chance against their common enemy. Since the advent of outsourcing in the US system of garment production in the early twentieth century, the primary methods of confronting the consequent race to the bottom it inaugurates, among other ill effects, in the garment sector arrived in two phases: first, the JA regime in Canada and the US and, then, the global anti-sweatshop movement. As American trade unionists and union-linked NGOs continued to push a modified tradition of the JA through organizing campaigns and holding brands responsible for labour conditions, the Europe-centric ITGLWF attempted to scale its social partnership model globally – typified by the development of GFAs.

The jobber–contractor system

Although there has been a great deal of research on the 'organizing model', the conclusions drawn from it rarely take into account the early precedent set by workers in the American garment sector. The omission of JAs in otherwise robust critiques of the social auditing regime and the exploration of what those agreements might mean for the twenty-first century is a loss for the field.

Figure 2.1 Price-settlement committee assesses clothing in order to determine price, ultimately settled between jobber, contractor, and union (est. 1950s)

Source: Retrieved from Kheel Centre ILGWU Archives.

Building union density, raising wages, and forcing employers to establish safe work environments have always required the use of innovative and intuitive organizing methods. Within the garment sector, the ILGWU made gains despite its vertical disintegration. In this structure, a retailer, such as a department store, like Macy's, held the top position; and it obtained goods through the next rung below, a jobber, that is, a brand, such as Calvin Klein. The jobber was responsible for designing goods, marketing them to the public, and supplying the fabric necessary for their construction to contractors. The contractor hired workers to manufacture these goods. This allowed unions to exert pressure on all three while only specifically targeting the jobber. At the turn of the twentieth century, when New York City was still the epicentre of domestic garment production, the ILGWU, due to its early adoption of this tactic, was the largest union in the sector, and confronted many of the same dilemmas found in the globalized industrial relations of the 1980s and onwards: subcontracting, mobile capital, and porous government protections. But globalization has now allowed capital to escape their orbit, and vastly expand the scope of its operations. Soon, other sectors, such as those in the capital-intensive manufacturing, adopted their own 'jobber–contactor' systems (that is, outsourcing) as a standard for GVCs.

The JA regimes were characterized by three mutually reinforcing contractual relationships: (*a*) the national industrial union negotiated contracts with a jobber over the designation of contractors, stipulating prices the jobber will pay to allow for fair wages and other provisions; (*b*) factory-level union representatives negotiated CBAs with direct employers or contractors; (*c*) the jobber gives long-term contracts to the designated unionized contractors who incorporate the pricing and other provisions from its agreement with the industrial union.

Confronting these structures a century ago, the ILGWU targeted not only the contractors, but the buyers (the 'jobbers') as well. The ILGWU maintained that the responsibility for labour conditions rested primarily with the jobbers, since contracted factories were completely dependent on them. The first such JA was born at Wiesen, Cohen, and Smith, a dress wholesaler, in 1922 (*NYT* 1922) and was hailed as the ILGWU's 'move to rationalise the chaos in the industry and create conditions for its own expansion' (Whalen 2008: 196). But it was not until the 1930s, when ILGWU locals went on strike while also boycotting retailers and threatening additional industrial action, that the agreements would expand and deepen. A 1955 Federal Trade Commission (FTC) ruling gives a synopsis of the ILGWU's history in its findings, revealing that the JAs had been won primarily through these and similar actions, issuing from the factory floor, in New York City cloak and suit sectors circa 1933, later the dress sector (circa 1936), and finally through actions in Los Angeles, where production had fled (circa 1942; FTC 1955).

The 1957 Garment Industry Proviso, an amendment to the National Labour Relations Act, recognized the 'joint employership' of both contractor and jobber within the garment sector. Joint employership had long facilitated the creation of a triangle bargaining system between the garment sector's three primary actors: workers (represented through a union), jobbers, and contractors. Triangle bargaining functioned as follows: a union negotiated a CBA individually with both a contractor and the relevant jobbers (initially with individual jobbers but later with employers' associations of jobbers as well as contractors); then, the jobbers negotiated an agreement with this contractor (Whalen 2008). Negotiations between the jobber and the contractor were essential for ensuring implementation because contractors required increased 'pass through' funds on increases in wages and benefits. The jobber could only terminate its relationship with a 'designated contractor' with 'a just cause' that was legally delineated in the JA. Triangle bargaining, which locked union jobbers into a symbiotic relationship with union contractors, remained the lynchpin for the success of the model.

As JAs proliferated, the membership of the ILGWU grew apace; it expanded from individual jobbers to a broad organized system, requiring jobbers to contract exclusively with a designated list of registered unionized factories. The agreements operated as follows: first, they held both the brands and the owners responsible for factory conditions; second, they ensured funding associated with providing living wages was 'ring-fenced' and not compromised; finally, they empowered workers on the shop floor to implement the measures that they themselves had negotiated (Anner, Bair, and Blasi 2012). The agreements in effect regulated the industry, 'abolish[ing] the "auction block"' (Schlesinger 1951: 103). Moreover, the JAs stabilized the labour market by requiring that jobbers keep the designated permanent contractors 'fully supplied with work'.

The mechanics of the JA forced the jobbers to work with union shops, while protecting wages. In addition, workweeks were set at 35 hours, and the jobber was made responsible for paying benefits (vacations, holidays, pensions, and supplemental unemployment benefits) into discrete and portable (that is, union-controlled) funds that followed workers from shop to shop. For every dollar worth of work put into a union contract shop, the jobber would pay an additional 33 cents into these benefit funds, increasing the cost by an additional 33 per cent above the wages paid at the union shops.[6] Finally, jobbers could only enlist as many contractors necessary to produce the jobbers' goods. JAs represented a comprehensive regulation of wages, hours, and working conditions. For the employer, it simplified things by taking wages and benefits

---

[6] Phone interview, Jeff Hermanson, 12 August 2013.

out of the competitive equation. Companies could, however, still compete in respect of design, quality, sales operation, purchases (such as textiles), and the management of the business.

Jeff Hermanson,[7] the ILGWU's former organizing director, who worked with the union from the mid-1970s to 1997, is now the Director of Global Strategies for Workers United-SEIU, and who helped form the International Union League for Brand Responsibility (IULBR) to organize a 'global JA' strategy. Hermanson states:

> In my experience, in order to force a brand or jobber to accept an all-inclusive agreement of the ILGWU type, it is necessary to mount a campaign that constitutes an existential threat to the brand or jobber and threatens to put them out of business. However, we were often able to get a partial jobbers agreement, covering a portion of a jobbers' contract factories, by causing significant economic and/or reputational damage, even though the existence of the business was not in danger. For an economically rational brand management, the question in such a case boils down to whether it costs more to continue to fight or to settle.

These agreements transformed industrial relations in the sector. They precluded labour cost competition and recognized, through legislative and legal precedent, that the jobber was the 'actual, if not legal, employer' of garment workers, not the subcontracted factory (FTC 1955). These and the aforementioned effects combined to curb the domestic fluidity of capital, answering the core dilemma over subcontracted labour that is now a global problem.

JAs heralded a new epoch in the life of the US garment worker. It dramatically bolstered trade union density and led to significant improvements in factory conditions and living standards. By 1938, *Life* magazine, in a 'Garment Workers at Play' cover story, declared that the era of sweatshops had ended: 'Thirty years ago ... [the garment industry] stank of sweatshops' and now 'the sweatshop is virtually gone'. By 1939, the contracts with the ILGWU were worth nearly $350 million (Wolfson 1950), a sum made even larger when considering the low capitalization of the garment sector. By ensuring that the buyers share in the responsibility for workers' rights, and exerting pressure through workplace agency and collective bargaining, JAs occasioned an almost exponential growth in union membership. Even in the mid-1950s, when American union density was at its domestic post-War peak of 35 per cent, a full 70 per cent of garment workers were unionized (Whalen 2008).

---

[7] Phone interview, Jeff Hermanson, 12 August 2013.

Figure 2.2 Striking dressmakers take a break in a diner, 1955

Source: Retrieved from Kheel Centre ILGWU Archives.

A blueprint for globalization

Early in the twentieth century, firms began popping up outside the production epicentre of Manhattan (labelled 'runaway' or 'out-of-town' shops), in other cities along the east coast. During the 1920s and 1930s, there was an exodus of shops to Connecticut, New Jersey, Pennsylvania, and Massachusetts. The then US Labour Secretary, Frances Perkins, wrote in 1933 that jobbers were contracting in neighbouring states because their 'labour laws were less stringent' (Pasachoff 1999: 76); as a result, they received nearly all the work of New York jobbers (Wolensky, Wolensky, and Wolensky 2002). Relocating the garment industry has always been easy, as Sol Chaikin, ILGWU president from 1975 to 1986, explained: 'It can be moved overnight because capital investment is low, machines are easily transportable and materials are comparatively light. Clothes are not steel, not copper, not lumber, not cement, not brick' (Wolensky, Wolensky, and Wolensky 2002: 25). But, the obvious value of JAs to local workers and their modularity allowed ILGWU organizers to successfully 'chase the work' and retain a 60 per cent density across the sector (Wolensky, Wolensky, and Wolensky 2002: 25).

From the 1940s through the 1960s, a combination of factors, including the Northeast labour shortage concomitant with World War II, large government contracts for military uniforms, the success of JAs, and the passage of the anti-union Taft-Hartley Act (1947), served to open the door for the relocation of factories within the so-called 'right to organize' states in the Northeast to the 'right to work' states in the South, as well as southern California.[8] As the ILGWU continued expending the resources 'chas[ing] the runaways', unions' negotiating power had begun to wane and the quality of contracts declined.[9] Sears, the large retailer, set up a contractor, Kellwood Inc., to produce most of their goods in Mississippi, Arkansas, Tennessee, and Kentucky – states which the ILGWU was still trying to crack into during the 1960s. The ILGWU was, however, successful in unionizing a segment of Kellwood and winning a CBA from contracting firms that were empowered through its agreements with jobbers (who had now become retailers) like Sears. Only 10 per cent of Southern and Southwestern (Texas and Southern California) firms were eventually unionized, compared to the 60 per cent in the Northeast (NY, NJ, CT, PA, MA, and RI) and 35 per cent in the 'Upper South' (VA, MD, and KY) and Midwest (IL, WI, IA, OH, IN, and MN). Despite a general weakening of domestic union power, the ILGWU's demands continued contributing to many successfully negotiated agreements. Meanwhile, cities in Canada – Montreal, Toronto, Vancouver, even Winnipeg – maintained high union density and a strong ILGWU presence. But though JAs continued to operate in Canadian production, local employment protections were relatively strong, making it an unattractive destination for runaway firms.

Initially, the ILGWU used 'bottom up' organizing strategies to force non-union jobbers to sign JAs. In several instances, the ILGWU declared a general strike of all the contractors in a particular industry to organize non-union jobbers and use the momentum created by the power of striking workers to 'clean up' the industry and sweep up any non-union contractors. However, by the 1970s, the ILGWU began to resort to more 'top down' strategies, with an over-reliance on retail pickets, returning to clandestine shop floor organizing in the late 1980s (Wolensky, Wolensky, and Wolensky 2002).

---

[8] In the 1960s, unions were pushing for labour rights centralization. Big capital responded by pushing for 'states' rights' (Harvey 2014), adopting the language of advocates of racial segregation.

[9] Phone interview, Jeff Hermanson, 12 August 2013.

Globalization of the industry was incremental, but the 1963 adoption of Item 807 of the US Tariff Code was a tipping point, opening the borders to capital flight. It allowed US firms to export cut fabric abroad and reimport the assembled and finished products duty-free (except on value added). Item 807 created tariff breaks for capital expenditure and raw materials sent abroad. This led to a boom in the cutting rooms of southern US cities like Miami and El Paso and an exponential expansion in sewing factories in free trade zones on the Mexican border and in the Dominican Republic. As described in detail in Chapter 7, the falling regulatory spatial inflexibility was driven, in part, by the success of the ILGWU, which meant falling structural power for workers (and with it the ability for the ILGWU to exercise associational power).

Nonetheless, through a protracted campaign of organization and strikes (a few four years long), the ILGWU was finally able to establish JAs that covered these cutting facilities under post-Item 807 conditions (for example, Calvin Klein) (Hermanson 1993). In the 1980s, clothing brand Calvin Klein established a 150-worker cutting facility in El Paso with sewing in Mexico. The ILGWU unionized the cutting facility but did not attempt to organize seamstresses in Mexico. The story of Calvin Klein in El Paso is representative of the ILGWU's larger failure to think beyond the border, dooming the JA strategy, and garment workers with it. Mexico's *maquila* system grew in tandem with Item 807, and then expanded beyond the border to the rest of Mexico with the passage of NAFTA (Collins 2009).[10]

While wages and conditions within the sector had matched those of autoworkers in the 1950s and early 1960s, by the 1970s and 1980s, after union-density plummeted, the garment sector had become one of the least worker-friendly industries in the country. As cutting facilities too began relocating in the late 1980s, the border seemed still a barrier too high for the ILGWU. As former organizing director Jeff Hermanson recalls, 'The "runaway shop" was a forerunner of globalisation in that it required the development of the communications and logistical infrastructure that was further developed in cross-border production.' Then, as now, the garment supply chain operated through 'bottlenecks', or economic monopsony, through which jobbers (brands and retailers) cast a multitude of small sellers into competition with one another for contracts. This allows the jobbers to set prices for products. Despite the more recent changes in scale, the essential relationship between workers, factories, and

---

[10] NAFTA, which was originally negotiated and signed by Ronald Reagan and Salinas de Gortari in 1992, passed by the US Congress and the Mexican Congress in 1993, signed by Bill Clinton in December 1993, went into effect on 1 January 1994.

jobbers has remained unchanged during the last hundred years.[11] In the first half of the twentieth century, an even higher degree of monopsony power (DMP) was hindered by a number of factors including regulated trade, jobbers that lacked a degree of monopoly power (relative to today's transnational brands) with less power to place downward pressure on suppliers, and limited access to capital and credit, which stunted the ability of new suppliers to enter the market. This quickly began to change in the latter third of the century.

In 1995, the World Trade Organization (WTO) was established to replace and expand the General Agreement on Tariffs and Trade (GATT). Whereas GATT was committed to free trade, it nonetheless exempted textiles and clothing, services, and agricultural goods. The WTO rid itself of these exemptions to promote freer trade in intellectual property, services, textiles, and clothing (Kiely 2005). By the late 1990s, outside of *haute couture* producers, the JAs and the US garment industry as a whole were on their last legs, victims of a paradigm shift in capital mobility that had cultivated a vast, now global, network of sweatshops. Between 1990 and 2004 alone, the number of workers employed in the textile or clothing-manufacturing sector in the US contracted by 60 per cent (Moran 2010). And in 2005, the *coup de grâce*: expiration of the MFA removed the last remaining restrictions on trade in the garment sector (Elbehri 2004).

The ILGWU and its inheritors, such as the global anti-sweatshop movement, have continued organizing in the US, at points of consumption, but the previously mighty union is a shadow of its former self. As capital began reproducing itself globally, the ILGWU (in its new incarnations UNITE, UNITE HERE, Workers United, and now Workers United-SEIU) was already devoting the bulk of its resources to maintain its hold on the fast-fading US garment sector. But in 1996, the last successful JA campaign was carried out.

In the 1990s, the ILGWU teamed up with Amalgamated Clothing Workers of America (ACTWU) and the ITGLWF to train and support 10 organizers in the free trade zones of the Dominican Republic, using the strategy of organizing a majority of workers into the union FENATRAZONAS and seeking recognition, striking when necessary (as it usually was), and only then

---

[11] Crucially, then as now, the sector remained largely inoculated against technological advancements, meaning that the barriers to entry remained low. Wolfson (1950: 33–34), describing the industry of the 1940s and 1960s, observes that 'in comparison with similar industries responsible for a similar volume of production, the [garment] industry is outstanding in the fact that a loft, a few sewing machines, pressing machines, a style, and fabrics constitute the chief form of capital investment.' She continues, 'The industry is one in which labour, rather than the machine, is the dominant factor. There is comparatively easy entrance into the industry on the part of the entrepreneur.'

pressuring the brands in the US to get their suppliers to recognize the union and negotiate. In this manner, FENATRAZONAS organized 10 free trade zone factories with over 10,000 workers and became one of the biggest unions in the Dominican Republic. The union, now known as FEDOTRAZONAS, continues to represent textile and apparel workers, and is now organizing the call centres that are replacing garment factories as the largest employers in the free trade zones. The ILGWU (later UNITE) used the same strategy in Honduras and Guatemala to win the first CBAs in *maquila*s in both countries. The turn to consumer campaigns came later, as UNITE's new leaders gave up on apparel worker organizing to concentrate on the 'air war' of pressuring corporations, arguing that worker organizing was expensive and often unsuccessful.[12]

Indeed, by the late-1990s, UNITE, having given up on an international organizing 'ground' strategy, besought governments to join together in the creation of an international agreement guaranteeing worker rights and protections (Hensman 2011). If the post-War welfare state represented the historical apex of state-based regulation, the neoliberal era marks its deepening nadir. Just as Reagan-era neoliberalism removed the ground under the American regulatory apparatus, Clinton-era neoliberalism effectively refused workers seat at the table altogether, ensuring regulatory impotence amid the emerging new economic world order.

At this time, several governments did attempt (half-heartedly) to protect workers' rights through 'social clauses', usually as side agreements to trade agreements like NAFTA, and voluntary 'codes of conduct' drawn up unilaterally by TNCs, and monitored and implemented by third-party organizations (both non-profit and profit-making enterprises) that actively excluded labour unions (Liubicic 1998). Trade union led governance initiatives often attempted to incorporate the organizing and campaign models of unionizing. These attacked profits at the points both of production and consumption, as the ILGWU had done. But unlike the ILGWU, which had organized industry-wide actions the

---

[12] It is critical to point out that transnational strategy from below was attempted but with inadequate resources coupled with daunting structural barriers – this became an impossible task. The ILGWU's (later UNITE) experience in organizing in the Dominican Republic, Honduras, and Guatemala in the 1990s, as well as the Kukdong campaign in Mexico (outlined in Chapter 1), is valuable, since it was mostly bottom-up organizing combined with some secondary pressure on the brands, and was successful in achieving CBAs without a full-fledged consumer campaign. An important element of these campaigns was the ILGWU (in Mexico) alongside the Solidarity Centre establishing a dialogue with the supplier companies' principals, who often maintained US offices to deal with brands. (Based on interview with Jeff Hermanson, 12 February 2019.)

US-led anti-sweatshop movement attempted to address industry-wide concerns (that is, demanding factory disclosure), while the results were largely limited to addressing problems as they arose at one factory at a time (Krupat 2002) – or 'hot shops'. Nonetheless, there were successes. By using codes of conduct to support shop floor organizing, workers won the first CBA by a Mexican independent trade union, in addition to codes assisting Latin American cross-border campaigns (Rodriguez-Garavito 2005). The anti-sweatshop campaigns of the early 2000s followed the same pattern. Workers would organize, brands would end orders, the organized factories would be shuttered, activists in the Global North would retaliate, brands would deny responsibility, and factories would often close again soon after. The 2005 Hermosa factory shutdown in El Salvador and the 2006 Gina Form Bra shutdown in Thailand were high-profile cases (despite Gina workers forcing the brand to pay into the severance), but the results remained the same.

There is a growing consensus that organizing remains critical and voluntary private governance initiatives such as corporate codes of conduct are not only unenforceable (Blackett 2000) but are also frequently part of a larger corporate marketing strategy (Seidman 2009), and/or designed expressly to prevent trade union involvement in workers' rights issues (Frundt 2004; Roman 2004). In a blistering appraisal of codes and audits in the garment sector, an extensive report by the AFL-CIO (2013) found that 20 years of initiatives had done little but provided corporate cover for declining wages and deteriorating factory conditions. In lieu of alternatives (or imagination), codes have been invoked as a 'necessary evil' (Gregoratti and Miller 2011: 87). And so, as IndustriALL (which had incorporated the ITGLWF) has set its sights on GFAs, to shore up weaknesses in the codes. The demonstration of worker power through organizing, locally and internationally, boycotts and industrial action, has its origin within the confrontational tradition of North American industrial relations but has hitherto been limited in geographic scope.

As US union density dropped by as much as a fifth during the early 1980s, due to deregulation, privatization, automation, and outsourcing – the cocktail of reforms that became known as 'neoliberalism' – a model of clandestine worker pressure and brand campaigns began to spread throughout (what was left of) the American labour movement. This was time tested for the ILGWU, however, which had been using this tactic in the US garment sector since the turn of the century. The anti-sweatshop movement incorporated elements of this ILGWU model – with less mapping and more emphasis on responding to factory struggles. They adopted much of the same confrontational stance, but failed nonetheless as the 'jobber–contractor governance system' – or 'outsourcing' – was expanded beyond US borders at breakneck speed.

Globalizing the European 'inside model'

In Europe, garment-sector trade unions developed a different kind of transnational model from their US counterparts, based on their own nationally bound system of industrial relations. The appearance of new world production systems and a deterritorialized legal order convinced European trade unions that state labour protections would need to be internationalized. The first such agreements obtained in the automobile industry were during the 1960s when US companies began offshoring to Europe. Company councils, consultative committees made up of workers and management charged with implementing labour agreements, expanded to some 60 in number during the 1970s but waned just as quickly with the weakening of the regulatory power of the social democratic state (McCallum 2013).

In the 1970s, Charles Levinson, general secretary of the International Federation of Chemical, Energy, and General Workers' Unions (ICEF), later the ICEM, proposed introducing representative bodies of workers into major globalizing industries. This would entice TNCs to come to the table with international union bodies and cover the company's subsidiaries. Studies located the failure of the Levinson strategy in its pursuit only of coordinating international trade union activity and never pursuing international collective bargaining (Gumbrell-McCormick 2000).

The first GFA[13] was signed in 1989 between the International Union of Foodworkers (IUF)[14] and Danone, a French-based international with 86,000 employees. It was heralded as a new tool in the fight for workers' rights (Miller 2004). As with the IUF–Danone agreement, over 80 per cent of GFAs have been signed with European TNCs, reflecting the European approach to industrial relations embedded in the GFA (Papadakis 2011). GFAs are bilateral agreements between a GUF and a TNC, often based on ILO Core Conventions, emphasizing freedom of association and the right to collective bargaining (Hammer 2005; Papadakis 2011). Unfortunately, GFAs rely on the voluntary participation of the TNC and only sometimes their suppliers, and do not formally bind suppliers to processes of collective bargaining (McBride and Teeple 2011). GFAs merely

---

[13] Sometimes referred to as 'international framework agreements' (IFAs). When first signed, the GUFs were called ITSs, and the agreements were called IFAs. When the ITSs began calling themselves GUFs, the IFAs became GFAs.

[14] The International Union of Food, Agricultural, Hotel, Restaurant, Catering, Tobacco and Allied Workers (IUF) is based in Geneva.

made clear the TNC's intention to respect workers' rights, and were negotiated from above to permit organizing efforts (Hensman 2011).

While GFAs may operate under a supposition of neutrality, without the additional presence of what Fung and Wright (2003: 260) call 'adversarial countervailing power' or 'a variety of mechanisms that reduce, and perhaps even neutralise, the power-advantages of ordinarily powerful actors', this is only nominal and delusory. Countervailing power can take many forms: workers can withdraw their labour through industrial action or they can build leverage through corporate campaigns. Fung and Wright (2013) maintain that the formation and maintenance of transnational collective bargaining must include a strategy that challenges the power of TNCs – otherwise a lack of countervailing power from below calls into question both the motivation of TNCs to sign agreements and the capacity of agreements to be enforced.

So what motivated TNCs to sign GFAs? Initially, GFAs were pursued with TNCs possessing a long history of partnership with unions at the national level, based mostly in Europe (Gallin 2008). These TNCs usually put up little resistance and the agreements operated as an extension of their traditional labour policies. Niklas Egels-Zandén (2009) finds that GUF involvement in governance is 'symbolically important' – TNCs sign GFAs to retain their positive internal relationship with trade unions and not out of fear of economic or public consequences. Papadakis (2009) also finds that GFAs rarely come out of protests and mobilization, and almost never result from strikes or industrial actions. Rather, the impetus behind a GFA can usually be attributed to the 'benevolence' of an 'enlightened' top manager, already committed to the 'virtues of social dialogue'. Like codes of conduct, GFAs offer a 'public relations triumph' (Stevis and Boswell 2008). The motivation for signing GFAs is therefore not the same as for signing domestic CBAs; generally CBAs are wrung from intransigent employers by worker actions that are inherently antagonistic and coercive, and can even present an existential threat, while GFAs are corporate gestures of accommodation designed to present a positive and benevolent image, which are rarely, if ever, tested.[15]

Similar conclusions are found in an ILO (2009) study assessing management views on GFAs. The study surveyed a quarter of all companies that had signed

---

[15] As one international trade union representative told me (interview, 14 December 2018): 'GFAs are so toothless, brands themselves approach IndustriALL to sign them, and brands write the initial draft. This was the case with the H&M GFA, which some North and South American unionists [came together] to prevent IndustriALL from signing, trying to use the resolution the IndustriALL Executive Committee had passed requiring GFAs to have "a binding dispute resolution mechanism", which the H&M GFA lacked; but to no avail, they signed it anyway.'

GFAs, finding that these had gained credibility, reducing risks to their investors and shareholders, even though GFAs are, by and large, informal and non-binding agreements. In fact, it was argued that GFAs have little to no impact on company profits, given that the associated costs (training, information dissemination) are easily absorbed by pre-existing 'corporate social responsibility' budgets. Herein lies a fundamental question: how can workers' wages and conditions improve at no additional cost to their employers?

In the 1980s, International Trade Secretariats worked in conjunction with the UN as a channel to reallocate resources from workers of the Global North to those of the Global South (Mathiason 2007). It was not until 2002 that, coinciding with the growth of GFAs, those secretariats started calling themselves GUFs. Underfunded and embedded in a culture of European 'social dialogue', GUFs are decidedly staff-run (that is, thoroughly bureaucratic) enterprises, possessing few links to rank-and-file 'membership' and little means to acquire them (Traub-Merz and Eckl 2007; McCallum 2013). Unlike national CBAs, GFAs are never negotiated or ratified by the membership of the GUFs. Indeed, examples of GUFs organizing workers from below against a hostile employer exist (McCallum 2013) – the GUF UNI-led campaign against security contractor G4S, for instance – but are exceptions. Nor do GUFs represent a united front; rather, they are often divided not only on spatial but also on ideological and sectoral grounds (Cumbers, Nativel, and Routledge 2008). However, unions of the Global South have at times held sway.[16] But on the whole, GUFs have mostly proven capable of shaking down the willing, and have yet to sufficiently prove their capacity to build international campaigns that oppose capital.

GFA advocates start from the position that rectifying poor working conditions under neoliberalism requires a universal application, operating beyond individual nation-states (D'Antona 2002), and filling a 'democratic deficit' in global governance (Niforou 2013). The establishment of such new rules is especially important regarding export processing zones (EPZs), where freedom of association either does not apply or is purposely not enforced. The supranational institutions currently in place, such as the ILO, offer no replacement for state regulation. According to Edo Fimmen (1922), the original purpose of the ILO was the creation of an international regulatory framework for labour, which would 'not merely adopt international conventions without

---

[16] A case in point is found when South Africa's powerful National Union of Mineworkers compelled the ICEM to adopt policies in support of transnational 'sympathy strikes'.

binding force but should pass international laws'. The ILO, however, 'failed to realise the high hopes of an international labour parliament with legislative and executor powers' at its foundation (Van Voss 1988: 524).

Despite the abundance of recent literature on GFAs, few researchers have explored how workers themselves attempt to bargain with their transnational employers, let alone union experience in efforts to organize in vertically disintegrated supply chains. This dearth of research may be explained by the limited data available regarding attempts – or successes – at organizing internationally and demanding cross-border agreements. As detailed in this brief history, attempts at international collective bargaining have been largely limited to the upper echelons of bureaucrat-run labour organizations, with few successes, especially in labour-intensive sectors like apparel and footwear production.

There is a clear disconnect between GUF or TNC actions and the workers or subcontracted suppliers in the periphery of production chains (Croucher and Cotton 2009; Papadakis 2011). Theoretically, GUFs push for partnership agreements to build external pressure that will strengthen local organizing – the so-called boomerang model (Keck and Sikkink 1999). Although Greven (2008) sees transnationalism – on paper, at least – as a result of diminishing union power, a dependency on transnational agreements reveals the weakness of global and local unions alike.

Martin Smith (2008: 8), a national organizer with British trade union GMB, describes the decision by GMB to categorically reject 'top down' partnership agreements within the domestic sphere as an approach that 'fail[ed] in its goal of organizing workers simply as it more often than not resulted in workers being approached by the union and management together after a deal had been struck'. Composed in inflexible language, not accounting for local specificity, GFAs, according to Smith (2008: 8), reflect only the concerns of management and a union bureaucracy remote from the shop floor, whose language frequently 'come[s] out of the same Wall Street legal firm'. They represent a movement towards top-heavy union culture, which, like the Designated Suppliers Program (DSP), deploys a *field of dreams* strategy to organize workers – an 'if we build it, they will come' method. Smith (2008: 9) concludes that 'our global campaigns will fail or become hijacked by corporate interests if we attempt to impose collective bargaining in an organization without the industrial strength to see it through. Or if we seek to apply organizing models from one corner of the world in every place at every time'. The motives for signing GFAs, McCallum (2013: 43) claims, may be more insidious: 'Most damning of all, because GFAs are technically joint ventures, occasionally it is the carefully crafted agreement language itself that serves to redirect worker activity toward channels that are acceptable to both union leadership and business interest, without workers ever having been consulted.'[17]

Most GFAs are in capital-intensive 'producer-driven' industries (Gereffi 1999; Hammer 2008) – that is, vertically integrated production processes with direct investment costs that workers can leverage to increase their bargaining power – and remain largely absent from labour-intensive sectors. Despite their growing popularity (91 had been signed by early 2013, up from 5 in 2000), even the strongest GFAs do little to hold employers accountable, nor can it be said with certainty that they cultivate stronger or more active unions (McCallum 2013). Even the 2008 UNI-G4S security guards' agreement, which triumphed over company resistance to the establishing of a security guard union in Bangalore, one of the most successful GFA-assisted efforts, led all the leaders to conclude that the GFA's role in negotiations was negligible – 'a waste of paper that we cannot afford' (McCallum 2013: 134) – which hamstrung the ability of local unions to take more militant direct action to avoid breaching the agreement (Kumar 2014b).

A chief organizing strategist for the SEIU, which deployed the GFA strategy against G4S, Stephen Lerner (2007: 32), has himself said:

> The time for these types of international framework agreements has come and gone. These general statements of principle are too weak and it is proven that they cannot be enforced. They should be abandoned in favour of agreements with language that concretely helps workers around the world win a union and higher standards. These new agreements should be part of plans to organise companies on a global basis to establish unions where they aren't as well as rebuild union strength in open shop countries where membership is in decline.

---

[17] One international trade union representative suggested that this occurs more than occasionally. That, in fact, GUF executives always construct, curate, and govern the GFAs (interview 20 December 2018), stating, 'Quite often the negotiations and enforcement are completely controlled by the GUF General Secretary and an "International Affairs" staffer from the European union that represents the corporate HQs or domestic manufacturing facilities. In the case of the H&M GFA, the GUF General Secretary worked with the Swedish International Affairs representative of a union, IF Metall, that represented no H&M production workers at all, simply because the Swedish owners of H&M were "comfortable" dealing with that union. Now the Swedish union is responsible for enforcing the GFA on behalf of more than one million production workers around the world. Some of them have unions that were not consulted in the negotiations of the GFA.'

There are successful cases nonetheless. Jane Wills (2002) found that, even without workplace conflict or democratic input, the IUF–Accor GFA was used to assist efforts to organize in the hospitality sector, that the strength of a GFA was predicated on the strength of the relevant local union (aside from enforceability, GFAs are often dependent on sector-wide union support) (Anner et al. 2006). In a nutshell, the weakness of GFAs consists in a model of management–worker cooperation, resembling the post–World War II labour–capital compromise (Munck 2008) – a failure of imagination that plagues trade unions to this day (Egels-Zandén 2009).

Garment sector transnational CBAs?

The primary obstacles in garment sector GFA negotiations are outsourced production and intense employer resistance. According to Welz (2011), only 9 per cent of the existing GFAs apply across the supply chain. The ITGLWF's first GFA in the garment sector was a backroom deal, years in the making (Miller 2008). Miller (2008) claims that the proliferation of the auditing regime in early 2000 and the resulting factory disclosure by major brands finally gave the ITGLWF what it needed to proactively pursue GFAs. The 2005 collapse of a knitwear factory in Bangladesh, killing 64, led to a series of discussions between a major buyer, Spanish clothing brand Inditex, and the representatives of the ITGLWF. In 2007, Inditex[18] signed a GFA with the ITGLWF – the first GFA in either the garment or textile sector and the first GFA to cover the entire supply chain (ETUF-TCL 2007).[19]

The ITG–Inditex GFA has created new opportunities for collaboration on training between Inditex and Turkish trade unions (Korkmaz 2013). One former researcher for ITG Turkish affiliate union, TEKSIF,[20] gave me his take: 'The agreement had no positive or negative effect on the union or workers until around three years ago when a new pilot programme targeted at Inditex suppliers was initiated by ITGLWF's successor IndustriALL [...] this is a pilot, but I'm sure we'll expand it and it will assist our trade union organizing.' However, despite Turkey's importance to Inditex, as one of its largest producers, with optimum turnaround times and convenient proximity to EU markets, Turkish unions were

---

[18] Inditex is one of the world's largest clothing companies, notable for its ownership of the brand Zara. The company owns 6,000 retail stores in 86 markets, with over 1 million workers producing in 40 suppliers countries (Inditex Group 2012).
[19] The next was the 2015 H&M– IndustriALL GFA (H&M– IndustriALL 2015).
[20] Phone interview, 17 March 2014.

not consulted during the drafting process. The TEKSIF researcher continued, 'When the ITG was formulating the GFA they did not consult TEKSIF. The problematic side of the GFA approach is that it came out of top-level negotiations, except maybe some Spanish unions since Inditex is a Spanish Multinational.' In another instance, the agreement led to the reinstatement of dismissed workers in Peru but failed to reinvigorate the union, which remained stagnant and weak (Miller, Turner, and Grinter 2011). In yet another case, the agreement was unable to combat what one comprehensive probe has called 'slave labour' conditions in Argentina (Roper 2013). The agreement did have an impact on white-collar workers at Inditex headquarters in Spain, at the top of the supply chain.[21] But like other GFAs, the Inditex–ITG agreement does not include a commitment to enforcement, but is only a mechanism for consultation.

Gregoratti and Miller (2011) have conducted the only known analysis of the impact of the Inditex–ITG IFA, focusing on River Rich, Inditex's primary supplier of knitwear from Cambodia. In January 2007, the Coalition of Cambodia Apparel Workers Democratic Union (C.CAWDU), an ITGLWF member, asked ITGLWF to pressurize Inditex on worker dismissal, full-time recognition, and maternity leave at River Rich. This set of demands, ignoring higher piece rate and other wage factors, was shaped by the ability of River Rich to pay, which itself depended on what Inditex was willing to give. The GFA does not question market supremacy, but only establishes a process to address concerns. As Gregoratti and Miller (2011: 96) put it, 'Clearly, sourcing policy and purchasing practices are variables over which the GFA approach, at present, have very little say'; the changing world economy has revealed the 'limited authority CSR departments have in commercial decision making'. Gregoratti and Miller found agreements rarely applicable beyond the short-term, immediate concerns, such as unfair dismissal, leaving systemic and structural inequities unaddressed.

River Rich represents an early test case for GFA applicability and as yet the only detailed study of Inditex compliance. Its authors highlight the conspicuous absence of language in the GFA that would bind Inditex to source from River Rich, leaving workers in a difficult and weakened negotiating position. And indeed in 2010, Inditex halted its River Rich production, when it was not obliged to continue it, a stoppage that extended, in part, to the supply chain. Gregoratti and Miller (2011: 97) suggest that the River Rich case sheds light on the weaknesses GFAs share with their predecessors: unenforceability ('a global union seeking to implement a GFA is no different from a global union seeking to enforce a multinational's code of conduct'), and efficacy in the sector ('the fickle

---

[21] Interview with IndustriALL employee, 23 July 2014.

nature of outsourced apparel production raises serious questions about the overall effectiveness and long-term sustainability of such an approach') (Gregoratti and Miller 2011: 85). They assert that an effective GFA must include a long-term supply agreement between the relevant multinationals and their external suppliers, a provision absent from current agreements.

Athit Kong,[22] the Vice-President of C.CAWDU, Cambodia's IndustriALL garment sector member union, claims that his union was unaware of the Inditex GFA until after the campaign, but knew that ITG had been involved in negotiating the agreement at River Rich. Athit stated that C.CAWDU had no involvement in drafting the GFA and in fact had 'never even seen the document'. Athit claims, 'It was worker power that allowed the GFA to have any power. In the absence of grassroots worker struggle the GFA provides a platform for negotiation and dialogue on an international level that might not already exist. Overall it is a good thing but is not useful by itself. The important part is always worker struggle.'

Fast-forward to Cambodia in 2013, and a four-month strike at the 6,000 worker SL Garments in Cambodia revealed the fault lines in the agreement. C.CAWDU led the charge, establishing local unions at both of SL Garment's two facilities in 2011, which, by 2013, encompassed the majority of workers. C.CAWDU is a member of both the newly formed IndustriALL (which includes the former ITGWLF) and the International Union League for Brand Responsibility (IULBR), also known as 'the League'. The Phnom Penh factory is the largest garment-processing factory in Cambodia and a critical bellwether for the state of the Cambodian working class. The strike ended after brands were pressured by the C.CAWDU, IndustriALL, the League, and the workers' rights NGO Clean Clothes Campaign to force SL Garments to negotiate with the union, with SL eventually agreeing to a list of eight main demands, including reinstatement of the terminated union leaders.[23]

The experience at SL Garments contradicts the argument that GFAs are a useful tool for the empowerment of workers and trade unions. As one outside negotiator[24] pointed out, 'Four major brands contract with SL Garments – Gap, Inditex, H&M, and Levi's – and Inditex has not responded sufficiently or pressured the factory to meet with workers to end the strike despite having an GFA.'

In July 2014, IndustriALL officials informed affiliated garment unions that they had renewed the Inditex–IndustriALL IFA. The renewal occurred

---

[22] Interviewed through the assistance of Liana Dalton on 6 May 2014.
[23] The strike at SL garments evolved into a national strike which was brutally repressed by Cambodian armed forces (Teehan 2014). The 3 December Agreement was signed by SL, C.CAWDU, and the Cambodia Ministry of Labour.
[24] Phone interview, 14 December 2013.

without the involvement of affiliates, such as C.CAWDU that has been locked in an ongoing and unresolved struggle with Inditex supplier SL Garment that IndustriALL had been supporting. Instead of utilizing the re-negotiation of the GFA as leverage (for example, conditioning renewal on Inditex first implementing the agreement signed months ago at SL), IndustriALL officials indicated that they planned to push Inditex on the issue after the agreement had already been signed, precisely when Inditex will feel the least vulnerable. By renewing the partnership with Inditex with no strings attached in the midst of a dispute, IndustriALL forwent the major point of leverage that the GFA affords in the first place.[25]

As is clear, the social model was translated onto the global stage and informs the strategy of GUFs. For example, IndustriALL presents itself as 'working with global brands' for the reinstatement of arrested or dismissed workers. For instance, 23 Cambodian labour activists were arrested in early 2014. Instead of launching a campaign against the brands that had more power to pressurize their outsourcing factories, IndustriALL 'work[ed] with' them to ask the Cambodian state for the workers' release, ignoring the fundamental conflict setting workers at odds with factory owners and brands, in favour of collaboration with short-term benefits. Yet this approach goes to the heart of the GUF ideology consistent with nearly a century of practice.

Because GUFs' strategy grew out of the social dialogue tradition, they tend to prioritize state targets over grassroots organizing. Although post-War Europe was initially a favourable climate for the cultivation of union power under this model (largely because of the power of labour in the aftermath of World War II), the subsequent innovations of capital have gradually exposed its fundamental weaknesses, initially top-heavy and entropic structure, far removed from the shop floor sources of worker power, but now increasingly symbiotic GVCs. As the balance of strategic and tactical innovation shifts to capital in the neoliberal era, only asymmetries of the power between GUFs and TNCs widen.

Hensman (2011: 285) argues that real global collective bargaining requires that unions 'evolv[e] a network structure rather than a top-down one'. She (2011: 301) describes a potential framework for successful transnational collective bargaining in a call for expanding the current codes of conduct:

> Codes could be reshaped to include purchasing practices, specifying that companies adopting them undertake to pay prices that enable suppliers to abide by them, rule out delivery schedules that cannot be met without compulsory overtime, and build stable relationships with suppliers so that they can invest in upgrading labour standards without fearing that

---

[25] Based on an interview with the IndustriALL representative, 10 July 2014.

their buyers will shift to cheaper suppliers. This would result in pressure to suppliers to invest and upgrade labour standards without fearing that their buyers will shift to cheaper suppliers. This would result in pressure to change being brought to bear on the companies that profit most from the labour production workers yet are inaccessible to collective bargaining by them. Including these issues, as well as workers' rights, in binding contracts between buyers and suppliers would enable both sides to take legal action in the event of violations by the other and would also allow unions to intervene.

On 10 February 2013, as activists in Manhattan protested Adidas' runway show at the New York Fashion Week, unions representing the workers producing Adidas products in Indonesia, El Salvador, Honduras, Nicaragua, Haiti, India, Cambodia, Bangladesh, Guatemala, and the Dominican Republic were delivering a letter to their bosses. They were announcing the formation of the IULBR and demanding Adidas to agree to collectively negotiate a brand agreement, mirroring the JAs that had helped the ILGWU to succeed (IULBR 2013b).

Internationalizing the campaign for a JA came from the Honduran union federation Central General de Trabajadores (CGT), allied activists, and organizations that grew out of the success of the earlier Fruit of the Loom campaign (highlighted in Chapter 5). Campaigners were emboldened and prepared to substantially widen their scope of operations, confident that their model could be spread to other countries.[26]

Confirming their intuitions, the JA model soon gathered steam across Central America. With the assistance of former campaigners from the US-based United Students Against Sweatshops (USAS), it spread even farther, to unions in Argentina, India, Bangladesh, Cambodia, Turkey, and Indonesia. From established unions affiliated with IndustriALL, such as C.CADWU and TEKSIF, to newer autonomous unions, such as south India's GATWU, a desire to form coalitions against unified targets became integrated with effective use of new communication technologies. Advocates for global governance understand the obstacles to establishing workers' rights under globalization – the decentred state, the weakness of the ILO, and so on. But as legal scholar Adelle Blackett (2000: 402) stresses, 'Workers' rights advocacy surrounding self-regulatory initiatives simultaneously understands, problematizes, and reinforces dominant conceptions of the globalisation process,' failing to meet the fundamental goals of labour law.

After exploring the potential legal hurdles, Allie Robbins (2011: 151) concludes that 'adopt[ing] a strategy of pursuing jobber agreements is [...] the

---

[26] Based on an interview with CGT leader Reyna Dominguez (31 August 2013) in Kumar and Mahoney (2014).

logical next step' for the anti-sweatshop movement. And yes, agreements can be made in national level courts, as the 2009 CGT–Fruit of the Loom agreement established, stipulating enforceability in US and Honduran courts; and the 2013 Bangladesh Accord on Fire and Building Safety, stipulating enforceability through the courts of the defendant's home country or a court of competent jurisdiction (AFBSB 2013; Kumar and Mahoney 2014). In other words, if there was a global JA in place and then a dispute arose in Indonesia filed against Adidas, it could be contested in either Indonesia or Germany, or even the US, if the goods are intended for sale in the US.

The new jobbers' demand borrows the core provisions of the old.[27] It includes an arbitration process and the resolution of disputes to designated arbitrators. If either party fails to observe the decision of the arbitrator(s), it can sue for breach of contract in any court of competent jurisdiction.[28] During the arbitration process, the text of the contract takes precedence. The expectation is that the contracts specify the choice of law – that is, which jurisdiction's decision would be relied on to interpret the contract where ambiguities exist or a contract provision is unlawful in the local jurisdiction.[29] The ILGWU model of organizing alone and employed domestically must be fit to the scale necessary to gain leverage over subcontracted and transnational configurations of capital. What distinguishes this demand for JAs is an intuitive combination of GFAs' 'global' reach with the antagonism of the ILGWU model.[30]

---

[27] Based on interviews with League leadership and staff (October–December 2013).

[28] It is possible that the JA would be limited to the home country of the complainant party or defendant party; or it could allow US courts as a universal option, which might be desirable, given that US courts have significant precedent related to jobbers' agreements.

[29] The League sought assistance in drafting the legal parameters of any agreement from Yale Law School's Transnational Development Clinic. Legal understanding of the jobbers are based on interviews with Mary Yanik of Yale Law School's Transnational Development Clinic (12 March 2013).

[30] The ILGWU tactic is only distinguished from that of the League by scale. Whereas the ILGWU had sought full unionization of contractors, to cover entire production networks (1,200 outsourced garment factories in the Adidas clothing commodity chain), the League's limited resources have confined its demands to applying agreements where there are active organizing campaigns. This global jobber agreement would cost brands significantly less than the original (as percentage of total profit), making it more palatable as a means of averting industrial actions and anti-corporate campaigns that can sully expensive marketing efforts. And though benefits may not be as extensive as ILGWU members previously had, the wage provision would take into account local and differential application of a

The JA proposal reaches along both the directions of the supply chain, beyond garment worker organizing, to include ancillary suppliers. A few IULBR member unions represent clothing retail and warehouse workers as well, a foothold which could be expanded strategically, applying additional upward pressure on the supply chain.[31] In February 2013, for example, SAE-A, a Korean manufacturer and Walmart supplier, was brutally suppressing the organizing efforts by members of the Nicaraguan League affiliate FESTMIT (WRC 2013b). Walmart contract workers then led a delegation to SAE-A offices in Los Angeles and New York with Warehouse Workers Unite demanding the SAE-A to begin bargaining with the union and to reinstate all the dismissed workers (Eidelson 2013).

Of course, there will always be challenges. The Designated Suppliers Program (DSP), a 2005 USAS initiative, attempted to channel consumer power, through licensed university apparel, to create space for the workers producing the apparel to organize. This included a set of labour rights qualifications but no specific plan for organizing workers, substantially limiting its ability to recruit factories into its 'DSP'[32] – that and an accusation that DSP violated anti-trust laws (before passing legal muster years later [USJD 2011]). The ILGWU's JA strategy crucially included retail boycotts to supplement shop floor organizing. As Vogel (2005) claims, consumer boycotting campaigns rarely influence consumer trends or corporate profits, and indeed are 'more bark than bite', and useful only as a tactic secondary to worker organization. Several ILGWU jobbers had contractors in Canada, and several Canadian jobbers had American production sites, and both

---

living wage. Finally, an agreement has the potential to give union's access to other plants, extending union neutrality to all producers in countries where workers are represented, similar to the CGT–Fruit of the Loom agreement in Honduras.

[31] League unions target not only brands but also the direct employers. Day-to-day industrial relations, however, are a matter to be negotiated in the factory-level CBA. Targeting specific employers instead of their governments allows workers in different locations and trades to coalesce around a unified set of demands. In the case of the JA, these help establish a ground supporting a workers' movement that does not end the moment a TNC signs an agreement. Importantly, the leadership comes from the trade unions themselves, with a commitment to move more decision-making to individual representatives despite geographic, resource, and language hurdles, to build workers' power directly from the shop floor.

[32] A September 2006 memo from the DSP working group lists only five possible DSP-qualified factories, showing the severe lack of qualified factories: Lian Thai (Thailand), Mexmode (Mexico), PT Dada (Indonesia), PT Kolon, and BJ&B of the Dominican Republic (closed in 2007, BJ&B went on to become a Knights Apparel subsidiary and Living Wage CSR-project Alta Gracia in 2010 [Kline 2010]).

were covered by the agreements; the legality of this practice was never challenged or litigated. JAs in the 1980s and 1990s also had provisions requiring payment of 'liquidated damages' to the union for production in other countries,[33] on the theory that this production 'damaged' the union, diminishing job opportunities for ILGWU members.[34] Unknown variables notwithstanding, the recognition of jobbers as employers with shared liability for the conditions, rights, and wages of garment workers was enshrined in the 1959 Garment Industry Proviso, which was a legislative provision that exempted garment workers from the prohibition on secondary boycotts or hot cargo clauses (Winefsky and Tenney 2002).

The interest here is on JA's international application; however, a more important question is whether such a strategy is as necessary as it once was, given the radical restructuring of production outlined in the book. The IULBR strategy is a longer one, intended to turn weaknesses into strengths gradually, through campaigns on both local and international fronts.[35] Organizers believe the cumulative economic effect will be sufficient to extract a JA from a targeted TNC. However, the changes in the GVC – with increasingly powerful suppliers – means more long-term contracts and greater value capture for suppliers – which in effect, due to the logic of competition, moves the GVC towards a JA-like environment for workers to organize within.

Building labour's power

Governance regimes' attempts to curb the outsized power of corporate actors – as inventive as they have been – have failed to resolve the fundamentally unequal power relationship joining capital to labour. The problem, Fung and Wright (2003: 259) emphasize, is that 'such schemes are often inattentive to

---

[33] Only a small portion of the funds acquired through this mechanism were directed to organizing projects in the Dominican Republic and Central America. Had a larger portion of the funds been used in this way, it is possible that a more powerful international organizing and bargaining capacity could have been built.

[34] Although it can also be argued that the liquidated damages provision for imports prioritized the bank balances of unions in the Global North over the rights of the outsourced workers in the Global South, emphasizing the millions of dollars generated in liquidated damages rather than leverage to ensure outsourcing conditions included freedom of association for the foreign contactors.

[35] The IULBR is also engaged in cross-border political pressure in the Global North, 'naming and shaming' brands as a form of what Keck and Sikkink call 'accountability politics' (1998, 1999).

problems of powerlessness and domination, thus seeming to suggest that if only the institutional designs can be constructed just right, then gross imbalances of power in the context of these can be neutralised'. Unlike top-down policy-making, which can effectively disempower the affected persons, a strategy from below can deepen democracy, giving, in this case, workers increasing say in policy formation. Fung and Wright (2003) consider a relationship vis-à-vis the state, but JAs wove democratic practice and empowered participatory deliberation through the entire process, from conception to consumption.

Andre Gorz (1967) developed the concept of 'reformist reforms', superficial concessions that actually further consolidate power in the hands of the already powerful, as compared with 'non-reformist reforms', intermediate objectives that create structural changes, consolidating working-class power. These Gorzian concepts have been a bright-line test for the radical efficacy of transnational social movements, like the 'global justice movement' (Bond 2004, 2008).

Through a Gorzian lens, 'inside models' and GFAs form a mode of transnational activity distinct from that of the JAs born out of the US labour movement. Campaigns for JAs were conceived as grassroots struggles, developing out of the shop floors, the streets, and shantytowns, where new forms of union organization can take place. Lacking the institutional support of a GUF does pose its own problems, namely questions of resources and legitimacy. But on the other hand, it means these struggles are not bogged down by the routine and bureaucracy that plague GUFs and can pursue unconventional methods in a dynamic fashion to reach the shared goal of building workers' power; the direct participation of the factory-level workers and their unions opens up new vistas for a powerful legitimacy of a different kind.

Modern labour history is a history of workers jockeying with capital for power, and the primary method of building worker power has been through collective bargaining – though this too has been utilized to smother militancy (see Chan and Hui 2014). In this context, the GFA represents a classic case of 'reformist reformism', serving as a means to ease the implementation of neoliberalism, exemplifying global labour's defeatism by dwelling on what Gorz (1967) calls 'what can be' rather than 'what should be'. The rising organic composition of capital – or simply the increased proportion of output contributed by machinery relative to labour – in the garment and footwear sectors at a global level presents new possibilities for challenging TNCs and allowing workers to organize and magnify their power and demands, with new mega-suppliers who are too-big-to-cut for TNCs. And though these campaigns are new, and there remain untested variables, the early signs are auspicious. GUFs today, beholden to a tradition of 'social dialogue', persist in pressing states to establish multi-stakeholder initiatives, bringing unions, companies, and civil society organizations together to improve worker protections. Campaigns outside these frameworks, meanwhile, have trained their crosshairs on brands, suppliers, and the state.

There is an unfortunate and ahistorical assumption that, before capital globalized in the 1970s, unions had agitated only against their immediate employers, ignoring, or unaware of, any larger contexts. As detailed earlier, workers in the US garment sector had long ago displayed their intuition in this regard, anticipating capital flight and pursuing staunchly grassroots initiatives. The (legally binding) JAs succeeded in: contractually locking in both jobber and contractor, dismantling the 'auction block', ensuring the 'pass through' of value from jobbers through contractors to workers, and strengthening worker solidarity across the sector. But by the late 1990s, trade union membership in the Global North was in steep decline. Gathering clouds or no, US unions had cut their teeth on organizing during 40 years of neoliberal onslaught. Before that, the US had never enjoyed the perks of a real welfare state the likes of those found across the Atlantic – and the innovative methods of survival developed therein were still, on occasion, remarkably effective. They had acquired a hard-won familiarity with the new, even more unsympathetic industrial relations climate, and were capable of using it to good effect. This form of labour campaign soon defined the American labour strategy and was later enlarged in the form of the global anti-sweatshop movement.

Both the European and US strategies proceed from analyses of the garment supply chain as having been from its earliest days a 'buyer-driven' sector, in which brands and retailers set prices (and therefore wages) while outsourced suppliers competed for brand orders (Gereffi 1994, 1999). This configuration obtained within the context of an evolving world economy is subject to swift and sometimes radical changes. But since the 2005 phase-out of the global quota arrangement, known as the MFA, introduced new volatility to the sector, the garment industry has become especially vulnerable to these vicissitudes. As I outline in great detail in subsequent chapters, production has consolidated, as larger suppliers absorbed smaller ones; and those large suppliers expanded vertically across the supply chain to textiles, warehousing, logistics, and even retail. This has led to an oligopoly among suppliers, creating greater value capture at the bottom of the supply chain, and more capital expenditure at the supplier-end introducing innovations in technology and production processes, capturing even more value. The relationships between the buyer and the supplier are moving in the direction of mutual dependence, and these dynamics inform the strategy. Greater value capture at the supplier-end not only lessens the power brands hold over prices but also creates more possible bargaining power for workers at larger suppliers, independent of brands.

Although some evidence suggests that an inside model approach has been effective within the borders of some European nation-states, a global strategy requires a flatly participatory methodology, collapsing the distance between the global negotiating table and shop floor power. Otherwise, the asymmetry of power in industrial relations will render agreements between labour and capital unenforceable. The JA approach organized the workers across the garment value chain in order to build power for all the workers whose labour it took to produce clothing, from the factory floor to the retail rack, and to internally regulate an industry structurally inoculated against top-down regulation. The model invoked by anti-sweatshop campaigns, and so concretely successful in contesting the power of TNCs, has been historically effective but hitherto limited in scope to the US and Canada.

PRESENT

3

China
A Strike at a Giant Footwear Producer

On the morning of 15 April 2014, 43,000 of the 60,000 workers employed in Yue Yuen's Gaobu factories in Guangdong Province downed tools and walked off the job. Within two weeks, the largest strike at a private company in Chinese history[1] had drained Yue Yuen of more than $60 million in lost profits and exacted benefits.[2] What was astonishing about this strike was that it occurred in the footwear sector – a decidedly 'buyer-driven' GVC – at facilities that exclusively produce for major buyers Nike and Adidas. Even more, the supplier was able to absorb the costs and workers were able to win some concessions in a historically low-value sector with the buyers unable or unwilling to relocate production to a different supplier.

The rise of Yue Yuen and its strike typifies capital–labour relations of the contemporary Chinese economy. Indeed, growth in Chinese industrial capacity outpaced labour, causing a pronounced power shift, since 'bosses are short of workers and workers are short of patience' (*Economist* 2010) despite reports of a manufacturing downturn in 2012 following a two-year strike wave (Barboza 2012). The export-oriented industrial provinces of Guangdong and Zhejiang in South China have become a hotbed of worker unrest (Silver and Zhang 2009) and since strikes exist in a legal grey area – neither outlawed nor permitted, thus sometimes allowed and other times repressed – it has made China the site of more wildcat strikes than any other country in the world (Friedman 2015).

---

[1] Some strikes in China have caused greater economic damage, for example in the ports or public sector, but in terms of the number of private-sector workers and the length of strike, Yue Yuen is among the 'largest recorded industrial disputes in living memory' (Borromeo 2014) and the largest at a single company in Chinese history (based on claims in Valdmanis [2014]).

[2] Yue Yuen workers previously conducted smaller strikes such as in 2008 in Dongguan over wages, with workers refusing to sign their contracts, resulting in a company lock-out (Gongchao 2014).

And as labour shortage and worker pressure mounted, employers were forced to accommodate, allowing real wages to rise by 12 per cent per annum since 2001.[3] Workers often succeeded in wresting double-digit salary increases from their employers (Friedman 2014). Indeed, 'by the end of 2010, Chinese media commentators were [already] declaring that the era of low-wage labour had come to an end' (Friedman 2012).

Here, I examine the 2014 strike at Yue Yuen in the Pearl River Delta (PRD) region of southeast China.[4] It contributes to the argument of the book that firms, adapting from assembly-only affairs to integrated monopolistic suppliers, transformed previously asymmetrical power imbalance between global brands ('buyers') and producers ('suppliers') to a more symbiotic relationship. Enhanced value capture by firms at the production-end may also, past a certain point, bridge the divide separating value capture from value creation in the footwear sector, calling into question established value chain theories, and bringing new emphasis to labour tactics against their direct employers.

The footwear value chain has remained labour-intensive and vertically disintegrated for the past half-century, and as globalization intensified, these dynamics were transformed from domestic to global production and consumption (Herrigel and Zeitlin 2010). The concentration of capital at the top of the supply chain – Nike and Adidas, for instance, control over 50 per cent of the global athletic shoe market (Merk 2008) – has only served to further entrench this structure, which remains a key obstacle to greater workers' bargaining power in the sector (Ross 2004; Armbruster-Sandoval 2005; Hale and Wills 2005b; Moran 2010).

These developments are linked to the issue of labour shortage in South China, which has been widely documented and contested. Elfstrom and Kuruvilla (2014) maintain that the growing labour shortage is driving increased labour unrest, while others argue that the issue is a shortage in industry-specific labour, specifically in labour-intensive GVCs (Cai 2015a). Regardless, this transition from labour surplus to labour shortage (sector-specific or otherwise) is linked

---

[3] This is also state policy, in part due to pressure from labour, but also as a strategy to steer the Chinese economy into a more 'value-added', technologically advanced direction (*Economist* 2015).

[4] The study is based on a combination of sources including news reports from on the ground, detailed accounts on the strike from Hong Kong–based NGOs, as well as five key informant phone interviews conducted with NGO workers at Hong Kong–based organizations. Company data were retrieved from Yue Yuen's annual financial statements at the Hong Kong Stock Exchange; Yue Yuen is listed in the Hong Kong Stock Exchange (retrieved through Capital IQ corporate database).

to the so-called Lewis Turning Point, a marker for the beginning of the end of labour surplus that can induce a structural transformation of labour-intensive industries to capital-intensive ones (Cai 2015a). The labour-market squeeze for labour-intensive producers is reflected in the dynamics of industrial capitalism. This process has contributed to the phenomenon identified as the 'organizational fix'. As we find in the other cases in this book, vertical and horizontal expansion signals a lurch away from the spatial fix, which was integral to absorbing garment capital crisis tendencies for the past century. When Yue Yuen began to grow, they purchased cost-saving technologies and expanded, often along the supply chain, erecting new barriers to entry as they grew, and thereby fundamentally increasing their own bargaining power with big brands like Nike and Adidas. At the same time, this helped to transform the bargaining power of Yue Yuen's workers.

Unmade in China

China has emerged as an economic superpower, recognized as 'probably the most remarkable economic transformation in history' (Stiglitz 2006: 1). But, as Peck and Zhang (2013) have argued, China represents a capitalist hybrid and cannot be boxed into either embedded neoliberalism or embedded socialism. However, Chinese labour unrest is not unusual but an outgrowth of capitalist development. Anner (2015: 292) categorizes China as an extreme example of 'authoritarian state labour control regime' in which labour is controlled by both legal and extra-legal apparatuses with the aim of limiting independent worker organization. To Anner (2015), it is the efficacy of this regime that is one primary explanation for China's continued dominance of global apparel and footwear production despite having wages that are four times higher than other Asian countries such as Bangladesh.

Nonetheless, the shape and the form of contemporary labour unrest within China are linked to the changing relationship between transnational capital and the Chinese state. Friedman (2015) argues that, since 2010, there has been a weakening of the alliance between capital and the Chinese state in the repression of strikes. He claims that both the Chinese central government and Guangdong provincial authorities sought a new means of accumulation and were even willing to ally with workplace radicals to realize these aims. At the same time, the central government continues to intensify its opposition to civil society by restricting the bounds of official tolerance, especially against individuals and NGOs involved with labour rights (Jacobs and Buckley 2015). For example, Zhang Zhiru, who operates a Shenzhen-based labour rights organization and was the principal legal consultant to the Yue Yuen workers on strike, was forced to close his organization after a series of state pressure tactics including police intimidation.

There is a clear contradiction between the interests at different governmental levels in response to strikes. The shift away from a centrally planned economy in the 1970s empowered increasingly autonomous provinces to institute market reforms. The result was a race to the bottom for neoliberal reforms with the most 'successful' provinces serving as 'models' and promoted across China (Friedman and Kuruvilla 2015). Friedman and Kuruvilla (2015) argue that this differentiated approach is necessary to accommodate a diverse set of employment relations across sectors and regions. Yet decentralization has also fostered a space in which capital can remain meaningfully autonomous from a central state while integrating itself into the provincial government. Friedman and Kuruvilla (2015) maintain that the state is now taking a gradualist and decentralized approach to reforming labour relations. This, in part, can explain the intranational variation, differentiated reactions by national and provincial officials, which was mirrored by the sole official union All-China Federation of Trade Unions (ACFTUs) to the Yue Yuen strike. The ACFTU is integral to the central government's changes in labour relations such as workplace organizing and collective bargaining. Yet, while capital is relatively autonomous at the provincial and municipal levels, labour is far more constrained, revealing an incongruence at the national and local levels (Friedman and Kuruvilla 2015).

As outlined in Chapter 6, the changing political and economic conditions in China has had a reverberating effect on the structure and bargaining power of actors within the global economy. This is particularly acute for the labour-hungry garment sector, since China produced the majority of global garment exports in the immediate years following the MFA-phase out. Thirty years of Chinese economic growth was predicated on policies that encouraged an export and investment–oriented development model that aimed to provide a seemingly endless supply of diligent workers. China's immense surplus labour was widely recognized as a primary source of its global comparative advantage (Knight and Song 2005; Kwan 2009). Indeed, Silver and Zhang (2009: 175) observe, 'These migrant workers were generally thought to be part of an inexhaustible supply of cheap labour waiting to be tapped in China's rural areas.'

Under previous policy dictates, the nail that stood up earned the billystick – with the state targeting human rights activists and strike leaders to enforce labour discipline, which ensured the ongoing investment from transnational capital. More recent events have shown that the central government has tended to look the other way during some labour unrest, even if – as was clear from the case of Yue Yuen – province officials continue to strong-arm strikers when they can.

This new policy of restraint by the central government would be in line with an IMF (2012) report that concluded that China's turn to services and away from investment and export–led growth accompanied both rising labour and raw material costs. Part of the calculus is the transformation of the Chinese working class as not only labourers but also consumers, who must be cultivated. Despite its success, China now stands at a major crossroads in which the days of export-oriented manufacturing as the driver of growth is reaching its zenith. Just as Japan found its investment-driven growth drying up in the 1980s, the sector is showing the slowdown of returns because of the emergence of weak points in the domestic economy from the finance or real estate sectors. Florian Butollo (2014: 13) points to an epochal 'turning point' in China with both Chinese political leaders and international observers sharing the view that the country must reorient towards a more sustainable model based on domestic demands.

As investment rates climbed to 50 per cent of GDP in 2014, the proportion of consumption fell to roughly 30 per cent. The government, acutely aware of the limitations of its traditional growth model, attempted to shift the economy to bolster consumption. There has been much debate regarding China's attempts to rebalance the economy away from labour-intensive industrial manufacturing towards household consumption. These debates were the sharpest following the release of China's twelfth five-year plan (2011–2015) which made explicit the government's move away from its single-minded drive to maximize growth towards a more balanced economic development model. This rebalancing talked more of the protection of the environment, expanding its 'social wage' through welfare provision, and enhancing consumption which materialized into policies such as raising the minimum wage at double the rate of real GDP growth since 2011. Additionally, this strategy includes an expansion in social security, a rebalancing of the developed coastal regions and the developing interior, and a move towards the technological upgrading of labour-intensive production.

Alongside these policies, the Chinese government introduced collective bargaining legislation, which, as Chan and Hui (2014) claim, is a transition from 'collective consultation as formality' through a kind of 'collective bargaining by riot' towards a 'party state-led wage bargaining' driven by a desire of the state to temper labour unrest (a quintessential Gorzian 'reformist-reform'). Indeed, Silver and Zhang (2009) argue that the introduction of a number of reforms was intended to directly stave off the growing unrest, moving away from a single-minded focus on attracting foreign investment, and promoting a 'new development mode' with the aim to reduce inequality. An initial step was the 2008 Labour Contract Law, which strengthened the ACFTU's role at the workplace and put into place the restrictions on the ability of firms to terminate employees without a just cause, and the Arbitration Law that allowed workers to bring cases against employers free of charge.

A significant proportion of the population has seen their incomes and standards of living rise alongside the GDP growth. The reinvestment into fixed capital, such as infrastructure, has expanded the benefits of growth to the countryside as well. However, the cost of living, in particular that of housing, has risen at a faster pace than that of the profits and wages in the manufacturing sector, resulting in a higher rate of returns for large land-owning capital than the GDP. Indeed, the Chinese '1 percenters' have been able to generate more wealth at a faster pace than their counterparts around the world (Sheng and Geng 2014).

These profits coupled with labour shortage increase workers' bargaining power. Indeed, Chinese workers have been winning a real medium wage increase of 17 per cent per annum since 2009, taking home nearly five times what they were in 2000. And since wages, which account for 20–30 per cent of manufacturing costs, were, in 2011, only 30 per cent lower in China compared to the lowest-paying American states, a mere gap of 10–15 per cent gap had to be bridged. By 2016, the market research firm Euromarket reported that Chinese factory workers' wages had hit $3.60, a three-fold increase from 2005. The wages of China's industrial working class stood at five times the hourly wages of India and equal to those in South Africa and Portugal (Yan 2017).

The first cracks in the outsourcing model of economic growth began to appear in the early 2000s. It is an advantage that it is coming to a close and with it, an escalation of labour unrest, rising wages, and labour shortage have resulted in growing bargaining power for the workers in South China. China's working population shrank (by 3.5 million) for the first time in 2012. There have been a few explanations for this. First, China's implementation of a 'one child policy' that began in 1978 and was formally phased out in 2015.

As a consequence of strict family planning and macroeconomic development policy, China may have reached a demographic transition in a little over 30 years that took comparable developed countries nearly a century to reach (Cai 2015a). Since the late 1970s, China first witnessed a persistent decline in its fertility rate followed by a sharp fall in the working age population and a growth in the elderly population. While official Chinese government figures are notoriously unreliable, the United Nations (2015) ranked China among the lowest per capital fertility rate, alongside the US, Brazil, Russia, Japan, and Vietnam, a sign of the consequent decline in working population to continue or to decline further.

Emerging markets, however, are entering consumer society's first bloom; and the strike-won wages are just beginning to disappear into iPhones and cineplexes. Years of wage suppression in the West, predicated on a neoliberal 'social contract' of cut-rate Chinese goods, are in a process of mutation. As Bruce Rockowitz, CEO of Li & Fung, which handles 4 per cent of China's exports to the US, claims that 'it is the end of cheap goods', and that none of the alternatives will come close to curbing costs and inflation like China has done. 'There is no next' after China, says Rockowitz, predicting that the price of goods will rise by 5 per cent per annum, optimistically, and that Li & Fung's sourcing operation has already seen an annual price increase of 15 per cent.

Many economists, even in the IMF, claim that China is reaching a point of labour scarcity, the so-called Lewis Turning Point, an 'inevitable' developmental phase when wages surge sharply, and industrial profits are squeezed, with a steep fall in investment. Whether China has indeed reached the Lewis Turning Point is a controversial and hotly debated topic both within and outside academia.[5] Answering this question is central to making sense of the Chinese labour market, wage levels, and competitiveness, and this carries larger implications for the global garment sector. From its earlier liberalizing days, China 'exemplified a dual economy characterised by unlimited labour supply, subsistence wage, and the existence of institutional barriers to labour mobility' (Cai 2015b: 1). Cai (2015b: 5) argues that the sign of an end to the unlimited labour supply in China marks a new phase with the labour market reaching an equilibrium: 'As China enters a new era demographically, the impact on the labour market is enormous. These changes will shape the course of China's future development.'

The data and the literature on the question remain split and seemingly contradictory. Steady increases in urban wages and other demand-side factors support the claim that China has reached the Lewis Turning Point. However, the supply-side data, such as a large rural reserve army of labour, suggest that this 'turning point' is yet to arrive. Such is the contradiction between rural surpluses and urban shortages of labour in China (Wang and Weaver 2013) – this is despite the urban population surpassing the rural in 2012 (Simpson 2012). However, these different populations are far from being fixed. Even the government figures, which exclude most migrant workers, between 2001 and 2011 show that the urban labour demand grew at an annual rate of 3.2 per cent, whereas the labour supply grew at 1.1 per cent, a shortfall that has continued in the years following (Cai 2015b). Most workers in the manufacturing sector are classified as migrants from rural areas and are more likely to be affected

---

[5] The debates about whether China has indeed reached the Lewis Turning Point have been discussed widely including in special issues of the *China Economic Journal* (2010) – which became an edited volume (Yiping and Cai 2015) – as well as in the *China Economic Review* (2011) and the *Journal of the Asia Pacific Economy* (2015).

by cyclical unemployment, resulting in a return to the villages and agricultural labour, where they would be seasonal and underemployed.

One possible explanation cited for conflicting data between rural and urban labour markets is the Hukou system. Under the Hukou system, Chinese law mandates that individuals register as either 'rural' or 'urban', excluding rural–urban workers from state-subsidized social reproduction at their urban residence. This creates a bifurcation between urban production and rural social reproduction (Schling 2014).[6] Thus, the state is able to heavily regulate the labour market, cleaving social reproduction from material production, rendering urban migrants as permanently temporary. Internal Chinese migration results in split-households and so-called left-behind children who remain in the care of grandparents in the village. Thus, China's internal 'care chain' means that 'elder care' is also an issue of 'child care', or the generational reproduction of labour power (Murphy 2004).

Whalley and Zhang (2006) use statistical modelling to demonstrate the significant role played by the Hukou system in intensifying relative inequality in China since the liberalization by restraining labour migration between rural regions and urban areas. As Whalley and Zhang (2006: 2) point out, 'Not having Hukou in urban areas means that migrants receive no education or health benefits and cannot purchase housing since title to it cannot be registered by them. Effectively, Hukou operates as a barrier to urban/rural migration in China and supports large regional wage differentials which labour markets do not compete away.' The Hukou makes durable the segmentation of the labour market, as Knight, Deng, and Li (2011) argue, which restricts the ability of surplus rural populations to move to cities. Naturally, this rural divide is generational in which rural areas are abundant in older workers and cities require younger workers who have fewer social care needs (Chan 2010a). Geographically differentiated labour markets and living standards reinforce these barriers across rural and urban areas and between provinces (Garnaut 2010).

In his original conception, Lewis (1954) distinguishes two areas of the economy: industrial and agricultural. To Lewis, it was the profit maximization of the industrial sector and the traditional agricultural sector which uses family units with allocations based on marginal productivity that explained the structural differences between these sectors. Rural areas are able to absorb surplus labour to a significantly greater degree than urban. As Wang and Weaver (2013: 4) put it, 'The agricultural sector thus acts as a "sink" for the industrial

---

[6] Simply put, social reproduction theory analysis 'the relation between labour dispensed to produce commodities and labour dispensed to produce people' in understanding the totality of capitalism (Bhattacharya 2017: 2).

sector.' In other words, traditional agricultural sectors can act as, as Marx (1867) termed, a 'reserve army of labour' for industrial capital. Across the Global South, labour is cheaper compared to their counterparts in the Global North for many factors, but one important factor is that subsistence is an essential element within reproduction. Unemployed workers may revert to subsistence production, but they still remain part of a reserve ever ready for (re-)proletarianization.

The state and large firms have attempted to counter this labour shortage. Manufacturers in the east and west will no doubt be following Apple supplier Foxconn's example to replace a million workers with a million robots to 'cope with rising labour costs'. In recent years, the world's largest contract manufacturer of electronics and China's largest private-sector employer, Foxconn, has made global headlines after a series of suicides and labour protests. In February 2013, Apple stocks tumbled by 2.4 per cent after Foxconn's announcement of a hiring freeze, and that they will be opening a 10,000-worker facility in Brazil while at the same time committing $10 billion to open factories in Indonesia. This dwarfs Apple's high-profile announcement of investment in high-tech capital-intensive factories with a skeletal labour force to operate the machines in the US.

The Chinese working class, so often caricatured in the West as either globalization's passive victims or its active vectors – as its stoic assemblers of sneakers or its eager army of blacklegs – have, in recent years, been busting this myth, and asserting themselves in ever-higher numbers. In the late 1990s, labour protests were largely marginal, leading to the mass layoffs and closing of state-owned industries. China is now described as the 'epicentre of world labour unrest' (Silver and Zhang 2009: 177).

This followed China's enterprise restructuring law in 1994 and the smashing of the 'iron rice bowl' to engender transnational production unencumbered by state-owned facilities (Silver and Zhang 2009). Younger workers, who moved from their villages in the interior to the industrial centres then rising in the southeast, during the 1980s and early 1990s, are proving rather uppity. Silver and Zhang (2009: 174–175) observe, 'The mass movement of capital into China and the deepening commodification of labour since the mid-1990s have been accompanied by a rising tide of labour unrest in China.'

As Duan Yi, a Chinese labour activist, attests, 'The new generation of workers born in the 80s and 90s are not like their parents. They want to make a life in the cities. So they are becoming better organised and more rebellious than ever before.' Even Chinese government figures paint a picture of burgeoning upheaval: the incidence of mass protests between 1993 and 2003 grew six-fold, from 10,000 protests to 60,000, from some 730,000 protestors to over 3 million (Silver and Zhang 2009). And this explosive growth of wildcat strikes and work stoppages, which has only accelerated since 2004, is all the more significant for its illicitness in the nominally socialist state – where independent unions are in fact illegal and strikes are often criminalized as 'disrupting social order', and all grievances – concerning workplace conditions, wages, the appointment rather than election of factory representatives – must be mediated through the ACFTU.

Despite the ACFTU's historical role as an appendage of the Chinese Communist Party and, by extension, of the state's export-led strategy, in the latter half of the 2000s the ACFTU began taking unprecedented steps towards organizing union branches at transnational firms. Embittered by the ongoing employer intransigence, in 2006, the ACFTU initiated a widely publicized, and ultimately successful, campaign of mobilizing workers at Walmart stores into the union (Baines 2015). However, the usefulness of that particular legal channel is demonstrated by the recourse en masse to extra-legal means.

Wick (2009) conducted a survey of six PRD factories producing in labour-intensive sectors (electronics, household appliances, cosmetics, and textiles) for the retailer Aldi. Immediately following the end of the MFA in 2005, investigators commissioned by the German SÜDWIND Institute visited Aldi garment suppliers in Jiangsu Province and were aghast at the working conditions stating that 'labour law violations […] are far worse than any recorded so far in Chinese factories' (Wick 2009: 1). Every factory that was investigated was in violation of Chinese law, and investigators found evidence of child labour; workers were required to work the first month free, pay deposits, were fined for missing work, workers' ability to resign was restricted, and many had to wait for nightfall to escape.

But these conditions began to change dramatically following 2005/2006. Wick (2009: 29) describes the changes in PRD:

> In recent years, however, these migrant workers have been demanding more from their employers and the government. Countless industrial actions take place in the PRD, including strikes, go-slows, road blockages and daring public demonstrations. High profile labour activist in exile Han Dongfang estimates that strikes of over 1,000 workers happen daily in the Pearl River Delta. Staff turnover is a huge problem – even for relatively good factories – as workers vote with their feet and change factories frequently in search of better conditions. One survey of IRC factories in the region revealed that company managers characterised 25 percent annual staff turnover as relatively low! Many factories were experiencing turnover of 35–40% each year. The PRD is facing a pronounced labour shortage, especially of skilled workers – a stark contrast to the queues of migrant workers looking for work outside factory gates in the 1990s. Factories are having to offer better conditions to attract and retain staff, while local city governments

have announced significant annual increases in the minimum since 2006 in order to help workers meet the high cost of living in the region (particularly in big cities such as Shenzhen, where the minimum wage is now the highest in the country at 1,000 RMB [113 EUR] per month)

But this is no exception. Silver and Zhang (2009: 178) identify recent changes in China as part of a historical response to crisis:

> If an analysis of the dynamics of historical capitalism leads us to predict that 'where capital goes, conflict follows', then this same analysis leads us to look for a number of predictable capitalist responses to the labour unrest and rising costs in China. For example, during the past 150 years, capital has responded to labour unrest by geographically relocating production in search of cheaper or more docile labour ('spatial fixes') and by introducing technological/organizational changes in the process of production ('technological fixes').

Workers in large Asian garment firms

In the labour-intensive footwear sector, tariffs were relaxed in the 1980s, which is one explanation for the consolidation of buyers and supplier firms in the 1990s. The concentration of production in China has been followed by the consolidation of capital in a fewer number of mega-firms (Azmeh and Nadvi 2014). Gereffi (2009) notes that China has undergone unprecedented development by leveraging its abundant and low-cost labour, land, electricity, and raw materials, taking the lead in upgrading a number of industries, with high- and medium-technology exports outpacing low technology by around 2008. The emergence of large-scale production and place-specific value chain agglomeration has led to the foreign investment–driven clusters of what have been called 'supply chain cities' in China, primarily in Guangdong and Zhejiang, and strategic coupling between TNCs, provincial governments, and their outsourced manufacturers. '[Supply chain cities] bring together multiple parts of the firm's supply chain – designers, suppliers, and manufacturers – so as to minimise transaction costs, take advantage of economies of scale, and foster more flexible supply chain management' (Gereffi 2009: 46). Gereffi (2009) argues that foreign-led clusters have concentrated in the South China provinces of Guangdong and Fujian mainly in low-cost manufacturing sectors, such as textiles and apparel, primarily due to government policy, low-cost labour, and relative proximity to major transportation centres.

The strike at Yue Yuen facilities reveals that Yue Yuen, which 'has emerged as a major economic powerhouse' (Appelbaum 2008: 73), is rapidly attaining oligopolistic power. Detailed in Chapter 6, monopoly power is not meant to imply a single seller exercising sole proprietorship of a market (a rare phenomenon), but, as in economic parlance, denotes a phase of capitalist development in which giant firms 'limit new competitors entering the industry, even if there are high profits' (Foster, McChesney, and Jonna 2011). The monopoly firm has an incredible capacity to generate profits assisted by economies of scale and scope (Baran and Sweezy 1969: 52). Ngai and Chan (2012) argue that Apple producer Foxconn has become a monopoly firm because of supply chain integration, mergers, and acquisitions. It is the ensuing dependence by large global brands that results in Foxconn's power to dictate price, output, and investment. The Yue Yuen strike and brand reaction demonstrates the burgeoning power of oligopolistic suppliers vis-à-vis oligopolistic brands as well as workers vis-à-vis suppliers. Yue Yuen's ability to influence the sector in fundamental ways comes through a combination of the strength of its productive capacity relative to its competitors and the scale, size, and mutual-dependence of its buyers.

The labour unrest escalating in China since 2004 has been the subject of extensive reportage and research (Silver and Zhang 2009; Friedman 2012). In the first quarter of 2014, China Labour Bulletin, a leading Hong Kong–based rights group, recorded 319 strikes in China, a 30 per cent increase from year to year, mostly in the manufacturing sector. Elfstrom and Kuruvilla (2014: 454) find that 'Chinese workers are increasingly using strikes and protests proactively to demand higher wages, better working conditions, and increased respect from employers'.

As a consequence of the labour shortage, changes in state policy, and workers' agitation, wages have increased by 7 per cent per annum and Chinese capital is losing its labour cost advantage. The new era of competition has thinned the herd, leaving larger amalgamated firms with enhanced production-side value capture (Azmeh and Nadvi 2014). These dominant firms have reinvested in labour-saving technology, deepening their advantages in Chinese clothing and footwear production (Zhu and Pickles 2014). Labour-intensive industrial firms within Guangdong Province, the scene of Yue Yuen's production, that once occupied a large segment of the province's economic geography, have left en masse.[7] Firms had to resort to a 'spatial fix' (Harvey 2006a), relocating to other areas of China and Asia, where labour was cheaper. Yue Yuen survived in situ only because it possessed sufficient resources to effect organizational and technological 'fixes', mitigating labour costs, while also relocating part of its production to Indonesia

---

[7] For extended research on strikes and footwear in Guangdong province, see Chan (2011).

and Vietnam. As a conglomerate spanning multiple phases of the production process, across several countries, Yue Yuen is maturing towards monopolistic power as formulated by Baran and Sweezy (1969), later expounded into the labour process (Braverman 1974), and finally into a globalized context (Foster, McChesney, and Jonna 2011). Although the firm has not acquired full monopoly power, its growth represents a trend: a departure from a comprador role, which saw domestic firms simply piggyback on transnational capital. Monopoly should be understood not as an anomaly, or aberration, but as a logical consequence of competition, and the consolidation it engenders. Monopolization 'is in the DNA of capitalism' (Foster, McChesney, and Jonna 2011).

But what does industrial upgrading and monopoly power mean for workers? Wible, Mervis, and Wigginton (2014) describe Yue Yuen's parent company Pou Chen as in league with Apple manufacturer Foxconn, 'connect[ing] vast underlying commodity and labour markets that are relatively hidden from public eye'. They maintain that this 'sprawling web of supply chains can raise living standards, improve conditions for workers, and help alleviate poverty'. Indeed, there has been an upsurge in the discussion of the relationship between the gains to capital, or 'economic upgrading', and working conditions and benefits, or 'social upgrading' (Barrientos, Gereffi, and Rossi 2011; Bernhardt and Milberg 2011). These debates move away from 'trickle down' theories based on the axiom that firm growth improves labour conditions. While these recent interventions make critical inroads into filling a lacuna within GPN/GVC/GCC frameworks, much of the analysis fails to see the inherent antagonism between capital and labour. Indeed, as Selwyn (2013) has articulated, the literature continues to frame capital–labour relations as mutually beneficial and a causal 'top-down' relationship mediated through elite institutions such as the World Bank.[8] The case of Yue Yuen brings the question of antagonistic subjective agency back to labour itself by demonstrating that workers gain power and increase their share of value through the combination of economic upgrading and the sheer dint of *force*.

As the case of Yue Yuen demonstrates, the growth of suppliers in labour-intensive production does not automatically 'raise living standards', but constitutes a dialectical process. The sheer size of Yue Yuen affords it the resources to endure minor episodes of labour unrest, outlasting and undermining workers, while pressing state and police into service as guarantors of its physical and financial stability. Size can prove a liability, however, by amplifying the effects of worker

---

[8] For a critique of attempts at establishing workers' rights through capitalist institutions, see Kumar (2015).

actions on commodity chains where large firms have integrated, fusing together successive phases of production. Appelbaum (2008: 82) observes, 'If production is concentrated in a few giant factories, work stoppages can have a significant impact not only on the factory itself, which may have significant capital investment, but also on the entire supply chain.'

Both Merk (2008) and Appelbaum (2008) published papers on the growth of Yue Yuen in 2008, six years before the strike was observed. In this chapter, I apply and build upon their work while exploring the changing political economy of, and power dynamics involved in, producing within garment and light manufacturing sectors in South China.

The case of Yue Yuen

Formed in 1969, Taiwan-based Yue Yuen Industrial (Holdings) Limited has become the world's largest manufacturer of branded casual and athletic footwear, producing 300 million pairs of shoes a year, or 20 per cent of the global production of sports and casual-wear shoes. They have over a half million workers in their factories, churning out goods for more than 30 different brands such as Nike, Adidas, Reebok, Puma, Asics, Under Armour, New Balance, and Timberland.[9]

Yue Yuen, a subsidiary of Pou Chen – a conglomerate controlled by the billionaire family of Tsai Chi Jue, grew quickly. 'From slippers, we made sandals. From sandals we made shoes. From shoes we made sports shoes,' recalls a member of Tsai's family (Merk 2008: 86). Today, the majority of Yue Yuen production is based in China's PRD region, but facilities can be found as far afield as Vietnam, Indonesia, and even the US. The firm maintains two primary divisions: one manufacturing footwear for transnational branded companies and the other, a much smaller division, for retailing in the Greater China region, selling brand name footwear directly to consumers, and as a wholesaler. In recent years, Yue Yuen has continued to expand, acquiring smaller firms in quick succession and growing at ~20 per cent per annum throughout the 2000s (for reference, the total market for athletic shoes grew only ~10 per cent per annum during the same period). In some years, Yue Yuen's net annual profits exceeded even those of its buyers like Adidas or Reebok (Merk 2008).

---

[9] Jeff Hermanson states that since the end of the MFA, Nike has gone from 1,000 suppliers to just 300, shifting away from Korean suppliers to Chinese for apparel production (interview, 6 February 2019).

In the 1970s and 1980s, Yue Yuen became indispensable to industry heavy hitters, attracted to its epochal innovations in cost and turnaround time. Indeed, both Reebok and Nike would go on to name it as their 'most important producer' (Merk 2008: 86). It is during this era that Yue Yuen incorporated the Original Design Manufacturer/Original Equipment Manufacturer (ODM/OEM) designation, signalling its entrance into the design field, and its ambition to bring all phases of production – from conception to distribution – under the Yue Yuen label. By the 1990s, it had relocated its production facilities from Taiwan to China, Indonesia, and Vietnam.

Yue Yuen now enjoys the advantages of scale. Assembly takes place in imposing facilities that employ as many as 10,000 workers and set the curve for inventory turnover, emptying and replenishing stocks of product a full 5 to 20 days faster than the industry competitors (Merk 2008). And, as it happens in competitive economies, strength has led to strength, and one advantage – well-leveraged – can develop into another: technology. Yue Yuen's labourers, though already the most numerous, can be said to do the least individually in the sector since they operate the most advanced (ergo *most automated*) equipment. While its buyers outsource more and more of their production, Yue Yuen expands and deepens its operations, integrating horizontally and vertically, and investing heavily in research and development. This has allowed Yue Yuen to market itself as a one-stop shop, 'full package' to global buyers, handling raw materials, assembly, design, and distribution of products. As one Morgan Stanley report noted, the 'smaller players without sufficient resources will find it difficult to match Yue Yuen's services to its customers' (Merk 2008). Valued at a comfortable $5.6 billion, Yue Yuen 'has emerged as an economic powerhouse in its own right' (Appelbaum 2008: 73).

Yet something is rotten in the state of Yue Yuen. On 15 April 2014, 43,000 workers would walk out.

A demand for social insurance

The strike at Yue Yuen was centred on the issue of social insurance. China's social insurance system dates back to the early 1980s and remains, to this day, an opaque and complicated affair that manufacturers either recklessly undermine or simply avoid. Chinese law stipulates that employees and employers alike are responsible for funding the employee social insurance accounts administered by the local government. Yet intransigence is the norm. While large employers do not calculate social insurance payments using the minimum wage, smaller employers find it easier to engage in complete non-compliance and hide in the lower end of government priorities. Workers depend on these accounts, which also include health, injury, maternity, medical, unemployment compensation insurance, and, crucially, pensions for what they hope will be relatively burden-free retirements, often to their ancestral villages. Yue Yuen, however, calculated its contribution using a basic wage not accounting for overtime. Although the average monthly Yue Yuen wage comes to about 3,000 yuan ($490) with the inclusion of overtime pay, workers reported employer contributions proportionate to an average of only 1,810 yuan ($296). China's central government confirmed the discrepancy and publicly accused Yue Yuen of 'wrongdoing', entreating them to take corrective measures. According to Agence France-Presse (AFP), labour rights activists had estimated arrears in the range of 100–200 million yuan ($16–32 million). In light of this, Yue Yuen employee contracts were deemed invalid. In 2014, workers discovered that the company had been engaged in the practice of miscalculating social insurance for years with, it appeared, the active collusion of local government officials. As the *Economist* (2014) observed, strikers' chants often mingled the lyrics highlighting government corruption and complicity with those that indicted Yue Yuen.

Yue Yuen workers complained that 'the factory has been tricking us for 10 years [...] the district government, labour bureau, social security bureau and the company were all tricking us together' (Gongchao 2014). And the problem, it appears, is endemic. According to the state newswire *Xinhua*, local officials often created legal loopholes specifically designed to attract capital. 'Some local governments even allow foreign companies to escape payments to attract their investments,' observes He Gaochao, a political scientist at Sun Yat-sen University (Valdmanis 2014).

Yue Yuen did not back down. Its (alleged) allies in government employed aggressive police tactics throughout the strike, detaining, arresting, and even hospitalizing protesters. *Xinhua*, however, reported little of the strike, and contradicted all reports of worker injuries, despite myriad claims by international press and activists. Eventually, employees, facing threats and an overwhelming police presence, began to trickle back but employed 'work-to-rule' tactics through work slowdowns.

However, by the strike's end, workers' demands had grown to include a new contract, better working conditions, better-funded government housing, an enshrined right to conduct a union election within the plant, concrete assurances against employer retribution, and a transparent and accountable government to execute and administer all the aforementioned demands. Thus, an economic demand – in this case, honesty in wage reportage (that is, pension and social insurance payments in accordance with the law) – gave rise in due course to further demands, for institutional and social reforms, and would consolidate and build upon economic victories.

Figure 3.1 Striking workers at Yue Yuen Facility, Dongguan, China, 23 April 2014

Source: Courtesy of IULBR sourced anonymously from Weibo.

A strike escalates

According to the activists, the strike had been set off by a Yue Yuen employee who, after putting in her paperwork to retire, discovered that her 20-plus years of service to the company – in a managerial role, no less – had left her with a mere 600 yuan (roughly $100) in social insurance, to sustain her through old age. Understandably upset, she stormed off to a company dormitory. Word spread.[10]

On 5 April 2014, several hundred workers at a Gaobu factory clocked in and promptly walked out; they then gathered at a bridge to block traffic. By 14 April, the strikers' numbers had swollen to 10,000 and had come to include workers from all six of Yue Yuen's Gaobu factories – among them even a few contingents from management. Though only partial, the strike was already significant in absolute terms, since the Gaobu factories accounted for 10 per cent of Yue Yuen's total output (Qi 2014). An army of riot police was dispatched.

---

[10] Phone interview, Taiwan-based labour activist, 24 August 2014. In addition, this account is supported by extensive Reuters interviews (Harney and Ruwitch 2014). Some claim that the company managers orchestrated the strike by encouraging frontline workers to walk out (Harney and Ruwitch 2014).

Meanwhile, on 15 April, 43,000 walked out. Yue Yuen responded by offering to sit down with workers; however, negotiations fell through when Yue Yuen refused to concede to any of the strikers' primary demands. 'It was rumoured,' according to workers,[11] that 'the company agreed to pay the full social insurance to be calculated from the date that workers returned to work, which would not include back pay, a central worker demand. Workers also wanted it in cash because they knew that they could never ensure enforcement of any agreement.' A group of worker representatives were then arrested with the purported help of officials of the state union ACFTU (Gongchao 2014). On 17 April, Yue Yuen announced publicly that it would pay the full social insurance calculated from 1 May, but not retroactively, and only on the condition that workers returned to work.

In the face of this offer, 'the workers [continued] striking, and the numbers ... probably increased' despite 'the factory releas[ing] a notice saying it [would] dismiss the workers if they continue[d]' (AFP 2014). AFP (2014) spoke to a Yue Yuen striker who said she and the other workers had been offered the welfare payments until 2016, but she was not satisfied. 'The factory could just leave in the middle of the year, and we might end up without welfare payments.'

By Friday, 18 April, the same day that the wives and children of jailed Gaobu workers demonstrated in front of the district office, 2,000 Yue Yuen workers in the neighbouring province of Jiangxi, responsible chiefly for producing Adidas shoes, joined the strike and walked out. The spread of the strike occurred without central coordination but organically as a consequence of the identification as a Yue Yuen worker outside the boundaries of a single factory, city, province, and, as we see shortly, beyond the border of the Chinese state itself. Francine Chan[12] described the strike's propagation, noting that, though 'some workers passed information through the social networking site Weibo and the instant messaging service Qq, [most of] the workers are older [and therefore] most of the news spread through word-of-mouth, [since] strike organisers had already developed contacts with worker leaders at other Yue Yuen factories during smaller strikes in the past'. Because of this, the workers were more than able to circumvent the news blackout imposed by government authorities. (The *Economist* [2014] reported that though foreign journalists were allowed onto Yue Yuen's property at Gaobu, Chinese citizens had been barred.)

On 21 April, Yue Yuen made a statement to the Hong Kong stock exchange, where it is registered, reassuring investors that it would return calm to the factory floor by raising workers' living allowance to 230 yuan ($37) per month,

---

[11] Phone interview, Francine Chen, Worker Empowerment, 24 August 2014.
[12] Phone interview, 24 August 2014.

and promised to make up the unpaid social security payments, though 'the contributions [could not] be quantified for the time being' (NDTV 2014). Workers were informed through loudspeakers and fliers distributed by the ACFTU. As one Taiwan-based labour activist stated,[13] 'Workers rejected this offer. Even if it sounds nice, workers didn't know how long they would be employed still and this was based on future earnings. There was also no way to enforce the agreement– plus the offer was tiny compared to the amount workers were owed.'

The following day, factory gates were closed to workers, to prevent them from pressing their timecards (and then leaving). Those who did manage to find their way inside were arrested when they still refused to work. In response to a call to arms by Taiwanese labour activists, a series of demonstrations sprang up in front of prominent international Adidas retailers, placing additional – albeit indirect – pressure on Yue Yuen (fortunately for the strikers, the recently formed International Union League for Brand Responsibility [IULBR] was already engaged in an ongoing campaign to exact worker protections from Adidas (see Chapter 2), whose retailers are conveniently ubiquitous – even compared to other major Yue Yuen partners, like Nike). Protests erupted in Istanbul, Melbourne, Bangalore, London, Taiwan, Hong Kong, New York, and elsewhere.

By 24 April, Yue Yuen had garrisoned its factories with riot police. Four days later, the company reported that 80 per cent of the workers employed at the Gaobu factory, where the strike had started, had returned to work (Qi 2014). Labour activists and workers, however, accused the government and the police of physically compelling workers to return (Yue Yuen, it was said, asked they 'rectify the situation'). The AFP (NDTV 2014) compiled testimonials from workers who claimed to have 'only returned because of intimidation'. One, who asked not to be named, stated, 'At the moment the factory is controlled by police.'

Eventually, the company agreed to pay full pensions, with an additional living allowance, starting 1 May 2014 – but without retroactive pay. The offer, announced over loudspeakers on Yue Yuen's corporate campus, elicited 'howls of derision' from picketers, who tore up copies of the ACFTU mediation letter in response (*Economist* 2014). The majority of the workers understood this to not be a victory, and the irony involved in considering it as such was palpable. Li, a 45-year-old sanitation worker, explained, 'The workers were not successful: the government is forcing us back to work' (NDTV 2014). Tan, a 17-year-old worker in the accessories unit said: 'Factory officials have warned us that those who make a fuss will be sacked without compensation,' therefore, 'the strike has

---

[13] Phone interview, 21 July 2014.

failed, we didn't get the result we wanted.' But despite misgivings and all, the workers accepted and the strike was lifted.

Yue Yuen estimated direct losses from the April 2014 strike at $27 million, with an additional $31 million in exacted concessions for 2014 alone (Qi 2014). By 3 May, days after the strike, shares of Yue Yuen had dropped by 4.6 per cent, to a five-month low. *Forbes* conceded that 'the strike and extra payments involving Yue Yuen [...] underscores the rising cost of doing business in China, the country's declining competitiveness for labour-intensive manufacturing and investment' (Flannery 2014).

The influence of the strike was nonetheless felt. On 21 July, workers at a Yue Yuen factory in the Chinese city of Zhuhai in Guangdong Province themselves struck over slow social insurance processing, prompting immediate corrective measures by company officials. 'At this point all the misunderstanding has been resolved,' company official Jerry Shum announced shortly after (Lin 2014). In mid-March 2015, around 5,000 Yue Yuen workers in PRD downed tools and walked out once again in opposition to the reorganization of the production process. In late-March and into April 2015, up to 90,000 footwear factory workers at Yue Yuen's Vietnam subsidiary Pou Yuen went out on a week-long strike, described as 'one of the longest and largest that has ever happened in Vietnam' (BBC 2015). Their demands mirrored those of Guangdong workers a year earlier, centring around social insurance distribution, while targeting changes in state policy. In response, the Vietnamese government announced that

Figure 3.2 Workers at Pou Yuen in Ho Chi Minh City gather for talks

Source: Reuters, 2 April 2015.

they would amend the law to incorporate workers' concerns. Although major brands reportedly monitored the Vietnam case closely, they did not shift orders away from the plant and stressed that their deliveries were unaffected by the strike (Barrie 2015). In February 2016, 17,000 workers at the Bien Hoa City plant struck in opposition to Pou Chen's intransigence with respect to Vietnamese law requiring 12 days of paid annual leave, and a raft of new reward-and-punishment measures; Pou Chen capitulated to workers' demands after four days and agreed to pay workers for strike days (Rogers 2016).

Brand reaction and geographic relocation

Even before the strike, Yue Yuen had begun relocating production inland from China's industrial southeast, away from the region's rising labour costs (Zhu and Pickles 2014). Despite rumours and reports to the contrary (Qi 2014), an Adidas spokesman confirmed with me[14] the official Adidas statement, 'The Adidas Group has a highly flexible supply chain in place. [And] in order to minimise the impact on our operations, we are currently reallocating some of the future orders originally allocated to Yue Yuen Dongguan to other suppliers. At the same time, we'd like to point out that we are not pulling out of the Yue Yuen factory in Dongguan and we have no plans to do so. A press release by China Labour Watch claiming this is incorrect.' A few months later, it was revealed that Adidas had indeed shifted a number of orders to other suppliers but 'at no point did [it] consider pulling out of the factory at Dongguan' (Borromeo 2014).

In the waning days of the Yue Yuen strike, Nike's the then chief executive, Mark Parker, mentioned at a press conference that Nike was mulling its own relocation of production, to follow the path of least worker resistance in China. But though 'we [that is, Nike] didn't move product out in this case, [we're] staying close to it. We've been in a position to do that […] we're always considering it' and that, despite maintaining 'close contact' with Yue Yuen, it had 'not yet taken a position on that' (Valdmanis 2014). He reassured the financial press that Nike had 'a factory base where [it] can move product around as [it needs to, in order to] make sure that [it doesn't] have issues with production'.

However far paying workers retroactively would have gone towards rehabilitating its corporate reputation, it was apparently not enough – and Yue Yuen refused. Presumably, the strike's end, in Yue Yuen's eyes, had put a cap

---

[14] Email correspondence, Ben Goldhagen, Adidas Marketing Director (UK), 24 April 2014.

on its responsibilities to labour. As a case in point, Nike's non-binding code of conduct includes a clause protecting worker compensation, asking that 'contractor employees are timely paid at least the minimum wage required by a country's law and provided legally mandated benefits' (Valdmanis 2014). Yet Nike made no public statements during the strike regarding labour conditions despite protests at their retail-end across the world, but instead reassured the investors on the potential relocation of orders in order to resume production.

Two months after the strike, an article in the *Guardian* (Borromeo 2014), titled 'How Adidas Supported Worker Rights in China Factory Strike', analysed how major brands responded to the strike.[15] As is commonplace during labour factory fires or collapse in the global garment sector, transnational brands immediately disassociated themselves. Similar to Yue Yuen, the brand Timberland, for example, stated that 'Timberland products are manufactured in some Yue Yuen locations [...] but not in the locations that were involved in the strikes' despite being featured prominently on Yue Yuen's website. While Nike stated that it was working closely with Yue Yuen, the company emphasized that this was not the brand's responsibility but an issue between workers, Yue Yuen, and the government.

The most far-reaching statement came from Adidas, 'Throughout the strike, the Adidas Group was closely monitoring the situation and in touch with our partner Pou Chen Group [...] Pou Chen Group was in direct discussion with the local government and the trade union federation to seek ways to address the concerns expressed by the workers [...] with respect to the arrest of two workers' representatives, Mr. Zhang and Mr. Lin, we were engaged with several labour groups in southern China, to try to determine where they were being detained and offered our support to secure their release. We also wrote to the Dongguan mayoral office, calling for [their] immediate release' (Borromeo 2014). Adidas' strategy was to place principal responsibility on the manufacturer and the local government while identifying itself as a third-party advocacy group who, alongside labour groups, were lobbying the local government rather than being an intimately enmeshed actor within the forces of production. Nonetheless, the recognition by Adidas that a modicum of responsibility must be assumed to 'address the concerns expressed by workers' is distinct from other brands. Indeed, this may reveal the efficacy of the global solidarity campaign of which Adidas was the sole target.[16]

---

[15] As an aside, the article series was sponsored by brand-retailer giant H&M.
[16] Major brands maintain longstanding corporate social responsibility (CSR) policies including 'codes of conduct' that protect legally mandated social security. Yet brands either failed to notice (signalling incapacity) or noticed but failed to intervene

The state and social reproduction

The Yue Yuen strike represents the most significant private sector strike over pensions in Chinese history,[17] an indication of changing labour demographics and an ongoing crisis of social reproduction in China. The shifting demand from wages towards pensions, housing, and other forms of social care is characteristic of China's ageing workforce, especially within labour-intensive manufacturing. How workers anticipate receiving pension payments shaped their decisions on whether to remain or leave the labour force.

The age for retirement in China is generally 60 for men and 50 for women and the workforce at Yue Yuen are mostly in their 30s and 40s, with many having worked at the company for a decade or longer. Women constitute 70 per cent of Yue Yuen's workforce, and a similar percentage of the workforce had been employed for five years or longer (Gongchao 2014), meaning they had accrued more for their pensions and, unlike the high turnover that plagues worker capacity building in the sector, many Yue Yuen workers had developed longstanding relationships. Ageing workplaces are a trend across Guangdong where labour shortage, especially of younger migrants from the countryside, has forced suppliers to find ways to retain employees for longer periods. Consequently, workers have shifted away from immediate wage-oriented demands, taking stock of a changing landscape across South China of factory closure, reorganization, and relocation. The longer a worker is employed, the greater the potential payoff after a closure or restructure; as such the possibility of closure moves social insurance–related demands to the fore among an ageing workforce. Nearly eight months after the end of the Yue Yuen strike, the *Wall Street Journal* (Magnier 2014) highlighted a burgeoning movement of Chinese migrant workers forging demands over pensions, with workers identifying the Yue Yuen strike and the subsequent agreement as the 'turning point' which 'sparked further worker actions', citing a number of strikes and employer concessions regarding social insurance for workers at electronics, apparel, and toy factories. For example, workers at China Qilitian Golf Articles, a subcontracted manufacturer for major brands based in Shenzhen in Guangdong, went on strike shortly after the Yue Yuen strike. Ji Jiansheng, a 42-year-old Qilitian worker, claimed, 'Yue Yuen's success has made a big difference' in their negotiations.

(implying complicity). Regardless, it contributes to mounting evidence of a failure in the regime of CSR and codes of conduct (Kumar and Mahoney 2014).

[17] Based on the assertion by Geoffrey Crothall of the China Labour Bulletin (*Economist* 2014).

The focus on social benefits is also important for Dongguan's population where nearly 80 per cent of its 8.3 million residents either moved in or are children of those who moved from other parts of China. Although a Guangdong Province law provides rural migrant workers entitlement to some social insurance since the late 1990s (Cheng, Nielsen, and Smyth 2014), the fusing of Yue Yuen's demands around social insurance reveals an intersection between spatiality, temporality, gender, and an ageing industrial working class in PRD.[18]

For a brief period, the central government enacted a number of pro-labour laws in an attempt to pacify growing worker unrest, responding in a 'paternalistic' fashion rather than acceding to the specific demands of workers (Friedman 2014), for example, enacting a 2008 labour law that required employers to contribute to social security payments. The Yue Yuen strike coheres with Friedman's (2014) characterization of labour unrest in China as a form of 'alienated politics' with workers unable to articulate larger politics despite antagonism towards their direct employers, the local government, and the official trade union. Yet, contrary to Friedman's claims, the strike spread to other factories and provinces, effectively communicating demands both internally and to the outside world despite a media blackout, and is therefore not entirely 'cellularized'. Within this context, Yue Yuen represents a clear example of a growing trend in South China of workers striking for full implementation of the law. Lee and Zhang (2013: 1504) have shown that the use of force has become undesirable as the market economy has reduced popular dependence on the authoritarian state. They maintain that the Chinese government developed a catalogue of measures to manage unrest, allowing a space for aggrieved citizens to obtain material concessions and symbolic rewards from the state, which they term 'bargained authoritarianism'. Increasingly, the state is resorting to clandestine rather than purely authoritarian means of reaching governmentality; that is to say, the authoritarian Chinese state has taken on a more 'paternalistic' character and is less antagonistic to the demands of workers. Workers do not see the state as an ally, but recent demands for implementation of the law is in marked contrast to previous movements in which a state legal framework could not be called upon.[19]

In the case of Yue Yuen, we see how the actions of workers, domestic manufacturer, and transnational capital are all informed in varying degrees by the

---

[18] In western China, there is an expansion of vocational schools that operate as a 'labour fix' for relocated factories of PRD.

[19] It appears this trend may be reversing under the rule of Xi Jinping, with many arrests of labour activists in the last few years, a shutdown of most labour NGOs operating in PRD, and more aggressive repression of strikes. The most recent example is the repression of the Jasic Technology workers (Pringle and Chan 2018).

state and its labour relations regime, rebutting value chain analysis that tends to downplay the state. Global commodity chains do not operate in a geographical–historical vacuum. The shifting capital–labour relations in China are place-specific and tied to broader domestic politico-economic changes. Recent years have seen the combined forces of a labour shortage and Chinese state policy away from low-technology, low-value manufacturing. This has helped to create an optimal environment to increase workers' bargaining power within China's labour-intensive sectors.[20]

Enhanced supplier-end value capture

Yue Yuen represents the 'ideal type' of this phenomenon within the sector whose size, integrated supply chains, and technologically upgraded factories led to reduced lead times and costs, aggravated the price differentials between Yue Yuen and its closest competitors, and made it increasingly prohibitive for transnational buyers to adopt alternative suppliers. Thus, through consolidation, Yue Yuen accumulates the necessary capital to invest in industrial upgrading, further reinforcing its market share, erecting insurmountable barriers to entry, and extracting their own economic rents. Through this process, Yue Yuen has accumulated considerable value in a historically low-value sector. Consequently, the firm has begun to exert greater influence in the global commodity chain vis-à-vis global buyers.[21]

Yue Yuen's power is measured within the commodity chain and against global buyers. The greatest power of brands in footwear is in their capacity to seamlessly move production at little cost to them but at great cost to producers and workers (see Armbruster-Sandoval 2005; Moran 2010). Despite threats, brands retained their relationship with Yue Yuen during the strike in spite of its

---

[20] The increase in workers' bargaining power is one explanation for the state increasingly resorting to repression on behalf of the employers. In the Jasic Technology case, outlined in Pringle and Chan (2018), the ownership of the firm is domestic, and the production (robotic welding equipment for industrial use) is an important part of Xi Jinping's 'Made in China 2025' plan, and this undoubtedly increases the desire to repress workers' industrial action. Indeed, the support for the workers by elite university students must have been an ominous sign for those who recall the origins of the so-called Great Proletarian Cultural Revolution at Peking University.

[21] The use of enhanced value in the case of Yue Yuen can be inferred by bringing together a range of factors such as upgrading, consolidation, and the fact that Yue Yuen's gross profits surpassed all but 2 of the over 30 brands it supplies for.

longevity and brand assurances to investors of their capacity to replace Yue Yuen. Brands did not move production to other suppliers after the end of the strike, which is unprecedented given the history of brands moving production after the mildest labour unrest. The difficulty of relocating production is tied to capacity but also related to intellectual property and further evidence of embeddedness of transnational brands with domestic firms. The growth of firms like Yue Yuen makes replacing it increasingly onerous. The size, in terms of net profits, of Yue Yuen now exceeds even those large branded firms whom it produces for, with Nike and Adidas as the only exceptions.[22] The effect of this should not be understated. The ability of buyers to dictate terms to suppliers has as much to do with barriers to entry as it does with monetary power.

Teresa Cheng, a labour activist, posited[23] that 'similar to Foxconn and Apple, brands could see the critical importance of keeping design functions within a trusted producer like Yue Yuen'. In other words, retaining production at Yue Yuen could be tied to both cost and the liability of shifting production. This represents a radical departure from previous brand action in garments and footwear production (Kumar and Mahoney 2014). Over the past decade, Nike, Adidas, and other branded companies have begun to consolidate both manufacturing and various phases of the supply chain under one roof by the so-called full-package producers like Yue Yuen. While major brands are outsourcing tasks, Yue Yuen is insourcing more functions, moving upstream on the global commodity chain. Large full-package agreements, like Nike's, function to lock-in the high barrier to entry for competitors. Consequently, Nike and Yue Yuen have become 'highly dependent on one another' (Appelbaum 2008: 80).

Yue Yuen's horizontal and vertical growth, alongside its enormous production capacity, has allowed the company a greater degree of leverage when signing agreements with transnational brands. In addition, by developing ODM/OEM design capability, Yue Yuen is able to expand into a higher value phase in the supply chain. As one director at a large Hong Kong shoe supplier reportedly told the *Wall Street Journal*, 'If Yue Yuen said today "I won't supply anymore to Nike" then Nike would be scared' (Merk 2008: 88). Instructively, the unwillingness or inability for major brands to relocate a noticeable proportion of its production from Yue Yuen, despite an increased risk of resurgent and costly labour unrest, reveals Yue Yuen's power in the value chain. Over time, this relationship becomes irreversible, with competing small and mid-size supplier firms melding

---

[22] Based on the annual Yue Yuen and brand report data (retrieved 24 April 2016).
[23] Phone interview, 15 July 2014.

into larger firms or vanishing altogether. The result is a deepening of Yue Yuen's power to dictate prices, and dramatically reconfigure the 'buyer-driven' paradigm described by Gereffi into a kind of *buyer–producer symbiosis*. This new mutually dependent relationship between buyer and supplier means increasing difficulty in identifying the drivers of GVCs and, as we see from the strike at Yue Yuen, forcing larger buyers to steel-reinforce their relationship with suppliers despite growing liability brought on by labour unrest. Symbiosis within the value chain is part of a larger trend of economic growth and purchasing power within emerging markets and falling consumption patterns within saturated economies.

Thus, Yue Yuen's fully integrated supply chains brought under one roof are capable of producing a competitively higher volume that is ready for market at considerable cost-savings for clients. Large full-package firms become increasingly dominant within the regime of just-in-time production, in which low-inventory and faster turnaround times are essential to capital accumulation. Yue Yuen's capacity has expanded so significantly that if Nike or Adidas chose to go directly to a standalone production firm in China instead of a supply chain integrated firm, 'the organizational costs might be too high to afford' (Lo, Wu, and Hsu 2014). Notably, despite its means, expertise, and strategic position, Yue Yuen has not produced its own brand. Doing so, despite the potential profits, would turn Yue Yuen from a high-value supplier into a direct competitor with its vital branded clients. Such is the relationship between Yue Yuen and the brands it produces for, but without being static.

Workers' power at Yue Yuen

Industrial geography strongly contributed to the labour–capital relations at Yue Yuen's primary facilities. Despite Guangdong Province housing 20 per cent of China production, in recent years the province has witnessed rising production costs due in part to a labour shortage. Yet Yue Yuen retained much of its production in Guangdong, unlike many other capital-light manufacturing firms, through a combination of organizational expansion and technological upgrading. Conditions of labour shortage were thus optimum for an escalation of labour demands and burdensome for the company to replace striking workers. In what Hobsbawm (1952) called 'collective bargaining by riot', workers at Yue Yuen do not have an independent union to mediate their concerns. What they have is a single official union, ACFTU, utilized, as Pringle (2013) and Howell (2008) have shown, to stifle their militancy. The risks of organizing such strikes are too high, due to government spies or company-side informers, so strikes are often seemingly spontaneous,[24] based on word of mouth, and both erupt and fizzle out with equal precision.

The size and longevity of the Yue Yuen strike is unprecedented in labour-intensive sectors but particularly remarkable is a singular demand coalesced against a single target utilizing the same tactic – the wildcat strike – across many different factories, provinces, and even countries over time, largely rebutting claims that '[in China] when workers do protest collectively, it almost never extends beyond a single workplace' (Friedman 2014: 1002).[25] The strike should not be viewed in isolation and reveals changes in labour–capital relations not only in global footwear but also across capital-light manufacturing sectors. These sectors once consisted of many small factories in which demands failed to cohere against a single employer, a notable difference to Yue Yuen, despite levels of workers' organization remaining uneven. Striking workers had an intuitive sense of Yue Yuen's power in the global supply chain and the efficacy of a large and escalating strike. Once the strike began at Gaobu in a historically militant and organized factory, it expanded to other factories and neighbouring provinces despite a lack of organization and a rejection of the official government union, with neighbouring strikes emerging even after the original strike had ended. For example, Yue Yuen HQ immediately capitulated to workers at the Zhuhai facility who struck for social insurance a few months after the end of the main strike, extending the counter-hegemonic power of the original strike to make gains for the Chinese working class beyond a single factory. As Henderson et al. (2002: 450) state, 'The source of power within the GPNs and the ways in which it is exercised is decisive for value enhancement and capture and thus for the prospects for development and prosperity.'

Enhanced value capture at supplier-ends also begins to change workers' strategies and tactics. As stated earlier, the employer contribution to social insurance is often under-calculated by larger employers and completely avoided by smaller firms. The profit margins of Yue Yuen motivated workers to action. As one activists[26] stated, 'I've never seen social insurance as a demand at smaller companies where there are many other difficulties. Workers I spoke to on the

---

[24] 'Spontaneity' of strikes is addressed in Leung (2015) through first-hand accounts of labour struggles in the jewel sector in Guangzhou.

[25] Similarly, the 2010 Honda 'strike wave' spread across the country coalescing around wage demands and the demand for an independent union. However, automobiles remain capital-intensive and as such, there is different workers' bargaining power than in footwear.

[26] Phone interview, 21 July 2014.

Yue Yuen strike knew exactly how much the company was worth and the issue that drove them was knowing the company could easily pay them.'

Shifting the terrain

The conventional wisdom of capital flows in footwear production is that profits are predicated on the global 'race to the bottom' where employers are able to choose from an almost unlimited number of producers in an arena with low barriers to entry. However, freer capital flows, labour shortage, and the rise of labour unrest and bargaining power can also contribute to the vanishing of smaller firms and an even greater enlargement of enormous suppliers. While a strike at a smaller firm would signal its death knell, Yue Yuen's size means it can absorb much of the liability brought on by labour unrest. This is indicated by both the $27 million cost of the strike, the company's ability to ensure the obedience of local officials and police, and the inability of brands to either effectively pressure Yue Yuen or move production significantly. However, as an outgrowth of Yue Yuen's capacity, it was able to agree to pay $31 million in workers' benefits. Despite the failures of the strike and continued reported difficulties in ensuring the enforcement of the agreement, the levels of compensation were unparalleled in the sector.[27]

By technological upgrading, organizational consolidation, and even relational rents, Yue Yuen 'locking-in' buyers, resulting in enhanced value capture at the bottom of the global value chain, of which its profit margins are but one indicator, in turn opening up a space for workers to finally make material demands on their direct employer. Simultaneously, however, the transformation to higher value capitals allows them to materially withstand sufficient economic pressure, such as undermining industrial action through its ability to absorb losses brought on

---

[27] Hitherto footwear workers of the Global South coordinated with Global North activists, targeting the spaces of high value capture in the supply chain – the brands. The Yue Yuen strike reveals the changes in consumption patterns and points of leverage. During the Yue Yuen strike, storefront solidarity actions against Adidas erupted around the globe, and in a significant departure the Yue Yuen strike saw retail targeted in cities of the Global South exposing the growth of Asia's proportion of global consumption (Russell 2014). Thus, the emergence of a multipolar world, in which products are produced and consumed within the Global South, hints at the prospect of multiple points of leverage for workers. It also counters the claim by Anner (2015) that China's 'authoritarian state labour control regime' prevents links between workers' international advocacy groups and workers.

by strikes, as well as wielding greater influence with the state apparatus, such as province officials and the police, in reproducing labour power.

Yet it would seem that the Yue Yuen strike, by pressing for labour-law compliance, was largely 'defensive' and it is still unclear if any enduring organization will develop from it, despite its clear influence on further strike actions and China's migrant workers' demands for social security. Indeed, the strike at Yue Yuen may represent another example of what Chan (2010) has called 'class struggle without class organization'. However, as the strike progressed and additional demands were added, the strike took on a more 'offensive' or proactive character similar to what Elfstrom and Kuruvilla (2014) have described in Guangdong's capital-intensive automobile industry. Still, the Chinese state's reaction remains inconsistent: in some instances, they stand aside during the workers' strikes, while, in the case of Yue Yuen, they returned to their authoritarian practices with a vengeance.

However, questions of capital flows are live ones. Since 2012, Pou Chen has continued to move production internally out of South China to Vietnam (a process that intensified following the introduction of the now failed Transatlantic Trade Partnership [TPP] in 2015), but there is no indication that brands have sought alternative producers to Pou Chen (Ting-Fang 2015). In 2016, Adidas unveiled a robot-operated, vertically integrated, large-scale 'speedfactory' in Ansbach, Germany, announcing future plants in Britain and France, with Nike also developing its own robot-operated shoe factory (AFP 2016). As a direct consequence of rising costs in Asia, Adidas and Nike are replacing humans with machines and 'returning' production to Europe, where shoes will be produced faster, with quicker turnaround times, and significantly reducing freight and labour costs.

Additional research is needed on how economic changes in China are affecting the spatial, technological, and organizational reconstitution of capital in labour-intensive production. The Yue Yuen strike draws an initial picture, namely of a restless, ageing Chinese industrial working class with greater bargaining power against a vertically integrated and enlarged domestic capital. In a strategy that traces its roots to the early 2000s, private sector workers are utilizing a legal framework by which to uphold their demands, and these demands are now spreading to other factories against a single enemy. Finally, economic leverage has spread out of the factory and against retailers, not only with allies in the Global North but by garment workers themselves in the Global South through person-to-person connections and material solidarity made possible by the emergence of a global consumer class. Thus, we see actions that are fortifying the bonds between workers across the region – development of worker's struggles to meet the development of capital. For as Marx (1848) stated, 'The real fruit of their battles lies, not the immediate result, but in the ever-expanding union of the workers.'

Thus, greater value capture at the producer-end is dramatically altering the questions of power and production. The Yue Yuen strike is a sign, a shift away from giant monopolistic footwear brands placing downward pressure on a seemingly endless reserve of small, powerless suppliers with an army of workers left unable to exert power. The case of Yue Yuen demonstrates that workers help shape the actions of the state, which attempts to placate them through legislation, and capital: by driving up labour costs and forcing vertical and horizontal integration, moving the struggle to the more direct and brutal organizational fixes, which are clearly in the workers' court – the point of production itself.

4

India

A Warehouse Workers' Struggle at a 'Full-Package' Denim Firm

Established in 1931, Arvind Mills, along with thousands of other producers, was born out of the demand for domestically produced fabric, part of Mahatma Gandhi's call for the boycott of imported fabric, or the 'Swadeshi Movement'. Arvind emerged as the sole survivor among 85 textile mills that made their home in Ahmedabad three decades ago entirely as a consequence of their decision to transform from a multi-product company to primarily a denim manufacturer. Until 1987, all available denim in India was imported. That year, Arvind became the first mill in the country to produce denim, a key initiator and beneficiary of India's 'denim revolution'.

Here, I explore the factors in India that led to the growth and concentration of denim, a less volatile section of the garment sector that due to limited seasonality and fashion-sensitivity valorize faster than others (like footwear and cotton commodity production).[1] To understand this phenomenon, I look at the struggle at a denim warehouse owned by Bangalore-based Arvind Group (hereinafter

---

[1] The study is based on an extensive field research conducted over a three-year period from 2012 to 2015 with four additional site visits every year between 2015 and 2019. Methods included participant observation, company data, and semi-structured interviews with workers, labour activists, and labour monitors. Much of the company data are derived from annual reports and corporate databases such as Capital IQ. A total of 27 interviews were conducted with Arvind workers, managers, union organizers, and international factory auditors. Interviews were conducted in person and, except for an English-speaking factory auditor, translated from Kannada. They were conducted with a recorder, and I took additional written notes on non-vocal speech that I observed. They typically lasted between 40 minutes and several hours, sometimes over the course of many months. Some names have been altered for anonymity.

'Arvind'). What we see is a transformation of relations in the sector between buyers and sellers, producers and consumers, and workers and bosses.

The case is but one demonstration of how the phase-out of the MFA brought with it an end to the regime of 'comprador capital' that had dominated Indian economic life from the early post-colonial days, allowing indigenous firms to piggyback on foreign corporations seeking access to cheap labour and raw materials. The post-MFA era has seen global competition weaken and the autonomy of smaller firms across the globe gradually removed altogether, leaving many to be absorbed into larger rivals, forced to merge, or simply vanish into the red. What remains, in a handful of countries, are a handful of mega megasuppliers, powerful enough to corner the supply chains of specialized products and intensify supplier-end value capture. Meanwhile, large retailer/brand oligopolies simultaneously benefit from growing profits brought on by economies of scale and integration, while becoming gradually dependent on increasingly oligopolistic suppliers. Thus, the 'buyer-driven' character of the value chain gives way to a kind of 'buyer–producer symbiosis'. In consequence, as we observe in the case of Arvind, labour's resistance adapts as well.

These developments are consistent with some of the findings by Tokatli and Kizilgun (2004) in the growth of Turkish jeans manufacturer Erak Clothing, which they link to the lifting of European quota restrictions in the mid-1990s. Similar to the case of Yue Yuen, we see that, until recently, Arvind was just another supplier-end firm, confined to low-value functions in the GVC. But, relatively quickly, it became a 'full-package' multinational that now embraces the full length of the value chain.

The development of economies of consistent size and scale has increased capitalist accumulation at the supplier-end, allowing for the introduction of new technologies that cause a 'cascading effect' (Nolan, Zhang, and Liu 2008) down the supply chain, expanding each link. The reverberations of this change, through production and the circulation of capital, result in a corresponding adaptation of workers' resistance in the garment sector that reflects the shift in the locus of power from spaces of consumption to production. The case of Arvind embodies a move towards symbiosis and the changing relationship of buyer and producer, from an asymmetrical high degree of monopsony power towards a more of synergetic interdependence.

The workers' struggle takes place between 2011 and 2015 at a warehouse in the south Indian state of Karnataka. The evidence supports the conclusion that India's emergent-specialized supplier firms are now better able to reorganize production in order to undermine workers' actions at a single factory, while also diminishing the leverage of brands, which are made more deeply rooted and are less able to 'cut-and-run' from their suppliers. However, as entire commodity chains are digested by single entities, the workers therein find themselves capable of larger scale operations too, with the potential for multi-phasic organization, allowing them to bring a *full-court press* against their newly amalgamated employers and avoiding the pitfalls of single-factory resistance (such as isolated contingents of victorious workers becoming casualties of the market). Thus, the evolution of managerial forms in the apparel industry, as in other sectors, engenders a reciprocal evolution in labour strategies, and within the case of this chapter indicated a distinct departure from traditional 'anti-sweatshop' campaigns, which historically targeted the buyers rather than the producers in the sector.

From mill to retail

India was relatively late to liberalization. It was not until the 1990s that export-oriented garment production began to proliferate in India, and only towards the end of the first decade of the 2000s that large Indian garment firms began establishing beachheads in transnational markets. The constitutive forces of 'liberalization' – increased access to foreign capital, greater domestic purchasing power, deregulated FDI, environment embeddedness – explain these changes. Gupta and Qiu (2013: 57) elaborate:

> Market liberalization was the root of unleashing this trading potential, by empowering the Indian firms to participate in the global capital and investment markets. Many firms, such as Moser Baer in optical media, Bharat Forge in auto components, Reliance in polyester yarn, Arvind Mills in denim fabric, and Zee Telefilms in satellite television channels, become global category leaders.

In the case of China, globalization matured before India; consequently, it also witnessed firm consolidation before India. For example, Appelbaum (2008) relates the history of the manufacturer Luen Thai Holdings, which created a 'supply-chain city' in Guangdong Province that includes a product-development centre, a 4,000-worker capacity on-site dormitory, and a 2-million square foot factory. For Luen Thai buyers (like Ralph Lauren, for example), it soon became a one-stop shop where designers met directly with both factory and textile mill technicians, bringing the whole supply chain under one roof (Appelbaum 2008).[2]

---

[2] Although Appelbaum (2008) uses the example of Liz Claiborne, they went out of business under this name and was sold to JC Penney shortly after the publication of that article. At the time, Liz Claiborne downsized its network of 250 suppliers in 35

An economy of scale geared towards producing primarily a single product is likely, for obvious reasons, to undercut more diversified competitors. In addition to Luen Thai, global suppliers such as Panarub (Adidas' exclusive cleats producer in Indonesia), Yue Yuen (detailed in Chapter 3), and Indian denim and clothing conglomerate Arvind provide examples, in this chapter, of large capital-holding companies that have upgraded to produce highly efficient specialized product lines and that have thereby become crucial 'strategic partners' for major brands.

India's post-reform period saw the emergence of large-scale home-grown companies in the 1990s, mostly within capital-intensive industries such as automobiles and steel. Acquisitions soon became the predominant mode of outward FDI. Between 2000 and 2006, 15 companies were responsible for 98 out of 306 overseas acquisitions, or 80 per cent of total value acquisitions (Gupta and Qiu 2013). Gupta and Qiu (2013) argue that Indian MNCs were able to internationalize through the organization and management of value chains suitable to emerging market settings and develop firm-specific advantages to cope with country-specific scarcity. They claim that most of the emergent companies had already developed in the pre-reform period, easing their transition to outward FDI. Arguably the most successful example of this growth is Tata, a single auto factory that effectively entered the international market and, in due time, acquired the iconic British automotive brand Jaguar. For the first time, Indian capital began to compete at an international stage, not as simply a *comprador*, as in the heyday of the British East India Company, when imperial capital commissioned local merchants for extractive purposes, but as a force of its own. The first generation of capital-intensive companies has long since gone transnational, producing and distributing wherever they please. Meanwhile, companies within labour-intensive sectors, such as garment production, remained tied down as compradors, subordinate to international buyers. However, as Merk (2014) points out, the recent decade has seen that these same home-grown companies are now emerging as large-scale manufacturers.

The radical reorganization and technological advancements of the manufacturing-end of the sector are discussed in depth in Chapter 6; however, similar changes are occurring in the nodes of the value chain which assist in the circulation of capital, specifically to warehouses and distribution centres. Conventional warehouses intended for long-term storage have been replaced

---

countries to only a handful, including Luen Thai. Under this plan Liz Claiborne and Luen Thai anticipate reducing staff by 40 per cent, which will cut costs and improve turnaround times, through logistic harmonization. A better example today is Ralph Lauren for whom Luen Thai is a 'strategic supplier'.

with massive, highly automated facilities designed to maintain a non-stop stream of goods. For example, Walmart's busiest warehouses operate 24 hours a day and seven days a week with 90 per cent of its goods turned over every day. This is coupled with radical advances in technology such as the use of bar codes to collect sales information, radio-frequency identification tags, predictive purchasing, and distribution models (Danyluk 2017). In addition, we have seen the growth, integration, and increasing importance of intermediary trading companies (such as Li and Fung) and logistics freight forwarding companies in managing the linkages between production and consumption (Smith and Pickles 2016). These advances in the Global North and South have catalysed the consolidation and vertical-integration of logistics and warehousing. This has only intensified global logistics as a key site of resistance against capital.

Evolving workers' strategies

The Asian garment firms, given a boost by liberalization, were able to establish widely dispersed supply chains without losing functional integration. They eliminated middlemen and inched ever closer to the source of their income, the customer. In the course of this ascension, retailers acted as proxies, affecting a shift from a producer-driven marketplace to one that is consumer-led. Tewari (2006) explains India's flourishing clothing production, despite relatively low sectoral FDI, as a result of a burgeoning domestic market. Bangalore, where much of Arvind's supply network is based, accounts for 30 per cent of India's garment production and 800,000 of its 6 million garment workers (Mallikarjunappa 2011). Since the mid-1990s, the top 20 to 30 textile and apparel firms have begun introducing domestic brands, like Parx (Raymond) and Indian Terrain (Celebrity Fashion Limited) (Jin, Kandagal, and Jung 2013).

Earlier, the divide between the source of value creation (production) and value capture (brands and retail) had forced workers to make demands on buyers, rather than their direct employers. As outlined in Chapter 1, this often had to be accomplished through Global North allies, like the Global Justice Movement's 'anti-sweatshop' campaigns of the 1990s and 2000s. Global North activists were asked to compel brands and retailers through secondary economic pressure or other tactics to take responsibility for the conditions in outsourced factories since they had the power to impose labour standards on suppliers. This kind of response sought to close the growing gap between workers and the brand executives that controlled the industry, with a few rather isolated successes limited to large institutional purchases (Kumar and Mahoney 2014).

The asymmetry of power between buyer and supplier also exists at the point of consumption. As Merk (2008: 82) states, 'Manufacturers produce shoes that are distributed and sold under the name of the contractor [that is, the brand] and little control is exercised over (retail) market outlets in Western countries. Generally speaking, their lack of control over large market outlets renders them dependent.' These socio-economic factors caused campaigns at the point of consumption to become an important lever against brands to achieve gains for workers at the point of production.

Conventional export-oriented units in the garment sector undermine worker campaigns to organize through systematic harassment and retaliatory dismissals. If a union is established, the company is likely to be driven from the market as transnational brands take orders elsewhere. The early campaigns to unionize in the 1980s and 1990s, therefore, had predictable results. As described by Kumar (2014a), the strategy of Bangalore-based Garment and Textile Workers' Union (GATWU), the largest independent garment union in India, has taken form within this context. In its early years, GATWU was involved with community organizing and establishing a women workers' front. Shortly after that, GATWU began to incorporate a brand strategy, targeting large global brands with the assistance of allies at the point of consumption. As outlined in detail in this chapter, under pressure during the struggle at the Arvind warehouse in Ramnagara, GATWU evolved practices targeting full-package suppliers while simultaneously placing secondary pressure on brands.

From a cotton mill to a full-package supplier

Arvind Limited is the flagship company of the Lalbhai Group, the largest manufacturer of denim in India, and among the top three manufacturers and distributors of denim in the world (Reuters 2007; Singh 2012). The company owns cotton mills, garment factories, and the distribution and retail outlets of cotton shirts, knits, khakis, and denim for major transnational brands of PVH Corporation (which include Tommy Hilfiger, Calvin Klein, IZOD, and Arrow) alongside Gap and others across South Asia and the Middle East.

Arvind was a well-known textile mill with trusted distribution channels throughout India producing high-quality traditional Indian clothing such as voiles, *dhotis*, and sarees. They had incorporated a dual distribution system for creating its own separate distribution channels of what became known as Arvind's Original Denim, a brand in itself. This eliminated middlemen between the manufacturer and the producer, representing Arvind's first step beyond textile mills. In 1986, Arvind began investing in increasing its production capability and erected its first denim facility with a capacity of 10 million metres per annum and under Arvind's 'renovision' strategy expanded its products marketed as 'high-quality premium niche' to the international market. Small-scale power looms simply could not compete with the large-scale, high quality, timely turnaround expected by US buyers. Sampler and Sarkar (2010: 74) state that these requirements 'meant that manufacturers would have to invest in capital-intensive technology, large scale as well as better management of operations'. The company's success in India quickly expanded outwards and it soon began selling its material to leading transnational brands of denim such as Levis, Wrangler, and Lee. Technological upgrading and increased capacity made Arvind an important partner to transnational brands and by 1990 it had opened offices in New York, Hong Kong, and London (Choudhury 2001). The growth of Arvind is also linked to the deregulation of the Indian garment sector. Until 2000, the sector was regulated to assist the small-scale manufacturing industry, precluding FDI through rigorous licensing requirements. In 2000, the union government relaxed these laws, which allowed the growth of firms like Arvind.

Jeans were inextricably linked to the aesthetic of the young urban Indian and with each successive year, with more expendable cash in the pockets of India's urban residents, the increased affordability of jeans saw an ever-expanding consumer base. By 1991, the company was selling 100 million metres of denim per annum and within a year they had upgraded a number of plants, further increasing production and cost-cutting. By the mid-1990s, Arvind had expanded across the supply chain with separate textile, garment, and telecom divisions to create harmonized supply chains that provided global brands with greater comparative economies of scale, increasing Arvind's capacity and profits.

Around the same time in the 1990s, Arvind expanded the consumer base of jeans outside of the urban centres to the villages, by creating an in-house low-cost brand RufNTuf. The strategy led to a second explosion of jeans, and Arvind sold over a million pieces within the first two months (Shah 2000). This massive expansion of Arvind's denim capacity was funded largely by domestic financiers and overseas financial institutions, the latter made easier in post-reform India (D'silva and Joseph 2014). Simultaneously, Arvind began using capital generated from denim sales to diversify its production portfolio, bolstering its non-denim technological upgrading by breaking ground on India's largest state-of-the-art shirting, gabardine, and knits facility. However, by the late-1990s, a shift in fashion trends led to a crash in denim prices and Arvind had to restructure its debts in order to repay its increasingly onerous international commitments. By 2001, Arvind had the 'distinction of becoming the first Indian corporation to restructure its entire debt in a single go' (D'silva and Joseph 2014: 46).

By the early 2000s, Arvind had 'moved on from being a commodity player to a value provider from South Asia' (Sampler and Sarkar 2010: 68). Arvind was initially hit hard by falling input prices and revenues brought on by the phase-out of the MFA in 2005 when China offloaded nearly 40 per cent of the world's denim, severely undercutting global denim prices and Arvind's competitive advantage. In time, however, the MFA would assist Arvind's market share, as already hard-pressed power loom or handloom weavers were now saddled with the cost of meeting India's central value-added tax.[3]

These smaller, member-controlled handloom cooperatives had been encouraged through a macroeconomic policy of the post-Independence Nehruvian state and were now collapsing under the weight of both international and domestic competitive pressures. As small capitals began to quickly vanish, larger capitals like Arvind took over, realizing exponential growth in their market share. Indeed, India would become a prime beneficiary of the post-MFA world, with the country rising to become one of the world's foremost cotton producers boasting a global market share of 25 per cent.

The emergence of a transnational producer–retailer

Today, Arvind is a conglomerate of seven diversified divisions with their own brands.[4] The expansion in Arvind's retail division is a crucial component of its comparative advantage and appeal to transnational clothing capital. Crucially, in 2007, Arvind magnified its brand and retail division with the creation of MegaMart in addition to Club America. Almost 45 per cent of Arvind's retail sales are its own brands while international brands account for the remainder. The company expanded its services to include low-cost product design for transnational brands by hiring a team of international fashion designers, which is the clearest indication of its extension to the high-value phases in the supply chain. A sign of Arvind's growing value to buyers is in its ability to negotiate stability of orders by requiring buyers to enter long-term purchasing contracts

---

[3] The state's relation to petty commodity producers has become increasingly ambivalent and contradictory. It both promotes policies that ostensibly encourage the sector, such as subsidies, self-help groups, and so on, while also authorizing policies that destroy it, such as the promotion of capital-biased technology (Harriss-White 2010).

[4] Brands include Flying Machine (jeans), RufNTuf (jeans), Newport (jeans), and Excalibur (shirts).

(Sampler and Sarkar 2010), lowering Arvind's liability in an inherently volatile fashion sector and aggregating its competitive market advantages.

By integrating various phases of the value chain, Arvind has kept its costs low, allowing it to invest heavily in research and development (R&D). Arvind spends 5 per cent of its annual turnover on R&D, leading to technological advances like the modified air jet looms as well as slasher technology in dying operations making Arvind's 'vertically integrated plant[s] among the most modern in the world' (Sampler and Sarkar 2010: 70). Arvind's technological advances have contributed to economic upgrading and a 50 per cent reduction in its manufacturing costs over time (Shukla 1998), allowing it to expand even more rapidly, further cornering the denim market and becoming an indispensable partner to transnational brands. This represents a departure from the low R&D investment that has become a trademark for Indian companies (Bound and Thornton 2012).

By 2011, Arvind began its transition to become a *transnational* full-package supplier. Importantly, Arvind announced it would set up a large-scale garment factory in Bangladesh (Ahmed and Nathan 2014). In addition, it secured long-term production, marketing, and retail packaged licensing contracts with major transnational brands across South Asia and the Middle East for PVH brands such as IZOD in 2011 (PVH 2011) and a 50:50 joint venture to open 500 stores with Tommy Hilfiger in 2012 (Bailay 2013). Then, in 2013, Arvind entered international undergarment retail by becoming the exclusive licensee for major undergarment markets and becoming licensed to sell Hanes in India.

In 2014, Arvind announced a mega e-commerce initiative, Creyate, to be included in its supplier packaging. In the same year, the company announced that it would enter a full-package agreement with the largest casual wear retailer in the US, Gap, expanding from production to distribution, marketing, and managing Gap's Indian e-commerce on its newly announced platform, in order to open 40 stores for Gap beginning in 2015. For Gap's South Asian debut, it chose to franchise with Arvind, with whom it had a long-standing relationship for denim manufacture, despite 100 per cent FDI being permitted in India for single-brand retailers.

Over the past decade, Arvind has seen year-on-year growth rates, doubling its annual revenue between 2004 and 2010 and doubling it again between 2010 and the end of 2014, with annual profits increasing by 26 per cent in 2011 and by 30 per cent in 2014 alone. Thus, Arvind's continual expansion geographically and across the value chain has increased its economy of scale and bargaining power in the clothing commodity chain to secure longer-term contracts. Off the back of its quickly valorizing denim sector, contracts now include the full breadth of clothing value chain, further cementing its relationship with buyers.

Arvind's strategy today is to provide transnational brands and large retailers with the full production package, from cotton mill to retail rack, having integrated most of the clothing commodity chain, including textiles manufacturing, garment production, marketing, design, with a vast network of ever-expanding retail outlets. It also aims to provide GPS-based fleet automation and management for logistics, as well as in-house warehousing facilities, and, crucially, invaluable access to India's retail market.

Arvind warehouse workers' struggle

One of Arvind's primary distribution sites was at a warehouse an hour's drive southwest of Bangalore in the town of Ramnagara. While Arvind owns the Ramnagara warehouse, the building itself is leased for another 20 years, according to one manager, who claims that Arvind owns only one of the three floors. In 2011, the Ramnagara warehouse handled cataloguing, inventory, and international distribution in South Asia and the Middle East, primarily for transnational brands owned by PVH.

PVH brands alongside Gant and US Polo were distributed through the Ramnagara warehouse. Arrow had established a long-term full-package contract with Arvind, which had first hosted the brand in India in 1993. In 2011, Arvind signed an eight-year full-package licensing contract, alongside a renewal option that would extend that agreement until 2029, to produce, market, and retail Izod throughout India, the United Arab Emirates, Kuwait, Bahrain, Qatar, Saudi Arabia, Bhutan, Madagascar, Seychelles, Oman, Yemen, Bangladesh, Nepal, Sri Lanka, and Maldives (PVH 2011). At the time, the major distribution node between the point of production and consumption was the distribution site in Ramnagara.

A contract company run by Arvind HR Manager Harsha technically employed the 150 warehouse workers. Despite the Indian Contract Labour Act of 1970 that prohibits contract employees from being tasked with 'core' activities, the practice of shell contract companies is endemic. The workers were predominantly from Ramnagara, around 50 were women, and a majority were low-caste dalits or categorized as other backward classes.

Before the beginning of the workers' unrest towards the end of 2010, the site was a 'pressing warehouse', which meant it had five areas of responsibility: ironing, fabric testing, fabric distribution, accessories distribution, and alterations. Warehouse worker Jayram[5] recounts the primary tasks,

---

[5] Interview, 11 October 2014.

Garments arrived inward and categorized into inventory, placed on racks and coded. The outward department received directions electronically from the head office specifying which garments, how many pieces, what sizes, and to which country. The system operator then gives the directions to helpers, who direct the pickers. Next the helpers bring clothes to a scanner while another registers the code and where the clothes will be delivered. Workers organize the clothes into boxes for the dispatcher to ensure it is picked up and ready to be taken to its destination.

During the seasonal rush, the numbers of interstate workers at the warehouse would swell with short-term 'job workers' brought in mostly from north India. As another worker, Ratnamma,[6] explained, 'A "job worker" is like a *coolie* (a worker for hire). They are brought in to work for the day and do not get any social benefits like healthcare or pensions and are paid by piece-rate rather than a salary, paid weekly rather than monthly, but their lodging and food are paid for by the factory.' Job workers end up costing the factory more in the short term, but flexible terms are essential within the seasonal garment sector and, as we will see in the case of Arvind, a crucial bulwark against worker organizing.

In November 2010, the General Manager (GM) of the warehouse called all the workers to the floor and announced that Arvind would close the warehouse, shifting work to a new warehouse in Hosakote (70 kilometres away). Since 2011, Arvind has built a number of new warehouses in and around Bangalore, in Whitefield, Hosakote, and Chintamani, to facilitate its growth. The reason given to workers for the movement was that the building had been leaking during the rainy season and would be prohibitively expensive to repair. The GM told the workers they could get employment in the new locations, but nearly all decided to stay in Ramnagara. A few asked if the company would provide a bus to Hosakote but the GM refused, offering two to three month's salary as a severance package for those who declined.

Santosh, a worker at Arvind,[7] recalls, 'None of us said anything after this announcement, we began discussing amongst ourselves, and one of the workers Nirmala had previously worked at an Arvind garment factory in Peenya Industrial Area in Bangalore which had a union fight a few years back. Nirmala tracked down the union contact from her sister who still worked there and that's how we joined the union.' Upon arriving, GATWU organizers asked how far the workers were willing to go, as Kempraju[8] recalls, 'We told

---

[6] Interview, 5 February 2013.
[7] Interview, 12 October 2014.
[8] Interview, 14 December 2013.

[GATWU organizers] that we were willing to lay our bodies in front of the gates to stop the closure.' Within days, 70 per cent of the workforce had joined the union. By December 2010, the workers were given some critical information. As Nirmala[9] recounts, 'A driver at the Arvind transport company SpeedX once worked in the warehouse and still had friends there. One of the workers at the warehouse received a call from the transport worker stating that he had heard Arvind had called a large number of trucks to Ramnagara. So we were ready.' The workers had strong suspicions that Arvind planned to move the equipment that night.

Another worker, Krishna,[10] recalls, 'We waited in a nearby forested area and at 9:30 we observed that one truck went in the gates and the warehouse lights went on. We immediately called all the workers and union officials.' By 10 p.m. there were 100 local workers assembled outside the factory gates alongside members from Suwarna, a popular Kannada-language news channel. The workers began picketing, laid down their bodies in front of the gates, and refused to let mover trucks leave the premises. The Arvind warehouse sits on the main artery that runs through Ramnagara and so word quickly spread. Local community organizations began rallying their own members and the crowd began to grow. Within a few hours, dozens of police arrived at the behest of the management. The crowd continued to swell and hundreds of community members, workers and their family put their bodies on the ground, picketed, and chanted. As Jayram[11] recounted, 'In the early morning the GM finally stepped out of the gates and announced that they would not close down the factory and the crowd erupted with celebration.'

In January 2012, after a year of union education and membership strengthening, GATWU submitted a charter of demand, which would have resulted in union recognition and collective bargaining at Arvind. The threshold for filing a charter of demands is 10 per cent of the workforce, and in the middle of 2012, the union density at Arvind had reached an unparalleled 70 per cent.

For most of 2012, the union would be attacked and its membership undermined. Kempraju,[12] another union leader at the warehouse, indicated how the warehouse management began exerting pressure on the union, 'Once our union became bigger [...] management offered union leaders money and promotions to switch allegiances, which turned to threats; then they began to

---

[9] Interview, 6 February 2013.
[10] Interview, 6 February 2013.
[11] Interview, 11 October 2014.
[12] Interview, 14 December 2013.

Figure 4.1 Garment workers on wildcat strike, 2016, Bangalore

Source: Courtesy of GATWU.

bring in contract workers mostly from [the northeastern state of] Assam, and finally they began to physically attack us.'

By November 2012, the abuse at Arvind had reached fever pitch. That month, a number of union-side workers were violently attacked by management-side workers at the direction of the HR managers. Following the attack, four union leaders were terminated from employment. An international campaign was initiated, primarily by the International Union League for Brand Responsibility (IULBR), of which GATWU is a member-union, with allies placing pressure on brands and workers, targeting Arvind retailers for pickets and actions in Bangalore and Mysore. After a month-long campaign and an investigation by an outside labour-rights monitoring group, the workers were rehired with back pay.

Reorganizing production to undermine the union

Over the course of the union campaign, it was revealed and later confirmed in a district labour court decision that Arvind operated unlawfully without a contract license and had failed to compensate workers legally mandated overtime. In addition, it came to light that management had begun laying the groundwork to convert the warehouse from a 'pressing warehouse' to a 'returns warehouse' following GATWU submitting a charter of demands.[13] A pressing warehouse is a primary node between in-house production and disintegrated international consumption, with clothes arriving directly from Arvind's manufacturing facilities and distributed directly to brand-name retailers. A 'returns warehouse' functions as a site for handling rejected garments, repackaging clothes originally destined for the international market into garments for domestic consumption.

By early 2013, Arvind began the 'returns warehouse' transformation with Ramnagara's pressing functions being moved to a new facility in Chintamani on the eastern part of Karnataka. Within a few months, the facility had become a 'returns warehouse'. A worker, Jayram,[14] described the returns warehouse tasks:

> If someone outside India returns a shirt produced by Arvind that now comes to our warehouse and we wash, iron, and repackage it. It's then delivered to Arvind's own discount retailer, such as MegaMart, and is sold usually at a 50% discount or 'buy 1 get 1 for free' deal. Older clothes that don't sell are also repackaged at the returns warehouse.

Santosh[15] believed this transformation of the warehouse was directly linked to workers' actions: 'It's clear why [Arvind management] did this. They know our union is strong and if we went on strike it would cost the company greatly as a pressing warehouse, but as a returns warehouse the impact would be minimal because those items are non-essential and not headed for international retailers.' The transformation from pressing to returns warehouse reduces liabilities by transferring international to domestic, core to peripheral, functions. Other workers shared similar suspicions, suggesting that a one-day strike alone at the pressing warehouse during the season would cost the company immensely, but as a returns warehouse, the impact would be negligible.

In November 2014, the union had 80 members, rising from its nadir of 25 at the end of 2013. The reasons for this increase are a few-fold. Unlike an industrial centre such as Bangalore, most of the workers in Ramnagara lived and worked near the factory. In essence, the relationship between the workers did not begin and end at the warehouse gates. Another claim cited by workers was the long history of trade unions in the city. Many of the workers' parents were former

---

[13] This is close cousin to what the ILGWU described as 'backbone shops' (pressing warehouse) and 'overflow shops' (returns warehouse).
[14] Interview, 11 October 2014.
[15] Interview, 29 September 2014.

silk factory workers. Indeed, working-class organization was not novel in a city known for its union-dense government-owned silk processing plants. Thus, the combined force of specific historic, spatial, and relational factors coupled with the changing composition of garment capital lent itself to an environment in which a high proportion of workers organized into the union in response to employer bullying and intransigence.

Even though the number of workers consistently hovered at 150 and the workload remained stable throughout, Arvind began replacing local Ramnagara workers with roughly 50 'job workers' brought in from Goa, Assam, and Orissa, up from 20 in 2010. In early 2014, after reading a company press release on the Internet, Arvind warehouse union members began demanding a 20 per cent increase in their wages, citing Arvind's profits and the announcement of the opening of 500 new stores.

Mangala[16] stated, 'When we approached management they opened a file and showed us that although they made profits, those were redirected towards opening more retail shops.' Despite the company's denials of profit numbers, union members continued to exert pressure on the company to increase workers' wages. As Rajanna[17] from Arvind stated, 'Smaller garment companies I have worked for have never had profits for us to demand higher wages from. They use their small profits to make us work more and for less money, and even when they do have profits they are not as publicly available as Arvind. [...] Even if Arvind lie to us we can find out the truth easily because it's a big public company.' Jayram[18] stated that workers have begun looking into other ways to pressure the company, 'We are now reaching out to Arvind production facilities near Ramnagara in Kengeri and textiles as well.'

Arvind employs 'job workers' despite having to pay for workers' individual lodging, transport, and three meals a day. As Krishna[19] states,

> [Arvind] are afraid of the union and don't hire local workers and because the 'job workers' are under constant supervision, we cannot access them. They're also much more fearful [...] they're in a different land and don't speak the language, with no community, and owe their food, bed, and transport to the company.

---

[16] Interview, 13 November 2014.
[17] Interview, 15 October 2014.
[18] Interview, 11 October 2014.
[19] Interview, 4 December 2014.

Jayram[20] adds, 'They withhold salaries earned by "job workers" until the end, so they are terrified that they'll lose that money by joining the union.'

Yet, despite its shortcomings, the campaign at Arvind had a number of successes including Arvind agreeing to pay overtime and, as Pratibha[21] from GATWU stated, 'Arvind responded immediately to the Karnataka state minimum wage increase in 2014, unlike all other major companies, and we believe that is because of the campaign in Ramnagara.' Another victory is that the union gained in its direct power vis-à-vis management. Jayram[22] stated,

> The campaign against the union exposed the management's tactics to everyone. They assaulted us, bribed the police, and dismissed us, which only emboldened workers' resolve. We're stronger because of Arvind's campaign against us.

Aggregated spaces of value capture and value creation

Arvind's growth can be attributed to a number of factors. It expanded from a cotton mill to become one of the largest retailers in India. However, many of Bangalore's large apparel production companies are yet to witness the kind of vertical-integration found in Arvind. For example, Bombay Rayon failed to upgrade and has now nearly shuttered down, a victim of Gereffi's 'buyer-driven' dilemma.

A few factors can explain this. Denim production is highly specialized and more capital-intensive, while the basic material, namely cotton, remains unchanged. Thus, there is a greater capacity for technological and economic upgrading. Furthermore, there is an enhanced ability to overpower potential competitors and, over time, to achieve a vertical expansion across the value chain. Arvind's initial success was due to its strategic investment decisions such as indigenous denim production and its expanding outside of urban spaces with its RufNTuf brand that combated rural scepticism of readymade clothing by creating low-cost bare bones pre-cut 'ready-to-stitch' jeans, while effectively transferring part of the labour process to the consumer. This functioned as an 'extra-market' mechanism to lower labour costs by relying on the unwaged work undertaken predominantly by women in the home.

---

[20] Interview, 6 February 2013.
[21] Interview, 15 October 2014.
[22] Interview, 11 October 2014.

Arvind's growth expanded quickly following the end of the MFA. Similar to Tokatli and Kizilgun's (2004) case study of the growth of a denim manufacturer in Turkey after European quotas were relaxed in the mid-1990s, the end of the MFA directly contributed to the growth of Arvind. In the case of Turkey, they claim that preferential treatment in European and US markets explained internal upgrading but not the expansion to higher value phases in the value chain. However, what we see in the case of Arvind is that these two processes are complementary. Through internal upgrading, Arvind increased sectoral barriers to entry. As a large capital-holding firm, Arvind further 'locks-in' its market share, expanding into more value-added activities of product development, branding, marketing, and retail, absorbing them into the full-package network.

Through vertical-integration and technological upgrading, firms like Arvind increase their proportion of profits by reducing the cost of production and expanding capacity. The capacity of these firms to move upstream in more value-added links in the global clothing commodity chain cemented their market power. Gereffi (2002) states that much of the power of global 'buyers' is in their ability to 'act as strategic brokers in linking overseas factories and traders'; yet what we see from companies like Arvind is the fusing of consumption and production under one roof, weakening the strategic power of these traditional 'brokers'.

While acknowledging that a distribution site is different from a production site, the struggle at Arvind's Ramnagara warehouse allows us to examine the early stages of this shifting dynamic between producers and buyers and between workers and their employers. One of the clearest examples of this change is the signing of long-term exclusive licensing contracts between major brands and Arvind that apply across South Asia and the Middle East. A number of PVH-owned clothing brands that were distributed through the Ramnagara site had signed long-term contracts shortly before or during the labour unrest at Ramnagara. Such long-term agreements had been pushed by Arvind and portend a departure from short-term purchasing orders, which are still a hallmark of assembly-only suppliers. The weakness of assembly-only suppliers is their dependence on buyers, but long-term contracts have the effect of 'locking-in' retailers and brands to large firms like Arvind and, in part, melding together disintegrated chains.

Arvind's expansion from textiles meant that it began at a higher valued phase than assembly-only production. It is not cost-effective to ship natural fibres in raw form, which gives textile industries in supplier countries a built-in advantage. The specifications of international buyers for these specialized products advantaged large-scale indigenous producers by intensifying supplier-end technological upgrading, organizational agglomeration, and supply chain integration. The strategy at Arvind is to focus on delivery to five or six large-scale customers in order to align delivery capacity to their sourcing calendar and ease the uncertainty of demand. By providing end-to-end 'full-package' services for a few large-scale brands, Arvind became an irreplaceable partner to key players in the international clothing market. The resulting production networks are a durable system of social capital, which is a precious competitive asset for global buyers.

As shown throughout, economies of scale – brought on by upgrading and social downgrading – undercuts competitors, allowing the firm to expand into the various phases in the production process, leading to the emergence of full packages, which bring down the costs of production for buyers. This results in higher volume orders for Arvind and a greater competitive disadvantage over competitors, more downsizing and closures for competitors, and an accelerated rate of expansion horizontally for Arvind. The final outcome is a combined force of greater value capture at the supplier-end of the commodity chain and fewer competitive options for buyers. In essence, Gap needs Arvind almost as much as Arvind needs Gap, a reality that will be further cemented if current trends continue.

Part of the 'full package' includes Arvind's retail chains that run across the country selling international brands as well as its own. Arvind and other such firms operate as gatekeepers to these emerging consumer markets, guaranteeing an immense shift in power vis-à-vis buyers. For example, US retailer Gap actively out the Indian market after heavy losses in the US. Expansion into the subcontinent became essential for Gap as a strategy to absorb and turn the tide on its own crisis of profitability. Despite the Indian government allowing 100 per cent FDI since 2012, Gap chose to join with their long-time manufacturing partner Arvind to become a vital partner in its entry into India's burgeoning consumer market, both online and offline. But retail reaches beyond India for Arvind with licensing and manufacturing for PVH across Asia and the Middle East, as well as being an official retailer of PVH in India. Thus, one can classify some large capital-holding garment suppliers in India, who were once comprador in nature, as now in the league of global multinational capital.

Most evidently, the shifting dynamic between buyer and producer is found by those involved in the struggle in Ramnagara itself. It became clear early on to those involved that the Arvind case revealed prescient clues to other cases that would open shortly after. Pratibha,[23] an organizer at GATWU, states while reflecting on the campaign, 'We did everything right. We put pressure on the brands, like PVH, we got an auditor in, we had a sympathetic brand representative, but the

---

[23] Interview, 2 November 2014.

company was still able to reorganise the task of the warehouse to diminish our power without diminishing their standing with brands.'

Specialization is not the only variable in buyer–producer symbiosis but represents a key path towards monopoly power. For example, Shahi Exports is one of the largest export-oriented garment manufacturers in India; however, they are not specialized. Shahi produces a large proportion of clothes for H&M, Gap, and other major brands in its 56 factories in India alone, yet have repeatedly violated basic labour rights in the face of frequent warnings from international monitoring organizations. As one auditor[24] at a prominent monitoring organization told me, 'Shahi knows we have been monitoring them since 2002, but they continue to openly violate basic workers' rights. H&M has been made known of Shahi's violations and have gone completely silent. It's because H&M knows that it will be too expensive to find another producer the size of Shahi. Shahi knows this and that's why they don't care.'

A new space for workers' power?

Many workers at Arvind maintain that the management was desperate to close the warehouse due to the union, but a combination of factors prevented them from doing so. This included: the long-term lease, the trade union campaign, potential legal violations, a possible international backlash, and, most importantly, the ability to internally reorganize and transform an inward–outward pressing warehouse for international buyers into a returns warehouse where goods are delivered to domestic in-house retailers – thus weakening the structural power of workers located at a strategic 'chokepoint' in the supply chain, and thereby considerably reducing the liability of worker unrest.[25]

Unlike domestic capital of South Asia of the past, Arvind is flexible, restructuring domestic and international functions to reduce risk. This *dual labour markets* strategy applies at multiple levels. First, Arvind provides its 'core'

---

[24] Interview, 21 November 2014.

[25] It has been argued that the battle against capital has now shifted away from struggles at the point of production to sabotaging the 'technical infrastructure of the metropolis', in other words, to circulation, distribution, transport, and consumption (The Invisible Committee 2009). But, as we will see in the case of the Arvind warehouse, although it represents an interface between production and consumption, unlike the immovable power of a port – a critical 'chokepoint' in the supply chain – a large shed in a dusty little town can be easily replaced or reorganized to render workers powerless in the chain.

employees, such as managers, designers, or others at high-value phases, with a wide breadth of employee benefits, whereas 'peripheral' workers, those employed through shell contractor companies at the low-value phases of production, remain subcontracted, heavily exploited, with few avenues for redress. Second, Arvind's phases of production for international brands are in-house, while its production for domestic retail and of its own brands are outsourced. They may deploy a similar strategy of transnational brands delinking production to reduce risk brought on by the instability of seasonality and fluctuating consumption patterns. Finally, as was accomplished during the struggle at the Arvind in-house warehouse in Ramnagara, a pressing warehouse was converted into a returns warehouse externalizing its labour from 'core' to 'non-core' functions. This partly insulates Arvind from major brands that might otherwise be compelled to place pressure on Arvind over labour violations, averting potential losses caused by work stoppages or strikes at a major artery in its distribution network. Thus, the flexibility of dual labour markets allows Arvind to use multiple methods to intensify downward pressure on subcontracted workers and reduce liability by cleaving production from consumption, while minimizing the efficacy of workplace actions.

The case of growing supplier-end firms like Arvind shows that large capital-holding companies are able to expend more capital to bring on expensive 'job workers' and have a growing number of alternative facilities to undermine workers' actions at a single warehouse. Arvind was able to invest in a number of substitute warehouses across the state and replace the work at Ramnagara. This capacity would be inconceivable a few decades ago or with smaller capital-holding firms. The workers' struggle at the Arvind warehouse represents a classic example in which greater market power and value capture for Arvind translates into a greater ability for capital to overwhelm and undermine labour at a specific facility. By maintaining a spatially aggregated production network, with numerous facilities distributed in the same area, Arvind can seamlessly turn the production process around from one facility to another, whether it is a full-grown production plant or a warehouse.

Despite reorganization and losing members, the trade union at the Ramnagara warehouse remained intact. However, the result is contradictory. A budding 'full package' capitalist environment can result in greater bargaining power from the point of production. As workers at Arvind indicated, company profits and high-profile deals can be used to bolster demands for a greater share of the value for workers. Information that was previously hidden became accessible to workers because of Arvind's growing and high-profile status. Arvind's sizeable value capture augmented workers' demands and strengthened the union, sharpening the antagonism between workers and their direct employer.

Alongside Arvind's growth across the supply chain, workers created their own mirrored 'labour networks' of Arvind and affiliated workers. For example, workers received information on Arvind's plans from a worker who had retained a contact at his old job within the Arvind logistics network. This information was critical in preventing the relocation. Moreover, Arvind's workers attempted to expand the membership of the union to include nearby Arvind textile and garment facilities to unify demands against a single employer, whereas, previously, smaller firms littered the landscape, creating impermeable barriers to unity.

Finally, the targeting of retail shops assisted an expansion in the labour network to include allied activists, urban unions, and Arvind retail workers. The Arvind campaigns highlight a growth in purchasing power in the Global South, the resulting boom in retail, and a shift in the power of workers to confront their employer at the point of sale. By targeting retail shops in Mysore and Bangalore both at Arvind-owned shops and their major brand buyers during the campaign, workers were able to attack both the point of production and the point of consumption to put pressure on their direct employers. Thus, the bridging of spaces of production and consumption while benefiting suppliers is also changing the relationship between global buyers and, now, *global* producers through a burgeoning retail market. But clearly, this is also helping alter the relationship between workers and their bosses by adding multiple points of leverage. The growth of consumer power in the Global South is a relatively new phenomenon and, potentially, another tool for workers within a new generation of 'anti-sweatshop' campaigns.

Arvind's growing client list also means a greater ability to survive the loss of a single contract even from a large branded company. The relationship between buyer and supplier continues to be asymmetrical in favour of buyers, but companies like Arvind are no longer entirely dependent on a single global brand. Arvind can increasingly withstand the loss of a single major client. Whereas with smaller assembly-only, single-factory suppliers, a single brand can become the ultimate decision-maker, and the breaking of a large purchasing contract has often resulted in the closure of the factory. Moreover, large firms like Arvind hold enough capital of their own to withstand the loss of a single contract. It is true that emergent firms like Arvind have not generated surpluses in the form of finance capital; rather, capital that is accumulated is immediately invested. Yet the liquidity and leveraging of assets afford large suppliers a degree of freedom not accessible to assembly-only suppliers.

These changing dynamics have informed GATWU's strategies. From its foundation in 2005, GATWU's strategy has gone from a reactive 'hot shop' form, followed by community organizing strategy to, from 2012 onwards, targeting brands' outsourced production by affiliating with the IULBR.

Following the struggle at Arvind, GATWU added another layer to its strategy to account for the changing nature of supplier-end capital. The symbiosis of buyer and supplier meant that workers could now leverage a greater degree of power against full-package suppliers across the supply chain buttressed by a corporate campaign against traditional Western brands. As Jayram[26] from GATWU stated,

> Three years ago our strategy was organizing the community through our women's organization and coverting community members into factory-level committees, from there we propped our union up. After that we moved towards targeting a single brand, organizing the outsourced company, and getting our allies in the West to put consumer pressure through brand campaigns. [...] As we see in Ramnagara, the land itself is the value because they don't have valuable machinery there, making labour organizing at a single facility a recipe for failure. [...] Its not like ten years ago, now even if we get a brand to tell a manufacturer to remediate a situation the manufacturer will refuse. I was in a meeting where it happened just like that. Now, we're starting to look at a strategy of organizing companies like Shahi or Arvind. With such large companies present in the sector you can no longer organize around a single factory or rely only on Western allies and expect it would sustain itself.

A mixed bag

Arvind is not an isolated case. In February 2016, the Indian central government announced its changes to the Employees' Provident Fund (EPF), India's pension scheme, including raising the retirement age and restrictions on workers' access. At 9:30 a.m. on 18 April 2016, 4,500 workers at a factory outside Maddur, between Mysore and Bangalore, at one of India's largest garment firms, Shahi Exports, walked out. In a report compiled by People's Union for Civil Liberties (PUCL 2017), they document how word quickly spread to Unit 14 Shahi Exports in Bammanahalli in Bangalore, 130 kilometres away, where workers walked out hours later. This compelled others at smaller firms to walk out as well. Later that day, 15,000–20,000 workers had congregated in Bammanahalli alone. Word spread to workers in Bangalore's Peenya-Jalahalli Industrial Area who joined in. The wildcat strike lasted two days and large sections of Bangalore and neighbouring industrial cities were shut down. The strikes were estimated

---

[26] Interview, 20 October 2014.

to have involved up to 100,000 workers. The police's brutal response is also well documented (PUCL 2017). Nonetheless, the strikes are cited as the reason for the central government's withdrawal of the proposed EPF changes.

Although these are just a few examples, they demonstrate the ability of demands to become harmonized across cities, states, or even countries at large factories under large firms. On the other hand, once such mass workers' actions would threaten the ability of the supplier to continue to produce for major brands since the liabilities would be too great. Now the power dynamics in the global garment industry is shifting from the unilateral power of brands to a more mutually dependent symbiotic relationship between global brands and big multinational production companies, with the original Taiwanese, Korean, Hong Kong, and Singaporean companies now being joined by Indian, Sri Lankan, Bangladeshi, and mainland Chinese companies. There are of course significant differences between how these different factions of capital function. The case of Arvind demonstrates how one type of big production company developed into a power unto itself and is able to deal with the brands as not quite an equal but symbiotic, as 'strategic partners'. Ongoing struggles at companies such as the Azim Group in Bangladesh, where the owner is a politically connected and powerful member of the national elite, is able to use violence with impunity against trade unionists, and stand up to transnational brands despite a number of brands cutting their relationship with the company, are examples of the growing power of garment firms across the subcontinent.

Of the 400 denim manufacturers worldwide, around 40 manufacturers account for slightly less than 30 per cent of the world output, whereas the largest retailers share more than 30 per cent of the markets among themselves (Sampler and Sarkar 2010). This incongruity shows that 'buyers' are still more powerful within the denim commodity chain; however, the output is not the only variable involved. Arvind's market power is linked not to its production capacity alone, but rather to its integrated value chain and access to the Indian consumer market, which provides substantial economies of scale, cost cutting, as well as shorter cycle and turnaround times for buyers.

As global brands continue to outsource more of the production process, companies such as Arvind continue to insource and expand into the export-oriented value chain. Arvind's one-stop shop offers global buyers cost-effective procurement of raw materials, shorter lead, inventory and transport times, and other cost benefits tied to an integrated supply chain. Despite buyers outsourcing to reduce their international production footprint, the signing of long-term full-package agreements has the effect of locking-in branded companies with higher value suppliers and reconfiguring the buyer–producer relationship. This results in further upgrading potential, erecting greater barriers to entry, and ensuring, in the long term, that a handful of specialized supplier firms ascend as capitals with a high degree of monopolistic power, who may eventually allow full-package firms to determine investment, price, output, and employment while being increasingly vital gatekeepers to Global South consumers.

The changing relationship from asymmetrical *buyer-driven value chain* to a mutually dependent *buyer–producer symbiosis* illustrated throughout this case study is best demonstrated by an anecdote from an auditor of an independent labour organization who had inspected the Ramnagara firings in 2012.[27] 'It's clear that a "brand pressure" campaign simply wouldn't work here,' adding, 'with companies like Arvind, from our experience, brands just don't have as much leverage anymore because Arvind now effectively controls all of PVH's production and sales in the entire region.' During the Arvind investigation, it became clear that PVH was not in an optimum position to negotiate with Arvind, and as the independent monitor later indicated, 'PVH cannot lose Arvind's business, since the kind of services that Arvind offers are only replaceable at a heavy financial cost to PVH. [...] PVH needs Arvind and Arvind needs PVH.' However, by mid-2019, all but a handful of the militants who had organized the campaign at the warehouse remained. On balance, we find that the story of growing supplier consolidation ultimately overwhelmed the power of workers at one logistics unit at Arvind. Had the workers been organized in a more automated phase, or been in a more central position in the value chain, they may have had a greater power to bargain with their employer.

Beginning with the post-colonial Nehruvian state, into the post-reform period, India's garment sector consisted primarily of a domestic comprador bourgeoisie. India's garment firms acted as go-betweens for transnational capital, who were required to 'partner' with an indigenous firm in order to operate in the country, a rapidly changing dynamic in recent years. Ramnagara represents a case in point; these changes in the sector are both obstacles and opportunities for workers. If these trends continue, garment workers, sector trade unions, and anti-sweatshop allies will need to reassess strategies and redirect their energies to target large 'full-package' firms across the supply chain and demand a greater share of production as done by GATWU.

---

[27] Interview, 19 October 2014.

5

Honduras
A Transnational Campaign at a Cotton Commodity Producer

On 14 November 2009, Fruit of the Loom (FOTL), the world's largest producer of T-shirts to the US market and the largest private sector employer in Honduras (Doh and Dahan 2010; Anner 2013), announced that it would reopen its garment factory Jerzees de Honduras (JDH), under the name Jerzees Nuevo Dia (JND), or 'New Day'. They had capitulated almost entirely to the demands of the union and international activists. The final deal, negotiated between FOTL workers and executives, included rehiring of 1,200 employees, a multi-million dollar payout to workers, and a commitment to extend union neutrality and access across its Honduran supply chain.

This is the story of a garment factory that was shut down by its owner in response to unionization, as so often happens.[1] But in this case it is also the story of how FOTL, the factory's TNC owner, suddenly reversed course and, in so doing, fundamentally altered how it approached labour relations. The embattled union drive overcame retaliatory sacking, death threats, and a nine-month factory shutdown, while keeping up morale and high participation to win an impressive package of wages and benefits and create the political space for a new wave of labour organizing in Honduras and abroad.

The garment and footwear sectors are not monolithic, of course, and evolve in different and uneven ways, with a great deal of intra-sectoral variety. Previous chapters outlined how the particularities of garment and footwear production – fashion trends, seasonality, and so on – are made for highly fragmented, labour-intensive, and low-value industries. The top-heavy power balance in these value chains allowed buyers to exert persistent downward pressure on suppliers, who were less and less capable of capturing enough value to upgrade. And that

---

[1] For more detailed history and case studies of such closings in Latin America, see Armbruster-Sandoval (2005).

pressure, like all *downward* market pressures, ultimately fell on workers, whose wages were further squeezed by employers with nothing more to give.

Since the production process depends on what is being produced, seasonality and fashion kept the garment and footwear GVC low-tech and vertically disintegrated, while the least seasonal and fashion-sensitive are the most valorized and vertically integrated. By way of illustration, my case studies focus on a few of the least seasonal and fashion sensitive products in the sector: jeans, casual shoes, and sports shoes; and this chapter's focus is on cotton T-shirts and undergarments.

I survey successful union campaigns in the export-oriented garment sector for clues as to what underpins that success and what it portends for the larger economy and labour's response. The union drive at a FOTL plant in Honduras drew attention from activists across the Anglosphere, who persuaded as many as 132 universities[2] to boycott FOTL's subsidiary Russell Athletic, costing FOTL upwards of $50 million (Davis 2010). The collegiate boycott was the largest since the campaigns targeting Apartheid in South Africa, and the largest of a single apparel brand in history.[3] The *New York Times*' Stephen Greenhouse (2009) heralded it as the student anti-sweatshop movement's 'biggest victory so far'. Organizers triumphantly announced that this was the first time in the history of the anti-sweatshop movement that 'a factory that was shut down to eliminate a union was later re-opened after a worker-activist campaign'. Moreover, it achieved the 'first company-wide neutrality agreement in the history of the Central America apparel export industry' (Doh and Dahan 2010).

And victory was snatched from the jaws of defeat, right as the situation went from bad to worse. Before the closure, in 2005, immediately following the MFAs expiration, the Central American Free Trade Agreement (CAFTA) was passed, making Latin America a testing ground for a new, even more freewheeling garment sector. In 2006, the JDH changed hands when Russell Athletic was acquired by FOTL (itself a subsidiary of Berkshire Hathaway, the holding company of Warren Buffett), which might choose to jettison assets after the acquisition. After the initial shuttering of JDH, the skies darkened again, and again. A military coup ousted labour-friendly Honduran President Jose Manuel Zelaya and the 2008 financial crisis gave FOTL a perfectly plausible alibi for any factory closures (despite labour watchdogs confirming suspicions that this

---

[2] This includes all the universities that participated in the boycott by either cutting, suspending, or, in cases where the university currently had no business relationship with FOTL, publicly agreeing to withhold orders until remediation.

[3] Comparison by value of contracts lost, based on interviews with former and current leaders of various anti-sweatshop and labour union organizations including USAS, the former UNITE, and the WRC.

closure was indeed punitive). But the triumph over those difficulties highlighted the importance of the relationship between product and production process and how labour can exploit an evolving GVC.[4]

The cotton commodity producer GVC

Each segment of the sector has its own political economy. Typically, the manufacturer of a garment purchases the cloth from a textile mill. But as we saw in Chapter 4, under the right conditions, certain products allow for more capital-intensive textile mills to grow as firms. In the Arvind case, for instance, a textile mill became a producer and later a brand, mostly due to its capacity for denim production. The strength of this cotton commodity-producer (henceforth 'commodity-producer') then lay in its being a brand, not a manufacturer.

Here, I examine the 'commodity phase' of the garment GVC – that is, where cotton undergarments, hosiery, knit shirts, socks, and sweaters are produced – and the producing firms that managed to grow and ascend the chain. While globalization ruined most manufacturers, leaving only a few weakened survivors, it was often a boon to large commodity-producers. The low margins in cotton commodity production – among the lowest in a low-margin sector – mean that manufacturers must control the minutest details of production, *from dirt to shirt* (this can be done directly or indirectly). In the late nineteenth century, for example, the low-margin Lancashire cotton industry, which was vertically

---

[4] For analysis, I rely heavily on multiple sets of interviews over a number of years with Jeff Hermanson. Hermanson joined the ILGWU as an organizer in New York City and left in 1997 as the Director of Organizing at the national level. He continued to organize JAs up to the time he left. He has since been a key advisor in the FOTL campaign and contract, helped start the IULBR, and is now retired after serving for several years as Director of Global Strategies at Workers United-SEIU (the present-day incarnation of the ILGWU via many mutations). Worker interviews were conducted in person and translated by Jack Mahoney, a labour organizer based in Central America at the time, which were part of Kumar and Mahoney (2004). Methods include semi-structured interviews with workers and organizers in Honduras and the US, as well as primary source data extracted from union notes, campaign e-mails, internal documents, CBAs, and labour contracts. Union organizing efforts in the global garment industry have few, if any, real successes, which is one explanation for the dearth of research in the area. Thus, to use a spatial metaphor, we are scouting territory with little previous exploration, even groping our way around in the dark.

specialized with separate spinning and weaving firms, declined, says Lazonick (1983), because of a failure to vertically integrate, which left it especially vulnerable to cheap foreign competition. Meanwhile, larger integrated cotton mills producing standardized textile commodities weathered the vagaries of the market and grew to become commodity-producers.

Early in GCC studies, Gereffi (1996: 438) noted a distinction between standardized and differentiated products and their respective value chains:

> [...] the distinction between standardised and innovative (or fashion-oriented) products is correlated with production technologies, the existence of domestic vs. global sourcing networks, and the degree to which firms are innovation or customer-driven [...] The U.S. Apparel sector has a standardised segment (e.g. cotton underwear, blue jeans, mens dress shirts, jogging suits) made up of products that are sold through the year, and fashion segment (eg. women's wear) which is sold in shorter buying seasons of 6–8 weeks in length. Standardised apparel is made by large, vertically integrated manufacturers (e.g. Levi-Strauss, VF corporation, Fruit of the Loom, Sara Lee) [...] the standardised vs. fashion segments are highly correlated with where production takes place (the United States or the Caribbean basin for standardised goods, Asia for fashion goods), how production takes place (large, assembly-oriented factories for standardised goods vs. Networked, OEM production for fashion goods), and the kinds of firms that are the 'drivers' of these segments (large U.S. Manufacturers for standardised items vs. U.S. Retailers and designers for the fashion segment).

The garment sector contracts work out for many reasons,[5] prominent among them being material and seasonality. Brands do not want to be saddled with equipment and factories that frequently outlive their use, and so handle seasonality with the help of contractors. The latter mitigate the risk of investment in capital intensive equipment and factories by using a flexible labour regime (thereby passing the risk on to workers) that can meet shifting goals, producing different articles for different seasons in different volumes. In this way, suppliers keep the lights on year-round. Fashion-sensitivity also prevents suppliers from producing a single product year-on-year, which could allow for enough value capture to result in more capital-intensity.

In a more standardized sub-sector, like denim, detailed in Chapter 4, vertical-integration is easier to achieve. The big jeans brands – Levis, Gap Jeans,

---

[5] But as Yueng and Coe (2015) point out, outsourcing carries its own risks (for example, the so-called bullwhip effect).

Wrangler, and Lee – sell all-weather garments with minimal fashion-sensitivity. This explains why, as Gereffi (1996) shows, denim was vertically integrated until the mid to late 1990s.

Hermanson[6] contrasts jeans with cotton commodity-producers, noting that, as globalization progressed, jeans brands began to move abroad and did not build their own factories:

> Since, they are more fashion-sensitive than a cotton t-shirt. There are more styles and there is more of a fashion component and there's more money to be made. Jeans brands have a little bit bigger margin so they don't have to control all the stages of production. [...] They can control production by their requirements on contractors – so indirect control. [For example,] they could say you have to have an automated pocket setter – so they force [the supplier] to buy that machine which requires additional financing. So basically, only the big jeans contractors – who are highly consolidated – will be able to make for Levis and Gap.

TNCs are increasingly liable to form 'strategic alliances' with suppliers, whereas the cotton commodity-producer produces internally through a wholly owned subsidiary. Commodity-producers globalize through joint ventures, acquisitions, or by starting from scratch (greenfield investment).[7] As Yueng and Coe (2015: 35) have argued, the cost–capability ratio responsible for the outsourcing vogue must be analysed in the context that 'it must be conceptualized in combination with the actor-specific capabilities of these lead firms and their suppliers in order to arrive at a complete picture of its causal influence on the formation and evolution of global production networks'. Capability and degree of monopoly power factor into whether firms internalize or externalize. Naturally, the higher the capability (technology, know-how, and so on), the greater the requirements for suppliers (barriers to entry).

For cotton commodity-producers, who are oligopolistic and capable of technological advancements (despite being in the low margin garment sector), the difficulties of operating in an uneven world, with suppliers of varying capacities, create the cost–capability ratios that incentivize in-house production. However, it is the combination of low capability needs and the attraction of low costs that has always incentivized outsourcing, made for a technologically stunted

---

[6] Interview, 22 November 2018.
[7] As Kaplinsky (2006) has documented, upgrading allowed brand commodity-producers to remain relatively inoculated against the progressively downward competitive price pressures placed on garment value chains.

sector, and opened the doors to globalization as its logical next step. Over time, however, the spatial limits on capital and the unfolding logic of competition led to a class of suppliers growing in size to become 'strategic partners' in increasingly symbiotic relationships with buyers. But not all garments are alike. Parts of the sector (footwear, denim, and cotton t-shirts/innerwear) lend themselves to standardization, since they are less vulnerable to seasonality and fashion. Commodity-producers, like FOTL, who have trouble finding capable suppliers, therefore, took to internalization.

Fruit of the Loom and vertical-integration

Outsourcing has always been a means of mitigating risk and lowering costs (via supplier bidding wars) while ensuring the stability and variability of orders. A century ago, the ILGWU called this the 'auction block system', suggesting that such monopsony power begat a kind of slavery. Indeed, a flexible GVC with high DMP required a workforce with next to no bargaining power. 'There is no security for workers in an insecure industry,' wrote Julius Hoffman (1941), an ILGWU VP (from Wolfson 1950). Worker demands, therefore, required a more 'stable' value chain, with higher margins and so on – that is, immediate employers with something to give.

Just as labour strength can reshape the GVC and implementations of the 'spatial fix' (see Chapter 2), so too can labour weakness. FOTL and Hanes both originated in so-called right-to-work states, in the US South, where they were able to avoid domestic organizing efforts (it is also probable that their example inspired northern brands to start outsourcing). Being in the South, FOTL and Hanes also benefitted from their proximity to cotton fields. These advantages notwithstanding, the cotton GVC is mostly determined by the commodity being produced.

Having supplanted the Dominican Republic in the late 1990s, Honduras' garment sector is now the largest within the Dominican Republic–Central America–United States Free Trade Agreement (DR-CAFTA) region. Its short lead times and preferential regional trade agreements gave it an edge over Asian competitors, and allowed it to break into the American market, upon which it then came to depend. The first textile plant in Honduras was established by a Taiwanese firm in 1999, and large-scale investment followed in the early 2000s, coinciding with the MFA phase-out and new preferential access for knitted fabrics. Five mills for knitted fabrics were established in this period, the largest of which was a joint venture between a Honduran firm and FOTL. And since the 2005 MFA phase-out and signing of CAFTA, at least seven more knit textile fabric plants have sprung up, all run by large North American commodity-producers. In this period, 72 per cent of all Honduras' exports were basic cotton T-shirts or underwear, mostly men's (Lopez-Acevedo and Robertson 2012). Honduran apparel producers employed 90,000 workers, and FOTL had become the single largest private sector employer in the country.

For FOTL, the structure of globalized production dovetailed with domestic production (vertical-integration). Consequently, the firm was heavily committed to Honduras. As Hermanson tells me,[8] 'Their investment there is huge. I think it's a 20-year investment at least. They not only bought buildings, they trained staff, their entire management in Honduras are actually Honduran. They were trained from the inside, they were brought to the US for that training. It's an immense investment in both material and human capital.' In 2002, FOTL was acquired by Berkshire Hathaway, and, in 2006, Russell Athletic became a subsidiary of FOTL. The investment numbers for FOTL and Russell Athletic are harder to separate now since they are merged in Berkshire Hathaway's annual reports. But any way you slice it, establishing 8–10 plants, with 11,000–12,000 employees, is no small undertaking.

FOTL approaches apparel manufacturing with scientific rigour, controlling every element and every stage. The ownership of this phase gives FOTL direct oversight and allows for investment and the application of new technologies. And by both owning *and* controlling every step in the production process, FOTL and other commodity-producers can reap more value.

FOTL's biggest customer is Walmart, for whom they produce at a scale dwarfing the entire operations of other companies. Because of the uniformity of production at FOTL, they can also engage in large-scale upgrading, which is why it was the first company in the sector to introduce lean production and to move towards modular manufacturing.

Dunning's 'eclectic paradigm' (1971) identifies three prospective advantages behind a firm's decision to go multinational with FDI: ownership, location, and internalization (OLI). FOTL had all three in Honduras. Its ownership-advantages as one of the world's three large cotton manufacturing brands (alongside Gildan Activewear and Hanes) included direct access to US cotton (and indirect US state support) and to markets at either end of the supply chain, allowing it to maintain steep capability requirements. Honduras also had a comparative advantage in terms of labour, which together with preferential trade agreements made for cheap transportation to the US market. Finally, and most importantly for me, is how internalization figures in the Dunning model. The reasons are

---

[8] Interview, 25 September 2016.

quite clear. According to the model, the more standardized the product, the more internalized the firm; the incentive/risk structure encourages this, just as it encourages the sellers of variable commodities to decentralize production through outsourcing. If you are producing plain white socks, you face less risk and can afford to continually invest in margin-stretching equipment. Capital-intensity and vertical internalization go hand-in-hand.

Like FOTL, Gildan and Hanes are commodity-producers that started as textile mills before ascending the value chain. FOTL and Hanes are rooted in the American South, in Kentucky and North Carolina, respectively, among the cotton fields, symbolizing the cruelty upon which American power was founded (Beckert 2014). While Egyptian cotton is desirable for textile goods, such as bedsheets and tablecloths, due to its strength and length, American cotton is considered the best in the world for shirts and innerwear.[9] The big three cotton commodity-producing firms vertically integrated early, and hence built their own factories where they moved. Since the 1980s, FOTL has produced only in Mexico, El Salvador, and Honduras. Noticeably, they have yet to open a facility in China.

Hanesbrands, or simply Hanes, which includes Hanes, Champion, Playtex, and over two dozen other name brands, grew out of a textile boom in North Carolina. As a rival, they mirrored FOTL – even in market share, with 35 per cent – until the late 1990s. It was then that Hanes started to 'de-verticalize' while FOTL shifted production to Honduras (Benko and McFarlan 2003). Nonetheless, 70 per cent of Hanes production in 2018 was still carried out internally in its 50-plus factories or by dedicated contractors. It is estimated that Hanes saved 19 per cent on production between 2015 and 2019 because of internalization (Weishaar 2018). The company has grown steadily through acquisitions as well (recently, Maidenform and DPApparel). In 2006, Hanes announced its intention to close US facilities while consolidating Central American plants and increasing its investment and sourcing in Asia. Hanes now has mills in Thailand, Vietnam, and China (Lopez-Acevedo and Robertson 2012).

Montreal-based Gildan is the youngest of the big three and has won the price war for years. Gildan manufactures blank cotton T-shirts and socks which are sold to major print screen printers, retailers, and brands that add designs and logos. It has kept costs low by integrating yarn spinning, knitting, dyeing, finishing, and cutting and sewing operations in 'cost-efficient' countries like Honduras and Haiti, while investing in state-of-the-art equipment and technology (Richter Consulting 2004). Although their quarterly reports boast

---

[9] This claim is of course contested.

of a vertically integrated twenty-first-century production system, their treatment of labour – especially in Haiti – is something out of the nineteenth century. The contractors that operate these factories were set up by Gildan, who thereby transferred ownership responsibilities to Haitian nationals while maintaining control of a fully integrated firm.[10] In 2010, Gildan purchased its first mill in Bangladesh (Lopez-Acevedo and Robertson 2012).

Vertical-integration, however, cannot be reduced to product mechanization. In 1983, as the White House was arming right-wing paramilitaries in El Salvador, Nicaragua, and other Central American states to counter a political 'pink tide', Ronald Reagan signed the Caribbean Basin Economic Recovery Act (CBERA), part of the larger Caribbean Basin Initiative (CBI). The CBERA comprised the economic, carrot/stick aspect of the siege. At the time, 90 per cent of apparel production was concentrated in Guatemala, Honduras, and El Salvador, countries that would be given preferential access to US markets in exchange for being 'anti-communist' and 'respectful of American property' (Lucero 2011: 14). Additional CBI provisions required participating countries to purchase inputs for textiles and apparel goods from the US. 'Textiles and apparels made from US components were,' in essence, 'fully duty-free and quota-free while those made with domestic components were subjected to trade barriers' (Lucero 2011: 14). This depressed a viable local industry to the benefit of US cotton commodity-producers, and 'the result was a vertically-integrated international production process' (Lucero 2011: 15).

As I will show in the workers' struggle at FOTL, vertical-integration increases spatial inflexibility, giving labour greater potential bargaining power. This proved a deciding factor in the case of FOTL. Immense direct investment by brands, and direct brand employment, combined with no alternative workforce during labour unrest gives workers significant leverage (compared to workers in outsourced garment factories). Foreign-owned companies, which are usually larger and much better-resourced, tend to pay more than domestic firms, because they invest more in workers, have more to lose, and are more productive (Doms and Jensen 1998; Ramstetter 1999). And, lucky for labour, they have more to give.

But that is by no means a fait accompli. Take Phillips-Van Heusen's (PVH) Camisas Modernas facility in Guatemala City, for instance. The factory was directly owned by PVH (which includes well-known brands such as Tommy Hilfiger, Van Heusen, Calvin Klein, IZOD, Arrow, and others) and therefore became the target of trade union organizers in the mid-1990s. A six-year campaign led to a collective bargaining agreement (CBA) between PVH and Sindicical de

---

[10] Interview, Jeff Hermanson, 25 September 2016.

Trabajadores de Camisas Modernas (STECAMOSA) in 1997 – the only CBA at the time in the entire Guatemala garment *maquila* industry. Workers won a first-year wage increase of 11 per cent, followed by 12.5 per cent the second; provisions for maintaining current employment levels and increased subsidies for transport and lunch; and the introduction of bonuses and grievance procedures. However, in 1998, PVH shuttered the factory (Armbruster-Sandoval 2005; Lucero 2011). According to Stephen Coats, Executive Director of US/LEAP, the factory closed because of the CBA (Armbruster-Sandoval 2005: 53).

As Jeff Hermanson recalls,[11] 'It was a tough fight [...] we used international leverage'. He adds that after settling on a negotiated contract, the company closed down after two years and after that 'PVH stopped owning factories. PVH gave up their own factories and operated production by contract completely. They basically decided to get out of the ownership business. That's a constant threat and is a strategy that is always open to Fruit of the Loom as well'.

The evolution of anti-sweatshop campaigns

A 1936 New York dressmakers' union pamphlet urged its members to strike, declaring: 'The union announces simply and straightforwardly that the insanity of the unrestrained jobber–contractor system cannot be permitted to continue unchecked.' As described in Chapter 2, to rein in the chaos, the dressmakers demanded a 'limitation of contractors', which was later called the 'designation of contractors' by the ILGWU. Following several mass strikes, the unions forced brands to exclusively do business with designated suppliers – unionized factories where brands agreed to pay a price high enough to guarantee fair wages to workers and reasonable profit to owners (Anner, Bair, and Blasi 2012). The necessity for direct engagement between brands and unions was so evident that, in 1959, the US Congress passed a labour law amendment allowing garment workers to picket and boycott the brands despite having no direct employment relationship[12] (Previant 1959).

Soon, early spatial fixes were forcing the union to play catch-up. When a brand pulled out of a union factory in New York City and gave the work to a non-union factory in Jersey City, unionists drove through the Holland Tunnel

---

[11] Interview, 25 September 2016.
[12] The then Massachusetts Senator John F. Kennedy spoke in favour of the amendment, known as the Garment Industry Proviso, an exception to the 'hot cargo' prohibition that prohibits picketing or boycotting secondary targets, a legacy that continues today.

to picket that factory and recruit its workers.[13] But when brands started sending the work to Santo Domingo and Jakarta, unionists could not keep up. While corporate executives had the resources to travel and communicate across borders, workers faced major obstacles in globalizing their movement, not least of which was the absence of a functioning global union alliance (Stevis and Boswell 2008).

Eventually, United Students Against Sweatshops (USAS) was formed in 1997, born out of the necessity to find new footing under globalization. The brainchild of student activists working with the Union of Needletrades, Industrial and Textile Employees (UNITE), a successor of the ILGWU, the aim of USAS was to leverage the $4 billion university apparel market. That market, in which brands receive licenses from the universities who collect royalties for the sale of apparel bearing their names and logos, totalled 1–2 per cent of US clothing sales (Krupat 2002). USAS grew to 150 chapters across the US, with thousands of students supporting far-away labour struggles by leveraging universities' licensing agreements with transnational apparel brands, citing their codes of conduct (USAS 2013).

Meanwhile, the Clinton administration's Secretary of Labour, Robert Reich, formed the Apparel Industry Partnership (AIP). Reich had been campaigning domestically against sweatshops, and the establishment of AIP set in motion the creation of the Fair Labour Association (FLA) to monitor apparel manufacturing. Transnational corporations were quick to fund the FLA and publicize their own codes of conduct, but union partners such as UNITE and the Retail, Wholesale, and Department Store Union (RWDSU) left the AIP in protest shortly after the formation of the FLA (Chatteri and Levine 2005). Student activists soon realized that such codes were hollow without a truly independent third-party monitoring of factory conditions. The FLA became, what Ross (2006: 52) calls, 'the exemplar of an approach to fighting labour abuse known as Corporate Social Responsibility,' adding that such initiatives, including the FLA itself, are 'almost useless'. 'Workers rarely know the codes exist, contractors evade the standards with relative impunity and lie to auditors, remediation of violations is slow, and violations are not public knowledge except as generalizations.' A global industry of for-hire auditors and accounting firms sprung up in response to the new, burgeoning market for factory investigations, but methodologies and credibility varied.

USAS activists were critical of the FLA and rejected the CSR, calling instead for the formation of an independent monitoring organization. When it was not provided, they formed their own in 2000, called the Workers' Rights Consortium

---

[13] Based on interview with Jeff Hermanson, 23 August 2013.

(WRC), and pressured their universities to join and fund it. By 2005, student campaigns had affiliated over 170 universities to the WRC, funding full-time factory investigators around the world. While major apparel transnationals had funded the FLA and made up its board of directors, the WRC was governed by a body comprised of university administrators, labour experts, trade unionists, and USAS activists. The WRC conducted independent and unannounced investigations and published reports with the help of shop floor workers who were interviewed off-site. The FLA, however, contracted external monitors who only published report summaries, after opaque processes (Chatteri and Levine 2005).

But eventually, it became apparent that even the WRC auditing regime was insufficient (Bartley 2009). After workers successfully organized a union or remedied a major labour violation, they could still be fired, as the brand 'cut and run', or face a factory closure, or a combination thereof. With few exceptions, such campaigns ended with retaliatory firings and denials of corporate responsibility, regardless of how scathing a report or how thorough an investigation was.

Several major campaigns illustrated this. Starting in 1998, US unions and anti-sweatshop organizations like USAS and WRC repeatedly intervened to support workers organizing at the BJ&B factory in the Dominican Republic, eventually pressuring Nike and Reebok to reverse the illegal firing of unionists. In a historic victory, the BJ&B union became the first in its country's free trade zones to win a CBA[14] (Esbenshade 2008). But the factory gradually began to lay off most of its workforce as Nike and Reebok shifted production to cheaper alternatives, and, a few years later, moved its entire operation to Vietnam and Bangladesh.

Meanwhile, the unionized Hermosa Manufacturing factory in El Salvador abruptly closed in 2005, stealing an estimated $825,000 it still owed workers. Those who organized and demanded their pay were blacklisted. Brands such as Adidas, Nike, and Russell Athletic insisted there was nothing they could do. University of Wisconsin student Jan Van Tol (Sexauer 2007) told the university newspaper, 'If Adidas' system requires this long to resolve even such an obvious case of labour rights violations as Hermosa, that system is obviously broken.' Activists proposed an overhaul.

In 2005, USAS, the WRC, and several universities launched an ambitious new campaign called the Designated Suppliers Program (DSP). The DSP echoed

---

[14] The first since the earlier victories of the 1990's ILGWU-ACTWU-ITGLWF organizing project, which resulted in 10 CBAs covering over 10,000 workers and the creation of the union that went on to organize at BJ&B and other garment and textile factories (including big Hanes and Gildan textile mills that are still alive and well).

UNITE's jobber agreements and the 1936 dressmakers' demand for 'limitation of contractors', but would make universities enforce it instead of unions. The programme would have universities require apparel brands to produce at least 75 per cent of clothing bearing the university's logo in factories where workers had a democratic trade union and earned a living wage. The representatives of USAS fanned out across the world to meet with garment unionists and develop a strategy.

Unfortunately, given the paucity of 'qualified' factories, DSP proponents were left hoping that, 'if they built it, they would come'. When BJ&B closed in 2007, the Dominican factory was one of the only five on the list of DSP-qualified factories.[15] Prospects for the programme were looking grim. Aside from an ever-shrinking list of qualifying factories, the DSP's opponents had begun alleging antitrust violations, triggering a review by the US Department of Justice (DOJ).[16] As this went on, the race to the bottom continued apace.

In 2007, at the nadir of the anti-sweatshop movement, a group of women in Choloma, Honduras, who were frustrated with their working conditions decided – in the face of tremendous odds – to form a union. But this situation was different. These workers were employed in a vertically integrated subset of the garment sector: a cotton commodity-producer. The combination of industrial context (a vertically integrated GVC) and subjective agency (workers organizing) proved incredibly effective and durable. These workers would revive the tradition of direct negotiations with TNC executives and reveal a capacity for reversing capital outflows.

A campaign at Fruit of the Loom[17]

Reyna Dominguez worked at JDH, in Choloma, the heart of the country's export-processing region. She sewed hooded sweatshirts that were trucked an hour north to the Caribbean port of Cortés, then shipped to the US – often

---

[15] Taken from a September 2006 memo by the DSP Working Group.
[16] The DOJ eventually approved DSP in 2011 (USJD 2011).
[17] There are also two additional papers describing the FOTL campaign. One is a working paper by Doh and Dahan (2010) that gives a general overview of students' role in the FOTL campaign, comparing it with the student campaign to divest from Sudan in protest of human rights violations in Darfur. And the other is a book chapter by Mark Anner (2013). Building on this work, I have assessed the campaign itself, its meaning for the structural power of workers to negotiate better terms and conditions, and its implications for the next chapter of the anti-sweatshop movement.

to universities. Production of exports for the US, especially apparel, was good business in Choloma following the DR-CAFTA.

One afternoon, in the summer of 2007, Dominguez and four other JDH workers walked into the Choloma office of a union confederation called the Central General de Trabajadores (CGT). They described their situation to Evangelina Argueta, coordinator of the CGT's union organizing in the *maquila*'s export-oriented assembly plants. Together, the women made plans to build a strong union of JDH workers, knowing it would likely bring harassment, retaliatory dismissals, and blacklisting.

Dominguez and her co-workers were not the only FOTL workers organizing, at nearby Jerzees de Choloma (JDC) workers began forming a union in March 2007 and soon affiliated with the CGT. In May 2007, workers at Petralex, a contract factory producing for FOTL, had also organized their own union and joined the CGT.

By July, managers at all three factories had begun firing unionists. JDC fired almost all 72 founding union members (WRC 2007), Petralex fired all 6 union officers, and JDH fired 25 unionists. By October, 145 workers had been unlawfully dismissed for union activity at JDC and JDH (WRC 2008). The union filed a complaint with the local labour ministry and alerted international organizations.[18] The WRC investigated and published reports. Students pressured universities to leverage their multimillion-dollar contracts to pressure FOTL to rehire the workers. Though many unionists were eventually rehired, FOTL soon announced plans to close JDC in July of 2008. In talks with the unions and WRC, the company agreed to transfer the fired JDC unionists to JDH, offering priority hiring at JDH for JDC workers after the latter closed.

Nevertheless, Dominguez and her fellow unionists at JDH pressed forward. On 11 July 2008, the union began negotiations with local management over a CBA. Negotiations reached an impasse on 3 October 2008, after management refused to budge on several issues, including wages. Under Honduran law, this meant FOTL would be obliged to submit to a mediation process at the local labour ministry. Instead, on Wednesday, 8 October 2008, FOTL announced it would close JDH, then its only unionized factory.

The factory finally closed on 31 January 2009. The next day, union leaders Moises Montoya and Norma Chavarria were at the University of Maryland, kicking off the first of multiple tours coordinated with USAS. The workers

---

[18] Honduran labour law is rarely enforced – a common practice in export-oriented countries. For more detailed analysis on labour law, state, and international capital, see Hensman (2011).

announced their objective: to turn universities, retailers, shareholders, and other business partners against FOTL until the company reopened the factory and finished negotiating with the union over working conditions.[19]

The 'Rein in Russell' campaign that followed[20] lasted from January to October 2009. The college boycott began to snowball as the union leaders spoke at public events organized by USAS activists and met with university administrators to convince them to terminate licensing contracts. Combining an 'air' and 'ground' strategy,[21] workers met with members of the US Congress,[22] travelled to the Omaha headquarters of Berkshire Hathaway, and joined USAS activists to distribute leaflets at retail stores selling FOTL products. While activists were expanding leafleting activities across the country, JC Penney informed the campaigners they would no longer sell FOTL products. Doug Morton, CEO of the retail chain Sports Authority, met with activists in Colorado in April 2008 and, soon after, announced Sports Authority would no longer stock FOTL. The Honduran workers' local union struggle had now become a comprehensive strategy focused on university licensing contracts, retail outlets, and even the NBA's relationship with FOTL subsidiary Spalding. The campaign was an all-out assault on the company's profits.

Notwithstanding the strategic role played by USAS and other organizations, the Honduran union leaders remained the protagonists of the campaign, not limited to the roles of messengers to advance another organization's agenda, as it often happens in transnational anti-sweatshop campaigns (Brooks 2007). In February 2009, two union leaders travelled to Omaha, Nebraska, to personally knock on the door of Berkshire Hathaway CEO Warren Buffett. Later that year, one union leader spoke at a Berkshire Hathaway annual shareholder meeting (dubbed the 'Woodstock for capitalists' [*WSJ* 2018]), directly confronting FOTL's then-CEO John Holland with stories of death threats and other labour abuse at JDH (Stop Sweatshops 2009). But most importantly, when FOTL was ready to

---

[19] Informed during interview with Dominguez who went on a separate 2009 campaign tour in the UK.

[20] See Anner (2013) for a detailed account of the campaign.

[21] Derived from military terminology, union campaigns often distinguish 'air war' tactics, like pressuring an employer via its clients, from a 'ground war', mobilizing workers.

[22] On 13 May 2009, 65 members of the US Congress sent a letter to Russell Athletic CEO John Holland expressing serious concern over labour violations (US Congress 2009).

discuss a settlement, it was the Honduran workers who negotiated face-to-face with top executives.

FOTL and the workers' union reached an agreement at a Washington, DC, meeting in November 2009. The consumer campaign ended and JND reopened its doors, rehiring 1,200 employees, and making a multimillion-dollar payout to workers. But workers were just getting started. In May 2011, after nine months of negotiations, JND and the union signed an impressive first CBA. It stipulated an immediate wage increase of 19.5 per cent, with another increase of 7 per cent to be implemented in January 2012 (USAS 2011, 2012). Additional wage negotiations in the summer of 2013 added another 9.5 per cent raise for most workers.

In October 2013, the legal minimum wage for factories in Honduras' free trade zones was 4,982.13 lempiras (US $245) per month. The JND unionists estimate the majority of JND workers earn over 8,000 lempiras (US $395)

Figure 5.1 A union sign attached to a sewing machine at JND reads, 'We demand fair wages.' 2 April 2013

Source: Jack Mahoney.

per month.²³ Workers also enjoyed rare benefits such as free lunch and free transportation to and from work – both major expenses for garment workers in the region, who may typically spend upwards of 20 per cent of their salary on bus fare and their factory's cafeteria.²⁴ Downtime resulting from sewing machines in need of repair were no longer counted against a worker's pay calculation, incentivizing management to keep equipment working safely and efficiently.

In September 2013, Reyna Dominguez reported that JND's production quotas were more reasonable than those of FOTL's main competitors, Hanesbrands and Gildan Activewear. She also noted that workers in those factories earned wages approximately 25 per cent lower and worked longer hours. Gildan, which competes directly with FOTL for shelf space at Walmart and other retailers, bragged that its 'low-cost manufacturing' was 'giving the retailers better margins' than FOTL (Altstedter 2012). That may well have been true. Gildan's production network is so notorious for labour violations – including refusals to pay minimum wage in Haiti and death threats against unionists in Honduras – that workers making Gildan products in four countries held a coordinated international protest in July 2012 (IULBR 2013a).

The November 2009 JND settlement agreement also included a unique provision whereby FOTL agreed to remain neutral during union drives at all its Honduran facilities, and another provision for phasing out 'collective pacts' – a Honduran form of employer-dominated representation (WRC 2009). The WRC had advocated forcefully for such a proactive measure, given the repeated violations of workers' freedom of association during the preceding two years. Asked why her negotiating commission decided to make this a priority in its talks with FOTL, Dominguez replied,

> We took the initiative to protect other workers, because obviously when they saw the successes of Jerzees Nuevo Dia, the rest of the workers would want to organise. So, to avoid the problems of firing and fear, this was important. [...] It has gone well. There are now three unionised Fruit factories.

And the success at JND did, in fact, inspire other FOTL workers to organize. Workers at Jerzees Buena Vista (JBV) would soon sign their own landmark agreement with FOTL, winning similar benefits. Workers at the VFI facility,²⁵ formerly Vanity Fair International, in Honduras and the Joya de Ceren factory

---

²³ Globally, statutory minimum wage typically functions as both a minimum and maximum wage for garment workers.

²⁴ Based on a number of worker interviews in August 2013.

²⁵ FOTL purchased the Vanity Fair Lingerie division from VF Corporation in 2007.

in El Salvador also formed unions. The 2014 FOTL and VFI workers agreed to a CBA, winning benefits like those at JND and JBV, while the Joya de Ceren workers won neutrality in 2017 through direct meetings between the union and local FOTL management.

From victory to victory

The success of the FOTL campaign is the result of a union drive model, developed through decades of labour struggles, taking root at a firm in a structural sweet spot, allowing for significant associational power for labour. But can the JND example be replicated? The extraordinary circumstances surrounding JND – specifically, the international attention it garnered – may be the reason for pessimism. However, while FOTL still outsources much of its production, all four union factories in Honduras and El Salvador are vertically integrated subsidiaries – which is the structural power workers of the sector lack. The factories also make up a planned 'industrial cluster' – part of a 'location agglomeration', in which the concentration of capital and labour reduces spatial costs (Sassen 1998; Scott 2009). Since the 1990s, FOTL has invested enormous sums in Honduras and El Salvador, splitting over 20,000 workers between the two neighbouring countries. Its Central American facilities include textile mills, which are much less mobile than assembly plants due to the large and expensive machinery involved and are run by seasoned management teams trained in the US. These sunk costs will keep work in Honduras and El Salvador regardless of union efforts.

Everything that was under a single corporate umbrella at the industrial cluster also made it impossible for FOTL to deny responsibility. The history of organizing in the garment sector is littered with efforts thwarted by the (purposeful) plausible deniability of TNCs employing contractors. But at a vertically integrated firm, workers can collapse the layers of bureaucracy between the CEO and a factory foreman. Webs of contracts and subcontracts, on the other hand, are designed to ensnare labour in impossible litigations, while indemnifying brands and letting them cut loose any hired firm caught on the wrong side of law.

Once there's a strong union, it can respond to and organize hot shop campaigns targeting specific issues at neighbouring factories. Jeff Hermanson, who was intimately involved in the ILGWU and FOTL campaigns, drew parallels:

> The big difference between the New York market and extending into Pennsylvania, New Jersey, Connecticut we had union density. We basically had control of the labour market which was won over 50 years of struggle. But by the 1970s we had lost control of the labour market. Here we are in

like 1910, where the unions are marginal in most markets. Therefore, we [now] have a tremendous amount of work to do. To become a player, we have to look at the overall industry, figure out who are the major firms, who are the lead firms, in order to become less than marginal in our own markets. By organizing Fruit of the Loom in Honduras, the CGT becomes a very powerful player in that labour market.

While negotiations finished up at FOTL, two new campaigns, using similar strategies, took off at outsourced facilities. In January 2009, two Nike subcontractors had shuttered in Honduras. The Hugger de Honduras and Vision Tex (for simplicity, 'H&VT') factories also denied their now-jobless employees $2.2 million in severance and other legally mandated benefits. The CGT representing the former workers of H&VT used the JDH strategy to fight back. Nike, the factories' largest buyer (Nike 2010), released an early public statement claiming plausible deniability that the 'factories who directly employ workers are responsible' and not the transnational brands who buy from them (Nike 2010). But after another set of tours with USAS forcing several universities to cancel their contracts, Nike signed a deal with the CGT on 23 July 2010, promising the owed severance and health benefits.

Because workers build momentum after big victories, the FOTL CBA set off alarm bells for garment TNCs. In January 2011, the PT Kizone factory in Indonesia closed and its owner fled, leaving 2,700 workers who were by law owed more than $3.3 million in severance. Buyers were cautiously apologetic: Nike quickly chipped in $500,000, the Dallas Cowboys $55,000, and brand intermediary Green Textile poured in another $1 million. But there was still $1.8 million outstanding. The final brand, Adidas, invoked plausible deniability. In response, PT Kizone workers joined with USAS to attack Adidas' university licenses, using advice on organizing and negotiating from CGT as well as Sitrasacosi, the union that had represented workers at Adidas contractor Hermosa.[26] By now, the two unions had joined others to form a new global coalition, later called the International Union League for Brand Responsibility (IULBR, also known as the League). The Kizone workers joined the League, which provided them negotiating advisors before and during their meeting with Adidas executives. In April 2013, Adidas and the ex-workers' union signed a settlement agreement, stipulating that Adidas would pay the outstanding severance – a first for the brand, and a sea change after its stubborn refusal to pay severance to the former Hermosa workers.

---

[26] The 250 workers at the Hermosa factory were left without jobs after its closure in 2005. Workers never fully received their legally mandated severance from Adidas or the factory.

Even after capitulating, both Nike and Adidas were careful not to admit direct liability, calling the payouts, respectively, a 'workers' relief fund' and 'humanitarian aid' (Greenhouse 2010; Adidas Group 2013). Semantics aside, what happened was unmistakable: TNCs had negotiated directly with the employees of subcontractors to whom they paid outstanding money owed for assembling their goods. Nike's speedy response to the Kizone case, in particular, even after paying the H&VT workers, demonstrated a recognition of the consequences TNCs now faced for violating labour rights. Nevertheless, even these victories were only stopgap measures, *tweaking* the power balance in a few far-flung localities.

A new day

The aforementioned examples offer a new path forward. As Compa writes, 'The CGT's success in Fruit of the Loom plants has led to a coordinating group of unions throughout Central America aiming to persuade more firms to respect their organizing rights.'

Since 2011, the CGT, an ad-hoc group of regional unions, has transformed into a global coalition of unions dedicated to bottom-up campaigns in the production networks of large transnational brands. Formally launched in 2013, the League is comprised of national union federations of garment, textile, and footwear factory workers in 10 countries, from El Salvador to Cambodia. At several union meetings, between 2011 and the League's public launch in February 2013, leaders from the CGT and FOTL workers' union delivered presentations on their victory, explaining how it was achieved, and urging the international unionists in attendance to take up similar strategies.[27]

Their story provided a case study in how much more effective negotiations are when they involve real stakeholders, without intermediaries. Dominguez was part of the union's negotiating commission in 2009 with the local JDH management and in the 2010 face-to-face with top FOTL executives, including CEO Rick Medlin, in Honduras and Washington. She reflected on the experience: 'In negotiations here in Honduras with the local plant management, they didn't have the power to make decisions about whether to give ten [lempiras] or more than ten when workers are asking for twenty. They didn't have the power to decide. [...] With them, we didn't achieve anything.' At a factory directly owned

---

[27] Based on interviews with numerous unionists across Central America, including CGT leaders and FOTL workers.

by a TNC, management has no need to worry about razor-thin margins and competition for contracts. 'If Rick Medlin says he can go five [lempiras] higher,' Dominguez said, 'he means it, instead of stalling. The top executives honour their word and have the power to make decisions.' After so much hemming and hawing in negotiations with middle management, frank dialogue was a relief.

Dominguez argued that feats like that at JDH could be achieved elsewhere, with other TNCs: 'This happened, and can happen with another brand, because of international pressure.' International pressure was definitely central to the FOTL campaign since most union efforts languish in obscurity. However, as we see from the other cases highlighted here, when firms enlarge and integrate (even if vertically disintegrated from large brands and retailers), they become the ones who must negotiate with shop floor workers. The FOTL case, for instance, laid the groundwork for direct negotiations between the CGT and Nike at H&VT, as well as between the PT Kizone ex-workers' union and Adidas, reifying the new 'responsibilities' of garment TNCs. These victories, however, cannot be disarticulated from the structural advantages workers have at commodity-producers in terms of bargaining power.

While the CGT is considered politically moderate compared to its explicitly left-wing national union counterparts, its members have taken a militant approach, emphasizing strikes and the importance of mass participation.[28] It led mass industrial actions with the Confederación Unitaria de Trabajadores de Honduras (CUTH) and Confederación de Trabajadores de Honduras (CTH) union centres against the 2009 military coup that ousted centre-left and Chavez-friendly President Manuel Zelaya (CGT 2009), where many CGT garment worker activists marched under the banner 'Feminists in Resistance'. This militancy might surprise theorists of 'labour imperialism', because the CGT once received funds from the US Department of State for a labour rights education programme.[29] The US government, of course, tacitly supported the coup by refraining from calling

---

[28] In the FOTL case, Anner (2011) points out that the CGT began acting more like a radical union after the introduction of the collective pacts – an inversion of the 'radical left flank'.

[29] The CGT had a programme with the AFL-CIO Solidarity Center funded by a grant from the US Department of State's Bureau of Democracy, Human Rights, and Labour. The Solidarity Center is the successor of the American Institute for Free Labour Development (AIFLD), which received US State Department funding to encourage innocuous 'business unionism', and, in some cases, worked to destabilize 'unfriendly' governments, including left-wing governments in Latin America (Scipes 2000, 2005, 2011). Some scholars maintain that the Solidarity Center continues the legacy of labour imperialism established under AIFLD (Bass 2012).

it such and losing no time in recognizing the new government (McLean, Shane, and Tse 2014).[30] But the evidence is clear that CGT leaders acted independently, uninfluenced by funding for a peripheral programme.[31]

The political goings-on in Honduras concurrent with the FOTL campaign touch on larger questions concerning worker organization vis-à-vis the state and empire.[32] Workers were fighting for their rights in the teeth of empire, in a client state hell-bent on attracting foreign investment. That the CGT succeeded, in the face of employer intransigence and an anti-labour government supported by a superpower, is nothing short of remarkable. The CGT–FOTL agreement fundamentally altered labour relations at the country's largest private employer. But the state was shut out of the process, showing that TNCs actually pulled all the strings – something the CGT intuited and the League later understood.

Lance Compa (2013) asserts that the Rana Plaza disaster 'should be a pivot point for the global apparel industry', but cautions against replicating the consumer-dependent strategies of the past. Instead, 'demands for change [should] start to focus on workers' right to form trade unions'. While arguing for stronger Bangladeshi unions, he refers to the FOTL case:

> The Kentucky-based company reopened the factory where the union dispute arose, rehired all employees, recognised the union and entered into good-faith bargaining. Now the renamed 'New Day' facility has a collective bargaining agreement with higher wages, better conditions, and a strong health and safety committee. Workers have maintained high productivity levels, and the company has added employees.

Anner (2011) describes the apparel export industry as embedded in what he calls a 'triangle of power', comprising brand-name clothing companies, local

---

[30] For a Marxist critique of international law, imperialism, and race, see Knox (2016). For an analysis of war and imperialism on development and, indeed, de-development, see Khadri (2014).

[31] In fact, on the contrary, the AFL-CIO Solidarity Center petitioned the post-coup government and the Organization of American States to protect CGT leaders from death threats related to their opposition to the coup, as mentioned in a leaked US State Department cable (Wikileaks 2009).

[32] The debate over US global power was revived by Hardt and Negri's (2001) contention that it was an *Empire* in decline. The idea that globalization has led to a weakening of the state's regulatory power is well founded, but recent scholarship suggests that more of the US sphere has been enlisted to help manage capitalistic crisis (Desai 2013), while Panitch and Gindin (2013) aver that numerous states act as satrapies, upholding an imperial system at America's direction.

166 | *Monopsony Capitalism*

suppliers, and the state. He argues that unions must target all three, which the CGT did. But as described earlier, little progress was made dealing with local management and local authorities; results only came when the union targeted the real capital-holders (which, being vertically integrated, was both the brand and the supplier).

Anner (2013) also observed that the FOTL campaign benefitted from having an 'empowering frame' rather than a 'victimization frame'. Though the latter may have attracted broader support, by evoking sensational images of helpless workers, it would likely have led to ineffective, top-down solutions. Anner describes a prominent photo used in the campaign's literature (Figure 5.1), portraying *the workers* as the protagonists in their own struggle (as opposed to, say, intercessors from abroad):

> Instead of depicting very young women in the campaign fliers, they used two older elected leaders of the factory union, one male and one female. And instead of depicting them as vulnerable victims, the image of the unionists was one of strength and determination. The solution suggested by the message and the image was one of worker organization through

Figure 5.2 JDH union leaders Moises Montoya and Norma Chavarria at University of Minnesota, 13 February 2011

Source: Minnesota Daily.

respect for internationally recognised freedom of association rights, not paternalism. This was a deliberate decision on the part of the Honduran unionists and their USAS allies. (Anner 2013: 33)

Over the course of the campaign, union leaders acquired the knowledge and the diplomatic skill necessary to convince university administrators to sever ties with FOTL and to finally get themselves seats across from the company's CEO. Sentiment still played a part, of course. One union leader often broke down at public events while describing her family's hardship after the factory closure and the death threats she faced for fighting FOTL. Virtually, every campaign document and press release made clear that the campaign would continue until FOTL gave in and restarted negotiations with the union.

Besides being a victory over sweatshop conditions, the FOTL campaign was an unmistakable success for *unions*. Greenhouse's article (2009), the first to announce the settlement, featured the word 'union' or 'unionized' twelve times, even as he chose to dwell on the involvement of US students in the campaign. That the Rana Plaza discourse today tends towards a 'victimization framing' ought to give one pause. While US unions and NGOs have since rallied to end 'deathtraps', two global union federations have negotiated the Accord on Fire and Building Safety (henceforth 'Accord') with the Bangladeshi government. The Accord aims to establish a new auditing system, an inspection programme funded by transnational brands (AFBSB 2013). The USAS too launched an 'end deathtraps' campaign following Rana to pressure universities to require the brands manufacturing their apparel to sign the Accord. But as Compa warns, 'The one-day visits and checklist-style monitoring routine in such efforts have not worked.'[33]

---

[33] This characterization of the Accord is not one that is shared by many labour-rights NGOs including WRC, ILRF, USAS, CCC, and others. These organizations maintain that the Accord is a model of an 'enforceable brand agreement' that has effectively forced major improvements in structural and fire safety in Bangladeshi factories. Unfortunately, despite the leverage arising from the Rana Plaza industrial catastrophe, and despite the millions of dollars spent on the Accord inspection regime, the Accord did not result in the strengthening of Bangladeshi garment worker unions, and thus the modicum of gains made will easily be wiped away once the inspection regime has officially ended, which has all but happened. Indeed, NGOs play a dominant role in many aspects of the Global South, from national policies to the construction of cities to the many labour-rights programmes identified here. As Davis (2006: 71) points out, this speaks to a new wisdom from the 1980s onwards that 'mandated the state ally with international donors, and, then, NGOs, to become an "enabler" of the poor'.

Structure and agency

The FOTL victory was made possible primarily by labour's 'objective' conditions of the structural power of vertical-integration (and its assorted sunk costs) coupled with the subjective agency of the associational power of a transnational campaign. Indeed, the union took stock of the crucial weakness of vertical-integration and exploited it while – among other things – leveraging the help of international activists. As Jeff Hermanson recalls, 'In the struggle to organise one plant, we basically waged a campaign against the whole company. We threatened the existence of the corporation itself and that put us in a power position relative to the corporation.' The Washington Agreement signed between the CGT and FOTL executives rendered the rest of FOTL's Honduran operations vulnerable to additional organizing. Soon, the CGT won union recognition at two additional plants.

If you recall, the factory Camisas Modernas, at a vertically integrated firm, was the site of a successful union drive too – but was then gradually shut down, marking the end of direct factory ownership for PVH. Jerzees de Honduras could face a similar fate if FOTL shifted production to, say, Asian contractors to better compete with Hanes and Gildan. And that may still be on the cards. The now-defunct Trans-Pacific Partnership (TPP) and subsequently the Comprehensive and Progressive Agreement for Trans-Pacific Partnership induced Hanes and FOTL to expand production beyond Central America to Vietnam. Both firms built their own factories. But FOTL contracts out the production of garments containing polyester and other synthetic fabrics. Intimate and athletic wear that contain synthetic fibre, for example, are produced by firms in Sri Lanka and Cambodia. Only cotton goods are produced in-house.

As previously mentioned, the cost–capability ratio of cotton production makes contracting disadvantageous to commodity-producers. Thus, Asian contractors actually have difficulty in competing with directly owned Central American facilities, which can stretch margins by exercising scientific control over the production process. That is a crucial advantage of vertical-integration. According to Hermanson, 'The control of every single element of the process down to the finest motion of the operator's fingers – the scientific wringing of the last inch of efficiency [...] when you're making underwear this is what you have to do to make a profit and remain competitive.' As mentioned earlier, the profits from in-house development are high enough to allow for steeper payrolls, even before labour organizes. 'In our most recent negotiations,' Hermanson says, '[FOTL executives] provided figures that showed that their wage and benefit costs are 25–35% higher than their direct competitors.'

The vertical-integration at FOTL had other advantages for workers too, aside from a boss with deep pockets. First, it meant that FOTL could not undermine labour with value chain monopsony... power (integration takes that out of the picture). Second, it meant increased control and capacity, allowing for greater economies of scale and greater technological investment with fewer transaction costs (a sunk cost in its own right). Third, the aforementioned sunk costs associated with larger investments in technology, skills, and organization. Fourth, those sunk costs functioned as entry barriers, helping the firm capture and hold market share.

And there are, of course, limits to what technology can do for a garment firm. Hermanson explains, '[These firms] do everything they can to develop the technology but there's not much you can do to a sewing machine – you can speed it up or get automatic thread cutters but at the end of the day there's got to be a worker that will feed the material into the machine.' Ergo labour control and relative capital-intensity. 'In terms of technological upgrading,' Hermanson continues,

> I think these firms are now reaching a plateau. The changes now taking place in the commodity sector are taking place on the distribution side. In other words, instead of sending everything to the US in containers and then breaking them down in the US to distribute to different buyers or different stores or the same buyer, [FOTL] has now expanded up the value chain and now operates distribution centres in Honduras. So, now they are pre-packing containers in Honduras that are shipped to the US, put on trucks and then driven to stores.

While distribution and packaging have historically been the responsibility of Walmart and the like, that now falls on FOTL.

If value chains are conceived as existing on a spectrum between buyer-driven and producer-driven, then FOTL factories are positioned next to light electronics. Foxconn, for instance, exercises complete control over production, reaping profits from every stage it brings in-house. But with that kind of control, companies lose mobility, exposing them to organizing campaigns like that which triumphed over FOTL. Those sunk costs can become albatrosses. FOTL subsidiary Russell Athletic, who operated JDH, became persona-non-grata at over 100 universities, costing them contracts with major retailers in need of collegiate logos.

The standardized goods in which cotton commodity-producers specialize have insulated them from the harsh world of modern garment production, dogged by fierce competition, low margins, volatile consumer demand, and uneven seasonality. The production of white socks and the like does not require laborious and fashion-specific cut-sew-trim operations, and so can be perfected through technology and other investments. This changes the composition of capital at the firm, as labour shrinks relative to constant capital. For workers, this is an opportunity. They can turn all those high-tech machines into expensive paperweights by simply withdrawing their labour. Such was the case at JDH and other FOTL factories in Honduras. Other examples of garment specialization include denim and footwear, whose contexts are outlined in Chapters 3 and 4, respectively. Because they too require greater degrees of capital expenditure than standard garment factories, they are also exposed to strategic worker action.

FUTURE

6

Cartels of Capital

In February 1972, Nixon went to China. While American bombers scoured the Vietnamese countryside with defoliants and explosive ordnance, killing and maiming its inhabitants by the millions, Richard Nixon arrived in Beijing, where flashbulbs popped on the tarmac, and a giddy American press corps – already primed to call this 'the week that changed the world' – went into ecstasy. An avowed anti-communist, no less, this president – the first to ever visit the People's Republic – had crossed the Pacific to extend a historic offer. Officially, it was peace. The US and China were not to be friends yet, but cordial acquaintances *agreeing to agree* on future agreements, eventuating in normalized relations.

By positioning the US – at arm's length – on China's side, Nixon and Kissinger had turned the mutual suspicion cleaving Sino-Soviet relations into an irreparable rift whose parties could now be dealt with on more favourable terms (Strategic Arms Limitation Talks [SALT] I, for example, was inked three months later). But this was not just an exercise in geopolitical manoeuvring, meant to isolate the USSR. There were other motives afoot, motives concerning the future of the world economy and America's place at its centre.

With the global financial and monetary system of Bretton-Woods deteriorating fast in the 1960s, it had become urgent that US monetary imperialism underwent transformation. First, by suspending gold convertibility of the dollar in 1971, US Federal Reserve Chair Paul Volcker removed the cap that was placed on America's balance of payments by tying it to a finite material. Next, an ingenious reversion: instead of acting as the world's creditor (drawing on its now-depleted gold reserves), the US would become its chief debtor, exploiting to the hilt that old saying, 'If you owe the bank $100, that's your problem. But if you owe the bank $100 million, that's the bank's problem' (the dollar's value being kept afloat by the petrodollar). By greasing the wheels of commerce, and the palms of politics, with a flood of American treasury bonds, it would remain the world economy's 'indispensable nation', still capable of exercising outsized authority – but now through a more elastic financial instrument. The US, of course, reserved the right to threaten war should anyone get any bright ideas and try to call in its tab. However, instead of underwriting reconstruction in Europe, which was largely whole again, it would use this liquidity to perfuse the late-industrializing nations – and in that regard, China, with its great reserves of labour, held the most potential.

And, indeed, Nixon's warm embrace had thawed party doctrine enough to allow for the rehabilitation of figures like Deng Xiaoping, a party elder whose pragmatic approach to economics – which strove to harness capitalism – had gotten him relegated to anonymous factory work. In the coming years, Deng would, after some jockeying, succeed Mao as a paramount leader and proceed to institute sweeping reforms, opening China up to flows of international learning, technology, and – most importantly – capital. The ensuing boom in manufacturing saw China become the new 'workshop of the world', replacing the US in labour-intensive manufacturing, which itself had taken over the de facto title from Britain. Meanwhile, America – the single biggest market for Chinese goods – would undergo a complementary transition, as its own capital-light industries gave way to services and leveraged consumption.[1]

The most salient of Deng's reforms was the creation of special economic zones, or SEZs, first in the southeast of the country, in Guangdong and Fujian Provinces, and then dotted up the coast and inland, as Beijing conferred the new status on several major ports and provincial capitals. This experimental designation – the brainchild of Xi Zhongxun, father of Xi Jinping and the then governor of Guangdong – allowed for relaxed regulatory regimes and the lifting of tariffs, with the aim of stimulating, but not revolutionizing, the economy.[2] Originally conceived as a quick way to stem the outflow of Guangdong Chinese into neighbouring Hong Kong, where wages and living standards were much higher, SEZs more than resuscitating the local economy, supercharged it. Soon, the designation became a means of creating boom towns by fiat. The first SEZ, Shenzhen, had been a sleepy fishing village just north of Hong Kong, with a population of about 30,000 in 1979 – or the size of Beloit, Wisconsin. But by 2018, only 40 years later, it had grown into an administrative area with over 20 million residents – the size of metropolitan New York City. Beijing accommodated the vast sums of FDI pouring into China by encouraging internal migration

---

[1] This arrangement tends to lock in austerity/underconsumption for Chinese workers, since it is based on the precondition of low-wage, labour-intensive industry. However, beyond low-wage/high-wage dichotomies, there is also a pattern in the neoliberal global order of 'producer-savers' (that is, Germany and China) and 'consumers-debtors' (US).

[2] These reforms did not start with China. Tariff-free zones, specifically, have a prior history – fragments of neoliberalism within the period of embedded liberalism (Feingold 2013).

to the SEZs and channelling new tax revenues into infrastructure (especially transportation networks) to keep down capital costs. This willingness to invest in infrastructure while suspending regulations (protecting labour, trade, and the environment) dovetailed nicely with China's natural advantages in raw materials and workforce size, and nourished a manufacturing revolution for transforming the country into an export powerhouse.

This process – the fall of the so-called Bamboo Curtain – is usually described in triumphalist terms, lauding the successful 'integration' of China into the world economy, its burgeoning skylines, and the emergence of a domestic nouveau riche. But such talk obscures the devil's bargain at the heart of it all, since it is the Chinese Communist Party (CCP) that steered this course and remains at the helm. Under Mao and his central planning regime, which used lessons gleaned from early Soviet history, the economy had been designed to achieve wage parity and maximum employment, and therefore to define any labour market out of the equation.[3] However, under Deng, the 'iron rice bowl' (public sector jobs guaranteeing steady pay and benefits) began to shrink as structural unemployment and worker competition were gradually reintroduced. In due time, it seemed that the CCP was organizing workers solely for the sake of capital – that is, to produce the labour market optimums necessary to attract yet more FDI (Knight and Song 2005). In terms of GDP, this new tack was a wild success: the economy took off like a rocket, growing at some 10 per cent per annum – the fastest pace recorded in history (Wang and Weaver 2013). By the late 2000s, the Chinese GDP had surpassed Japan's to become the world's second largest.

The majority of early FDI, however, came not from the West, but from the Han diaspora in Taiwan, Hong Kong, Macau, and Singapore (Yang 2006), which was given special privileges (Yeung 2000, 2004), allowing it – and select firms in Malaysia and South Korea (Merk 2014) – to form what became known as 'dragon multinationals'. These firms grew rapidly and became gravity wells for outsourced production, especially in the most labour-intensive sectors. Bulk purchasing orders flooded in from Western clothing brands.

The mass shift in global production towards China and other emerging economies transformed the GVC, allowing TNCs to capture substantially larger surpluses. These new profits were owed to the difference in 'markup' caused by 'global labour arbitrage', or international unequal exchange relation. And so, as unit labour costs in China dropped, the cost advantages of production there grew.

---

[3] 'Labour markets' should be understood simply as the interaction of the available supply and demand of labour.

The GVC is a market-based construct, however, and subject to the shifting tensions between buyers and suppliers. These are not well understood by governments, which are often beholden to the economic theories of yesteryear. Despite their good intentions, no current system of classification can accurately depict GVC dynamism. Descriptions of the flows from bigger to smaller boxes still leave the interstitial spaces unexplained.

However, identifying what influences GVCs is essential for understanding today's economic geography. This chapter attempts to draw out these factors and build on them. Using Kalecki (1971) and Robinson (1969), I identify the degree of monopsony power (DMP) as the principal variable in bargaining, such that higher DMP necessarily leads to a higher share in value obtained by the lead firm. The spatial specificities of production, combined with changes in the distribution of value, lead to consolidation and change in DMP. And because capitalism is always evolving, so must the study of the GVC. When the balance of competitive forces resolves temporarily into a symbiotic state, it limits the spatial fix (that is, capital flight) for buyers (thus lowering DMP), which, in turn, provides suppliers more bargaining power.

Capitalistic competition, therefore, produces oligopolies at either end of the value chain, leading to crisis of profitability and attempts at new 'fixes'. This harkens back to Adam Smith (1776), who argued for an inverse relationship between profit and capital stock caused by intensified competition and consequent innovation. Hilferding too argued that in certain specific historical conditions, competition could actually hinder long-term accumulation (Durand and Lege 2013).[4]

My central argument is two-fold: First, the garment sector (and vertically disintegrated value chains generally) is animated by the logic of competition, which moves it inexorably in the direction of consolidation, thereby reducing the monopsonistic power of buyers. Second, changes in the value chain are reflected in the bargaining power of workers. The first will be addressed in this chapter and the second in Chapter 7.

Predicated on the deregulation of trade, the underlying logic is as follows[5]:

1. Increase in the lead firm's DMP allows them to capture a higher share of value.

---

[4] Durand and Lege (2013: 4) state, 'In Marx's view, competitive pressure constrains individual capitalists to invest in order to adopt the more modern productive techniques that lead to an increasing capital intensity of production and then a tendency of the rate of profit to fall due to a rise in the organic composition of capital.'

[5] This specific formulation was devised by myself and Giorgos Galanis (2018).

2. As the share of value obtained by the lead firm increases, the source price falls placing increasing downward pressure on suppliers. The number of firms who are able to meet those price demands therefore shrinks.
3. As the number of competing supplier firms shrinks, DMP decreases in the global garment sector, which moves the GVC away from a buyer-driven state and towards a supplier-driven state, oscillating according to buyer–supplier symbiosis (or a symbiotic steady state).
4. As DMP decreases and the lead firm moves towards a perfect market steady state, the share of value it obtains becomes smaller.
5. This decrease in the share of value obtained by the lead firm constitutes a crisis of profitability which may lead, among other things, to:
   - An increase in the number of supply firms, which, in turn, increases DMP. A return to step 1.
   - An increase in vertical-integration by the supplier firm.
   - Direct investment in new 'fixes' – innovations in finance, technology, product, or organization that open new frontiers in profit-seeking – to steer out of the crisis (Silver 2003).[6]

Monopoly and monopsony in the GVC

So far as GVC analysis is concerned, monopsony and monopoly can be regarded as different sides of the same coin when it comes to the bargaining process. But it is important to take into account their different externalities. The externalities involved in increased monopolization of suppliers, for instance, allow us to understand the consolidation process and its effects.

A firm is said to have a monopoly when it is the sole seller of a good in a market. Similarly, an oligopoly is a market dominated by a *limited number* of sellers. A monopsony, however, is the inverse of a monopoly, meaning a market with a single buyer. And, oligopsony, by extension, is the inverse of an oligopoly, meaning a market with only a *limited number* of buyers. Here, I define the degree of monopoly as the relative degree of oligopoly in a market and the degree of monopsony as the relative degree of oligopsony in the value chain. Oligopoly and oligopsony both describe markets with imperfect competition, that is, a stark asymmetry in the balance between buyers and

---

[6] These are often combined, as in the establishment of new, technologically advanced supplier factories on new, low-wage ground, for example, in Ethiopia and Kenya.

sellers. It follows from this, of course, that the degree of monopoly (the ratio of sellers to buyers) in a market is the inverse of the degree of monopsony (the ratio of buyers to sellers). Changes in this ratio, however, may be accompanied by other effects.

In the case of GVCs, both monopoly and monopsony can be used for the study of value distributions between supply (sellers) and lead firms. The degree of monopsony or monopoly influences not the price but the share of value obtained by each type of firm in the bargaining process. For this reason, I refer to the relative bargaining power of the lead firm as its DMP and to the relative bargaining power of a supply firm as its degree of monopoly power.

I approach GVC typology as a spectrum which is, on the whole, buyer or producer driven. Because of this, I connect the degree of monopsony (or monopoly) power with certain GVC characteristics. For instance, GVCs are primarily buyer driven because of relatively low barriers to entry for sellers, and this produces a high DMP, advantaging buyers.

To avoid contradictions, it is important to distinguish between the bargaining process taken as a *static* balance of powers and as a *dynamic* rebalancing. In a static, 'snapshot' assessment, the degree of monopoly power possessed by seller firms is, as discussed, simply the inverse of the degree of the monopsony power possessed by lead firms. But this is not the case in medias res. An increase in a seller firm's degree of monopoly power means, *in concrete terms*, a consolidation of firms, and this produces more than an immediate and corresponding increase in bargaining power; it also leads to greater market share, and therefore higher profits, which can be invested in marketing, R&D, expansion, and other means of further augmenting profits. Because of this cascade of secondary effects, which under judicious management can be turned into positive feedback loops, growth (or decline) in the bargaining power of firms often proceeds in volatile fits and starts, in which the balance of power may suddenly shift after one or the other side has hit a 'tipping point' and picked up *momentum*.

Assume, for simplicity, that there are no costs for the lead firms. The total GVC value then is comprised of the lead firm's share, the supply firm's share, and the latter's costs. If we assume a constant value share for the lead firm, a decrease of costs, in this situation, necessarily leads to an increase in value share for the supply firm.

Global competition and GVC

Capitalism – our prevailing economic system, driven by profits and competition – has until now been only a faint and secondary presence in the GVC and GPN literature.[7] I aim to make it central.[8] Under capitalism, firms compete in order to capture the maximum possible portion of the total social product. This portion, the firm's 'maximized profits', is the highest revenue for the lowest cost. To achieve this, firms employ pricing strategies, marketing, R&D, and so on, to give them advantages over competitors. And it is through such competition that successful firms increase their share of the market and their profits. Cost-reduction is paramount, especially for labour-intensive garment suppliers, who rely almost exclusively on downward pressure on wages to lower costs, since the vertically disintegrated structure they inhabit prevents them from investing in technology and other means. And, given the limitations of that structure, the only ways they have to stretch their revenue–cost differentials (that is, their profits) from the other end (that is, their revenue) are through the intensification of labour or its extension. Because the garment sector subsists on influxes of high variable capital and low constant capital, the survival of firms in the market is wholly dependent on their ability to get more labour for less.

Competition exerts this pressure across the garment sector (horizontally), as well as down the value chain (vertically). In Marxian terms, the global buyer must outsource larger and larger portions of its chain while trying to control commodity production indirectly through the labour process (that is, by passing the burden of costs down the chain). However, these processes are neither monotonic nor unidirectional, since there are several variables always in play, including competition, the vagaries of profit, suppliers, and the pliability/agency of labour. Anwar Shaikh (2016), in theorizing on *real competition*, states:

> Competition within an industry compels individual producers to set prices that keep them in the game, just as it forces them to lower costs so that they can cut prices to compete effectively. [...] In this context, individual capitals make their decisions based on judgments about an intrinsically indeterminate future. Competition puts seller against seller, seller against buyer, buyer against buyer, capital against capital, capital against labour, and labour against labour. *Bellum omnium contra omnes.*

---

[7] For Marxian economics, the goal of capitalist production is the realization of 'value' and 'surplus-value', which is to say, the sale of commodities for prices above the cost of production, allowing the capitalist to accumulate profits. For the Keynesian, Kaleckian, and Post-Keynesian schools of economics, the concepts of 'markup' and 'profit margin' are utilized in reference to prices minus costs. Due to the limited scope of this book, I will be using the concept of value in the broadest sense.

[8] This section is influenced by the ongoing research on the role of competition in shaping GVCs conducted with Giorgos Galanis and Panagiotis Iliopoulos.

This state of perpetual competition is always remaking the composition of capital. And a close analysis of its dynamics can offer valuable insight into the evolutionary tendencies of capitalism and provide a theoretical foundation for analysis into the importance of spatial allocation of production and shop-floor-level labour negotiations. By pursuing this angle, I aim to enrich the GVC/GPN literature, which has heretofore concerned itself primarily with the 'technological characteristics of products and processes' (Gereffi, Humphrey, and Sturgeon 2005).

That being said, so far as competition and market power have figured in the GVC/GPN literature, it is important to take stock of them before advancing the discussion. Coe, Hess, and Dicken (2008) and Mahutga (2012, 2014), for example, take the measure of a firm's power by the height of the barriers to entry in its market. For the former, that power is a function of its possession and control of assets necessary to the production process. But for the latter, entry barriers are functions of the economy, having to do with economies of scale in production and distribution and the availability of alternative partners and suppliers. Oligopoly and oligopsony power are implied in Mahutga but are not explored. Similarly, Milberg and Winkler (2013), in their investigation of the 'new wave of globalisation', emphasize the lead firms' corporate strategies (cost-reduction, production flexibility, and coverage of local markets). They conclude that offshoring is a competitive strategy allowing lead firms to increase, on the one hand, their market power, captured by a Kaleckian markup, and, on the other, their monopsony power, by exploiting the *spatial flexibility* of the supply base and labour force.

What remains underdeveloped, however, is the conflictual nature of capitalism, which reaches peak expression through garment sector competition (while obviously rendering the labour theory of value). Scholarship has remained by and large beholden to the neoclassical concept of perfect competition that assumes competition is just a function of the number and size of price-taking firms. The alternative to this quantity view holds that competition is a turbulent process, the messy and haphazard reorganization of a market, as capitals merge and migrate, and rival firms strive unceasingly for greater market-share. This is the competition found in the classical tradition of Smith, Ricardo, Marx, and later in Schumpeter and a few others (Schumpeter 2010; Moudud, Bina, and Mason 2013; Shaikh 2016). For them, competition is a Darwinian struggle for greater and greater profits. It is the impetus behind efficient new technologies and the constant reorganization of production. Capitals wage war on two fronts: with each other, for higher surplus-value and larger market-share; and with labour, for more work and an even larger share of the proceeds (Selwyn 2012; Moudud 2013; Shaikh 2016).

The success of a firm under capitalism depends on its ability to compete and remain competitive. And competitiveness, in a market, often requires constant innovation, improving the means of selling or of producing. And the more competitive a firm becomes, the more power it accumulates. And the more power a firm accumulates, the more market share it can acquire from its horizontal competitors, which, in turn, enlarges the share of value it can capture from suppliers and labour, bringing down input-prices.

This capacity to acquire market share from horizontal competitors, and thereby capture greater value, is a firm's oligopoly power. *Oligopsony power*, on the other hand, is the capacity of a buyer-firm to capture more value from suppliers and labour through downward pressure on supplier margins (Steiner 2008) and/or the greater exploitation of labour. More oligopoly or oligopsony power may result in greater value capture and consequently greater control of the GVC governance structures. The firm with the greatest market power is, in GVC parlance, the lead firm, and drives the structural changes to the GCC/GVC/GPN. Other lesser capitals that are unable to compete at the same level will thus be made subordinate. This is the process by which competition remakes production systems within capitalism. In other words, governance structures evolve as well, in response to fluctuations in the balance of market power.

Bringing competition into industrial organization theory allows for a new formulation of power as the motor of market dynamics and, *through the process of competition*, ultimately, of changes in governance. The analysis of power in the value chain follows the logic of competition, between capital and capital (whose battlefield is the market) and between capital and labour (whose battlefield is the site of production). As discussed earlier, this process resolves into situations of either oligopoly or oligopsony power. In other words, oligopoly and oligopsony power are measures of a firm's ability to maximize profits. Inevitably, this leads to concentration, as argued by Mandel (1968: 38): 'Capitalism was born of free competition and is inconceivable without competition. But free competition produces concentration and concentration produces the opposite of free competition, namely, monopoly.'

From capitals to capital

In *Capital Vol. 1*, Marx (1867) briefly discusses his law of the Centralization of Capitals: 'it is concentration of capitals already formed, destruction of their individual independence, expropriation of capitalist by capitalist, transformation of many small capitals into a few large ones. [...] The laws of this centralization of capitals, or of the attraction of capital to capital [... are that] larger capitals beat the smaller. [...] Competition rages in direct proportion to the number, and in inverse proportion to the magnitude of the antagonistic capitals. It always ends in the ruin of many small capitalists, whose capitals partly pass into the hands of their conquerors, partly vanish.'

Marx maintained that the concentration of capital – that is, the progressive expropriation of the many bourgeois by the few – was an immutable law of capitalism. In the *Communist Manifesto*, Marx and Engels argued that this continuous expropriation results not in the preservation of property, but its eventual destruction. This phenomenon can be observed from early industrial capitalism, for example, coal mining in France and Belgium, on through the twentieth century, for example, the consolidation of the automobile industry in the US and England, where hundreds of firms that had sprung up in the late nineteenth century had been winnowed to fewer than 10 by the mid-twentieth century (Mandel 1968).

Marxists conceived monopoly capital, or the domination of a market by a single firm, as the inevitable result of competition. Baran and Sneezy, in their work *Monopoly Capital* (1966), expand on this claim by positing firms as 'the system's prime movers', and downplaying the role of state intervention. Firms' size and market power, and the consequent ability to prevail upon governments to fix the rules of the game (so the inmates run the asylum), ensure the devolution of markets into monopolies.

According to Bruce Norton (1983), capitalist firms are animated by a singular 'growth urge', which explains their behaviour when 'seeking to reinvest a fixed fraction of past profit income in physical capital stock' (Norton 1983: 2). Norton describes the firm as a self-determining and self-sustaining growth system, embodying the relationships between several variables – chief among them, saving and investment spending.

All was manifest to Marx, who observed this tendency a century and a half ago. Indeed, all that government restriction can do under capitalism is slow the process.[9] In other words, competition is a phase at best and a formality at worst, as capitals merge and centralize. In the garment sector, this phenomenon was amply illustrated by the consolidation that followed the MFA phase-out, which I will detail later. That the 'growth-urge' of capital achieves its final stage in entropy is one of capitalism's major internal contradictions, as formulated by Marx.[10]

---

[9] In some cases, regulation can hasten concentration, as smaller capitals cannot afford the added costs, and big capital supports these regulations for their effect of eliminating competitors.

[10] Marx argues that this is one of capitalism's great internal contradictions. Concentration in one link of the value chain is liable, of course, to produce a chain reaction going down

Other changes in the global economy – namely financialization and the advance of technology – have only hastened consolidation. Financialization, for one, put new emphasis on 'share value', which by itself can induce mergers and acquisitions (M&A) (Froud et al. 2000). Fold (2002) describes how the cocoa sector, for example, suddenly fell under the spell of share value, and larger cocoa firms quickly gobbled up their smaller competitors. Managers have become preoccupied with financial performance and cash management, leading them to target for M&A any company whose shares are deemed undervalued relative to asset values. As Coe and Yueng (2015: 40) state:

> As suppliers strive to reduce their cost-capability ratios and take on more value activity in lead firms' global production over time, they are inadvertently subject to the same ruthless financial discipline as their lead firm customers. To begin with, the sheer financial costs to suppliers increase exponentially when they upgrade from subcontractors to full package producers and contract manufacturers. Under the guise of supply chain rationalization, lead firms driven by financial considerations are included to source from fewer, but larger, suppliers in order to achieve greater economies of scale and lower unit purchase prices.

Large capital-holding firms now reinvest their surplus in labour-saving technology, transforming what Marx called the 'organic composition of capital' as labour-input falls, freeing up additional funds for marketing, R&D, and other means of increasing market share (that is, more of what was 'variable capital' can be converted into 'constant capital' or, in this case, primarily its subset 'fixed capital'). This effectively raises the market barriers to entry and, in GVC terms, reduces the DMP of the value chain since fewer firms can compete.

Another distinction, however, must be made between short- and long-term capitalist development. Although business cycles ebb and flow, long-term

---

the length of the GVC (Ghemawat 1990). The supremacy of Google among search engines, for example, led to Marriott Hotels buying Starwood as well as the acquisition of two rivals by online travel site Expedia in 2012 and 2015. Adrian Wooldridge (2006) has predicted 'the rise of superstars', a small group of giant companies (some old, some new) that are once again going to dominate the global economy, through a surge of M&As, eventuating in a small group of individuals owning the majority of the world's wealth. 'The McKinsey Global Institute, the consultancy's research arm, calculates that 10% of the world's public companies generate 80% of all profits. Firms with more than $1 billion in annual revenue account for nearly 60% of the total global revenues and 65% of market capitalization' (Wooldridge 2006).

development demonstrates what Marx called the tendency of the rate of profit to fall, as the portion of constant capital employed by firms rises relative to variable capital, the ultimate source of value. As Marx predicts in the *Grundrisse*, capitalism will increasingly come to rely on 'dead labour' (technology and so on) and less and less on 'living labour' (workers).

Mandel (1968: 37) explains how the organic composition of capital affects concentration by erecting higher barriers to entry: 'The greater the organic composition of capital in an industrial branch, the greater is the concentration of capital, and conversely, the smaller the organic composition of capital the smaller the concentration of capital.' Mandel continues: 'Why? Because the smaller the organic composition of capital, the less capital is required at the beginning in order to enter this branch and establish a new venture. It is far easier to put together the million or two million dollars necessary for building a new textile plant than to assemble the hundreds of millions needed to set up even relatively small steel works.'

The monopolization of manufacturing is a self-sustaining process whereby consolidation contributes to automation and automation contributes to consolidation. This can be observed recently at each stage of the GVC, from the cotton field to the retail rack. This is most evident – though it is a late arrival – in some of the garment and footwear producers (outlined herein in this volume), though workers in those parts of garment manufacturing most susceptible to valorization have seen their capital–labour ratio change. Marx argued that competition makes firms strive for efficiency, leading to continual advancements in labour-saving technology, a process that is accelerated by consolidation. This is true for most sectors where we find that the capital–labour ratio has grown steadily, especially during periods of extensive consolidation, like the 1990s. While the capital–labour ratio remained steady between 2000 and 2008, it began to grow around 2012. Moody (2017: 56) observes that 'competition was engendering not only mergers but increased capital accumulation and technology as well'. Indeed, competition, consolidation, and automation work in harmony. Moody notes that 'merger movement related investment has made a difference in the overall size of manufacturing firms [which] can be seen in how those corporations with assets value over $1 billion rose from 71% of total assets in 1990 to 87% in 2010'.

Consolidation and the GVC

Even if sometimes faintly, Marx's theory of monopoly capital can still be detected in the current GCC/GVC/GPN discourse. Though rarely mentioned specifically, it does figure, for instance, in the theoretical lineage of Hopkins and Wallerstein (1994), via the foundational work of Gereffi and Korzeniewicz (1994), who coined the GCC, and argued that 'monopoly and competition are key to understanding the distribution of wealth among the nodes in a commodity chain' (Gereffi and Korzeniewicz 1994: 2). In their work, the differential power of firms across the value chain depends on the 'capacity of some capitals to generate barriers to entry, which is in turn premised on their relative monopoly over some strategic "scarce asset", that is, one which expresses the capacity to actively participate in the development of the forces of production' (Starosta 2010: 440). An asset's scarcity is therefore relative: a function of entry barriers.

Hymer's microeconomic studies analysed the role of specific factories in helping firms obtain monopolistic advantages. What distinguished these particularly successful factories, he concluded, were the possession of superior technologies, scale, product differentiation, distribution networks, and privileged access to finance. Theories of monopoly capitalism have been heavily influenced by industrial economics and the structure–conduct–performance (SCP) paradigm. And according to SCP, profitability depends heavily on concentration. Conventional economics describes competition and monopoly as opposite ends of a spectrum, so that an increase in competition results in a decrease in monopoly (Sawyer 1988). What this view regards as 'atomistic' competition is, I assert, more accurately interpreted as a DMP, since the phenomenon described is specific to the inter-firm bargaining process between buyers and suppliers. DMP provides a useful framework for understanding the GVC's natural dynamism, while placing competitive states within a more coherent spectrum split between 'buyer' and 'producer' driven chains – that is, those possessing monopsony or monopoly, respectively.

Michal Kalecki (1971), who in the 1930s wrote that economies were by nature oligopolistic/monopolistic rather than competitive, has been a critical influence on the understanding of the relationship between vertical competition (what I call degree of monopsony power [DMP]) and monopoly. As Sawyer (1988: 52) remarked, 'It is of some significance that [Kalecki] talked of the degree of monopoly rather than the degree of competition for the one sense that they could be used interchangeably (negatively related of course). But such a usage does focus on monopoly rather than on competition, and also suggests a counterposing of competition and monopoly.'

The formulation of DMP in the GVC draws inspiration from Robinson's (1969) concept of labour market monopsony and from Kalecki's (1971) 'degree of monopoly'. In Kalecki (1971), a firm's degree of monopoly is determined by institutional factors, such as industrial concentration and trade union strength, and affects the markup that can be added to costs (both fixed and variable). That markup then affects the share of revenue given to workers as pay.[11]

Degree of monopoly can also be read, of course, as degree of concentration, and understood as a virtual oligopoly by a few firms accumulating larger and larger surpluses (in both absolute and relative terms), while growing their market share. The shuttering of small- and medium-sized firms thus signals the conquest of a market by larger firms. Kalecki (1954), however, argues that this growth begins to abate in its later stages, when there are fewer avenues left for innovation. What we see in the garment sector is a fall in the DMP and an increase in the degree of monopoly among supplier firms, demonstrating how 'filling up a space' in capitalism restricts mobility, as highlighted by Sawyer (1988: 51): 'First, the growth of scale of firms means that structural oligopoly/monopoly has emerged. Second, there are increasing restrictions on the mobility of capital. Both of these would point the direction of a move away from competition in the Marxian sense.'

In the era of globalization, 'strategic alliances' have emerged as an alternative strategy, but M&As remain the primary means for obtaining market power. According to Merced and Cane (2011) in the *New York Times*, 'Global dollar volume in announced mergers and acquisitions rose 23.1% in 2010 to $2.4 trillion.' Worldwide M&A activity more than doubled from 2002 to 2007, before the global financial crisis. But American firms have since begun another round of blockbuster mergers – some $10 trillion worth. And though the US still accounts for 34 per cent of global deal volume, the biggest trend in M&As in 2010 was the growth in emerging markets, particularly in the Asia-Pacific region, where deal volume jumped 43.5 per cent according to Merced and Cane (Kopf, Vehorn, and Carnevale 2013). Foster, McChesney, and Jonna (2011) remark, 'Wherever one looks, it seems that nearly every industry is concentrated into fewer and fewer hands.' They observe that once competitive sectors like retail are now controlled by 'enormous monopolistic chains [...] and the new firms and industries spawned by the digital revolution have quickly gravitated to monopoly status. In short, monopoly power is ascendant as never before'.

The recent work by Moody (2017: 57) agrees with this conclusion that the wave of consolidation is an outgrowth of crisis. However, he offers a different explanation. Moody believes that the emerging trend of consolidation is not 'monopoly capital' as it is articulated by neoclassical quantity theory (competition

---

[11] The term 'monopsony capitalism' is used by Joel Magnuson (2008) in *Mindful Economics* to describe the power of Walmart. However, I arrived at the term independently.

in which fewer capitals compete less). He states that, in fact, 'concentration and centralization are functions of competition, the effort to capture more profit by capturing more market share – in this case partly by absorbing the competition as well as increasing fixed capital'. Indeed, this 'battle of competition', Moody maintains, 'pushes each firm to compete more effectively by increasing the productive force of labour as much as possible. Competing firms, in effect, leapfrog as each attempts to become more efficient through the application of still more capital, and the competition tends to increase the intensity as the stakes grow greater.'

There is definite sense in Moody's (2017: 58) thesis that 'competition, consolidation or centralization, and the push for greater productivity' are central to the survival of contemporary capitalism. However, he argues that engineered depression (that is, the Volcker Shock, 1981–82) helped to break up large vertically integrated conglomerate firms, causing them to spin off inefficient non-core units to focus on core competencies. For a time, this increased competition.[12] The garment sector remains unaffected by these specific interventions since the growth of larger, consolidated firms, is a more recent phenomenon. Indeed, it was trade liberalization that resulted in a fall in DMP, fundamentally altering the bargaining power of different actors along the value chain, particularly the suppliers and supplier labour (more on that in Chapter 7). Just as many workers competing for few jobs in unregulated labour markets push their wages down, so too does downward pressure in an unregulated high DMP environment result in falling source prices.

It follows from the logic laid out above that a fall in the sourcing prices of buyers results in the disappearance of uncompetitive firms and the consolidation of big firms into even bigger firms. This is an 'organizational fix', or an integration of once exogenous phases into the value chain (which also places certain limits on the 'spatial fix'). Consolidation, therefore, produces two chief effects. The first is an increase in DMP through a reduction in the number of supplier firms, and the second is that consolidated firms are able – through improved coordination and the pooling of resources – to achieve a reduction in production costs.

---

[12] Similar arguments can be found in Christophers (2016) in which the state and law function to level out historical imbalances in a 'monopoly–competition dialectic'. Let us call this a kind of 'legal fix', a legislative mechanism to encourage and discourage monopolies and competition to absorb capitalism's inherent drive towards monopoly. However, it is difficult to imagine this 'fix' in the context of the global supply chain, given the principally transnational dimensions of monopsony capitalism.

The rise of consolidated firms in the global garment sector has a material basis in the logic of capital itself. In the 'buyer-driven' sector, supplier firms (and the nation-states they occupy) are under constant downward pressure by global buyers to cut costs, produce greater volumes of goods at quicker intervals, to stock less inventory, ensure labour discipline, and so on. After some time, this thins the herd, leaving a smaller number of firms to absorb the production capacity. Consolidation is not therefore anomalous, but structural. It shortens the time of production, circulation, and distribution. In recent decades, firms associated with the 'developing world' have become adept at generating 'value-added' activities across the value chain. In describing what they call the 'cascade effect', Nolan, Zhang, and Liu (2008) argue that, since the 1980s, there has been a growing concentration across the value chain through the merger of non-core activities brought about by the intense downward pressure of large buyers. They (2008: 45) explain that 'at every level there has taken place an intense process of industrial concentration, mainly through merger and acquisition, as firms struggle to meet the strict requirements that are the condition of their participation in the system integrators' supply chains'.

Drawing closer to GVC literature, Gereffi (2014: 14–15) observes, 'Today, we are entering a very different era. [...] Consolidation was growing at both the country and supply chain levels in a number of hallmark global industries, such as apparel.' The growth of oligopolistic firms at either end of the value chain results in what I call buyer–producer symbiosis or a symbiotic steady state. Simply put, this is a 'symbiotic' power relationship in the garment or footwear industry that develops between large transnational buyers and large transnational producers – an effect of consolidation that limits the use of spatial fixes in disintegrated (historically) high DMP sectors. Symbiosis leads to a fall in the lead firm's value share accompanied by innovative new 'fixes' for the crisis. GVCs are fluid formations, and just as 'the increase[ed] disaggregation of value chains [...] allow[s] new kinds of lead firms to capture value' (Pickles and Smith 2016: 25), the consolidation of supplier-end capitals allows new kinds of supplier firms to capture value.

Buyer–producer symbiosis, however, is more than a simple transactional relationship; rather, it resembles one-half of Gereffi's (1994: 95) formulation, 'show[ing] how "big buyers" have shaped the production networks in the world's most dynamic exporting countries, especially in the newly industrialised countries of East Asia'. Per Starosta (2010: 437), 'The concept of governance was originally devised to depict the diversity of authority and power relationships that give overall coordination to the division of labour within the commodity chain.' In this light, the introduction of 'symbiosis' is an addition to the taxonomy of power relationships, emerging out of giant capitals on either side of historically low DMP GVCs.

Take the global footwear industry, which is the focus of Chapter 3. Footwear is an object lesson in these long-term trends because it was the sole clothing industry not encumbered by the MFA. The relatively untrammelled growth and globalization of footwear production resulted in greater oligopoly of buyers. They were able to accomplish this because they had highly monopsonistic relationships with manufacturers in markets with low barriers to entry (Schmitz and Knorringa 2000).

Eventually, competition compelled smaller manufacturers to consolidate. This caused a fall in DMP, producing an increase in share-value for manufacturers and giving them more weight in negotiations with buyers. Fast forward to the present day, Adidas and Nike, who together control over 50 per cent of the world market for sport and casual shoes (Merk 2008), have announced that they will be opening fully automated production facilities in Germany, France, the US, and the UK (Manthrope 2017). This can be read as a response to a symbiosis in the footwear industry that has created a crisis in profitability and left the major brands exposed.

An October 2017 *Financial Times* article ('Nike's Focus on Robotics Threatens Asia's Low-cost Workforce' – Bissell-Linsk 2017) described how accelerating automation in footwear production has put developing countries at risk of losing their manufacturing bases. Nike, in particular, has been automating an increasing number of tasks, such as laser-cutting and glueing, due to growing production costs in Asia. Sridhar Tayur, a professor at Carnegie Mellon University, explains, 'The very-low labour costs in Asia are no longer that low [and] the pressure has been mounting for a long time to either move to a super low-cost place or to automate more' (Bissell-Linsk 2017). That the company is working exclusively with Flex, the highly automated manufacturer of Fitbit, illustrates the falling monopsonism in the footwear value chain. Chris Collier, Flex's chief financial officer, confirms, 'Together [Flex and Nike] are modernizing the footwear industry,' and that 'this is a long-term, multibillion-dollar relationship for us, [that] is not measured in the scope of years but decades'. In the same article, analyst Jim Suva asserts, 'We believe the apparel industry is likely to watch this closely. And if it is successful, we could see more room [for automation] to come.' In the future, changing economic geographies, combined with the apparel industry GVC's trend towards symbiosis, may result in the spread of similar technological fixes elsewhere.

Value chain power asymmetry

Firms compete on two fronts: horizontally, with other capitals in the same market, and vertically, with suppliers and buyers. Every link between the two ends of the value chain expresses a market relationship corresponding to its position, and the more profitable firms accumulate either oligopoly or oligopsony power.

It follows that every exchange between firms at different levels of production is a confrontation between a seller, embodying a given oligopoly power, and a buyer, embodying a given oligopsony power. Each firm tries to leverage its respective power to capture more value from the exchange, and the result is an agreed-upon price for the good or service in question. The difference between the oligopoly power of sellers and the oligopsony power of buyers can be read as vertical power asymmetry and distinguished from the power asymmetry emerging from horizontal power asymmetry, between firms in the same market.

Firms with greater market power tend to capture more value from their partners, both backwards (suppliers) and forwards (customers). A large and powerful buyer (brands or retailers), for example, will have greater oligopsony power relative to a group of small and geographically dispersed suppliers. The vertical power asymmetry differential will, therefore, be high, meaning the buyer can capture more value from exchanges with the suppliers. Meanwhile, suppliers, which are also capitalist firms, producing goods and services for profit, are still competing horizontally with one another for market share (that is, to capture value upstream). The opposite forces apply to manufacturers/suppliers with greater market power (for example, automakers). If the supplier is more powerful than the buyers, it will be able to exert oligopoly power and set higher prices, capturing more value from every transaction with buyers. Vertical and horizontal market pressures will determine how the most competitive/powerful firms (the lead firms in GCC/GVC) eventually remake governance structures.

The long-term corporate strategies of lead firms are forged by competition, which determines the technological and geographic organization of production (outsourcing, for instance, is the effect of buyer compulsion to find ever cheaper suppliers). Similarly, competition drives suppliers to develop their own corporate strategies that capture more value upstream, downstream (from buyers), and at the site of production (from technology, labour, and so on). What shakes out is a series of inter-firm vertical power asymmetries.

There are numerous examples from the GCC/GVC/GPN literature, which illustrate this conception of competitive dynamics and their shaping of governance structures in global capitalism. In the preceding chapters, I have shown that the garment sector is the archetypal buyer-driven chain, dominated by brands and retailers exercising monopsonistic power over numerous small suppliers, usually in low-cost developing economies. The garment sector has experienced significant changes since the MFA expired in 2005. Trade has liberalized, giving large retailers the 'spatial flexibility' they need to shift production en masse to the cheapest, smallest, and weakest suppliers available, significantly altering the value distribution. In turn, monopsonistic pressure on those suppliers (to reduce costs, decrease production time, ensure labour discipline, and so on) has endangered less competitive suppliers, leading them to consolidate or die off. The result is a turnabout; the merged suppliers have acquired oligopoly power and made themselves indispensable (Galanis and Kumar 2018).

But this process is by no means unique to the garment and footwear sectors.[13] The early US automotive industry, for instance, saw Ford pitting its product line against that of General Motors (GM), resulting in the quick depletion of fixed capital investments, and an eventual spending shift towards 'advertising, brand-name identification, distribution and financing' (Schoenberger 1994). The appearance on the international market of Japanese automakers, however, challenged the oligopolistic stability of Ford and GM, confronting them with more competitive pricing, and forcing a relocation of production to Portugal, Spain, and Latin America (Schoenberger 1994). And so, the 'globalization of markets' begets the 'globalization of production' and spurs 'excellence in governing spatially dispersed networks of plants, affiliates and suppliers' (Sturgeon and Florida 2000). In response, the mass of struggling suppliers in the new, lower-rent locales extend their spatial capabilities, merge with one another, and integrate *vertically* with second-tier suppliers (Sturgeon and Florida 2000). And since the Japanese went global, yet another generation of automakers has emerged fully formed from domestic markets to compete on the world stage – this time from China and India. The likes of India's Tata Motors and China's Geely have made their presence felt in the international market with aggressive business and marketing strategies, including the acquisition of European and American supply bases and brand names such as Jaguar Land Rover (Tata) and Volvo (Geely).

Also notable in this respect is the US electronics sector (personal computers, data management, and telecommunications), which faced similar international competition from Asia. Many large, hierarchically organized multinationals found themselves on the wrong side of history when cheap electronics flooded international markets in the 1970s and 1980s. Production was eventually

---

[13] Contemporary trucking and airline sectors, for instance, following deregulation witnessed a reduction in market concentration, and an increase in new firms. But this trend reversed quickly after a rapid succession of mergers, acquisitions, and bankruptcies that led to the growth of oligopolies.

reorganized and transformed into a modular network, with various activities outsourced to technologically competent suppliers (Sturgeon 2002).

Degree of monopsony power in the GVC

The centrality of the DMP in GVCs, which I helped formulate with Giorgos Galanis (Galanis and Kumar 2018),[14] is important to understanding how value chains operate. Monopsony, according to Robinson (1969), is a market with multiple sellers and a single buyer, or, in labour market terms, a single firm and more workers than are needed. Here, instead of a single firm and many workers, I consider a single lead firm and many supply firms.

Beggars cannot be choosers in the market, and suppliers competing for orders from buyers in a situation of DMP must be willing to reduce their prices. In Kalecki (1971), a firm's degree of monopoly determines the markup allowable for costs (both fixed and variable). That markup then affects how income is divvied up between workers and capitalists. As explained earlier, DMP affects the value share obtained by lead firms for given output prices.

Imagine you are an Indian or a Cambodian capitalist who wants to establish an export-oriented garment factory with relatively little start-up capital. Your first major expenditure would be a decrepit facility (for which the state has generously kicked in funds) in an export processing zone on the outskirts of a city (which has its own assortment of tax and cost benefits). Your next expenditure is on rudimentary machines for sewing, knitting, cutting, and pressing. Piece of cake, so far: your costs are a fraction of what you would have needed for an automotive factory. A high DMP confers the ability to enter GVCs with minimal capital investment, giving brands outsized power. And the stronger brands are, the more is the pressure felt by suppliers. Just as an employer benefits from operating in a deregulated environment with a large reserve army of labour, so too does the buyer from thousands of hungry suppliers competing for its business (Cook 1977; Porter 2008). Eventually, the stronger suppliers absorb the weaker. This causes monopsony to fall, leveling the playing field as the surviving suppliers use their new resources to evolve (technologically, organizationally, and so on) and raise the barriers to market entry, entrenching their position. If you got in on the

---

[14] My work with Giorgos Galanis attempts to bridge these two approaches using the same Post-Keynesian literature which has lately been enriching economic geography (Galanis and Kumar 2018). For examples, see Milberg and Winkler (2013); Onaran and Galanis (2014); Stockhammer, Durand, and Ludwig (2016); and Stockhammer (2017).

ground floor and climbed to the top, you are sitting pretty. Increased market share means you are able to capture more value than ever from transactions with buyers, and higher entry barriers mean you have effectively pulled the ladder up.

It is hard to deny that a multitude of suppliers competing for the interest of a few buyers are at great disadvantage, at least for a time, and this understanding colours much of the GVC literature. Monopsony has frequently been invoked in this sense, either explicitly or implicitly (Abernathy et al. 1999; Milberg and Winkler 2013; Anner 2015; Azarhoushang et al. 2015; Nathan, Saripalle, and Guranathan 2016; Mayer and Phillips 2017).

Nathan and Kalpana (2007) articulate that the dominant asymmetry in early globalization of the oligopolistic buyers in monopsonistic value chains 'leads to a corresponding asymmetry in bargaining power. Lead firms are able to utilise their buying power to beat down suppliers' prices'. This is supported by Mayer and Phillips (2017) and Milberg and Winkler (2013), who show that growing monopolistic buyers leads to greater monopsony, and greater power, in the value chain. These are all critical factors shaping the GVC, particularly, upgrading (the 'technological fix'), which cannot be delinked from consolidation (the 'organizational fix') as necessary to raising barriers to entry and affecting a larger shift in power between buyers and suppliers.[15] In light of this, one must consider DMP as essential to value share and power in the GVC. The original Gereffi binary illustrated how buyers control value chains but featured DMP only by way of implication – thus downplaying its significance as the mechanism by which buyer-driven GVCs give way to 'symbiotic' relationships between oligopolistic buyers and increasingly oligopolistic suppliers. Degree of monopsony power does this by indirectly compelling the consolidation of suppliers, which reduces the absolute number of suppliers while increasing the relative power of each remaining supplier.[16]

---

[15] Silver (2001) sees organizational and technological 'fixes' as one and the same, combining them into a 'technological–organizational fix'.

[16] This emergence of an 'organizational fix', an integration of once exogenous phases in the value chain, and the growth of large capital-holding firms at both production and brand/retail ends result in competition between 'fractions of capital' and weakening the hegemony of capital in its antagonism with labour (Mezzedra and Neilson 2013). A combination of the geographic limits of the state, alongside an emergence of a multipolar economic landscape of power, positions the developmental states as a mediator between the dominant 'fraction' of transnational brands and 'comprador' domestic suppliers to meld a 'total' capital. Thus, such fractions in capital and distribution of value within the supply chain may provide an additional advantage for workers bargaining at the point of commodity production.

More concretely, monopsony power is the capacity for lead firms to extract a higher value than in a 'perfectly competitive' market. DMP encapsulates this connection. Where DMP is low, lead firms tend to retain direct control over capital-intensive phases of the GVC, while subcontracting out more labour-intensive functions to hierarchical suppliers managed by the lead firm.

The MFA and GVC dynamics

The most significant event in recent garment sector history has been the expiration of the MFA, whose phase-out ended place-based restrictions on production, leading to changes in industry composition, trade, and employment patterns. Initially established with the backing of Global North garment and textile unions to check the globalization of garment and textile sectors with a regulatory apparatus, the MFA introduced a quota system which ultimately did not staunch production outflow so much as spread it more thinly (among some 200 plus countries). Over the course of its 30-year existence, the MFA was renegotiated four times, and had mutated in the process, before being replaced by the 1995 Agreement on Textiles and Clothing (ATC), which marked a transition period, drawing down regulations until full phase-out in 2005 (Dunford et al. 2016). While the MFA and ATC were still in effect, many developing countries had lobbied for their annulment, to open unabated flows of capital. But eventually, those same countries realized that China's advantages in infrastructure and labour costs would draw the bulk of post-MFA relocations, and so began calling for its extension (Loong-Yu 2005).

The end of the MFA/ATC quota system on 1 January 2005 inaugurated a new era of intense competition and price pressure (Frederick and Staritz 2012). With a freer hand now, global brands shifted production away from many small countries and into a few large ones – and, as feared, China absorbed the bulk of the relocation. The US and the EU attempted to reverse this windfall by invoking the protectionist clause in China's WTO agreement, but only after the sabre-rattling had settled could they extract another agreement – with the EU but not the US – extending quotas through 2007 (Loong-Yu 2005).

GVCs must be understood as operating under governance structures that evolve in tandem with the shifts in the balance of market power, especially in the garment sector (this fact has been fleshed out empirically through the course of this book). As mentioned earlier, the mid-1990s were the beginning of the end for the MFA. Signed in 1974, it had established import quotas for garments and textiles produced in the Global South and, during its existence, provided one of the few checks on the globalization of garment and textile sectors.

The MFA period witnessed a mass exercise of what David Harvey (2006a) calls the 'spatial fix', whereby firms (and/or capitalism) try to resolve crisis of profitability through geographic reconfigurations – that is, by removing production to cheaper locales. The spatial fix under the MFA's quota system, however, led to much more diffuse and far-flung migration. In Chapter 7, I introduce and explain the concept of *spatial inflexibility* in relation to labour agency, which partly builds on this theory. And, as in Harvey (2006a), production, reproduction, and the reconfiguration of space are front and centre in my analysis of GVC structure and its relation to political economy writ large.

Despite the strictures imposed by the MFA, buyers were nevertheless able to deploy spatial fixes and draw increased value to the top of the chain. And as the MFA era came to a close, the power gap between buyers and suppliers only widened. Anner, Bair, and Blasi (2012: 7) noted that international apparel prices dropped as the MFA phased out (1995–2005).

> The drop in the price paid per square meter of imported apparel coincides with the phase out of the MFA, which began in 1995. A part of the decline can be attributed to a shift away from suppliers located in relatively higher paying countries (e.g. Mexico and the Dominican Republic), to countries with much lower labour costs (e.g. China, Vietnam) whose exports to the U.S. had been quota-constrained. Yet, it also reflects a growing concentration of retailer power vis-a-vis suppliers, where, as a result of monopsonistic supply chain structures, retailers and major brand manufacturers are increasingly able to squeeze lower prices from their ranks of global suppliers.

They link this phenomenon to two factors coinciding with the end of the MFA. First, freed from quotas, buyers began shifting production from regions with relatively high labour costs (that is, Mexico and Central America) towards those with lower labour costs (that is, China and Southeast Asia). Second, this migration was made possible by the 'growing concentration of retailer power vis-a-vis suppliers, where, as a result of monopsonistic supply chain structures, retailers and major brand manufacturers [were] increasingly able to squeeze lower prices from their ranks of global suppliers.' QED: lifting trade restrictions on trade increases DMP and, in consequence, value share for buyers. Frederick and Staritz (2012) concur, showing that the MFA added indirect costs to quota-constrained countries like China, because the quota required them to 'purchase' the rights to another country's allocation.

The work of Feenstra (1998) supports the centrality of DMP as well by highlighting the parallel between the 'disintegration of production' in the international economy and the 'integration of trade'. Gereffi, Humphrey, and

Sturgeon (2005: 80) observe too that 'the rising integration of world markets through trade has brought with it a disintegration of multinational firms, since companies are finding it advantageous to "outsource" an increasing share of their non-core manufacturing and service activities both domestically and abroad'. Frederick and Straritz (2012: 58) find that the post-MFA era is one of accelerated consolidation, in which buyers are using their newfound power (that is, increased DMP) to now demand that manufacturers also develop and design products, in addition to handling inventory management, stock holding, logistics, and financing: 'The objective of buyers to concentrate on their core competencies and reduce the complexity of their supply chains has [only grown in significance].'

The rapid and widespread consolidation following the MFA is acknowledged throughout the literature. Gereffi (2013: 16), for example, states that

> one noteworthy consequence of global consolidation is the growth of big GVC producers and intermediaries, which tend to offset to some degree the power of global buyers. [...] Especially after the termination of the Multi-Fibre Arrangement (MFA) for apparel in 2005, and giant contract manufacturers and traders (such as Foxconn in electronics, Yue Yuen in footwear and Li & Fung in apparel) have considerable clout. India and Brazil have also generated their own manufacturing multinationals, such as Tata and Embraer.

Frederick and Staritz (2012: 57) also describe how the MFA's end and the greater choice it afforded buyers, resulting – after a competitive shakeout, following the GVC dynamics described above – in a focus on larger, consolidated suppliers:

> Buyers have had a greater choice after the MFA phaseout, and sourcing decisions have focused on the most competitive suppliers who offer consistent quality, reliable delivery, large scale procession, flexibility, and competitive prices. Thus, manufacturing requirements have increased and become more sophisticated. Buyers have also been striving toward more cost-effective forms of supply chain management and to reduce the complexity of their supply chains; hence they tend to focus on large and more capable preferred suppliers, with whom they develop strategic partnerships. This trend has led to a consolidation of the supply chain, reducing the number of supplier countries and firms within countries.

Post-MFA merger-mania has touched every segment of the garment GVC, and even spread to adjacent sectors. 'In summary,' Gereffi (2014) remarks, 'concentration is growing across different segments of GVCs, and this co-evolution of concentrated actors appears to have two main implications for GVC governance in at least some cases, a shift of bargaining power toward large domestic producers vis-a-vis global buyers; and an affinity between geographic concentration in large emerging economies such as China and India and organizational consolidation in GVCs.'

By the mid to late 2000s, DMP had peaked. Source prices had fallen and fewer and fewer suppliers were able to compete. What survived was a coterie of powerful mega-producers in labour-rich countries (Appelbaum 2008; Lopez-Acevedo et al. 2012; Azmeh and Nadvi 2014; Merk 2014), which had developed increasingly symbiotic relationships with large retailer/brand oligopolies.

For all intents and purposes, the metastatic growth of firms is an inherent feature of capitalism. As Hymer (1976: 441) notes, 'Since the beginning of the industrial revolution there has been a steady increase in the size of manufacturing firms, so persistent that it might be formulated as a general law of capital accumulation.' But that growth, however, hit a ceiling in the Global North during the 1970s, engendering a series of spatial fixes, and a relentless 'race to the bottom' for global manufacturing. My schema holds that the globalization of production increases DMP, giving buyers a greater value share, who, in turn, apply more pressure on producers. That pressure reduces the number of suppliers able to compete, thereby decreasing DMP and putting the breaks on the race to the bottom.

Indeed, in the current era, people like Fernandez, Frederick, and Gereffi (2011: 19) are questioning the continuing usefulness of the race to the bottom: 'In today's post-MFA environment, apparel firms in developing countries need to seek out new sources of competitive advantage to support their growth. Long-term viability of the "race to the bottom" sourcing strategy in the current global context is questionable and indeed industry experts note that firms are now looking for alternative sources of competitiveness.'

Merk (2014: 263) outlines how global brands started buying from fewer suppliers in fewer countries to reduce costs associated with logistics, warehousing, and turnover time. China, the biggest beneficiary of the MFA phase-out, grew its garment export market share from 16 per cent in 2000 to 40 per cent in 2012 (Russell 2014). Consequently, trends in the value chain began to change.

Garment sector consolidation

The deregulation that made globalization possible was motivated in part by the desire of buyers to intensify competition among suppliers while enlarging the available pool of firms. But the ensuing battle royale wound down as suppliers consolidated. The repetitive nature of this phenomenon (the continuous moulting of capitalism) is perceived as periodic 'waves' of consolidation (via M&As).

Historically, in the US there have been six major waves, the most recent of which began in 2003 and is ongoing. Each successive wave is an attempt by capital to remedy, or 'fix', a profitability crisis (Moody 2017). In the garment sector, the spatial and technological/organizational fixes are inversely related, so far as the limits for one are the opportunities for the other. In the waning years of the MFA era, and after, those firms that have survived competition have done so by increasing their size and productivity.

In the wake of the economic crisis during the early 1970s, capital, as it so often did, exploited the chaos to initiate a deregulatory response – neoliberalism – one of whose chief goals was the reorientation of Global South policies of import-substitution investment (ISI) towards export-oriented industrialization (EOI). A growing consensus asserted that EOI was necessary for the development of the underdeveloped countries in Latin America and later Asia that lacked the internal markets to support a robust ISI programme. Over time, a rising tide would lift all boats. And, to an extent, this did accelerate development. However, that acceleration, after the MFA and the 2008 crisis, was confined to China, India, and other larger emerging economies once production consolidated (Gereffi 2014).

The germ of concentration, of course, is in competition itself and it has grown steadily as globalization and deregulation have intensified competition, and have swept up more and more industries, including garments. The opening up of China, the liberalization of India, and the fall of the Iron Curtain have all hastened this process, including the eventual concentration of production in a handful of labour-rich countries. Gereffi (2014: 15) explains that 'this influenced the globalisation process, as GVCs began to concentrate in these giant countries that offered seemingly exhaustible pools of low-wage workers, capable manufacturers, abundant raw materials and sizable domestic markets. Thus, China became the "factory of the world", India the world's "back office". Brazil had a wealth of agricultural commodities, and Russia possessed enormous reserves of natural resources plus the military technologies linked to its role as a Cold War superpower'. Concentration would get additional boosts after 2000, with the rise of domestic consumer markets in emerging economies, and after 2008, with the decline in Global North exports. During this period, Gereffi (2014: 16) discerns 'explicit efforts of GVC lead firms to rationalise their supply chains in order to deal with a smaller number of highly capable and strategically located suppliers'.

Global South suppliers, who once piggybacked on transnational capital, have themselves now begun to operate as giant contractors and lead firms in GVC coordination. And so, the efforts of brands to reduce costs and consolidate control over GVCs have been their own undoing. As per Marx, 'Offshoots split off from the original capitals and start to function as new and independent capitals. [...] With the accumulation of capital, therefore, the number of capitalists grows.'

Gereffi (2014) connects the consolidation of production within a few countries to the consolidation of suppliers. The correlation, he argues, is caused by the concentration across the entire GVC, from suppliers to intermediates to buyers. Eager to reduce transaction and monitoring costs, buyers ask themselves, 'How can we "rationalise" our supply chains from 300–500 suppliers to 25–30 suppliers?' (Gereffi 2014: 15), and inevitably begin working with fewer and larger suppliers. In the similar vein, Yeung (2007) uses the example of the electronics sector to argue for the emergence of an organizational, as opposed to spatial, fix within labour-intensive GVCs, driven by and for lead firms. This strategic 'choice' analysis, however, has been criticized as 'presuppos[ing] that all other capitals do not have the power to contest that organizational leadership and will therefore have no choice but submissively to accept to valorise at a lower rate of profit' (Starosta 2010: 440).

Gereffi's work, therefore, supports my own contention that a fall in buyer source prices hastened the consolidation of manufacturers. However, again, this phenomenon is not a top-down decision made by buyers; rather, it is simply how market competition shakes out. To reiterate, a GVC buyer's DMP to a large extent determines the share of value within its reach. And a rise in DMP allows buyers to exert more pressure on producers, producing a positive feedback loop. Conversely, when DMP falls, the GVC becomes more 'producer-driven'. And consolidation accelerates.

However, both I and the 'rationalist' consolidation theorists understand that M&As are part of a larger developmental process. Mega-suppliers, for instance, are beneficiaries of the Global South's 'rising power' (Nadvi 2014). Their growth reflects a global transformation of the economy. Horner and Nadvi (2017) identify three factors behind this change. First, nearly half of global manufacturing is now sourced from the Global South. Second, the Global South's internal markets accounted for 32 per cent of global consumption in 2010 and are estimated to increase that share to nearly half by 2025. Third, South–South has replaced South–North as the dominant current in global trade. But for all the entry barriers that have been surmounted, there remains a great deal of red-tape holding back growth – namely the rent-seeking laws governing copyrights, design, and brand names (Gereffi 2014).

The logic of DMP is manifest in the growing number of supplier firms that have evolved from lowly cut-make-trim operations into 'full-package' productions, verging on multinationalism. Azmeh and Nadvi (2014: 709) note 'the emergence of large Asian suppliers as central players in the organizational restructuring of production and trade,' which are now 'co-leads' or 'strategic and pivotal' firms, 'effectively shaping the overall design of the global architecture of the garment value chain.' 'Geographically,' they add, 'these leading multinational garment manufacturers have built extensive dispersed and functionally integrated value chains that are spread pre-dominantly in Asia but also extend to Africa, the Middle East, and Central America.'

The Global South even receives most of its own FDI now (UNCTAD 2011). And though the regional economy suffered during the 2008 crisis, as industrial sectors, like metals and electronics, contracted, other sectors, like garments and textiles, food and beverage, and automotives, experienced minimal pain and bounced right back (UNCTAD 2011). The robustness of (mostly Asian) garment manufacturers, following the MFA, is attested throughout the literature (Chiu 2007; Appelbaum 2008; Fernandez-Stark, Frederick, and Gereffi 2011; Rotunna, Vezina, and Wang 2012; Gereffi 2014; Merk 2014). The 'dragon multinationals', especially, are rising stars, currently internationalizing across mainland China, Southeast Asia, and Africa (Yang 2006).

The sector begins to change dramatically after the MFA, when consolidation picks up speed. Global brands streamline production by purchasing from fewer suppliers in fewer countries, reducing the associated costs (logistics, warehousing, turnover time). Soon, they source directly from the countries that produce textiles and clothing. This is especially noticeable in 'labour-rich' countries, though official data is difficult to access. Merk (2014: 263) elaborates, 'From the global buyer's side, purchasing departments often place the majority of their orders with a relatively small number of key suppliers.' He cites the example of Nike where 20 per cent of contracted factories produce 80 per cent of Nike's total volume. Merk continues, 'This trend towards concentration has further been accelerated by the cessation of the MFA in 2005. Many lead companies have decided to reduce the number of suppliers they use drastically and consolidate their orders in fewer countries and with fewer suppliers.' This, in effect, rewards consolidation, as Merk states, 'To minimise logistics costs and turnover time, retailers increasingly source from countries that can produce both textiles and clothing.' By way of example, he cites Puma and Gap, which, in the year following the MFA phase-out (2005–2006), reduced the number of suppliers by 107 and 615, respectively. Finally, consolidation at the point of the brand/retail encourages consolidation at the point of production, in that 'they prefer to place orders with large suppliers capable of handling large volumes'.

The ascent of supplier firms marks a steep decline in the DMP of buyers. Crucially, it was a high DMP that initially led low-value small and mid-size firms to merge, so that they might survive the intense downward pressure exerted on them by buyers while competing with one another. This move into value-added phases of the GVC has transformed it, fundamentally remaking the buyer/supplier balance of power.

A prominent sign that producers are capturing more value is upgrading. A 2011 report (Fernandez-Stark et al.) showed expansion in the intangible services that occur before and after garment production in the value chain. In the survey, researchers found upgrading activity in the Asian garment sector but not in Africa, where production is still confined to assembly. In Sri Lanka, cut-make-trim (CMT) facilities have upgraded to full-package production plus design. In Bangladesh, facilities have transitioned into full-package production as well as the OEM (original equipment manufacturer) stage.

The same study found that the pre-existing infrastructure in Turkey, where the garment sector already accounted for 80 per cent of exports, allowed its suppliers to fast forward into full-package production during the 1980s. Today, full-package suppliers make up 60 per cent of the global garment sector, and frequently subcontract low-level work out to places like Egypt and Morocco. This trend accelerated after 2000, when Turkey's full-package firms graduated to design work (ODM) and brand development (OBM). Lead times consequently shrank to under four weeks and local brands thrived, elevating Turkey into a centre for fashion and design that could boast of long-term design contracts with retailers like M&S (Fernandez-Stark, Frederick, and Gereffi 2011). As mentioned in Chapter 2, the long-standing centrality of the garment industry to the Turkish economy (chief exports: T-shirts, sweatshirts, underwear, socks, men's shirts, and trousers) gave it a leg-up, allowing for easier upgrading and a streamlined, vertically integrated local sector.

Similarly, the garment sector in Sri Lanka, which accounts for 50 per cent of its exports, has been able to rapidly upgrade since 2000 with the benefit of duty-free access to EU markets (as part of the generalized scheme of preferences, or the GSP/GSP-plus scheme). Sri Lanka's multinational suppliers are now opening up vertically integrated factories in Africa and Jordan, as well as textile facilities in India and Bangladesh. By the 2000s, the Sri Lankan garment sector had weaned itself off FDI, and 80–85 per cent of factories were owned by Sri Lankans (Fernandez-Stark, Frederick, and Gereffi 2011). As DMP fell between 2008 and 2014, the number of garment factories in Sri Lanka halved, while export share to the US and the EU remained constant, and the larger Sri Lankan suppliers rapidly expanded. Now only four mega-suppliers – MAS Holdings, Brandix, Polytex, and Hirdaramany – employ 75,000 of the country's 230,000 garment workers, while raking in 25 per cent of total garment export earnings (Merk 2014).

The fourth largest global exporter of garments, Bangladesh, has seen its own knit and woven sectors advance in the last decade from CMT to OEM full-package operations with sourcing and logistics under the same roof. Although, like many other domestic garment industries, the Bangladeshi sector was seeded by FDI, it is now in mostly local hands (Fernandez-Stark, Frederick, and Gereffi 2011). The largest, most capital-intensive firms, however, remain foreign-controlled. South Korean mega-supplier Youngone Holdings, for example, has an annual turnover of $1.5 billion, production sites across China, Vietnam, and

El Salvador, with 17 factories in Bangladesh, and employs over 60,000 workers (Merk 2014).Consolidation has hit the Philippines also, where, Hurley (2005) notes, only 5 of the 1,500 registered garment firms account for 20 per cent of the domestic garment industry's outputs. There is also increasing evidence of garment sector consolidation in Bangladesh and across Latin America.[17]

Limits to the spatial fix?

The 2008 crisis was an economic pivot point.[18] A combination of factors, including state policy, labour shortages, and strikes, has since begun to raise labour costs in South China's Pearl River Delta region, endangering profit margins. The *Wall Street Journal* warns that Chinese industry will be forced into making tough decisions 'once the global factory floor for clothes and toys pushes through a transition to higher-value manufacturing in industries such as cars, aircraft and electronics' (Chu 2015). I explain what this means for workers' bargaining power in the next chapter.

A 2012 survey conducted by the American Chamber of Commerce found that only 73 per cent of US firms in Shanghai were profitable, down from 78 per cent in 2011 and 79 per cent in 2010, an ongoing slide it attributed to rising labour and logistical costs, a shrinking labour supply, and the emergence of domestic competition. Another 2012 survey found that almost half of the US manufacturers and importers in China were considering moving out of the country altogether for the same reasons (and that 26 per cent did). The anxiety is understandable. China is in the throes of internal economic turmoil (including a rebalancing of power between labour and capital and burgeoning consumer

---

[17] At the 2019 American Association of Geographers Annual Conference, discussant Jennifer Bair agreed with my contention on the rise of consolidation in Latin America but disagreed on whether this resulted in rising workers' bargaining power. Fellow participant Stephen Frenkal also agreed in his talk that he had witnessed increased firm consolidation in Bangladesh but like Jennifer Bair felt that this did not necessarily mean greater power for workers.

[18] Since the post-War Golden Age, advanced capitalist economies have stumbled from crisis to crisis, losing momentum. This Pyrrhic retreat, historic slowdown in capital accumulation (growth of gross capital formation), is manifest in declining rates of both production growth (GDP growth) and investment (investment as a percentage of GDP). The present crisis is therefore a single stage in a larger, longer downturn (Durand and Lege 2013).

markets), while also overseeing the shift to a new status quo in global trade, with a deficit-West and a surplus-East.

Because they are now, effectively, the two poles around which world trade revolves, a comparison of the US and China – which is to say, the world's largest consumer and its largest producer, respectively – allows us to take the pulse of the global economy. Between 2007 and 2012, for instance, US consumers had debt grow by some 10 per cent. Meanwhile, in China, where there are more active credit card accounts than there are people in the US, it ballooned an astonishing 67 per cent (UPI 2013). And it was in 2012 that GDP output in China from services (transport, retail, real estate, and so on) reached new heights, outperforming industrial sectors for the first time since 1961 (*Economist* 2013). Such is the speed of this transition, from the world's supply-side workshop to its next great marketplace, that manufacturing balance sheets in China and the US may soon converge (Fox 2018).

With that convergence looming, capital will be forced into yet another spatial fix – likely setting up shop in emerging economies. And once those emerging economies – Indonesia, Peru, Mexico, and Eastern Europe – mature into service economies as well, driving up local labour costs, where will capital go after that? Much of Africa, populous as it may be, lacks the readymade infrastructure necessary for large-scale manufacturing (Fernandez-Stark 2011). And though Vietnam and India have variously been touted as the 'next China', a host of political factors makes such prophecies unlikely.

But as Silver and Zhang (2010: 184) caution, the enduring advantages of China do not make large-scale capital flight a forgone conclusion, at least not anytime soon: 'If anything, rising real wages will make China even more attractive as a site of investment as the relative global weight of the Chinese market increases further.'

But over the long run, collapse appears inevitable. Capital is prone to crisis and as David Harvey observes, 'Capital never solves its crisis tendencies, it merely moves them around.' Yet we live in a finite world, meaning that the spatial fix is a tactic with built-in obsolescence: there are only so many viable destinations. Part of the reason for capital's continual innovation is that each new fix chases a frontier that is already vanishing.

Harvey and Lefebvre argue that capitalism's survival is contingent on the creation, or discovery, of new space, and of finding, through hook or crook, endless lebensraum. Lefebvre (1976) asserts that if this geography does not exist, it is necessary to invent it, to continue extracting maximal surplus value – and that this is the chief historical means by which capitalism has contained crises and endured.

The maintenance of capitalism, according to Lefebvre (1991), is accomplished – at least in part – through the domination of physical spaces. Harvey took this notion, added another dose of Marx, and applied it to the globalization of capital in his *Limits of Capital* (2006), which elaborated the theory of the spatial fix, or the use of geography by capital to neutralize crises. Immanuel Wallerstein and others argue that capitalism emerged out of the surpluses accumulated by petty sixteenth-century merchants and traders (the devil makes work for idle surpluses). As capitalism developed through the centuries, colonial plunder and other surpluses were successfully reabsorbed by the system, subsidizing the growth of managerial classes and large-scale industrialization. By the 1970s, however, things came skidding to a halt: advanced economies could no longer absorb their own surpluses.

Harvey (2001) traces the intellectual heritage of his spatial fix through Marx to the late Hegel, a thread that then was woven into the anti-imperialism of Luxembourg, Hobson, Lenin, and Bukharin, with empirical reference to the depressions of 1873–1896 and the early twentieth century. Harvey (2006a) insists that the spatial fix is only a short-term solution. When a place becomes a variable, everything tied to terra firma begins to depreciate. And, as Harvey (2006a) points out, those assets are hard to replace, and each new space only spreads resources more thinly. The spatial fix, therefore, staves off tomorrow's crisis, while setting up the Big One.

As decades of recent history attest, spatial fixes are clearly a significant obstacle for labour. In this chapter, I have shown that they can also lead to *organizational fixes*, such as when suppliers expand, vertically or horizontally, to become large oligopolistic firms, capable of throwing their weight around the GVC.

And since buyers relate to suppliers much like suppliers relate to labour, it follows that there is a great sleeping power in the workers, whose collective action can remake the GVC and – at the very least – enlarge labour's share of captured value.

7

Labour's Power in the Chain

On 17 September 1982, David Dubinsky died aged 90. An obituary in the *New York Times* described a life of commitment to the ILGWU, where he had served as President for more than three decades, from 1932 to 1966 (Raskin 1982). Born in what is now Belarus, at the age of 13 he was already working as a unionized baker and, during the failed Russian revolution of 1905, took inspiration from a mass rally for the Jewish Workers Union, or Bund. The next year, at the age of 14, he was elected its Assistant Secretary. And after several arrests for union-related activities, including attempts to organize strikes, he escaped from police custody while en route to Siberia. In 1911, he appeared in New York City. By 1932, the 5 feet 4 inches Dubinsky was running an American union: the ILGWU, which had been organized out of New York City's garment district. Buoyed by the jobbers' agreement (JA) strategy, union membership soared under his leadership. His detractors, however, accused the Belarusian of supporting imperialism, undermining strikes, and 'collaborating with manufacturers to fleece the consuming public' (Weinstone 1946: 13). The end of Dubinsky's presidency coincided with the end of an era, as the jobbers' strategy concluded, and globalization swept the garment sector out of New York City and London and into the Third World. As Chapter 2 details, in the early twentieth century, the ILGWU was forced to confront a new, vertically disintegrated business model, one that would become a commonplace across industrial capitalism and spread across the world. This system of outsourced production made direct negotiations with low-value employers very difficult, leading to a war of attrition.

On the face of things, it is the suppliers/producers who are responsible for the wages and working conditions of shop floor labour, since they are the ones who set wage policy and maintain the factories. But suppliers – however villainous or well-intentioned their owners may be – operate within the limits imposed on them by buyers through the value chain. And when buyers have high degree of monopsony power (DMP), they can demand a lot for very little, pushing down margins and giving labour much less to bargain *for*.

But the ILGWU's efforts were not entirely in vain. Concerted actions at the points of production as well as consumption have forced contractors to include the price of labour in source price negotiations with suppliers. These JAs also effectively 'ring fenced' any additional labour costs that contractors might incur, affording garment workers more wiggle room to bargain (Anner, Bair, and Blasi 2012: 22). This is an important beachhead for workers. As Anner et al. (2013: 5) observe, 'The principal cause for the persistent violation of workers' rights in the global apparel supply chain is the pricing mechanism between buyers and their suppliers.' What workers can demand of the contractors employing them cannot, therefore, be separated from source prices.[1]

Firms deploy a wide variety of strategies and tactics to survive and thrive under competition. From complex pricing manoeuvres to product innovations, differentiation, and marketing, all aim to create and exploit a loyal base of consumers. But in addition to drumming up business, firms also need to cut the costs of *doing business* (the one brings more money in while the other lowers the cost of getting it, and the difference is profit). And cutting costs is accomplished through new technologies, scientific management, outsourcing, and so on, anything and everything that does the same for less, within reasonable bounds. The third front in the enterprise, of course, is the competition itself, whose own positions and activities in the market must be considered by firm management. Every day competition rewards competent firms, who best their rivals through gumption, cost-effectiveness, or wily connivance, with bigger chunks of the market and higher profits.

Likewise, labour – in its efforts to self-determine and resist subordination – is in competition with the bosses over who gets a bigger slice of the pie. It does this by combining workers into associations and trade unions and through organizing

---

[1] Much analysis of labour in the garment GVC assumes a high DMP and therefore a low structural and associational power for workers. Therefore, the only methods deployed by workers have been to protest outside the workplace. Anner (2011: 16) explains: 'High worker turnover rates result in weak structural and associational (organizational) power for labour (Silver 2003; Wright 2000). But workers are not powerless. First, as Sydney Tarrow suggests, resource-poor actors often turn to protest because disruption is a form of power (Tarrow 1998). At the same time, the harsh conditions in buyer-driven value chains allow grievances to be framed in terms of basic human rights that resonate with broader publics. Since control lies on the retail and brand-name manufacturer end of this commodity chain, left labour unionists will have an incentive to form alliances with activist organizations such as women's groups, human and labour rights organizations, and student organizations and can maximise the shaming mechanisms as they pressure leading apparel firms through consumer-oriented campaigns.'

campaigns for better working conditions and pay. Organized labour can, among other things, pressurize political institutions to implement regulations, shielding workers from the worst predations of capital.

Employment relations can in part be explained by the conflicts between capital and labour. Labour is, after all, the only living and subjective factor in production. It performs tasks that vary in time, intensity, skill, quality of outcomes, the faculties used, oversight, and so on. In Marxian terms (Marx 1867), labour is an employer's 'variable capital'. Variable, in that it is elastic; the degree of exploitation involved (and, therefore, profitability) can be increased by cutting pay, extending the work day, or intensifying the work day.

Braverman (1974) believes labour-power has an 'intelligent and purposive character, which gives it infinite adaptability' and 'infinite potential'. But the capitalist cannot exploit the *infinite potentials* of labour-power, since these are 'limited to the subjective state of the workers, by their previous history, by the general social conditions under which they work, as well as the particular condition of the enterprise, and by the technical setting of their labor' (Braverman 1974). Instead, the capitalist desires only to get the most labour-power for the least money. This application of the profit motive reduces labour to an input comprised of fungible workers who, if they are to keep their livelihoods, must reach given quotas within given time frames while toiling under a production regime devised by the capitalist. Any resistance by organized labour will initiate a bargaining process between employer and employees. And how that bargaining process shakes out will largely be determined by capital's relative oligopsony power.

In other words, the state of capitalism at any given time depends on the strength of labour. Because capital's raison d'être is self-expansion, as long as there are different capitals, they will compete for profits or additional fragments of the total available capital (minus costs). However, a firm can also *free up* any capital used in its own operations that is deemed superfluous. It is here that capital confronts labour, which is the ultimate source of revenue, but also a cost. To achieve maximal productivity (that is, to draw maximal revenue), firms impose discipline on labour, coercing a set intensity of work. But to achieve minimal cost, firms pay as little as labour, and the available pool of labour, will bear. In order to achieve both a semblance of autonomy and a standard of living for workers better than subsistence (or worse), labour must assert itself through associational power, structural power, or a combination thereof. To reiterate the argument made in Chapter 6, competition drives down GVC DMP by reducing the number of suppliers to a few large firms that have greater bargaining power vis-à-vis buyers. Here I analyse how these changing dynamics involve labour and its own bargaining process.

Labour bargaining power and global governance

Recent policy papers have highlighted the importance of global supply chains to labour relations, emphasizing, among other things, the roles of skill (OECD 2017) and international labour standards (ILO 2015). What is neglected in the discussion, however, is worker agency, specifically its exercise through collective bargaining. The GCC, GVC, and GPN literatures dwell mostly on how lead firms figure in the power balance, portraying them as prime movers in the production process as well as the broader chain activity and enmeshed political structures. This framework is sometimes criticized as being too 'firm-centric'.

The treatment of chains/networks as static power balances between buyers and suppliers has obscured the role of labour, rendering it an exogenous factor in production. Much of the literature seems to have forgotten that the underlying thrust of the GVC – and capitalism itself – is the relentless accumulation of capital, leading to a turbulent and uninterrupted evolution, forever changing the character of production. Here, I treat labour not as an exogenous factor of production, or a variable in the cost function, but as a dynamic and decisive element in production, co-determining the value chain and its political environment. Ultimately, it is the third major force shaping the GVC, alongside buyers and suppliers. By bringing labour back into the equation, I intend to fill a glaring blind spot in a literature that is already preoccupied with questions of power and governance.

GCC/GVC/GPN approaches are also limited by how they conceive of power. They frequently regard it as a function of the technical and organizational position of each firm in the value chain, isolated from the competition. For Gereffi, Humphrey, and Sturgeon (2005), power is simply the 'degree of coordination' and 'asymmetry' achieved by lead firms vis-à-vis suppliers in the value chain. For the GPN, power is the influence firms, institutions, and stakeholders have over a production network. Power, by these estimations, primarily concerns decision-making and resource allocation, in which leverage comes from the firm's position in a production network (Henderson et al. 2002; Dougherty 2008; Coe and Yeung 2015; Yeung and Coe 2015).

Labour is, however, an active agent within production, exerting a pressure on the GVC in proportion to its organization and activity. But, in much of the literature, it is conspicuously absent, or present only as a spectator, even in the GPN, which tries to formalize labour as 'collective power'. Indeed, as I have argued here, GVC's competition is comprised of three fronts: a horizontal contest between capitals producing similar commodities; a vertical tug-and-pull between suppliers and buyers; and an intra-firm conflict between capital and labour. Each of these battles over value distribution creates an evolving configuration, affecting linked governance structures.

But more literature is cropping up addressing what firm-centrism leaves out. This has appeared in a few waves: one organized and published by the *British Journal of Industrial Relations* (*BJIR*), in 2013 and 2018, and another coming out of *Competition and Change* in 2013, and a 2018 special issue of *Human Relations*.

An early attempt to include labour in a GVC framework was undertaken by Frenkel and Kuruvilla (2002), who argued that patterns in labour relations are the combined effect of three factors: competition, industrial peace, and employment-income protection. Later, Riisgaard and Hammer (2011) analysed labour through the prisms of power and drive in the banana and flower value chains, with a special focus on international solidarity. Despite a few divergences with my own views, there is much to be gleaned from Riisgaard and Hammer whose work guides some of this chapter's analysis. In particular, how the power of suppliers vis-à-vis buyers affects labour, and how the power of labour affects the supplier–buyer relationship. Long-term contracts, the current relationship between suppliers and buyers, and the control buyers have over suppliers, and so on, are all shaped in part by the relative strength of labour. As Riisgaard and Hammer (2011) observed, the strengthening of supplier firms depends on labour.

Another forerunner, the *BJIR* 2013 special issue 'Across Boundaries: The Global Challenges Facing Workers and Employment Research' (Jackson, Kuruvilla, and Frege 2013), explained national employment relations in the context of global production, circulation, and consumption. Lakhani, Kuruvilla, and Avgar (2013) were among the first to marry theories of the GVC to employment relations. Their framework helped move firm-centric employment relations research towards a networked analysis, providing a foundation for something beyond the level of case studies. But their work was incomplete, so far as it treated GVC evolution as a top-down, automatic affair. As I demonstrate, rather than unidirectional, this process is dialectical.

In that same year, 2013, Selwyn argued against the 'automatic' interpretation of GVC change in a *Competition and Change* special issue titled 'Putting Labour in Its Place' (Taylor, Newsome, and Rainnie 2013). Although Selwyn made several valuable contributions, the argument against social upgrading in the ILO's Decent Work Agenda is most useful here. Selwyn's thesis – that improvements in labour conditions do not simply 'trickle down' but are won by workers – does colour the thinking behind this book. Comparing and contrasting the bottom-up and top-down interpretations, as readers of the recent literature are liable to do, is a very instructive process, immensely enriching one's understanding of how value is *actually* created and distributed.

The 2018 *Human Resources* special issue 'Global Supply Chains and Social Relations at Work: Brokering Across Boundaries' (Reinecke, Donaghey, and Wilkinson 2018) spotlighted brokerage and supply chain *intermediaries*. But those are bit parts; my focus is on the GVC main cast: buyers, suppliers, and labour.

Finally, we have the *BJIR* 2018 symposium, 'Corporate Social Responsibility and Labor Standards' (Jackson, Doellgast, and Baccaro 2018), which also concerns itself primarily with what is secondary. As I have argued throughout, a corporation – whether it be supplier, buyer, or other – is animated, above all, by the profit drive. And under that compulsion, meaningful labour standards can only be established where the rubber meets the road, and material conditions (structural power) constrain worker agency (associational power). Questions of corporate social responsibility (CSR) are window dressing. Mark Anner's piece on wildcat strikes, and the 'sourcing squeeze' in Vietnam from the same issue, however, is useful213 grounding for several of the theories developed here.

Structural power in the GVC

Erik Olin Wright's (2000) formulations of *associational* and *structural power* are valuable assets for analysing bargaining power in the GVC. Under Wright's rubric, structural power is the 'power that results simply from the location of workers within the economic system' (Wright 2000) and labour's ability to interrupt the production process and thereby exact concessions from employers. Associational power, however, is the collective power that emerges from the representative institutions and organizations of workers. Dimensions of associational power include union density, collective bargaining agreement coverage, and the participation of labour collectives in firm and non-firm decision-making.

Meanwhile, employers design and employ business strategies that extend or intensify work, reduce wages, and so on. Often, they attack the associational and structural power of labour directly, erecting obstacles to unionization such as the dispersal – through one means or another – of work; enacting systems of control over production and labour processes; and prevailing upon politicians to dilute the regulatory frameworks that legalize union power (Cumbers, Nativel, and Routledge 2008; Selwyn 2012; Flecker, Haidinger, and Schönauer 2013).

In response, labour leverages its associational and structural powers and expands; it rallies the shop floor, establishes representative institutions, and promotes pro-labour legislation, at both the national (laws) and the international (GFAs) levels (Riisgaard and Hammer 2011; Shaikh 2016). And, when all its ducks are in a row, labour initiates economic struggles. Wright sees the relationship between capital and labour as a fluid 'class compromise', shifting with the balance of power. But it is more complicated than what Wright (2000) suggests, especially with regard to GVCs. Although 'polarization' (that is, buyers, producers, and labour) is a useful analytic tool for exploring how the specificity of place figures in capital–labour relations (encompassing a multitude of interactions, hierarchies, and antagonisms), its greatest virtue lies in its universality.

Structural power is an especially significant feature in GVCs, where production formations require a system of tiered production that is decentralized and reintegrated through the vicissitudes of the market, allowing labour – if it can – to interdict capital accumulation at key junctures. Labour, therefore, possesses great latent power in countries, regions, particular economic activities, even specific firms, which have acquired a central position in a value chain or production network.

The 'positioning' of labour in the production process is also distinguished by two different aspects: *marketplace structural power*, which arises from the relative tightness of a labour market (in terms of skills, unemployment rate, and non-wage income), and *workplace structural power*, arising from the position of labour in 'tightly integrated production processes, where a localised work stoppage in a key node can cause disruptions on a much wider scale than the stoppage itself' (Silver 2003: 13). However, the latter is more important in GVCs, where labour is systematically deskilled.

The bargaining power of labour, of course, corresponds to its structural power. And while the cynical but savvy exploitation of uneven development led to a system of world production centred on the Global North, it appears that the next stage of development is already on the horizon. In 2010, for instance, the economies of the Global South accounted for half of all FDI inflows – a first. This fact, coupled with the year-on-year increase in FDI outflows from those same economies – the UNCTAD (2011: xii) report notes that 'emerging economies are the new FDI powerhouses', and that most outflows stayed within the Global South – indicates their growing significance as sites of production and consumption, and as sources of investment. And, as mentioned earlier, as a region, industry, or firm becomes more important and profitable, the higher the stakes that associated labour can exploit (that is, the higher its relative structural power). While the ILGWU innovated a strategy of applying pressure at both the sites of production and consumption, workers in the Global South are now less and less reliant on the Global North, especially as retailers turn to the Global South for new consumers. Both Yue Yuen and Arvind campaigns saw Global South garment workers chart new territory for international, South–South solidarity, as they successfully targeted retailers and brands at the shopfront level.

Power and network centrality

Insights from network theory allow for a more concrete understanding of labour's power position, of what it depends on and how it is affected by changes in global production, like outsourcing. Networks are *graphs* consisting of connected *nodes* or *points*. The lines that connect the nodes are called *links* or *edges*. The literature on GPNs imagines production as a network of interconnected activities executed by firm and non-firm actors – labourers, national states, intergovernmental entities, and so on. Each actor in a production network is a node, and each node is connected to the other nodes through links. These links represent established relationships.

Since the analysis of GPNs uses networking theory, one would expect a more rigorous application. However, the study of network structural properties is limited. Take, for example, network centrality, a fundamental concept in network theory emphasizing the importance of nodes. While Coe and Yeung (2015) admit that networks have structural properties affecting the larger power balance, they dwell instead on the relational characteristics of networks and conceptualize power being 'as much a structural property as a contingent and contextually defined practice among interconnected actors in a network' (Coe and Yeung 2015: 66). Nevertheless, the structural properties of networks remain valuable to the study of global production networks, especially with regard to labour.

Labourers employed in the 'key nodes' of globally integrated production systems possess greater bargaining power (workplace bargaining power) vis-à-vis capital, which can affect the entire value chain and production network. However, as Silver (2003) points out, subcontracting and 'vertical disintegration' were introduced to erode that power. Spatially and organizationally flexible production systems are therefore a tool for controlling labour costs by constraining labour's power.

To better understand power relations from the position of labour, it is necessary to study the network properties of global production, including *network centrality* that captures the importance of node positioning within networks. There are also now other *centralities* in network theory, each shedding light on 'different aspects of the position that a node has, which can be useful when working with information flows, bargaining power, infection transmission, influence and other sorts of important behaviours on a network' (Jackson 2008: 62). Network centrality is a function of the structural positioning of nodes in a network. Freeman (1978) introduces four families of centrality: *degree*, *betweenness*, *closeness*, and *neighbours' characteristics* (Jackson 2008).

A node's degree of centrality is 'the number of links that involve that node' (Jackson 2008: 51). For example, a node linked with five other nodes has degree 5 and is more central than a node with only one link (that is, degree 1). Betweenness centrality is the 'frequency with which a point falls between pairs of other points on the shortest or geodesic paths connecting them' (Freeman 1978: 221). If one takes stock of all the shortest possible paths (which are called *geodesics*) in a network, the node that shows up most frequently is the one which has the highest betweenness centrality. The third measure, closeness, is a measure of the distance between nodes defined as the 'inverse of the average distance between *i* and any other node' (Jackson 2008: 64). The closer a node is to other nodes, the more 'central' it is. The last family of centrality is *Neighbours' Characteristics*. These are measures based on 'the premise that a node's importance is determined by how important its neighbours are' (Jackson 2008: 65) – with 'importance' being a function of centrality. For example, *Eigenvector Centrality*, a variant of this family, emphasizes nodes linked to other highly linked nodes. On top of the centralities, Freeman (1978: 227) underlines the importance of *Graph Centrality*, which captures the 'tendency of a single point to be more central than all other points in the network'.

Network centrality adds to our understanding of capital–labour relations as well as labour's structural power. The greater the centrality of a firm in the production network, the greater the importance of associated labour and therefore the greater its latent bargaining power.

In the end, of course, capital–labour relationships are co-determined through struggle, and the confrontation of labour's associational and marketplace power with capital's oligopoly and oligopsony power. However, firm centrality is nonetheless a useful proxy for gauging the latent workplace power of labour in value chains and production networks since their respective strategic positions are two sides of the same coin.

The myriad organizational, spatial, and functional factors that affect the number of nodes in a GVC/GPN will by extension affect centrality and the relative power of firms. Whenever lead firms implement business strategies promoting flexible production systems, for example, and start outsourcing, they dilute the centrality of supply firms, whose labour forces are thereby weakened as well. Vertical-integration, on the other hand, creates 'mega-suppliers' whose workforces are strategically significant. The fewer the nodes in a network, the higher the centrality of suppliers and more bargaining power involved, for both firms and labour.

The conflict between capital and labour in each GVC segment does not occur in isolation but usually as the result of larger market forces. And whenever capital wants to undercut labour, it can move to vertically disintegrate, narrowing the topmost circle of competition while enlarging the bottom. As case studies in this volume attest, the latent power of workers lies in the relative power of suppliers vis-à-vis buyers. An increasing number of scholars are now using competition and market power to explain the dynamics of organizational structures under globalization. Selwyn (2008: 157), for instance, argues, 'Capital–labour relations are based on an inherently conflicting and ongoing process (sometimes hidden and sometimes open) where each class attempts to maximise their share of the surplus created in the process of accumulation. Various authors recognise this dynamic process, but argue that contemporary globalization has reduced significantly labour's power to appropriate a greater share of surplus.'

Degree of Spatial Inflexibility

As I have argued, it is the combination of material conditions and subjective worker agency that produces bargaining outcomes, good or bad. To concretize this idea, let us treat the buyer-driven and producer-driven value chains as two ends of the same spectrum. Here, I introduce the concept of *degree of spatial inflexibility* (DSI) which is central to workers' structural power. DSI is the scope of geographic possibility within which production can take place. In other words, the constraints on how global buyers can move production to optimize capital accumulation. A low DMP results in a high DSI and thereby greater bargaining power for workers.

DSI builds on David Harvey's 'spatial fix', which is capital's use of space to temporarily resolve crises of profitability. There are two sometimes overlapping forms: *regulatory* and *market*. *Regulatory DSI* is the set of geographic limits imposed on capital by states, supranational bodies, and trade agreements, and was strongest during the post-War embedded liberalism. *Market DSI* is the set of de facto geographic limitations that are baked into a given stage of capitalist development – during early capitalist development, for instance, crude technology, insufficient surpluses, and a tiny bourgeoisie-constrained market growth, producing a high DSI. During advanced capitalism, however, the drives to centralize, redistribute wealth upward, and erect high entry barriers eventuate in a handcuffing of garment buyers, for instance, to a fixed few mega-suppliers.

Take the history of the garment sector, where state-level regulation began in the nineteenth century. Previously, any structural power possessed by labour owed to the localized nature of capital and of work, in other words, *Market DSI*. Tilly (1995: 7) observes of this period, that 'although people exercised some individual rights as members of communities, churches, households, and other organizations, workers' rights generally took a categorical form, applying to individual workers only in so far as they qualified as bona fide members of local trades'.

By the 1850s, however, the legal grey area in which early labour activism operated gave way to more formal collaboration with employers and the state. Through a form of 'collective bargaining by riot' (Hobsbawm 1952) workers won, for example, the legal right to strike, to associate, a set of unemployment benefits, and state support for barring foreign labour: that is, *Regulatory DSI*. Of the burgeoning regulatory apparatus, Tilly (1995: 13) writes that 'controls [were instituted] over the stocks and flows of persons, diseases, other biota, pollutants, weapons, drugs, money, other capital, technology, information, commodities, political practices and cultural forms within well-delimited territories'. Tilly (1995: 8) continues, 'States that could conscript, tax, and police could also regulate working conditions, organise schools, and build highways. At the same time, concentration and nationalization of capital gave workers connections and central objects of claims they had not previously known.'

By the 1930s and again in the early 1970s, a high degree of regulatory DSI had given labour a longer lever with which to move the economy, a newfound power manifest through the trade union movement and collective bargaining agreements. Before the crisis of the 1960s and 1970s, Western garment workers, particularly in the US and the UK, had been shielded by protectionism. This capped the monopsonistic power of buyers and confined the ILGWU need to 'chase the work' within the US and parts of Canada. Even then, however, the ILGWU relied on a degree of a market DSI. They distinguished between what they called the 'backbone shops', which were essential to the jobber's business, and the 'overflow shops', which were used in seasonal peaks. Jeffery Hermanson[2] tells me that the backbone shops were powerful during the era of domestic garment value chain, stating that 'brands depended on these [backbone] shops for capacity and specific production ability; and if we organized them and could stop their operation, we stood a good chance of winning a confrontation with the jobber'. He contrasts the strength of the backbone with the weakness of the 'overflow shops': 'We would concentrate on organizing strong majorities in the backbone shops, while simply sending one or two workers to work in an overflow shop, to be in position to know what was going on inside, as we could then agree with the employer to put aside the jobber's work during the strike.'

The crisis, however, inaugurated a new era of trade liberalization – that is, a lower degree of regulatory spatial inflexibility, as capital spilled over into the Third World, significantly isolating the ILGWU.

However, Global North trade unions attempted to mitigate garment capital outflow with the 1974 MFA, which had been preceded by the Short-Term Cotton

---

[2] Interview, 12 February 2019.

Agreement (1961) and the Long-Term Cotton Agreement. The MFA partially constrained major import markets (US, Canada, and Europe) by establishing import quotas. The result, however, was a production apparatus that was spread more thinly, and whose regulatory DSI was too low to prevent spatial fixes should workers in any one location flex their associational muscle. The end of the MFA was also the end of the industry's regulatory DSI. Global buyers then steered production into a handful of cheap but labour-rich countries. Deregulation led simultaneously to higher DMP (and therefore greater value capture for buyers) and lower DSI (and therefore less structural power for workers). As manufacturers began consolidating in response to the intense competition for contracts in those labour-rich countries, buyer DMP gradually contracted, giving rise to what I call market DSI. By this point, suppliers had become mature firms, guarding their market positions with high entry barriers (via technology and so on), and exercising increasing heft within the GVC.

Before this latest stage set in, labour had been launching campaigns organized around a rights-based framework (codes, audits, and so on), but did not have enough footing to fight a globalized, vertically disintegrated industry. But now, centralization and market DSI have rendered the relevant workforces much more important, substantially increasing their relative structural power. They are no longer so disposable.

Regulatory and market DSIs each have their own drivers, underlying logics, and developmental contexts. But both – especially the former – constrain production, and therefore DMP, value distribution, and, critically, the power of buyers in the GVC.

For Harvey, globalization is simply the modern expression of the spatial fix, a geographic mechanism for capital expansion, whose origins he traces back to 1492. He teases the concept out of Marx's observation that capital is the 'annihilation of space through time'. Later, capitalism's spatial fix used deregulation to open new frontiers (that is, to negate regulatory DSI). Market DSI is developed out of Marx's (1867) theories of capital concentration and centralization and describes a situation in which the maelstrom of competition leaves only a few large and increasingly interdependent firms. Here, inflexibility is the culmination of untrammelled market forces. Regulatory and market DSIs sometimes overlap and are often complementary phenomena. But they can also be inversely related. Using Harvey as foundation, DSI puts the production, reproduction, and reconfiguration of space front and centre in analysing the contours of the GVC and the political economy of capitalism itself.

Although DSI best describes the vertical relationship of buyers and producers, it can also be seen in other, more producer-driven sectors, like the automotive industry. The allocation of market power that guaranteed the stable, oligopolistic conditions of the American auto industry unravelled not only because of Japanese competition but also because of the relative strength of its unions.

According to Katz (1997), the US automobile industry's high levels of unionization were the effect of the United Automotive Workers (UAW) organizing from the 1940s until the end of the 1970s, when international competition from Asia and Germany threatened America's Big Three automakers (Chrysler, Ford, and GM). The powerful UAW represented Canadian auto workers as well until 1985, when the Canadian Auto Workers (CAW) union was established.

Here, we find that autoworkers had high associational power due to both regulatory and market DSIs. And for that reason, US automobile firms responded to international competition by changing how production was organized. First, they outsourced it to low-cost regions in Europe, Asia, and Mexico, and to the independent American auto parts sector, which had much lower union density. At the same time, they implemented labour policies carefully skirting the collective bargaining agreements made with the UAW.

Labour and wage distribution

There is still much debate in academia over wage distribution. The neoclassical school understands international wage differentials as a harmonious expression of marginal productivity (generally linked to education level and human capital). Perfect, or near perfect, markets are an a priori assumption for their growth theory, and wages are indexed to marginal productivity. By this view, a worker can obtain a raise by simply being more productive. Bargaining, collective or individual, never enters the picture, since workers receive what the market determines, and surplus value is a fiction. Worker agency is negligible.

According to the standard neoclassical growth model, production has two inputs: capital and labour. Labour's share derives from the production function, so wages should correlate with profits. And yet the standard production function cannot explain a profit share that increases as wage share decreases – because it assumes they are linked. That may have been reasonable in the post-War era, but the late 1970s proved to be the beginning of a new, clarifying period. Post-Keynesian/Neo-Kaleckians, such as Onaran and Galanis (2014), have improved on the profit-led growth model, showing that the global decline in labour share since the late 1970s/early 1980s has contributed significantly to the overall decline in economic growth. Stockhammer (2015) assesses macroeconomics of income distribution from the standpoint of political economy. He analysed 43 developing countries and 28 advanced countries over a period of 37 years (1970–2007) in order to understand why wages have fallen. Stockhammer takes account of welfare state retrenchment, financialization, globalization, and technology when considering the tug-and-pull between labour and capital, and the effect on income distribution over time. Like Onaran and Galanis (2014), Stockhammer concludes that 'wage shares' are not linked to productivity.

Despite the 'mainstream' popularity of the neoclassical growth model, it has – understandably – little purchase in GCC/GVC/GPN literature. Here, I draw on the tradition of Post-Keynsian/Kaleckian economics, for which income distribution depends on the degree of monopoly; and the tradition of Goodwin, for whom income distribution depends on unemployment levels. The latter takes a more neoclassical redistributive approach, formulating an inverse relationship between labour share and growth (profit-led growth), while the former describes how more equal income distribution contributes to growth (wage-led growth). Both approaches, however, have their fans and have been influential in non-neoclassical macroeconomics for the last half-century.

I maintain that the relationship between growth and income distribution can be explained with reference to Kalecki *as well as* Goodwin. And I am not alone in such cross-pollination. There is, in fact, a wide array of scholarship informed by both traditions (for example, Stephen Marglin and Amit Badouri, whose research has spawned innumerable studies). Unemployment, of course, affects the bargaining power of workers. And Kaleckians maintain that a high degree of monopoly increases a firm's bargaining power. These ideas have made significant inroads outside the neoclassical school (Skott 1989; Chiarella and Flaschel 2000; Taylor 2004; Chiarella, Peter, and Franke 2005; Carpe et al. 2011; Dutt 2016; Shaikh 2016).

Malcolm Sawyer (1988: 55) inquires about the role of trade unions in influencing real wage distribution. He bases his work on Kalecki (1971) who argued that the pressure placed by trade unions (or similar workplace action) could impact real wages. Sawyer states trade unions may make greater demands on employers where profit margins are high. In addition, Sawyer states that 'the effect of a money wage push by unions depends on the firms' ability to pass on the wage increase as a price increase'. Since the number of competitors decreases the ability for this ability to 'pass on' wage increases, the increased monopoly power of the firm increases the possibilities for workers' bargaining. Sawyer concludes, 'Hence, the structure of wage determination (eg. decentralised or centralised) may be relevant of the determination of money wages and their impact on prices and real wages. [...] The degree of monopoly is seen as modified by activities in the labour market, and hence the real wage is influenced by the labour market.'

Outside of neoclassical economics, wage rates are in fact affected by bargaining. In Neo-Marxian economics, wages (or 'markup'), for example, often depend on the unemployment rate (the reserve army of the unemployed), and in

Post-Keynesian–Kaleckian economics, wages depend on degrees of monopoly power or relative growth rate (analytically, the same as the rate of exploitation). In the Goodwin Class Struggle Model (1967), Richard Goodwin uses a Marxian–Keynesian approach to explain the relationship between class conflict, employment as a proportion of the total labour force, and wage/labour share as a measure of national income. Economic booms produce a rising employment–population ratio, which drives wages and wage share higher. This creates a profit squeeze and often a reaction. After another boom, the cycle is repeated. The bargaining process (or 'class conflict') is triggered by fluctuations in the unemployment rate. Expanding on Goodwin's work, however, German Marxist Stephan Kruger identifies labour scarcity as *but one part* of the larger struggle by working people to defend wages. Nevertheless, trends in profit and wage share generally follow the vagaries of class struggle.

There is a rich body of literature in GVC/GPN/GCC arguing that the bargaining process is shaped in part by the power relationships within GVCs, and by upgrading within the factory (Knorringa and Pegler 2006; Coe, Hess, and Dicken 2008; Selwyn 2012; Gereffi 2014). Riisgaard and Hammer (2011: 5), in scrutinizing the cut flower and banana GVCs, conclude that 'analyses of labour in the global economy need to take account of how GVCs shape the terrain for labour to build international networks, strategies, and campaigns for labour rights. Furthermore, analyses of GVC restructuring and governance itself need to integrate the role of labour in shaping global value production as well as in "actively produc[ing] economic spaces and scales in particular ways"' (Herod 2001: 46).

Economic geography and international political economy assume a greater degree of market imperfection than is usually tolerated in neoclassical growth theory. Indeed, the question of *power* is central to GVC analysis, especially as smaller firms become large firms. Indeed, there is an endless number of studies that prove or attempt to explain why large firms pay higher wages and offer greater benefits than small ones (Lester 1967; Brown and Medoff 1989; Burdett and Mortensen 1998). The conclusions are varied, ranging from larger employers seeking high-skilled employees, greater capital-intensity, and greater efficiency to a mechanism to forestall unionization, less able to monitor workers, and so on. While these tell part of the story, what we find with the case in this chapter is a combination of workers' organization and mobilization in conjunction with employers finally being capable of both absorbing greater wage increases and remaining in the GVC.

And the relationship between firm growth and the power of workers in the value chain is developed in detail by 'economic upgrading/social upgrading' debates. Tied to the ILO's 'Capturing the Gains' research programme, which launched in 2009, these debates help answer a critical question: how do upgrading and firm consolidation affect workers? In the literature spurred by the ILO initiative, upgrading is divided into capital upgrading (the use of new machinery/technology) and labour upgrading (making workers more productive as workers). Social upgrading, on the other hand, refers to improvements in working conditions, and worker protections and rights (Barrientos, Gereffi, and Rossi 2011). Barrientos, Gereffi, and Rossi (2011) note that social upgrading usually results from a complex bargaining processes. The question is whether economic upgrading necessarily translates into social upgrading. As Gereffi and Fernandez-Stark (2016) point out, 'Within manufacturing, if we compare industries that can be classified as relatively low-tech (apparel) […] a key task for the GVC analysis is to explain the conditions under which the economic upgrading of firms and the social upgrading of workers can be mutually reinforcing.'

Many of the case studies in GVC/GPN research highlight instances of just such a mutually reinforcing relationship and of how workers and capital co-constitute while shaping the chain/network. Posthuma and Nathan (2010) observe that upgrading among firms in India is uneven and sector-dependent, and that garment suppliers largely remain 'locked-in' at low value-added and low-wage tiers. However, Tewari (2010) shows that even where Indian garment firms *are* upgrading, social upgrading is far from inevitable. Labour-market 'intermediaries' – 'new' unions, community groups, and buying agents – are another set of variables that must be considered. Caswell and De Neve (2013) take this further in a study of the Tiruppur garment cluster, bringing local social relations, the regional economy, and cultural environment into the equation.

Important here is Selwyn's (2013) 'labour-led' social upgrading. For Selwyn, the struggles of workers in horticulture to 'transform their structural power into associational power in order to extract concessions from capital constitutes a core determinant of the relations between economic and social upgrading. Put differently, if workers are able to organise in the face of capitalist management systems designed to raise the rate of exploitation, then they raise, significantly, the possibilities of achieving some form of social upgrading' (2013: 83–84). If workers can organize despite capital's machinations – to intensify labour, to atomize workers – that's half the battle.

Sigmann, Merk, and Knorringa (2014: 19) apply Selwyn's 'labour-led' social upgrading model to Wright's (2000) concepts of associational and structural power while analysing the Freedom of Association (FoA) protocol in Indonesia's footwear industry. The Indonesian workers' struggle benefited from a strong transnational solidarity network, which helped it implement the FoA protocol (meanwhile, there was a clear conflict between suppliers and buyers over value capture). The protocol was partially successful in applying the gains from labour struggles across the country's entire sector to eliminate competitive advantages. Sigmann, Merk, and Knorringa identify this as an example of labour-led social upgrading since 'it allows acts in the athletic footwear industry in Indonesia to move from a situation of confrontation to one that has the potential to catalyse cooperation'. They draw a direct link between the power of suppliers vis-à-vis buyers to that of workers vis-à-vis suppliers: 'In GVCs negotiations between unions and athletic sportswear producers are enmeshed in the negotiations with brands.'

As I have argued, higher value capture at the point of production makes the relevant workforces more important, and therefore potentially more effective agitators. The relationship between economic upgrading and social upgrading is not automatic, of course – it is established by workers. The results are varied. As we saw from the struggle of workers at Fruit of the Loom, capital that is 'locked-in' may capitulate to a transnational workers' campaign to avoid the high cost of relocation or fragmentation. However, in the Arvind case study, capital's response to worker agitation may be to use surpluses for reorganizing production and transport, and to house expensive interstate employees, thereby atomizing and isolating workers. Or, as in the case of China's Yue Yuen strike, it may use surpluses to try and absorb the cost of the strike and outlast workers.

Critically, wage distribution in the garment sector needs to take account of gender. Systematic feminization of the sector has been a function of both skill and power. About 95 per cent of those employed in the garment industry are concentrated in the production segments of the value chain. These are the ones with the lowest 'skill' and are the most gendered; as the firm upgrades and expands vertically, the required skill levels grow with them (Fernandez-Stark, Frederick, and Gereffi 2011). In CMT, the skills required of workers revolve around operating machinery that sews, cuts, or presses clothing. And the bargaining power of workers is further complicated by issues of race, caste, and gender.

At first glance, it makes little economic sense for a factory owner to exclusively seek out women labourers. In many cases, that would necessitate the additional costs of providing a legally mandated crèche (as in India, per the Factories Act 1948) and/or maternity leave (also in India, per the Maternity Benefit Act 1961), which can disincentivize the hiring of women (Frankel 1997; Rangaraju and Kennedy 2012). In the low-value garment sector, such costs might price a firm out of the market. Yet 80 per cent of the garment industry workforce is comprised of women (Dicken 2007) now as it was in turn-of-the-twentieth-century New York and London. Women-only hiring practices produce a clear, gendered division of labour within the factory. Highly skilled tailors, security guards, and managers are positions filled by men, and seamstresses, cutters, pressers, and helpers – the lion's share of work – is given to women, since it is characterized as 'women's work' (in essence, 'unskilled'). Despite the historical continuity, the acute feminization under globalization compounds pre-existing gender norms. Women sew, cut, press, and clean what men design; women operate machines that men service; women work on the factory floor while men stand guard; women toil while men manage, and so forth. 'Women's work' invariably results in less pay than what is defined as 'men's work'. In addition to questions of skilled and unskilled labour, workers are hindered by gendered ideas of self-organization and power.[3] In one illuminating interaction (Jobs with Justice 2007), a factory manager from Gurgaon near Delhi explains why he and other managers prefer women on the shop floor:

> Researcher: Why are your workers mostly female? Are there significant differences in productivity?
> Manager: No, no significant differences in productivity. Just, men together tend to form groups and lobbies because they have spare time.
> Researcher: I don't understand. What groups?
> Manager: Oh, they get involved in politics. [...] Women are easier to handle. They're docile, easier to control.

Hiring a workforce with diminished expectations regarding workplace control and pay makes exploitation notionally easier, limiting the liability associated with workplace action (Ghosh 2009). To fight this strategy, GATWU tried to turn the tables. As Mangala, a seamstress at a leather good factory on Mysore Road tells me, 'We are trying to organize the union, but some skilled tailors don't want to join us because they are above us; the security guards are with the management who beat our brothers and husbands; they are men just like the management, and we are women; we organize as women workers because that is who we are.'[4]

To state the obvious, trade unions are not exempt from sexism.[5] Rohini Hensman (2011: 22) claims in her studies of Indian trade unions that women were at a great disadvantage, and the number of women at meetings 'could

---

[3] A compelling example is found in Sharmila Rudrappa's (2012, 2015) description of the relationship between the garment and the surrogacy industries in India: 'In Bangalore, the garment production assembly line is the main conduit to the reproduction assembly line, as women move from garment factories, to selling their eggs, to surrogacy' (2012: 23). In a further indictment of garment sector conditions, women in the reproduction assembly line describe it as 'more meaningful' and 'creative' than that of the garment factory (Rudrappa 2012: 23).

[4] Interview, 23 December 2012.

[5] Look no further than a history of garment sector unions and the gender divide between the elected leadership and the rank and file.

be counted on the fingers of one hand or, at most, two'. 'It goes along,' she continues, 'with the notion of the working class that ignores the work done in the home (mostly by women) and with a notion of class struggle that marginalises working-class women and children and fails to challenge the gender division of labour and relations of domination and subordination between men and women.' This tension exists the world over, and most union bureaucracies and leaderships are still dominated by men – a reality confirmed by Mark Anner (2011: xvii) in his research on the garment sector in Latin America. Rohini Hensman (2011: 22) sheds light on its prevalence in the Indian labour movement, which 'showed very clearly that the problems of women as wage labourers could not be separated from their subordination in the family and broader social oppression, and therefore a labour movement that neglected these latter concerns (domestic violence, sexual harassment, and gender discrimination, for example) was not genuinely representative of the working class as a whole'. This adds another obstacle to the possibilities of an international labour movement already riven by caste, language, religion, race, borders, and the legacies of imperialism.

The acute feminization of labour carries on at global capital's behest, turning gender norms into profit and reifying social divisions. Women are the lowest rung of the social ladder and that fact is used to justify paying them the lowest wages in the factory.[6] And by doubling down on society's sexism, factories are also able to divide workers (as workers) into two separate camps.

Workers' bargaining in consolidated garment firms

Network centrality is a form of 'structural power', whereas size is a form of a 'contingent power' (it is more relative than relational). The different measures of power outlined earlier (centrality and size) are not binary, are often overlapping, but almost always complimentary in one direction or the other. Indeed, size can lead to centrality, just as centrality can lead to size. Centrality is typically found in vertical relationship, whereas size is a horizontal one.

Let us return to GATWU in Bangalore. In March 2019, GATWU's protracted campaign against California-based Avery Dennison was already a year and a half in and taking its toll on workers' morale. Avery Dennison is a radio-frequency identification (RFID), tag, inlays, and label manufacturer that designs and supplies for nearly every major apparel brand in the world. The vertically integrated firm supplies to roughly 130 brands,, with factories in over

---

[6] For detailed work on the notion of gender and skill, see Phillips and Taylor (1980).

52 locations worldwide. Through consolidation and automation, the firm has developed a high degree of monopoly power in the past decade. Thus, full-time workers at Avery Dennison (30 per cent of the shop floor) earn nearly four times the salary of a regular garment factory worker in the same industrial area. The remaining 70 per cent are contract workers who earn roughly double the average garment worker salary in the area.

They are a 'second-tier supplier' who does not supply directly to brands but rather supplies to their suppliers. They design, manufacture, and deliver their products. Simply put, it is gargantuan in size but not central in the network. In terms of distance, it is far from the centre. However, advanced technology and global reach make it an inimitable partner to suppliers as well as brands. It could be read as a three-node exchange. A *brand/retailer* has power over *CMT manufacturer* and *Avery Dennison*, and while all three are in contact, the exchange relationship is only unidirectional. However, the suppliers, even large and powerful ones, have no choice but to contract with Avery Dennison since there are few alternatives and Avery Dennison retains a non-exchange relationship with the brands. As Jayram,[7] GATWU organizer, tells me, '[Avery Dennison] are designing and printing the stickers. They're designing the tapes and printing the tapes. The supplier has no choice but to contract with Avery Dennison. For example, Avery Dennison was afraid of the worker action and so sent their workers and installed a machine inside of Shahi Exports and they produce the labels and tags for the brands produced by Shahi.' Indeed, more often than not, the brand dictates whom the supplier must purchase the fabric, thread, labels, and other essential accessories from.

Thus, this distinction between size and centrality informs the tactics employed by actors within the value chains. Since September 2017, GATWU has attempted to unionize the Bangalore factory of Avery Dennison, its primary unit in South Asia, after 47 contract workers were laid off. To GATWU, this makes them both a very tough adversary, since no single brand or supplier has much leverage with Avery Dennison, as well as a particularly strategic target. Indeed, its size, vertical-integration, capital-intensity, and large capital holdings make it ideal for the union.

It is for this reason that the management brought in yellow unions in two other plants in India (in Gurgaon and Pune) as well as their factory in Sri Lanka.[8] In Bangalore, the company has recognized the Centre of Indian Trade Unions, or CITU, the union affiliated with the Communist Party of India (Marxists),

---

[7] Interview, 20 February 2019.
[8] For example, in Pune, the factory is represented by the far-right Shiv Sena union.

for its full-time employees. Although historically feared by managers, employers now favour the Karnataka state CITU for their record of signing sweetheart deals with management and undermining strike activity. Avery Dennison is also well known for paying off officials in the labour ministry. Thus, a large capital-holding firm while integrating, investing, and largely staying-put still has the power to withstand independent labour organizing drives.[9]

Beyond these factors, the union's inability to put pressure on global buyers, since they are central in the network but technically far from Avery Dennison, and the futility of putting pressure on suppliers who are still dependent on buyers despite their direct economic relationship, makes it hard for the workers and their union to assert formal associational power despite labour market power ensuring significantly higher wages. This is in spite of high union-density in the factory (more than 90 per cent) and a robust international solidarity campaign. Here, we see firms with high organic composition and, therefore, under greater risk of labour unrest and associated sunk costs. Nonetheless, its distance from the centre (via buyers) and high barriers to entry (via suppliers) make it difficult for workers to use secondary pressures to force the company's hand to the negotiating table. GATWU's failure to put secondary pressure is because neither suppliers nor brands have an alternative, with the latter being able to escape even nominal responsibility. Thus, Avery Dennison is not susceptible to secondary pressure but *is* highly susceptible to shop floor action. Indeed, if workers took strike action, Avery Dennison could be crippled and thereby workers could take full advantage of their structural power.

GVCs, thus, evolve with industry antagonisms, reflecting the ebbs and flows of class struggle. A clear example where size and network centrality work in tandem is global logistics. Kim Moody's *On New Terrain* (2017) analyses how consolidation changes the balance of power in the logistics industry. He argues that conglomerates are better placed to resist isolated strikes since they can rely on other sites of production. Arvind (Chapter 5) is an example of labour unrest that resulted in the reorganization of production from a core activity (pressing warehouse) to a peripheral activity (returns warehouse). This reorganization – made possible through consolidation – was used to undermine the bargaining power of militant workers at any single production site. But despite such pitfalls along the way, consolidation eventually creates the conditions in which 'larger firms compete, the combined workforce of more and more firms is relatively larger, and the new production methods and links [are] more vulnerable. In the long run, this is a situation that makes the industry more susceptible to unionization, as was

---

[9] Interview, Jayram, 20 February 2019.

the case in the 1930s after the 1916–29 merger wave that produced corporate giants such as General Motors, John Deere, and Union Carbide' (Moody 2017: 49–50).

As I argue in Chapter 6 and demonstrated in the empirical chapters, the concentration of capitals contributes to R&D reinvestment, a portion of which is allocated to labour-saving technology. Moody explains that 'like the formation of larger firms along definite industrial lines, greater capital intensity offers expanded opportunities for successful direct action and increased power in collective bargaining' (Moody 2017: 56). This insight dovetails with that of Lund-Thomsen and Lindgreen (2018: 87), who write of GVCs in labour-intensive sectors, 'If suppliers earn lower unit rates over time, workers also tend to receive lower wages. If suppliers must reduce lead times, workers will have to engage in overtime work. Thus, the optimum point for suppliers and workers is inherently linked.' And Anwar Shaikh (2016: 751) writes that 'capital-intensive industries will also tend to have high levels of fixed costs which will make them more susceptible to the effects of slowdowns and strikes. At the same time, because labour costs are likely to be a smaller portion of their total costs, such industries are able to tolerate wage increases'.

But the new potentialities that confront the workforces of ascendant businesses, who are more dependent on them, remain just that: *potentialities*. Indeed, many have observed that it is in those sectors most effective at exploiting workers, and therefore most competitive, where one finds labour's worst adversaries. The more that capital accumulates, the more difficult it is to extract additional surplus value – a fact that can dampen worker power. As the ratio of capital to labour (in terms of firm outlays) grows, the power of workers as a class may fall. In the words of Marx (1867: 799), 'It follows therefore that in proportion as capital accumulates, the situation of the workers, be his payment high or low, must grow worse.' This is of course a generalization, but the case of Yue Yuen (Chapter 4) offers a concrete example of how larger capital-holding firms can undermine workers' attempts to exploit the 'sunk costs' of fixed capital – in part, by buying off provincial officials, the police, and courts, a degree of government capture beyond the capabilities of smaller firms.

In the current context, concentration and consolidation have not only increased exploitation but have also made firms more vulnerable to agitation. Selwyn (2008) applies the so-called bullwhip effect – in which small disruptions in a supply chain link lead to larger disruptions elsewhere – to labour unrest and global competition. He cites changes to the global distribution sector, where the introduction of new technologies and radical reductions in delivery time have become the main theatres of competition. Technological innovations – namely bar codes, high-speed conveyers with advanced routing and switch controls, reliable laser scanning of incoming containers, and increased computing capacities – facilitated 'time–space compression', making the GVC more interdependent, and allowing for lean production, lead distribution, and just-in-time deliveries.

The recent history of the United Parcels Service (UPS) provides an object lesson on how an emphasis on time pressures labour, increasing work intensity and provoking labour. Selwyn (2008: 164) remarks, 'Whilst these innovations, particularly those in the labour regime, took place with the acquiescence of labour unions and reflected the latter's weak associational power, it altered but did not diminish workers structural power.' In 1997, the 185,000 members of the UPS Teamsters Union struck, bringing UPS's global supply chain to a grinding halt. Within two weeks, only 10 per cent of UPS deliveries were at normal capacity and the company was losing $50 million a day. In due time, the workers won a 25–35 per cent five-year pay rise, and the union retained control of the employee pension fund. As Selwyn (2008: 164) concludes, 'For all its global and labour regime restructuring,' 'UPS's Achilles Heel was the capacity of its workforce to withdraw its labour and disrupt the entire UPS supply chain (Selwyn 2009: 194). The globalization of the distribution industry supply chain and the decreased lead-times only accentuate UPS's vulnerability.' Selwyn (2008: 167) also adduces several auto factory strikes in the 1990s, which were successful for similar reasons, observing that 'workers' ability to disrupt production is in some ways intensified, precisely because of firms' attempts at time–space compression'.

It is the GVC's changing composition (reflecting larger processes in global capitalism) combined with surpluses at the point of production and network centrality that renders the system vulnerable to labour pressure, widening the aperture for strategic uses of associational power to win a higher value share for workers. Florian Butollo (2014: 361) comes to similar conclusions, drawing parallels between early twentieth-century Fordism and recent history in China. In both periods, he points out, the benefits to labour were not 'passive modification of the labour process as a consequence of technological change. Quite the contrary [...] the decisive moment that lead to a transition of the mode of regulation towards an acceptance of trade unions, the implementations of collective bargaining, and the construction of the welfare state was a series of militant labour conflicts during the years of the Great Depression'. 'Workers' agency,' he continues, 'needs to play a prominent role in aligning economic development in a way that allows it.'

Finally, to bring it to the garment sector, the cases here reveal a number of distinct phenomena in the garment GVC and industrial relations. First, an increase in the scale and market diversification of specialized Southern suppliers (that is, the emergence of the mega-supplier) shifts the power balance between them and the Northern buyers, weakening the bargaining power of Northern buyers. These changes bring both obstacles and opportunities for workers. The various codes of conduct or auditing regimes were helpful at the level of discourse to assist the workers' campaign – but that is the limit of their utility. However, the implications of this dynamic on workers' rights depend, in part, on where the Northern buyer stood on the issue of labour rights. On the one hand, buyers relentlessly search for firms with labour costs that are low and undergird the global race to the bottom. On the other hand, Northern brands are highly scrutinized by NGOs, consumer groups, and anti-sweatshop activists in their own countries, and, as a consequence, can be relatively more responsive (compared to Southern suppliers) to demands for labour protections. Diminishing Northern buyers' bargaining power could negatively impact workers' rights, at least in the short term.[10] Thus, the strategy deployed for two decades, which relies on the dual pressure of Northern NGOs and anti-sweatshop activists, becomes less effective. However, the mega-supplier itself can now be more actively scrutinized through a 'direct' spotlight from the inside – from the shop floor – with workers shifting the strategy by more directly targeting their employers and bringing local and international media and allies for secondary pressure.

---

[10] See Mosley and Uno (2007), Greenhill et al. (2009), and most recently Adolph et al. (2017) on the Shanghai effect.

Conclusion

The Twilight of the Sweatshop Age?

The only constant is change.

– Heraclitus

In a course I teach on the dynamics of global capitalism, I begin with two sets of photos: garment and auto factories at the turn of the twentieth century and at the turn of the twenty-first. Students can see that the auto factory has undergone radical change, transforming the shop floor from a labour-intensive environment to one that is capital-intensive and reliant on advanced machinery. Robots now piece and fuse parts in an automated rhythm where previously workers had toiled by hand. The garment factory, however, looks much the same, with its rows of women hunched over sewing machines. While the demographics and pace may have changed, the factories, machinery, and value chain structure seem to exist outside of time, isolated from the developments that have transformed the rest of the global economy.

There's much that is striking about this pairing. First, autoworkers generally have higher union density now than garment workers and earn significantly higher wages because of it – despite all the assembly being done by robots. Second, it captures the sheer durability of the sweatshop within the garment sector. As I demonstrate in this book, the regulatory regime that had once enforced a degree of spatial inflexibility finally dwindled to nothing with the 2005 MFA phase-out. And the emergence of market spatial inflexibility, which gives labour new openings, can only occur if the flows between supplier and buyer are unrestricted. With this change, and a capable labour movement, there is hope yet that garment factory workers may close the gap.

A radical restructure of production

On 30 November 2018, the High Court of Bangladesh implemented a restraining order – passed days earlier – mandating the closure of the Dhaka office of the Accord for Fire and Building Safety ('Accord') and forcing its staff to leave the country. Introduced following the tragedy at Rana, the Accord had been heralded as an auditing regime finally capable of remedying the inhumane and often downright dangerous conditions that were endemic to Bangladesh's garment industry. However, the High Court's November restraining order, which pre-empted a negotiated 2021 Accord extension, was the result of concerns over inadequate government scrutiny. Despite attempts to appeal the decision and claims by Accord officials that factory monitoring was being conducted through third parties, by mid-April 2019 the Supreme Court of Bangladesh had delayed for the eighth time the attempts by Accord officials to challenge the High Court's decision to end its activities. The Accord has now all but ceased to operate. But the fate of the Accord was bound up with its very premise: instituting an auditing regime for an industry under the auspices of a government captured by that industry. To workers, however, the Accord's departure was of little consequence. In January 2019, 50,000 garment workers walked out for over a week. They blocked Savar's main arteries and demanded higher wages, only to be met with tear gas and rubber bullets – resulting in the death of one worker and injury to 50 more.

For the first time since the 1990s, a spectacular tragedy brought sweatshops back into the international spotlight. A massive garment factory collapsed, floor upon floor, crushing many of its occupants. Although the fight to improve working conditions in the garment industry was taken up as a cause célèbre in the previous decades, introducing the term 'sweatshop' into the common vernacular, and spawning several broad-based movements, the Rana Plaza disaster proved a monument to the complete and utter failure of Western activism: 1,134 workers perished. And it was no isolated incident. Two weeks later, a fire at a garment factory owned by the Tung Hai Group in Pakistan's Mirpur district killed eight people. In 2005, in the same neighbourhood as Rana Plaza, a nine-storey garment factory collapsed, killing 73. In 2012, some 117 people died when a fire broke out at the Tazreen Fashion factory in Dhaka. At least 262 garment workers died and another 600 were seriously injured when Pakistan's Ali Enterprises caught fire in September 2012, just a month after an inspection by a for-hire auditor earned the factory a widely respected but corporate-backed Social Accountability International accreditation (Walsh and Greenhouse 2012; AFL-CIO 2013).

Although the Rana Plaza disaster renewed concern for the victims of globalized capital, the long history of anti-sweatshop activism, its defeats, small victories, and lessons, seemed all but forgotten. Anti-sweatshop activists and global union federations (GUFs) were using the same playbook unaware of or simply ignoring the transformation of power relations occurring within GVCs. While the industry's auditing regime is widely recognized as a failure, there is little idea of what to do next. Frequently, the solutions offered are simply new auditing regimes, without any mind paid to why previous auditing regimes failed.

Strikingly, worker power and agency are wholly absent. But in Bangladesh, as in New York City after the Triangle Shirtwaist fire, the answer will likely come from workers. Of course, non-union workers are unlikely to blow the whistle since they have little protection from reprisals (Barnett 1992), but union workers are less afraid (Weil 1992), and as a result, their factories are safer (Grunberg 1983). However, questions of worker safety cannot be disentangled from larger social questions concerning the power of workers as a class.

Bangladeshi unions led the charge. By August 2013, 45 garment factory unions had been registered with the Bangladeshi government since the start of the year, a dramatic increase over the 2 – in total – which had been registered in the preceding three years (JDL 2013). By September 2013, 200,000 garment workers had taken part in mass protests, shutting down hundreds of factories, and demanding a 250 per cent increase in the minimum wage. Factory owners sublimated blame, claiming that their hands were tied since brands were unwilling to pay more (Burke and Hammadi 2013). In November, the government announced support for a 77 per cent increase in the garment worker pay – but the new $66.25/month minimum wage would still be the world's lowest. And so workers rejected that proposal, demanding $100/month instead, and taking to the streets. In the days that followed, workers destroyed several factories and shut down a hundred (Alam 2014) – part of a long tradition of 'collective bargaining by riot' (Hobsbawm 1952). Five days after the collapse at Rana, the fugitive Sohel Rana was arrested at the Indian border at Benapole as he attempted to escape into West Bengal.

In 2015, Sohel Rana was given a three-year prison sentence for not declaring his personal wealth. However, proceedings dragged on and no witness would come forward to give evidence. According to the prosecutor, Mizanur Rahman, 'Some witnesses [had] already gone missing.' This case 'created a culture of impunity', remarked Mohammed Ibrahim, one of the 41 labour activists arrested after mass walkouts over pay in 2016. Those walkouts cost over 1,500 garment workers their jobs, and 'none', Ibrahim said, 'have been reinstated'. 'The garment owners have become more powerful since the disaster.' Nazmul Huda, the cameraman who had snuck into Rana Plaza the day before its collapse to document a support beam fissure that workers had been complaining about, was now among those detained for 42 days for 'inciting' workers to protest. He was tortured and is desperate to flee the country (Jahan and Alam 2016).

Clearly, the sweatshop saga is complicated. The growth of large capital-holding firms in the Global South is not in itself a cause for celebration, though it does endow the workforces of those firms with greater potential bargaining power. A central question to the re-emergence of the sweatshop was why it continued in particular sectors (garments, footwear, and toys) and not in others – despite the subsumption of all manufacturing sectors into the globalized process. As I have argued throughout this book, there were particularities in a sector that, despite material gains made by trade unions for their class, were left with a value chain that remained vertically disintegrated, buyer-driven, and technologically underdeveloped. This intensified a global 'race to the bottom' magnifying the asymmetry between suppliers and buyers. Gereffi (1994) and others have noted the maintenance of a high degree of control by global 'buyers' (transnational brands and major retailers) despite the globally dispersed and outsourced suppliers. Globalized brands exercised monopsony power over producers through their ability to select from a large pool of outside firms for almost every phase of the value chain – textiles, production, transportation, processing, warehousing, and so on – to capture the lion's share of the value in the garment and footwear industries. Suppliers unable to reach the price demands of these transnational brands risked the loss of orders or even closure. This dependence left manufacturers in a state of perpetual instability, unable to muster the capital necessary to escape the orbit of brand power and pursue their own development, and with the possibility of losing a purchasing contract an inexorable existential threat. The result was that garment workers had the lowest bargaining power of any industrial sector.

Contrary to what neoclassical economists might have you believe, workers at the level of the firm do not get what they deserve – they get what they demand from what is available. In the cases covered by this book – Yue Yuen, Arvind, and Fruit of the Loom – large firms endured expensive strikes, workplace actions, and transnational boycotts. Using their vast resources, they prevailed upon governments to deploy police on their behalf, while also hiring private security and strongmen. They reorganized and outsourced. But for all their advantages, workers hold more potential than ever in these shops.

It has been six years since the Rana Plaza disaster and the global anti-sweatshop movement is at an impasse. History suggests that prioritizing a new auditing regime, code, or GFA, no matter how comprehensive, will ignore the roots of the problem, which are structural. For decades, transnational brands have leveraged GVCs to reap enormous profits – with scant regard for workers. But there is a change in the air.

In this book, I considered workers at large capital-holding firms in China, India, Honduras, Vietnam, Cambodia, and Indonesia. These factories were of relatively high organic composition in firms that were 'backbone' shops. I looked at campaigns testing the limits of the social order, stretching it until the seams started to show, and it became possible to glimpse another world where bosses come to the proverbial table, hat in hand, to hash out agreements with those who assemble their goods. When labour unions, activists, and advocates marshal their resources – financial, moral, political, and human – to support smart, focused, bottom-up organizing in large, increasingly integrated firms, garment workers will transform their industry. Safety issues in Bangladesh are only a symptom.

This 'race' is an integral part of the sweatshop renaissance under globalization. Yet the 'sweatshop' category is a somewhat arbitrary one. To many, it is a symbol, evoking ranks of underfed women and children, tending sewing machines, and – quite literally – sweating as they labour. To others, it is a technical thing: the absence of labour standards. I myself operate under the working definition that a 'sweatshop' is a workplace where labour has essentially no bargaining power. Of course, all labour has *some* power (there is a tacit threshold, somewhere around subsistence, beyond which a boss will always force labour's hand). But the capacity for collective bargaining, to improve wages and conditions, is, I believe, the most important determinant for identifying a sweatshop.

My book traces the changing DMP in the global value chain. The growing dependence of buyers on large, centralized suppliers indicates that shop floor labour too has become centralized and potentially more powerful. The empirical chapters demonstrate this phenomenon by example. The logic is as follows: deregulation produces high DMP, increasing the value share for the lead firm. This intensifies competition, which exerts downward pressure, winnowing the number of suppliers while shrinking DMP. Shrinking DMP leads supplier firms to consolidate, increasing their shares of value and facilitating self-investment, which raises entry barriers. The value chain settles into a symbiotic steady state, balancing oligopolistic firms at either end of the chain. Chapter 5 shows how product standardization can obviate outsourcing. As the Fruit of the Loom case shows, standardization brings opportunity for labour. For TNCs to continue to maintain power and manage domestic suppliers through the market, they need high DMP. And as DMP falls, a new era comes into view. Once barriers to entry have been established it is impossible to tear them down and return to high DMP. Brands and retailers could find other 'fixes' – vertical-integration, direct technological investment, or other methods to overcome the liability of GVC symbiosis. Whether this is indeed the twilight of the sweatshop age or a new race to the bottom may ultimately depend on the self-organization and demands of the working people.

This process has larger implications as well. Recent Chinese history, for one, resembles that of the US during the crisis of the 1960s and 1970s. Labour agitation wins higher wages and broad social reforms, creating diminished labour output while saddling employers with new costs that made room for a higher 'social wage'. In the next phase, capital automates and outsources. But the current transition may temporarily deepen the crisis of accumulation. Capital depends on the Chinese state to act as comprador, managing its billion workers, but as its discipline softens, the world economy threatens to destabilize.

Marx wrote that the history of mankind should be understood as succeeding modes of production, of which we are in the stage called capitalism. However, the internal contradictions of this stage, like those of its predecessors, can precipitate a new organization of society. And the workings of those contradictions against the forces of inertia (that is, conservatism) is an expression of historical élan vital. The only constant is change.

Global labour's bargaining power

Georg Lukacs (1971) wrote in *History and Class Consciousness* that a crisis is can bring the outlines of capitalism *as a system* into view. With this in mind, I analyse ruptures and their effects on the composition of labour-intensive GVCs and workers' bargaining power, and how international solidarity, illegal strikes, workplace disruptions, and so on, alter the balance of power. Applying historical analysis to the internal logic of GVCs, I forecast likely transformations in the sector and draw out the larger implications. In service of this, my three case studies home in on the stretch between the 2005 crisis and 2015, the 10th-year anniversary of the MFA's end.

The garment and footwear industries are 'starter' sectors, that is, training wheels in the course of economic development. Starter sectors offer clues to the direction of capitalist development by paving the road – sometimes literally – for more advanced industries. Within these sectors, there are products that are ephemeral by nature, sensitive to seasonality and fashion, and those which are not, and therefore subject to standardization and mechanization. I have examined three of the most valorized parts of the garment sector to which these categories apply: footwear, jeans, and cotton commodity production. I use Yue Yuen, Arvind, and Fruit of the Loom, respectively, as they are 'ideal types' (to borrow Max Weber's expression), which – as per Baran and Sweezy (1969: 15) – 'display with sharpness and clarity what may appear in everyday economic life in a disguised form, difficult to recognise and easy to misinterpret'. By analysing the most valorized parts of underdeveloped sectors, we can see where capital is going and how it is getting there. How capital affects the shop floor and how the shop floor affects capital are the two questions on which the value chain turns.

Any material analysis of the world must recognize that capitalism creates two opposing enemy forces: chiefly, the forces of labour and the interests of capitalists. The two have been at loggerheads since the transition to capitalism. But under globalization, this conflict has reached a fever pitch, throwing the stakes into sharp relief. Indeed, the struggles of workers are universal and transhistorical. 'Workers of the world unite, you have nothing to lose but your chains!' – the popular adaptation of Marx is both a call to arms and a recognition of the common aspirations that bind us.

I conclude that sweatshops occur where surpluses are limited and production is diffuse and isolated from consumption. Competition and the recent MFA phase-out, however, have created a centralized industry, with a few mega-firms in a few locations. Large, consolidated supplier firms are already flexing their new muscle. Oligopolistic power is being turned into larger surpluses, which are being stretched with finance and put into labour-saving technology and other entry barriers. This can be explained by changing labour markets, falling source prices, increased self-financing, the creeping march of finance capital, among other factors. However, I advance a general theory of GVCs. When buyer DMP falls, suppliers ascend, giving workers the high ground.

The changes in the value chain, however, cannot be disarticulated from larger transformations in capitalism. As I have laid out in Chapter 7, limits on the mobility of transnational capital – what I term 'spatial inflexibility' – create new openings for workers. Throughout this book, I revisit the ILGWU's jobbers' strategy as an example of regulatory spatial inflexibility, one in which nation-states allowed workers to 'chase work' under a single, unified regime of regulated wages, hours, and working conditions. The spatial limits on garment capital – that is, its geographic fixity – meant that workers could demand more of employers, despite the points of value capture and creation being on opposite ends of the value chain. For employers, the jobbers' agreement took wages and benefits out of the equation.

Now, intense market pressure has led manufacturers to consolidate, upgrade, and integrate vertically. This places spatial limits on capital and value capture at the point of production, giving workers greater potential bargaining power as manufacturers accrue the means to better undermine labour agitation. Oligopolization and the rising organic composition of capital mean that wages, hours, and benefits have a reduced role in competition.

However, even if there is a shift in the balance of power, in which contractors increase their influence vis-à-vis brands, both contractor and brand will remain significant players, and need to be engaged – ideally, though pressure – as in the triangular jobbers' agreement–style bargaining system. Just as the ILGWU once targeted 'backbone shops' (the large contractors upon which jobbers depended for their competitive edge), modern labour must identify and target the 'backbone' suppliers of today while simultaneously pressuring TNCs. If this model of bottom-up strategic organizing can go global under the flag of an international solidarity campaign, it could open the door for sector-wide global collective bargaining.

An understanding of how capital evolves and how the internal logic governing competition reshapes value chains can help improve workers' understanding of where they are situated (temporally and spatially) and how best to leverage that position. What is broadly understood as the global anti-sweatshop movement continues to rely on an outdated campaign model designed to fight a static industrial power arrangement. But firms, countries, and entire regions are now ascending the value chain. By targeting large, vertically integrated firms, workers – as demonstrated here – are evolving their strategy on the fly, to great effect. If these efforts advance, and continue picking up steam, the sweatshop could – in due time – be reduced to historical memory.

Bibliography

Abernathy, Frederick H., John T. Dunlop, Janice H. Hammond, and David Weil. 1999. *A Stitch in Time: Lean Retailing and the Transformation of Manufacturing: Lessons from the Apparel and Textile Industries.* New York: Oxford University Press.

AFBSB. 2013. 'Accord on Fire and Building Safety in Bangladesh.' *International Labor Rights Forum.* Available at: http://www.laborrights.org/creating-a-sweatfree-world/resources/bangladesh-fire-and-building-safety-agreement.

AFL-CIO. 1988. *Numbers That Count: A Manual of Internal Organizing.* Department of Organization and Field Services, AFL-CIO.

———. 2013. *Responsibility Outsourced.* Available at: www.aflcio.org/content/download/77061/1902391/CSReport.pdf.

AFP. 2014. 'Thousands of Workers Strike at China Shoe Factory.' *AFP.* April 16.

———. 2016. 'Reboot.' *The Guardian*, May 25.

Ahmed, Nazneen and Dev Nathan. 2014. 'Improving Wages and Working Conditions in the Bangladeshi Garment Sector: The Role of Horizontal and Vertical Relations.' Available at: http://www.capturingthegains.org/pdf/ctg-wp-2014-40.pdf.

Alam, Julhas. 2014. 'Bangladeshi Garment Workers Riot over Wages.' *Spokesman Review.* Available at: http://www.spokesman.com/stories/2013/nov/12/bangladeshi-garment-workers-riot-over-wages/. Accessed on 4 January.

Amsden, Alice. 1989. *Asia's Next Giant.* New York: Oxford University Press.

Anderson, Jeremy, Paula Hamilton, and Jane Wills. 2011. '21 The Multi-scalarity of Trade Union Practice.' *Handbook of Employment and Society: Working Space* 383.

Anner, Mark. 2011. *Solidarity Transformed: Labor Responses to Globalization and Crisis in Latin America.* Cornell University Press.

———. 2013. 'Workers' Power in Global Value Chains.' In *Transnational Trade Unionism*, edited by P. Fairbrother, M.-A. Hennebert, and C. Levesque, 24–41. New York: Routledge.

———. 2015. 'Labor Control Regimes and Workers Resistance in Global Supply Chains.' *Labor History* 56(3): 292–307.

Anner, Mark, Jennifer Bair, and Jeremy Blasi. 2012. 'Buyer Power, Pricing Practices, and Labor Outcomes in Global Supply Chains.'

Anner, Mark, Ian Greer, Marco Hauptmeier, Nathan Lillie, and Nik Winchester. 2006. 'The Industrial Determinants of Transnational Solidarity: Global Interunion Politics in Three Sectors.' *European Journal of Industrial Relations* 12(1): 7.

Appelbaum, Richard P. 2008. 'Giant Transnational Contractors in East Asia: Emergent Trends in Global Supply Chains.' *Competition & Change* 12(1): 69–87.

———. 2009. 'Big Suppliers in Greater China.' *China and the Transformation of Global Capitalism* 65–85.

Arndt, Sven W. and Henryk Kierzkowski. 2001. 'Introduction.' In *Fragmentation: New Production Patterns in the World Economy*, edited by Sven W. Arndt and Henryk Kierzkowski, 1–16. Oxford: Oxford University Press.

Armbruster-Sandoval, Ralph. 2005. *Globalization and Cross-border Labor Solidarity in the Americas*. New York City: Routledge.

Arnold, Dennis. 2013. 'Social Margins and Precarious Work in Vietnam.' *American Behavioral Scientist* 57(4): 468–487.

Arrighi, Giovanni. 2000. *Globalization, State Sovereignty, and the 'Endless' Accumulation of Capital*. Vol. 129. Lanham: Rowman and Littlefield.

Aschoff, Nicole. 2013. 'Imported from Detroit.' *Jacobin Magazine*. Available at: https://jacobinmag.com/2013/04/imported-from-detroit/.

Azarhoushang, Behzad, Alessandro Bramucci, Hansjörg Herr, and Bea Ruoff. 2015. 'Value Chains, Underdevelopment and Union Strategy.' *International Journal of Labour Research* 7(1/2): 153.

Azmeh, Shamel and Khalid Nadvi. 2014. 'Asian Firms and the Restructuring of Global Value Chains.' *International Business Review* 23(4): 708–717.

Bailay, Rasul. 2013. 'US Apparel Retailer Gap in Joint Venture Talks with Arvind Brands.' *The Economic Times*. Available at: http://articles.economictimes.indiatimes.com/2013-11-29/news/44575485_1_arvind-brands-arvind-ltd-joint-venture.

Baines, Joseph. 2015. 'Encumbered Behemoth: Wal-Mart, Differential Accumulation and International Retail Restructuring (Preprint).' *Handbook of the International Political Economy of Production* 149–166.

Bair, Jennifer. 2009. 'Global Commodity Chains: Genealogy and Review.' In *Frontiers of Commodity Chain Research*, edited by J. Bair, 1–34. Stanford, CA: Stanford University Press.

Bair, Jennifer and Florence Palpacuer. 2012. 'From Varieties of Capitalism to Varieties of Activism: The Antisweatshop Movement in Comparative Perspective.' *Social Problems* 59(4): 522–543.

Bair, Jennifer and Gary Gereffi. 2001. 'Local Clusters in Global Chains: The Causes and Consequences of Export Dynamism in Torreon's Blue Jeans Industry.' *World Development* 29(11): 1885–1903.

Ballinger, Jeff. 2009. 'Finding an Anti-sweatshop Strategy That Works.' *Dissent* 56(3): 5–8.

Banks, Andy and Jack Metzgar. 1989. 'Participating in Management: Union Organizing on a New Terrain.' *Labor Research Review* 1(14): 7.

Baran, Paul A. and Paul M. Sweezy. 1966. 'Monopoly Capital.' *Monthly Review Press*.

Barboza, David. 2012. 'China's Economy Slows as Exports and New Orders Decline.' *New York Times*, August 1.

Barnett, Tim. 1992. 'A Preliminary Investigation of the Relationship Between Selected Organizational Characteristics and External Whistleblowing by Employees.' *Journal of Business Ethics* 11(12): 949–59. DOI:10.1007/BF00871961.

Barrie, Leonie. 2015. 'Pou Yuen Strike Underscores Vietnam Challenges.' *Just-Style*. April 9.

———. 2018. 'Lesotho Workers Win 62% Jump in Minimum Wages.' *Just-Style*. August 24.
Barrientos, Stephanie, Gary Gereffi, and Arianna Rossi. 2011. 'Economic and Social Upgrading in Global Production Networks.' *International Labor Review* 150(3–4): 319–340.
Bartley, Tim. 2009. 'Standards for Sweatshops: The Power and Limits of Club Theory for Explaining Voluntary Labor Standards Programs.' In *Voluntary Programs: A Club Theory Perspective*, edited by Matthew Potoski and Aseem Prakash, 107–132. Cambridge, MA: MIT Press.
Bartley, T. and S. Smith. 2008. 'Structuring Transnational Fields of Governance: Networks, Legitimation, and the Evolution of Ethical Sourcing.' Working Paper. Indiana University.
Bass, George Nelson III. 2012. 'Organised Labor and US Foreign Policy: The Solidarity Center in Historical Context.' FIU Electronic Theses and Dissertations. Available at: http://digitalcommons.fiu.edu/etd/752. Accessed on 15 August 2013.
BBC. 2015. 'Thousands on Strike in Vietnam over Insurance Law.' *BBC*. April 1.
Beckert, Sven. 2015. *Empire of Cotton*. Penguin Books.
Benko, Cathleen A. and Warren McFarlan. 2003. *Connecting the Dots: Aligning Projects with Objectives in Unpredictable Times*. Harvard Business Review Press.
Bernhardt, Thomas and William Milberg. 2011. 'Economic and Social Upgrading in Global Value Chains.' Capturing the Gains Working Paper.
Bhattacharya, Tithi. 2017. *Introduction: Mapping Social Reproduction Theory*, edited by Tithi Bhattacharya. Pluto Press.
Bhaduri, Amit and Stephen Marglin. 1990. 'Unemployment and the Real Wage: The Economic Basis for Contesting Political Ideologies.' *Cambridge Journal of Economics* 14(4): 375–393.
Bissell-Linsk, Jennifer. 2017. 'Nike's Focus on Robotics Threatens Asia's Low-Cost Work-Force.' *Financial Times*, October 22. Available at: https://www.ft.com/content/585866fc-a841-11e7-ab55-27219df83c97.
Blackett, Adelle. 2000. 'Global Governance, Legal Pluralism and the Decentered State: A Labor Law Critique of Codes of Corporate Conduct.' *Indiana Journal of Global Legal Studies* 8: 401.
Blecher, M. J. 2002. 'Hegemony and Workers' Politics in China.' *The China Quarterly* 170 (1): 283–303.
Boston, Sarah. 1987. *Women Workers and the Trade Unions*. London: Lawrence & Wishart.
Bonacich, Edna. 2001. 'The Challenge of Organizing in a Globalised/Flexible Industry: The Case of the Apparel Industry in Los Angeles.' *The Critical Study of Work: Labor, Technology and Global Production* 155–178.
Bond, Patrick. 2004. 'Top down or Bottom up? A Reply to David Held.' *Opendemocracy on-Line* 23. Available at: http://www.ukzn.ac.za/ccs/files/Bond%20crit%20of%20Held.pdf.
———. 2008. 'Reformist Reforms, Non-reformist Reforms and Global Justice: Activist, NGO and Intellectual Challenges in the World Social Forum 1.' *The World and the US Social Forums: A Better World Is Possible and Necessary*.

Borromeo, Leah. 2014. 'How Adidas Supported Worker Rights in China Factory Strike.' *The Guardian*.

Bound, Kirsten and Ian W. B. Thornton. 2012. *Our Frugal Future: Lessons from India's Innovation System*. London: Nesta. Available at: http://www.nesta.org.uk/sites/default/files/our_frugal_future.pdf.

Braun, Rainer and Judy Gearhart. 2004. 'Who Should Code Your Conduct? Trade Union and NGO Differences in the Fight for Workers' Rights.' *Development in Practice* 14(1–2): 183–196.

Braverman, Harry. 1974. 'Labor and Monopoly Capital.' *Monthly Review Press*.

Breitenfellner, Andreas. 1997. 'Global Unionism: A Potential Player.' *International Labour Review* 136(4): 531.

Brenner, Neil. 1999. 'Beyond State–Centrism? Space, Territoriality, and Geographical Scale in Globalization Studies.' *Theory and Society* 28(1): 39–78.

Bronfenbrenner, Kate. 2007. *Global Unions: Challenging Transnational Capital Through Cross-Border Campaigns*. Cornell University Press.

Brooks, Ethel C. 2007. *Unraveling the Garment Industry: Transnational Organizing and Women's Work*. Minneapolis: University of Minnesota Press.

Brown, Charles and James L. Madoff. 1989. 'The Employer-Size Wage Effect.' *Journal of Political Economy* 97(5): 1027–1059.

Buhmann, Karin. 2006. 'Corporate Social Responsibility – What Role for Law? Some Legal Aspects of CSR.' *Emerald Insight*.

Buhmann, Karin and Florian Wettstein. 2017. 'Business and Human Rights: Not Just Another CSR Issue?' In *Corporate Social Responsibility: Strategy, Communication, Governance*, edited by Andreas Rasche, Mette Morsing, and Jeremy Moon, 379–404. Cambridge: Cambridge University Press.

Burawoy, Michael. 1979. *Manufacturing Consent: Changes in the Labour Process Under Monopoly Capitalism*. Chicago: University of Chicago Press.

Burdett, Kenneth and Dale T. Mortenson. 1998. 'Wage Differentials, Employer Size, and Unemployment.' *International Economic Review* May 1: 257–273.

Burke, Jason and Saad Hammadi. 2013. 'Bangladesh Police Clash with Garment Workers Protesting over Wages.' *The Guardian*. September 25. Available at: http://www.theguardian.com/world/2013/sep/25/bangladesh-police-clash-garment-workers.

Butollo, Florian. 2014. *The End of Cheap Labour? Industrial Transformation and 'Social Upgrading' in China*. University of Chicago Press.

Cai, Fang. 2015a. '16 Demographic Change and Its Consequences for the Labor Market.' *Managing the Middle-Income Transition* 453.

———. 2015b. 'Approaching a Neoclassical Scenerio: The Labor Market in China After the Lewis Turning Point.' In *Debating the Lewis Turning Point in China*, edited by Huang Yiping and Fang Cai. Routledge.

Campling Liam, James Harrison, Ben Richardson, and Adrain Smith. 2016. 'Can Labour Provisions Work Beyond the Border?' *International Labour Review* 155(3): 357–382.

Carpe, Matthieu, Carl, Chiarrella, Peter Flaschel, and Willi Semmler. 2011. *Financial Assets, Debt and Liquidity Crises*. Cambridge University Press.

Carswell, Grace and Geert De Neve. 2013. 'Labouring for Global Markets.' *Geoforum* 44: 62–70.
Cashore, Benjamin. 2002. 'Legitimacy and the Privatization of Environmental Governance: How Non-state Market-Driven (NSMD) Governance Systems Gain Rule-Making Authority.' *Governance* 15(4): 503–529.
Castells, Manuel. 1996. 'The Space of Flows.' *The Rise of the Network Society* 1: 376–482.
Carty, Victoria. 2010. 'The Internet and Grassroots Politics: Nike, the Athletic Apparel Industry and the Anti-Sweatshop Campaign.' *Tamara Journal for Critical Organization Inquiry* 1(2).
Cerny, Philip G. 1997. 'Paradoxes of the Competition State: The Dynamics of Political Globalization.' *Government and Opposition* 32(2): 251–274.
Chan, Anita. 2011 'Strikes in China's Export Industries in Comparative Perspective.' *The China Journal* 65: 27–51.
———. 2015. 'Introduction.' In *Chinese Workers in Comparative Perspective*. Cornell University Press.
Chan, Anita. 2018. 'The Relationship between Labour NGOs and Chinese Workers in an Authoritarian Regime.' *Global Labour Journal* 9(1): 1–18.
Chan, Chris King-Chi. 2010a. *The Challenge of Labour in China*. London: Routledge.
———. 2010b. 'A China Paradox: Migrant Labor Shortage Amidst Rural Labor Supply Abundance.' *Eurasian Geography and Economics* 51(4): 513–531.
Chan, Chris King-Chi and Elaine Sio-Ieng Hui. 2014. 'The Development of Collective Bargaining in China: From "Collective Bargaining by Riot" to "Party State-Led Wage Bargaining".' *The China Quarterly* 217: 221–242.
Chatteri, Aaron and David Levine. 2005. 'Breaking Down the Codes.' Center for Responsible Business, UC Berkeley Working Paper Series.
Cheng, Zhiming, Ingrid Nielsen, and Russell Smyth. 2014. 'Access to Social Insurance in Urban China.' *Habitat International* 41: 243–252.
Chiarella, Carl and Peter Flaschel. 2000. *The Dynamics of Keynesian Monetary Growth*. Cambridge University Press.
Chiarella, Carl, Flaschel Peter, and Reiner Franke. 2005. *Foundations for a Disequilibrium Theory of the Business Cycle*. Cambridge University Press.
Chibber, Vivek. 2003. *Locked in Place: State-Building Band Late Industrialization in India*. Princeton University Press.
———. 2011. *Capitalism and the State*. Available at: http://www.youtube.com/watch?v=R5R-9X_BtP4&feature=youtube_gdata_player.
Chiu, Catherine C. H. 2007. 'Workplace Practices in Hong Kong-invested Garment Factories in Cambodia.' *Journal of Contemporary Asia* 37(4): 431–448.
Choudhury, Pran K. 2001. *Successful Branding*. Universities Press.
Christophers, Brett. 2016. *The Great Leveler: Capitalism and Competition in the Court of Law*. Cambridge: Harvard University Press.
Chu, Kathy. 2015. 'Garment Maker Retreats as China Shifts Policy.' *The Wall Street Journal*. December 2. Available at : http://www.wsj.com/articles/garment-maker-succumbs-to-shift-in-chinas-policy-1449082802.

Chua, Charmaine, Martin Danyluk, Deborah Cowen, and Laleh Khalili. 2018. 'Introduction: Turbulent Circulation: Building a Critical Engagement with Logistics.' *Environment and Planning D: Society and Space* 36(4): 617–629.

Cini, Michelle. 2001. 'The Soft Law Approach: Commission Rule-Making in the EU's State Aid Regime.' *Journal of European Public Policy* 8(2): 192–207.

Coe, Neil M. and Martin Hess. 2013. 'Global Production Networks, Labor and Development.' *Geoforum* 44: 4–9.

Coe, Neil M., Martin Hess, and Peter Dicken. 2008. *Journal of Economic Geography* 271–95.

Collins, Jane. 2009. *Threads: Gender, Labor, and Power in the Global Apparel Industry*. University of Chicago Press.

Commons, John. 1977. 'Report by the U.S. Industrial Commission' Volume XV, 1901. In *Out of the Sweatshop: The Struggle for Industrial Democracy*, edited by L. Stern 44–45. New York: Quadrangle.

Compa, L. and T. Hinchliffe-Darricarrere. 1995. 'Enforcing International Labour Rights through Corporate Codes of Conduct.' *Columbia Journal of Transnational Law* 33: 663.

Compa, Lance. 2001. 'NAFTA's Labour Side Agreement and International Labour Solidarity.' *Antipode* 33(3): 451–67.

———. 2004. 'Trade Unions, NGOs, and Corporate Codes of Conduct.' *Development in Practice* 14(1–2): 210–215.

———. 2013. 'After Bangladesh, Labour Unions Can Save Lives.' Available at: http://articles.washingtonpost.com/2013-05-26/opinions/39544959_1_labour-unions-lance-compa-labour-relations.

Cook, Karen S. 1977. 'Exchange and Power in Networks of Interorganizational Relations.' *The Sociological Quarterly* 18: 62–82.

Cowen, Deborah. 2014. *The Deadly Life of Logistics*. Minneapolis: University of Minnesota Press.

Crouch, Colin and Streeck Wolfgang, eds. 1997. *Political Economy of Modern Capitalism*. London: Sage Publications.

Croucher, Richard and Elizabeth Cotton. 2009. *Global Business, Global Unions*. London: Middlesex University Press.

Cumbers, Andrew, Corinne Nativel, and Paul Routledge 2008. 'Labor Agency and Union Positionalities in Global Production Networks.' *Journal of Economic Geography* 8(3): 369–387.

D'Antona, Massimo. 2002. 'Labour Law at the Century's End: An Identity Crisis.' *Labour Law in an Era of Globalization*.

Danyluk, Martin. 2017. 'Capital's Logistical Fix: Accumulation, Globalization, and the Survival of Capitalism.' *Environment and Planning D: Society and Space*.

Davis, Mike. 2006. *Planet of Slums*. Verso.

Davis, Rowenna. 2010. Victory Looms. *New Internationalist*. January 1. Available at: http://newint.org/columns/currents/2010/01/01/workers-rights/. Accessed on 20 April 2014.

De La Merced, Michael J. and Jeffrey Cane. 2011. 'Confident Deal Makers Pulled out Checkboooks in 2010.' *New York Times*, January 3.

Desai, Radhika. 2013. *Geopolitical Economy*. London: Pluto Press.
Deyo, Frederic C. 1989. *Beneath the Miracle: Labor Subordination in the New Asian Industrialism*. University of California Press.
Dicken, Peter. 2007. *Global Shift*. London: Sage Publications.
Doh, Jonathan P. and Nicolas M. Dahan. 2010. 'Social Movements and Social Networks: An Evolutionary Perspective on Contemporary US Student Advocacy Campaigns.' Available at: http://www.egosnet.org/jart/prj3/egos/resources/dbcon_def/uploads/summer_workshop_papers/W-009.pdf.
Dominelli, Lena and Ankie Hoogvelt. 1996. 'Globalization and the Technocratization of Social Work.' *Critical Social Policy* 16(47): 45–62.
Doms, Mark E. and J. Bradford Jensen. 1998. 'Comparing Wages, Skills, and Productivity Between Domestically and Foreign-Owned Manufacturing Establishments in the United States.' In *Geography and Ownership as Bases for Economic Accounting* 235–258. University of Chicago Press.
Dougherty, L. Michael. 2008. 'Theorising Theory: Origins and Orientations of Commodity Chain Analysis.' *The Global Studies Journal* 1(3): 29–38. DOI: 10.18848/1835-4432/CGP/v01i03/40929.
D'silva, Bernadette and Annie Beena Joseph. 2014. 'A Study on the Implications of Corporate Restructuring.'
Dunford, Michael, Robin Dunford, Mirela Barbu, and Weidong Liu. 2016. 'Globalisation, Cost Competitiveness and International Trade: The Evolution of the Italian Textile and Clothing Industries and the Growth of Trade with China.' *European Urban and Regional Studies* 23(2): 111–135.
Dunning, John H. 1977. 'Trade, Location of Economic Activity and the MNE: A Search for an Eclectic Approach.' In *The International Allocation of Economic Activity*, edited by Bertil Ohlin, Per-Ove Hesselborn, and Per Magnus Wijkman. London: Macmillan.
———. 2000. *Regions, Globalization, and the Knowledge-Based Economy*. Oxford: Oxford University Press.
Durand, Cedric and Légé Phillipe. 2013. 'Regulation Beyond Growth.' *Capital & Class* 37(1): 111–126.
Dutt, Amitava Krishna. 2016. *Growth, Distribution, and Uneven Development*. Cambridge University Press.
Economist. 2010. 'World Economy.' July 29.
———. 2013. 'Industrial Eclipse.' April 15.
———. 2014. 'Danger Zone.' April 26.
Egels-Zandén, Niklas. 2009. 'TNC Motives for Signing International Framework Agreements: A Continuous Bargaining Model of Stakeholder Pressure.' *Journal of Business Ethics* 84: 529–47.
Egels-Zandén, Niklas and Peter Hyllman. 2006. 'Exploring the Effects of Union–NGO Relationships on Corporate Responsibility: The Case of the Swedish Clean Clothes Campaign.' *Journal of Business Ethics* 64(3): 303–316.
Eidelson, Josh. 2013. 'I Jumped to Save My Body: Walmart Slammed Over Nicaragua Stabbings and Bangladesh Fire.' *The Nation*. April 18. Available at: http://www.

thenation.com/blog/173921/i-jumped-save-my-body-walmart-slammed-over-nicaragua-stabbings-and-bangladesh-fire.

Elbehri, Aziz. 2004. 'MFA Quota Removal and Global Textile and Cotton Trade: Estimating Quota Trade Restrictiveness and Quantifying Post-MFA Trade Patterns.' In *Economic Research Service, USDA*. Paper Prepared for the 7th Annual Conference on Global Economic Analysis, Washington, DC. Available at: http://www. Ecomod. net/conferences/ecomod2004/ecomod2004_papers/318.Pdf And https://www.gtap.agecon.purdue.edu/resources/download/1861.pdf.

Elfstrom, Manfred and Sarosh Kuruvilla. 2014. 'The Changing Nature of Labor Unrest in China.' *ILR Review* 67(2): 453–480.

Emmelhainz, Margaret A. and Ronald J. Adams. 1999. 'The Apparel Industry Response to 'sweatshop' Concerns: A Review and Analysis of Codes of Conduct.' *Journal of Supply Chain Management* 35(3): 51–57.

Esbenshade, Jill Louise. 2004. *Monitoring Sweatshops: Workers, Consumers, and the Global Apparel Industry*. Temple University Press.

———. 2008. Going up Against the Global Economy: New Developments in the Antisweatshops Movement. *Critical Sociology* 34(3):453–470.

Esping-Andersen, Gosta. 1999. *Social Foundations of Postindustrial Economies*. Oxford University Press.

ETUF-TCL. 2007. 'ITGLWF/Inditex: First International Framework Agreement in the TGL.' European Trade Union Federation of Textile, Clothing and Leather.

Evans, Peter. 1997. 'The Eclipse of the State? Reflections on Stateness in an Era of Globalization.' *World Politics* 50(1): 62–87.

———. 2010. 'Is It Labor's Turn to Globalise? Twenty-First Century Opportunities and Strategic Responses.' *Global Labour Journal* 1(3): 352–379.

Fairbrother, Peter and Nikolaus Hammer. 2005. 'Global Unions: Past Efforts and Future Prospects.' *Industrial Relations* 60(3): 405–431.

Featherstone, David. 2012. *Solidarity: Hidden Histories and Geographies of Internationalism*. London: Zed.

Feenstra, Robert C. 1998. 'Integration of Trade and Disintegration of Production in the Global Economy.' *Journal of Economic Perspectives* 12(4): 31–50.

Feingold, Joel. 2013. 'Worker Struggle in the American Export Processing Zonez [1934–1962]. https://www.academia.edu/9037988/Worker_Struggle_in_the_American_Export_Processing_Zones_1934-1962_2013. Accessed on January 10, 2019.

Fernandez-Stark, Karina, Stacey Frederick, and Gary Gereffi. 2011. *The Apparel Global Value Chain: Economic Upgrading and Workforce Development, Technical Report*. Center on Globalization, Governance and Competitiveness, Duke University.

Fimmen, Edo. 1922. 'The International Federation of Trade Unions: Development and Aims.' IFTU. Available at: http://library.fes.de/pdf-files/netzquelle/01299.pdf.

Flanders, Allan. 1968. 'Collective Bargaining: A Theoretical Analysis.' *British Journal of Industrial Relations* 6(1): 1–26.

Flannery, Russell. 2014. 'Shares in Nike Drop to 5 Month Low After Controversial China Strike Ends.' *Forbes*. May 3.

Flecker, Jörg, Bettina Haidinger, and Annika Schönauer. 2013. 'Divide and Serve: The Labour Process in Service Value Chains and Networks.' *Competition & Change* 17(1): 6–23.

Fold, Niels. 2002. 'Lead Firms and Competition in "Bipolar" Commodity Chains: Grinders and Branders in the Global Cocoa Chocolate Industry.' *Journal of Agrarian Change* 2(2): 228–247.

Foster, John Bellamy, Robert McChesney, and Jamil Jonna. 2011. 'Monopoly and Competition in the Twenty-First Century.' *Monthly Review* 62(11).

Fox, Justin. 2018. 'U.S. Manufacturing Isn't Dwindling Away (or Booming).' *Bloomberg*. March 7. Available at: https://www.bloomberg.com/view/articles/2018-03-07/u-s-manufacturing-isn-t-beating-china-but-it-s-not-doomed.

Frankel, Judith. 1997. *Families of Employed Mothers: An International Perspective*. Taylor & Francis.

Frenkel, Stephen J. 2001. 'Globalization, Athletic Footwear, Commodity Chains and Emloyment Relations in China.' *Organizational Studies* 531–562.

Frenkel, Stephan and Sarosh Kuruvilla. 2002. 'Logics of Action, Globalization, and Employment Relations Change in China, India, Malaysia, and the Philippines.' *Industrial and Labor Relations Review* 55: 387–412.

Frederick, Stacey and Cornelia Staritz. 2012. 'Development in the Global Apparel Industry After the MFA Phase Out.' In *Sewing Success?*, edited by Lopez-Acevedo, Gladys, and Raymond Robertson. Washington DC: World Bank.

Freeman, Linton C. 1978. 'Centrality in Social Networks Conceptual Clarification.' *Social Networks* 1(3): 215–239. doi: 10.1016/0378-8733(78)90021-7.

Freidberg, Susanne. 2003. 'Cleaning Up Down South: Supermarkets, Ethical Trade and African Horticulture.' *Social & Cultural Geography* 4(1): 27–43.

Friedman, Eli. 2009. 'External Pressure and Local Mobilization: Transnational Activism and the Emergence of the Chinese Labor Movement.' *Mobilization* 14(2): 199–218.

———. 2012. 'China in Revolt'. *Jacobin*.

———. 2014. 'Alienated Politics'. *Development and Change* 45(5):1001–1018.

———. 2015. *Insurgency Trap*. Cornell University Press.

——— and Sarosh Kuruvilla. 2015. 'Experimentation and Decentralization in China's Labor Relations.' *Human Relations* 68(2): 181–195.

Froud Julie, Colin Haslam, Sukhdev Johal, and Karel Williams. 2000. 'Shareholder Value and Financialization: Consultancy Promises, Management Moves.' *Economy and Society* 29(1): 80–110.

Frundt, H. J. 2004. 'Unions Wrestle with Corporate Codes of Conduct.' *WorkingUSA* 7(4): 36–69.

FTC. 1955. In the Matter of the California Sportswear a Dress Association, Inc.

Fung, Archon and Erik Olin Wright. 2003. 'Countervailing Power in Empowered Participatory Governance.' In *Deepening Democracy: Institutional Innovations in Empowered Participatory Governance*, edited by Archon Fung and Rebecca Abers. Verso.

Galanis, Giorgos and Ashok Kumar. 2018. A Dynamic Spatial Model of Global Governance Structures. Post-Keynesian Economics Society. Working Paper 1804.

Gallin, Dan. 2001. 'Propositions on Trade Unions and Informal Employment in Times of Globalisation.' *Antipode* 33(3): 531–549.

———. 2008. 'International Framework Agreements: A Reassessment.' In *Cross-Border Social Dialogue and Agreements: An Emerging Global Industrial Relations Framework*, 15–41.

Garnaut, Ross. 2010. 'Macro-economic Implications of the Turning Point.' *China Economic Journal* 3(2): 181–190.

Seidman, Gay. 2009. *Beyond the Boycott: Labor Rights, Human Rights and Transnational Activism*. Gay W. Seidman Russell Sage Foundation.

Gereffi, Gary. 1994. 'The Organization of Buyer-Driven Global Commodity Chains: How U.S. Retailers Shape Overseas Production Networks.' In *Commodity Chains and Global Capitalism*, edited by G. Gereffi and M. Korzeniewicz, 95–122. Westport: Praeger.

———. 1996. 'Global Commodity Chains: New Forms of Coordination and Control Among Nations and Firms in International Industries.' *Competition and Change* 4: 427–439.

———. 1999. 'International Trade and Industrial Upgrading in the Apparel Commodity Chain.' *Journal of International Economics* 48(1): 37–70.

———. 2002. 'Outsourcing and Changing Patterns of International Competition in the Apparel Commodity Chain.' Paper presented at the conference on Responding to Globalization: Societies, Groups, and Individuals, Hotel Boulderado, Boulder, CO, April 4–7, 2002.

———. 2009. 'Development Models and Industrial Upgrading in China and Mexico.' *European Sociological Review* 25(1): 37–51.

———. 2014. 'Global Value Chains in a Post-Washington Consensus World.' *Review of International Political Economy* 21(1): 9–37.

Gereffi, Gary and Karina Fernandez-Stark. 2016. *Global Value Chain Analysis: A Primer*. Retrieved from https://dukespace.lib.duke.edu/dspace/handle/10161/12488.

Gereffi, Gary and Miguel Korzeniewicz. 1994. *Commodity Chains and Global Capitalism*. Westport: Praeger.

Gereffi Gary, John Humphrey, and Timothy Sturgeon. 2005. 'The Governance of Global Value Chains.' *Review of International Political Economy* 12(1): 78–104.

Ghemawat, Pankaj. 1990. 'The snowball effect.' *International Journal of Industrial Organization* 8(3): 335–351.

Ghosh, Jayati. 2009. *Never Done and Poorly Paid: Women's Work in Globalising India*. New Delhi: Women Unlimited.

Gibbon, P. 2001. 'Upgrading Primary Production: A Global Commodity Approach.' *World Development* 29(2): 345–363.

Gibbon Peter, Bair, Jennifer and Stefano Ponte. 2008. 'Governing Gobal Value Chains: An Introduction.' *Economy and Society* 3: 315–338.

Goodwin, Richard. 1967. 'A Growth Cycle.' In *Socialism, Capitalism, and Economic Growth*, edited by Carl Feinstein. Cambridge, UK: Cambridge University Press.

Gongchao. 2014. 'The New Strikes in China'. April.
Gorz, Andre. 1967. *Strategy for Labor: A Radical Proposal*. Boston: Beacon Press.
Gramsci, Antonio. 1992. *Prison Notebooks*. Columbia University Press.
Greenhill, Brian, Layna Mosley, and Aseem Prakash. 2009. 'Trade-Based Diffusion of Labor Rights.' *American Political Science Review* 103(04): 669–690.
Gregoratti, Catia and Doug Miller. 2011. 'International Framework Agreements for Workers' Rights? Insights from River Rich Cambodia.' *Global Labour Journal* 2(2): 84–105.
Greven, Thomas. 2008. 'The Challenge of Generating Cross-border Support.' *International Centre for Trade Union Rights* 15(3): 6–7.
Grunberg, Leon. 1983. 'The Effects of the Social Relations of Production on Productivity and Workers' Safety: An Ignored Set of Relationships.' *International Journal of Health Services* 13(4): 621–634.
Guest, David E. and Riccardo Peccei. 2001. 'Partnership at Work: Mutuality and the Balance of Advantage.' *British Journal of Industrial Relations* 39(2): 207–236.
Gumbrell-McCormick, Rebecca. 2000. 'Globalisation and the Dilemmas of International Trade Unionism.' *Transfer: European Review of Labour and Research* 6(1): 29–42.
Gupta, Vipin and Renfeng Qiu. 2013. 'The Rise of the Indian Multinational Corporations and the Development of Firm-Specific Capabilities.' *Journal of Business Theory and Practice* 1(1): 45.
H&M-IndustriALL. 2015. 'GFA Between H&M and IndustriALL.' Available at: http://www.industriall-union.org/sites/default/files/uploads/documents/GFAs/hm-industriall_gfa_agreed_version_09-09-2015.pdf. Accessed on February 14, 2019.
Haas, Peter M., John A. Hird, and Beth McBratney, eds. 2009. *Controversies in Globalization: Contending Approaches to International Relations*. CQ Press.
Hale, Angela and Jane Wills, eds. 2005. 'Introduction.' In *Threads of Labour*, 1–15. Wiley-Blackwell.
Hammer, Nikolaus. 2005. 'International Framework Agreements: Global Industrial Relations Between Rights and Bargaining.' *Transfer: European Review of Labour and Research* 11(4): 511–530.
———. 2008. 'International Framework Agreements in the Context of Global Production.' In *Cross-Border Social Dialogue and Agreements: An Emerging Global Industrial Relations Framework* 89–111.
Hanagan, Michael P. 2003. 'Labor Internationalism: An Introduction.' *Social Science History* 27(4): 485–499.
Hardt, Michael and Antonio Negri. 2001. *Empire*. Cambridge, MA: Harvard University Press.
Harney, Alexandra and John Ruwitch. 2014. 'In China, Managers Are the New Labor Activists.' *Reuters*. June 1. Available at: http://www.reuters.com/article/2014/06/01/china-labor-strikes-idUSL3N0O929U20140601.
Harris, Nigel. 2003. *The Return of Cosmopolitan Capital: Globalization, the State and War*. IB Tauris.

Harrison, Ann and Jason Scorse. 2010. 'Multinationals and Anti-sweatshop Activism.' *The American Economic Review* 100(1): 247–273.

Harriss-White, Barbara. 2009. 'Globalization, the Financial Crisis and Petty Production in India's Socially Regulated Informal Economy.' *Globalization* 12 3-2009.

Harvey, David. 2001. 'Globalization and the "Spatial Fix".' *Geographische Revue* 2: 23–30.

———. 2005. *A Brief History of Neoliberalism*. Oxford University Press.

———. 2006a. *The Limits to Capital*. Verso Books.

———. 2006b. *Spaces of Global Capitalism: Towards a Theory of Uneven Geographical Development*. London: Verso Press.

———. 2014. 'Contradictions of Capitalism and the New Urban Question: David Harvey and Andy Merrifield.' *Birkbeck*, University of London, April 3.

Hassel, Anke. 2008. 'The Evolution of a Global Labor Governance Regime.' *Governance* 21(2): 231–251.

Haworth, Nigel and Harvie Ramsay. 1988. 'Workers of the World, Untied: International Capital and Some Dilemmas in Industrial Democracy.' In *Trade Unions and the New Industrialisation of the Third World*, edited by Roger Southall, 306–331. London: Zed Books.

Heery, Edmund. 2002. 'Partnership Versus Organising: Alternative Futures for British Trade Unionism.' *Industrial Relations Journal* 33(1): 20–35.

Heery, Edmund et al. 2000. 'Organizing Unionism Comes to the UK.' *Employee Relations* 22(1): 38–57.

Henderson, Jeffrey, Peter Dicken, Martin Hess, Neil Coe, and Henry Wai-Chung Yeung. 2002. 'Global Production Networks of Economic Development.' *Review of International Political Economy* 9(3): 436–463.

Hensman, Rohini. 2011. *Workers, Unions, and Global Capitalism*. Columbia University Press.

Hermanson, Jeff. 1993. 'Organizing for Justice: ILGWU Returns to Social Unionism to Organise Immigrant Workers.' *Labour Research Review* 1(20): 8.

———. 2004. *Global Corporations, Global Campaigns: The Struggle for Justice at Kukdong International in Mexico*. American Center for International Labour Solidarity.

———. 2013. 'Global Corporations, Global Campaigns: the Struggle for Justice at Kukdong International in Mexico.' In *The Community Development Reader*, 304–310. Routledge.

Herod, Andrew. 1997. 'From a Geography of Labor to a Labor Geography: Labor's Spatial Fix and the Geography of Capitalism.' *Antipode* 29(1): 1–31.

———. 2001. *Labor Geographies: Workers and the Landscapes of Capitalism*. Guilford Press.

Herrigel, Gary and Jonathan Zeitlin. 2010. 'Inter-firm Relations in Global Manufacturing: Disintegrated Production and Its Globalization.' In *The Oxford Handbook of Comparative Institutional Analysis*, edited by Glenn Morgan, John L. Campbell, Colin Crouch, Ove Kaj Pedersen, and Richard Whitley, 527–564. Oxford University Press.

Herrnstadt, O. E. 2000. 'Voluntary Corporate Codes of Conduct: What's Missing.' *The Labor Lawyer* 16: 349.

Ho, Laura, Catherine Powell, and Leti Volpp. 1996. '(Dis)assembling Rights of Women Workers Along the Global Assembly Line: Human Rights and the Garment Industry.' *Harvard Civil Rights: Civil Liberties Law Review* 31: 383–414.
Hobsbawm, Eric J. 1952. 'The Machine Breakers.' *Past & Present* 1: 57–70.
———. 1995. *Age of Extremes*. London: Abacus. Available at: http://www.andreversailleediteur.com/?livreid=712.
Hoffman, Julius. 1941. *Labor Information Bulletin* 8(5), May 1941.
Holloway, John. 2002. *Change the World Without Taking Power*. London: Pluto Press.
Hoffman, W. Michael. and Robert E. McNulty. 2009. 'International Business, Human Rights, and Moral Complicity: A Call for a Declaration on the Universal Rights and Duties of Business.' *Business and Society Review* 114(4): 541–570.
Hong, Jane C. 2000. 'Enforcement of Corporate Codes of Conduct: Finding a Private Right of Action for International Labourers Against MNCs for Labour Rights Violations.' *Wisconsin International Law Journal* 19: 41.
Hopkins, Terence K. and Immanuel Wallerstein. 1994. 'Commodity Chains in the Capitalist World-Economy Prior to 1800.' In *Commodity Chains and Global Capitalism*, edited by Gary Gereffi and Miguel Korzeniewicz. Westport: Praeger.
Howell, Jude A. 2008. 'All-China Federation of Trades Unions beyond Reform?' *The China Quarterly* 196: 845–863.
Howse, Robert. 1999. 'The World Trade Organization and the Protection of Workers' Rights.' *Journal of Small and Emerging Business Law* 3: 131. Available at: http://www.gongchao.org/en/texts/2014/new-strikes-in-china#sdfootnote12anc.
Hsien, Nien-hê. 2017. 'Business Responsibilities for Human Rights: A Commentary to Arnold.' *Business and Human Rights Journal* 2(2): 297–309.
Huang, Yesheng. 2003. *Selling China*. Cambridge University Press.
Hughes, Alex Louise. 2006. 'Learning to Trade Ethically: Knowledgeable Capitalism, Retailers and Contested Commodity Chains.' *Geoforum* 37(6): 1008–1020.
Hughes, Alex Louise and Suzanne Reimer. 2004. *Geographies of Commodity Chains*. Psychology Press.
Humphrey, John and Hubert Schmitz. 2002. 'How Does Insertion in Global Value Chains Affect Upgrading in Industrial Clusters?' *Regional Studies* 36(9): 1017–1027.
Hurley, Jennifer and Doug Miller. 2005. The Changing Face of the Global Garment Industry. In *Threads of Labour: Garment Industry Supply Chains from the Workers' Perspective*, edited by Angela Hale and Jane Wills, 16–39. Malden: Blackwell Publishing.
Hyman, Richard. 2005a. 'Trade Unions and the Politics of the European Social Model.' *Economic and Industrial Democracy* 26(1): 9–40.
———. 2005b. 'Trade Unions and the Politics of the European Social Model.' *Economic and Industrial Democracy* 26(1): 9–40.
Hymer, Stephen. 1979. *The Multinational Corporation: A Radical Approach*. Cambridge: Cambridge University.
ILO. 1998. 'Declaration of Fundamental Principles and Rights at Work.' Available at : http://www.ilo.org/public/english/standards/decl/declaration/text.

———. 'Global Employment Levels in Textile, Clothing and Footwear Industries Holding Stable as Industries Relocate.' Press Release. ILO: Geneva. October 16. Available at: http://www.ilo.org/global/about-the-ilo/newsroom/news/WCMS_007911/lang--en/index.htm.

———. 2005. *Promoting Fair Globalization in Textiles and Clothing in a Post-MFA Environment*. Geneva: ILO.

———. 2009. *Assessing the Social Impact of IFAs (2008–2009)*. Available at: www.ilo.org/public/english/dialogue/ifp dial/downloads/xborder/ifa-survey-2008-09.pdf.

———. 2015. *World Employment Social Outlook: The Changing Nature of Jobs*. Geneva: ILO.

IMF. 2012. 'People's Republic of China: 2012 Article IV Consultation.' IMF Country Report No. 12/195.

Inditex Group. 2012. *2012 Annual Report*.

IndustriALL. 2014. 'More Solidarity for Cambodian Workers.' Available at: http://www.industriall-union.org/more-solidarity-for-cambodian-workers.

Invisible Committee. 2009. *The coming insurrection* (Vol. 1). Aware Journalism.

ITGLWF. 2007. 'Press Release: Time to Move to Life after Corporate Codes of Conduct.' Available at: http://web.archive.org/web/20080113030942/http://itglwf.org/DisplayDocument.aspx?idarticle=15453&langue=2.

IULBR. 2013a. 'First Public Declaration.' Available at: http://www.union-league.org/first_declaration.

———. 2013b. '2013: A Year in Victories for Garment Workers Worldwide.' Available at: http://www.union-league.org/2013_victories.

Jackson, Matthew O. 2008. *Social and Economic Networks*. Princeton, New Jersey: Princeton University Press.

Jackson, Gregory, Virginia Doellgast, and Lucio Baccaro. 2018. 'Corporate Social Responsibility and Labour Standards: Bridging Business Management and Employment Relations Perspectives.' *British Journal of Industrial Relations* 3–13. DOI: 10.1111/bjir.12298.

Jackson, Gregory, Sarosh Kuruvilla, and Carola Frege. 2013. 'Across Boundaries: The Global Challenges Facing Workers and Employment Research.' *British Journal of Industrial Relations* 51(3): 425–439. doi: 10.1111/bjir.12039.

Jacobs, Andrew and Chris Buckley. 2015. 'In China, Civic Groups' Freedom, and Followers, are Vanishing.' *New York Times*, February 26.

Jahan, Sam and Shafiqul Alam. 2016. 'Rana Plaza Everywhere – Danger Still Haunts Bangladesh.' *Dawn*. April 23.

JDL. 2013. *Steps Taken by the Government on RMG*. Ministry of Labour and Employment.

Jenkins, R. 2001. *Corporate Codes of Conduct: Self-Regulation in a Global Economy*. Geneva: United Nations Research Institute for Social Development.

Jin, Byoungho, Parvathi M. Kandagal, and Sojin Jung. 2013. 'Evolution Patterns of Apparel Brands in Asian Countries Propositions from an Analysis of the Apparel Industry in Korea and India.' *Clothing and Textiles Research Journal* 31(1): 48–63.

Jobs with Justice. 2007. *First Tier Garment Exporters in Delhi: Industry and Company Perspectives.*

Kabeer, Naila and Simeen Mahmud. 2004. 'Globalization, Gender and Poverty: Bangladeshi Women Workers in Export and Local Markets.' *Journal of International Development* 16(1): 93–109

Kalecki, Michal. 1971. *Selected Essays on the Dynamics of the Capitalist Economy.* Cambridge: Cambridge University Press.

Kaplinsky, Raphael. 2006. *How Can Agricultural Commodity Producers Appropriate a Greater Share of Value Chain Incomes?* Cheltenham: Edward Elgar and FAO.

Katz, Harry C. 1997. 'Industrial Relations in the US Automobile Industry an Illustration of Increased Decentralization and Diversity.' *The Economic and Labor Relations Review* 8(2): 192–220.

Keck, Margaret E. and Kathryn Sikkink. 1998. *Activists Beyond Borders: Advocacy Networks in International Politics.* Cambridge University Press.

——. 1999. 'Transnational Advocacy Networks in International and Regional Politics.' *International Social Science Journal* 51(159): 89–101.

Kelly, John E. 1998. *Rethinking Industrial Relations: Mobilization, Collectivism, and Long Waves.* Psychology Press.

Keohane, Robert O. and Joseph S. Nye, eds. 1972. *Transnational Relations and World Politics.* Cambridge: Harvard University Press.

Khadri, Ali. 2014. *Arab Development Denied.* Anthem Press.

Kiely, Ray. 2005. *The Clash of Globalisation: Neo-Liberalism, the Third Way and 'Anti-Globalisation.* Historical Materialism. Brill Academic Press.

Kingsnorth, Paul. 2012. *One No, Many Yeses: A Journey to the Heart of the Global Resistance Movement.* Simon and Schuster.

Klein, Naomi. 2000. *No Logo.* Canada: Knopf.

——. 2007. *The Shock Doctrine: The Rise of Disaster Capitalism.* New York: Allen Lane.

Klett, Erin, John-Paul Ferguson, and William A. Douglas. 2004. 'An Effective Confluence of Forces in Support of Workers' Rights: ILO Standards, US Trade Laws, Unions, and NGOs.' *Human Rights Quarterly* 26(2): 273–99.

Kline, John M. 2010. 'Alta Gracia: Branding Decent Work Conditions.' *Will College Loyalty Embrace 'Living Wage' Sweatshirts.* Available at: http://ibd.georgetown.edu/document/1242775279540/Alta_Gracia_Web_Final.pdf.

Knell, John and Great Britain. 1999. *Partnership at Work.* DTI. Available at: http://www.dti.gov.uk/ER/emar/emar7.pdf.

Knight, John and Lina Song. 2005. *Towards a Labour Market in China.* Oxford: Oxford University Press.

Knight, John, Quheng Deng, and Shi Li. 2011. 'The Puzzle of Migrant Labour Shortage and Rural Labour Surplus in China.' *China Economic Review* 22(4): 585–600.

Knorringa, Peter and Lee Pegler. 2006. 'Globalisation, Firm Upgrading and Impacts on Labour.' *Tijdschrift Voor Economische En Sociale Geografie* 97(5): 470–479.

Knox, Rob. 2016. 'Valuing Race? Stretched Marxism and the Logic of Imperialism.' *London Review of International Law* 4(1): 81–126.

Kohli, Atul. 2004. *State-Directed Development*. Cambridge University Press.
Kolk, Ans and Rob van Tulder. 2002. 'The Effectiveness of Self-Regulation: Corporate Codes of Conduct and Child Labour.' *European Management Journal* 20(3): 260–271.
Kopf, Jerry, Charles Vehorn, and Joel Carnevale. 2013. 'Emerging Oligopolies in Global Markets: Was Marx Ahead of His Time?' *Journal of Management Policy and Practice* 14(3): 92–99.
Korkmaz, Emre Eren. 2013. 'How Spanish Unions Support Unionisation in Turkey ~ Global Labour Column.' *Global Labour Column*, Corporate Strategy and Industrial Development. Available at: http://column.global-labour-university.org/2013/12/emre-eren-korkmaz-introduction.html.
Kreider, Aaron. 2002. 'Mobilizing Supporters to Sit-In: High-Cost and High-Risk Activism in the Student Anti-sweatshop Movement.' Doctoral Dissertation, University of Notre Dame.
Krupat, Kitty. 2002. 'Rethinking the Sweatshop: A Conversation About United Students Against Sweatshops (USAS) with Charles Eaton, Marion Traub-Werner, and Evelyn Zepeda.' *International Labor and Working-Class History* 61(1): 112–127.
Kucera, David. 2001. *The Effects of Core Workers Rights on Labour Costs and Foreign Direct Investment: Evaluating the Conventional Wisdom*. Vol. 130. International Institute for Labour Studies.
Kumar, Ashok. 2014a. 'Interwoven Threads: Building a Labor Countermovement in Bangalore's Export-Oriented Garment Industry'. *City* 18(6): 789–807.
———. 2014b. 'Securing the Security.' *City* 356–359.
———. 2015. 'Global Workers' Rights Through Capitalist Institutions? An Irreconcilable Proposition.' *Historical Materialism* 23(3): 215–227.
———. 2019a. 'A Race from the Bottom? Lessons from a Workers' Struggle at a Bangalore Warehouse.' *Competition and Change*.
———. 2019b. 'Oligopolistic Suppliers, Symbiotic Value Chains and Workers' Bargaining Power: Labor Contestation in South China at an Ascendant Global Footwear Firm.' *Global Networks* 19(3): 394–422.
Kumar, Ashok and Jack Mahoney. 2014. 'Stitching Together: How Workers Are Hemming Down Transnational Capital in the Hyper-Global Apparel Industry.' *WorkingUSA, Building International Labor Solidarity* 17(2): 187–210.
Kwan, Fung. 2009. 'Agricultural Labour and the Incidence of Surplus Labour: Experience from China During Reform.' *Journal of Chinese Economic and Business* 7(3): 341–361.
Lakhani, Tashlin, Sarosh Kuruvilla, and Ariel Avgar. 2013. 'From the Firm to the Network: Global Value Chains and Employment Relations Theory: From the Firm to the Network.' *British Journal of Industrial Relations* 51(3). DOI: 10.1111/bjir.12015.
Lazonick, William. 1983. 'Industrial Organization and Technological Change: The Decline of the British Cotton Industry.' *Business History Review*. Vol LVII (Summer 1983).
Leary, Virginia A. 1996. 'Workers' Rights and International Trade: The Social Clause (GATT, ILO, NAFTA, US Laws).' *Fair Trade and Harmonization: Prerequisites for Free Trade* 2: 177–230.

Lee, Naeyoung and Jeffrey Cason, 1994. 'Automobile Commodity Chains in the NICs: A Comparison of South Korea, Mexico, and Brazil.' *In Commodity Chains and Global Capitalism*, edited by Gary Gereffi and Miguel Korzeniewicz. Westport, Conn.: Greenwood Press.

Lee, Chang Kwan and Yonghong Zhang. 2013. 'The Power of Instability.' *American Journal of Sociology*. 118(6): 1475–1508.

Lefebvre, Henri. 1976. *The Survival of Capitalism: Reproduction of the Relations of Production*. Translated by Bryant F. New York: St. Martin's.

———. 1991. *The Production of Space*. Nicholson-Smith D (Trans.). Malden, MA: Blackwell.

Lenin, Vladimir. 1999. *Imperialism, the Highest Stage of Capitalism*. Sydney: Resistance Books.

Lerner, Stephen. 2007. 'Global Unions: A Solution to Labor's Worldwide Decline.' *New Labor Forum* 16(1): 23–37.

Lester, Richard. 1967. 'Pay Differentials by Size of Establishment.' *Journal of Industrial Relations* 7(1): 57–67.

Levi, Margaret. 2003. 'Organizing Power: The Prospects for an American Labor Movement.' *Perspective on Politics* 1(01): 45–68.

Levy, David L. and Aseem Prakash. 2003. 'Bargains Old and New: Multinational Corporations in Global Governance.' *Business and Politics* 5(2): 131–150.

Lewis, W. Arthur. 1954. 'Economic Development with Unlimited Supplies of Labour.' *The Manchester School* 28(2): 139–191.

LIFE. 1938. 'Garment Workers at Play.' *Life Magazine*. August 1.

Lin, Liza. 2014. 'Adidas, Nike Supplier Yue Yuen Says Work Stoppage Ended.' *Bloomberg*. July 22. Available at: http://www.bloomberg.com/news/2014-07-22/adidas-nike-china-supplier-yue-yuen-cites-work-stoppage.html.

Liubicic, Robert J. 1998. 'Corporate Codes of Conduct and Product Labeling Schemes: The Limits and Possibilities of Promoting International Labor Rights Through Private Initiatives.' *Law and Policy in International Business* 30: 111.

Lo, Chu-Ping, Shih-Jye Wu, and Su-Ying Hsu. 2014. 'The Role of Overseas Chinese-Speaking Regions in Global Sourcing.' *China Economic Review* 30: 133–142.

Locke, Richard and Monica Romis. 2006. 'Beyond Corporate Codes of Conduct: Work Organization and Labour Standards in Two Mexican Garment Factories.' MIT Sloan Research Paper No. 4617-06.

Locke, Richard, Greg Distelhorst, Timea Pal, and Hiram Samel. 2012. 'Production Goes Global, Standards Stay Local: Private Labor Regulation in the Global Electronics Industry.' Available at: http://papers.ssrn.com/sol3/papers.cfm?abstract_id=1978908.

Loong-Yu, Au. 2005. 'The Post MFA Era and the Rise of China.' *Asia Labour Update* Issue 56. Asia Monitor Resource Centre.

Lopez-Acevedo, Gladys and Raymond Robertson. 2012. *Sewing Success? Employment, Wages, and Poverty Following the End of the Multi-fibre Arrangement*. Washington DC: World Bank.

Losada, Mònica Clua. 2010. 'The Retreat of the Union: The Transport and General Workers' Union Strategies of Renewal in the 1990s.' Paper to be presented at the 60th Political Studies Association Annual Conference, Edinburgh 29 March – 1 April.

Lu, Su-Ping. 1999. 'Corporate Codes of Conduct and the FTC: Advancing Human Rights Through Deceptive Advertising Law.' *Columbia Journal of Transnational Law* 38: 603.

Lucero, Christina M. 2011. 'The Central American Free Trade Agreement: Effects on Labor in the Mogul Sector.' College of Liberal Arts and Social Sciences Theses and Dissertations. Chicago: DePaul University.

Lukacs, Georg. 1971. *History and Class Consciousness: Studies in Marxist Dialectics*. Cambridge: MIT Press.

Lund-Thomsen, Peter and A. Lindgreen. 2018. Is There a Sweet Spot in Ethical Trade? A Critical Appraisal of the Potential for Aligning Buyer, Supplier and Worker Interests in Global Production Networks. *Geoforum* 90: 84–90.

Magnier, Mark. 2014. 'China's Migrant Workers Struggle for Pensions.' *The Wall Street Journal*. December 26. Available at : http://www.wsj.com/articles/chinas-migrant-workers-struggle-for-pensions-1419637851.

Magnuson, Joel. 2011. *Mindful Economics: How the US Economy Works, Why It Matters, and How It Could Be Different*. New York: Seven Stories Press.

Mahutga, Matthew C. 2012. 'When Do Value Chains Go Global? A Theory of the Spatialization of Global Value Chains.' *Global Networks* 12(1): 1–21.

———. 2014. 'Global Models of Networked Organization, the Positional Power of Nations and Economic Development.' *Review of International Political Economy* 21(1): 157–194.

Majmudar, Madhavi. 2008. 'Trade Liberalization in Clothing: The MFA-Phase Out and the Developing Countries.' *Development Policy Review*.

Mallikarjunappa, N. L. 2011. 'Observance to International Labor Standards: A Study on Selected Unites in Bangalore Apparal Cluster.' *International Referred Research Journal* 3(26).

Mandel, Ernst. 1968. *Marxist Economic Theory*. London: Merlin Press.

Mani, Mohan. 2011. *Garment Sector and Unionization in India*. Bangalore: Cividep-India.

Manik, Julfikar Ali and Jim Yardley. 2013. 'Scores Dead in Bangladesh Building Collapse.' *New York Times*, April 24, sec. World/Asia Pacific. Available at: http://www.nytimes.com/2013/04/25/world/asia/bangladesh-building-collapse.html.

Manthrope, Rowland. 2017. 'To Make a New Kind of Shoe, Adidas Had to Change Everything.' *Wired*, October 4.

Maquila Solidarity Network. 2007. *Emergency Assistance, Redress, and Prevention in the Hermosa Manufacturing Case*. Report prepared for the Fair Labor Association by the Maquila Solidarity Network.

Maree, Johann. 2009. 'Trends in Collective Bargaining: Why South Africa Differs from Global Trends.' In *IIRA World Congress*. Available at: http://www.ilera-directory.org/15thworldcongress/files/papers/Track_4/Wed_P4_MAREE.pdf.

Marx, Karl. 1867. *Capital, Volume I*. Harmondsworth: Penguin/New Left Review.

Marx, Karl and Frederic Engels. 1848. *The Communist Manifesto*. Wiley Online Library.
Massey, Doreen. 1984. *Spatial Divisions of Labour: Social Structures and the Geography of Production*. London: Macmillan.
Mathiason, John. 2007. *Invisible Governance: International Secretariats in Global Politics*. Kumarian Press.
Mayer, Frederick W. and Nicola Phillips. 2017. 'Outsourcing Governance: States and the Politics of a "Global Value Chain World".' *New Political Economy* 22(2): 134–152.
McBride, Stephen and Gary Teeple. 2011. *Relations of Global Power: Neoliberal Order and Disorder*. University of Toronto Press.
McCabe, Donald L., Linda K. Trevino, and Kenneth D. Butterfield. 1996. 'The Influence of Collegiate and Corporate Codes of Conduct on Ethics-Related Behaviour in the Workplace.' *Business Ethics Quarterly* 6(4): 461–476.
McCallum, Jamie K. 2013. *Global Unions, Local Power*. Ithaca: Cornell University Press.
McDowell, Linda. 1992. 'Doing Gender: Feminism, Feminists and Research Methods in Human Geography.' *Transactions of the Institute of British Geographers* 17(4): 399–416.
Mead, Donald C. 1984. 'Of Contracts and Subcontracts: Small Firms in Vertically Disintegrated Production/Distribution Systems in LDCs.' *World Development* 12(11/12): 1095–1106.
Merk, Jeroen. 2008. Restructuring and Conflict in the Global Athletic Footwear Industry. *Global Economy Contested: Power and Conflict Across the International Division of Labour. Rethinking Globalizations*, 79–97. New York: Routledge.
———. 2014. 'The Rise of Tier 1 Firms in the Global Garment Industry.' *Oxford Development Studies* 42(2): 277–285.
Mezzadra, Sandro and Brett Neilson. 2013. *Border as Method*. Duke University Press.
Mezzadri, Allesandra. 2014. 'Backshoring, Local Sweatshop Regimes and CSR in India.' *Competition & Change* 18(4): 327–344.
Milberg, William and Deborah Winkler. 2010. 'Trade, Crisis, and Recovery.' In *Global Value Chains in the Postcrisis World*, edited by Olivier Cattaneo, Gary Gereffi, and Cornelia Staritz, 23–73.
——— and Deborah Winkler. 2013. *Outsourcing Economics: Global Value Chains in Capitalist Development*. Cambridge University Press.
Miller, Doug. 2004. 'Negotiating International Framework Agreements in the Global Textile, Garment and Footwear Sector.' *Global Social Policy* 4(2): 215.
———. 2008. 'The ITGLWF's Policy on Cross-border Dialogue in the Textiles, Clothing and Footwear Sector: Emerging Strategies in a Sector Ruled by Codes of Conduct and Resistant Companies.' Available at: http://nrl.northumbria.ac.uk/676/.
———, Simon Turner, and Tom Grinter. 2011. 'Back to the Future? A Critical Reflection on Neil Kearney's Mature Systems of Industrial Relations Perspective on the Governance of Outsourced Apparel Supply Chains.' *A Critical Reflection on Neil Kearney's Mature Systems of Industrial Relations Perspective on the Governance of Outsourced Apparel Supply Chains (November 18, 2011)*. Available at: http://www.capturingthegains.org/pdf/ctg-wp-2011-08.pdf.
Moody, Kim. 2017. *On New Terrain*. Chicago: Haymarket Books.

Moran, Peter. 2010. 'The Race to the Bottom.' In *Social Studies and Diversity Education*, edited by Elizabeth E. Heilman, Ramona Fruja Amthor, and Matthew Missias. Taylor & Francis.

Mosley, Layna and Saika Uno. 2007. 'Racing to the Bottom or Climbing to the Top? Economic Globalization and Collective Labor Rights.' *Comparative Political Studies* 40(8): 923–948.

Motlagh, Jason. 2014. 'The Ghosts of Rana Plaza.' *VQR*.

Moudud, Jamee K. 2013. 'The Hidden History of Competition and Its Implications.' In *Alternative Theories of Competition. Challenges to the Orthodoxy*, edited by Jamee K. Moudud, Cyrus Bina, and Patrick L. Mason, 27–55. London: Routledge.

Moudud, Jamee K., Cyrus Bina and Patrick L Mason. 2013. 'Introduction.' In *Alternative Theories of Competition. Challenges to the Orthodoxy*, edited by J. Moudud, C. Bina and P. L. Mason, 1–12. Routledge.

Munck, Ronald. 2008. 'Globalisation, Contestation and Labour Internationalism.' In *Global Economy Contested: Power and Conflict Across the International Division of Labour*, edited by Marcus Taylor. Routledge.

Murphy, Rachel. 2004. 'The Impact of Labour Migration on the Well-Being and Agency of Rural Chinese Women.' In *On the Move*, edited by A. Gaetano and T. Jacka, 227–62. Columbia University Press.

Murray, Robin. 1971. 'Internationalization of Capital and the Nation State.' *New Left Review* 67 (May–June): 84–109.

Nadvi, Khaled. 2014. '"Rising powers" and Labour and Environmental Standards.' *Oxford Development Studies* 42(2): 137–150.

Nathan, Dev and V. Kalpana. 2007. *Issues in the Analysis of Global Value Chains and Their Impact on Employment and Incomes in India*. ILO.

Nathan, Dev, Madhuri Saripalle and L. Guranathan. 2016. 'Labor Practices in India.' ILO Asia-Pacific Working Paper Series.

NDTV. 2014. 'Huge China Strike Peters out as Workers Cite Intimidation.' *NDTV.com*. Available at: http://www.ndtv.com/article/world/huge-china-strike-peters-out-as-workers-cite-intimidation-514996. Accessed on 5 November.

Ngai, Pun and Jenny Chan. 2012. 'Global Capital, the State, and Chinese Workers.' *Modern China* 38(4): 383–410.

Nielson, Brian and James Pritchard. 2008. 'Big Is Not Always Better: Global Value Chain Restructuring and the Crises in the South Indian Tea Estates.' In *Agri-Food Commodity Chains and Globalizing Networks*, 35–48. London: Routledge.

Niforou, Christina. 2013. 'International Framework Agreements and the Democratic Deficit of Global Labour Governance.' *Economic and Industrial Democracy*. Available at: http://eid.sagepub.com/content/early/2013/05/28/0143831X13484815.abstract.

Nolan, Peter, Jun Zhang, and Chunhang Liu. 2008. 'The Global Business Revolution, the Cascade Effect, and the Challenge for Firms from Developing Countries.' *Cambridge Journal of Economics* 32: 29–47.

Norton, Bruce. 1983. 'The Accumulation of Capital as Historical Essence: A Critique of the Theory of Monopoly Capital.' Association for Economic and Social Analysis: Discussion Paper Series.

Nova, Scott and Isaac Shapiro. 2012. *Polishing Apple*. Economic Policy Institute. Available at: http://www.epi.org/publication/bp352-polishing-apple-fla-foxconn-labour-rights/.

NYT. 1922. 'Contract Will End Dressmakers' Strike Jobber Signs First Agreement with Contractors' Association to Stabilise the Industry. Assures Union-Only Labor.' *New York Times*. Available at: http://query.nytimes.com/mem/archive-free/pdf?res=F50F1EFE38551A738DDDA80894D1405B828EF1D3.

O'Connell, Paul. 2018. On the Human Rights Question. *Human Rights Quarterly* 40(4): 962.

OECD. 2017. *Skills Outlook, 2017: Skills and Global Value Chains*. Paris.

Ohmae, Kenichi. 1993. 'The Rise of the Region State.' *Foreign Affairs* 72(2).

Onaran, Özlem and Giorgos Galanis. 2014. 'Income Distribution and Growth: A Global Model.' *Environment and Planning A* 46(10): 2489–2513.

O'Rourke, Dara. 2003. 'Outsourcing Regulation: Analysing Nongovernmental Systems of Labor Standards and Monitoring.' *Policy Studies Journal* 31(1): 1–29.

Outhwaite, Opi and Olga Martin-Ortega. 2017. 'Monitoring Human Rights in Global Supply Chains: Insights and Policy Recommendations for Civil Society, Global Brands and Academics.' BHRE Policy Paper. University of Greenwich.

Panitch, Leo and Sam Gindin. 2013. *The Making of Global Capitalsim*. London: Verso.

Papadakis, Konstantinos. 2009. *Signing International Framework Agreements: Case Studies from South Africa, Russia and Japan*. International Labour Organization. Available at: http://ideas.repec.org/p/ilo/ilowps/445545.html.

———. 2011. *Shaping Global Industrial Relations*. UK: Palgrave Macmillan.

Parmet, Robert D. 2005. *The Master of Seventh Avenue*. New York: New York University Press.

Pasachoff, Naomi. 1999. *Frances Perkins: Champion of the New Deal*. Oxford University Press.

Pasture, Patrick. 2002. 'A Century of International Trade Unionism.' *International Review of Social History* 47(2): 277–289.

Patel, Seth Newton. 2013. 'Have We Built the Committee? Advancing Leadership Development in the US Labor Movement.' *WorkingUSA* 16(1): 113–142.

Peck, Jamie and Jun Zhang. 2013. 'A Variety of Capitalism…with Chinese Characteristics?' *Journal of Economic Geography*, 1–40.

Perea, Juan F. 2011. 'The Echoes of Slavery: Recognizing the Racist Origins of the Agricultural and Domestic Worker Exclusion from the National Labor Relations Act.' *Ohio St. LJ* 72: 95.

Phillips, Anne and Barbara Taylor. 1980. 'Sex and Skill: Notes Towards a Feminist Economics.' *Feminist Review* 6(1): 79–88. DOI:10.1057/fr.1980.20.

Pickles, John and Adrian Smith. 2016. *Articulations of Capital*. Wiley Blackwell.

Piketty, Thomas. 2013. *Capital in the 21st Century*. Harvard University Press.

Porter, Michael E. 2008. 'The Five Competitive Forces That Shape Strategy.' *Harvard Business Review*, 1–18, January 1.

Posthuma, Anne and Dev Nathan. 2010. 'Introduction.' In *Labor in Global Production Networks in India*, 1–36. Oxford University Press.

Poulantzas, Nicos. 1978. *Classes in Contemporary Capitalism*. Verso.

Prashad, Vijay. 2007. 'The Third World Idea.' *The Nation*, May 17.
Previant, D. 1959. 'New Hot-Cargo and Secondary-Boycott Sections: A Critical Analysis.' *Geo. LJ* 48: 346–349.
Pringle, Tim. 2013. 'Reflections on Labor in China.' *South Atlantic Quarterly* 112(2): 191–202.
——— and Anita Chan. 2018. 'China's Labour Relations Have Entered a Dangerous New Phase, as Shown by Attacks on Jasic Workers and Activists.' *South China Morning Post*. September 19.
PUCL. 2017. 'Thread and Tension: An Account of Historic Uprising of Garment Workers.' Available at: http://puclkarnataka.org/wp-content/uploads/2018/12/GW_-Protest-Report-english-book.pdf. Accessed on January 12, 2018.
PVH. 2011. 'Phillips-Van Heusen Licenses IZOD in India, Middle East.' February 16. Available at: http://www.pvh.com/investor_relations_press_release_article.aspx?reqid=1529618.
Qi, Liyan. 2014. 'Yue Yuen Strike Is Estimated to Cost $60 Million.' *Wall Street Journal*, April 28, sec. Business.
Rangaraju, M. S. and S. Hanuman Kennedy. 2012. *Innovation in Management Challenges and Opportunities in the Next Decade*. Allied Publishers.
Raiborn, Cecily A. and Dinah Payne. 1990. 'Corporate Codes of Conduct: A Collective Conscience and Continuum.' *Journal of Business Ethics* 9(11): 879–889.
Rainnie, Al, Andy Herod, and Susan McGrath-Champ. 2011. 'Review and Positions: Global Production Networks and Labor.' *Competition and Change* 15(2): 155–169.
Ramstetter, Eric. 1999. Comparisons of Foreign Multinationals and Local Firms in Asian Manufacturing over Time. *Asian Economic Journal* 13(2): 163–203.
Raskin, A. H. 1982. 'David Dubinsky – A Reporter's Memoir.' *New York Times*, September 19.
Raworth, Kate and A. Coryndon. 2004. *Trading Away Our Rights: Women Working in Global Supply Chains*. Oxfam.
Reich, Robert. 2012. 'The Factory Jobs Aren't Coming Back.' *Salon*. February 17. Available at: https://www.salon.com/2012/02/17/the_factory_jobs_arent_coming_back/.
Reinecke, Jukiane, Jimmy Donaghey and Adrian Wilkinson. 2018. 'Global Supply Chains and Social Relations at Work: Brokering Across Boundaries.' *Human Relations* 74(4).
Reuters. 2007. 'Arvind Mills to Issue Warrants to Promoters.' September 28. Available at: http://in.reuters.com/article/2007/09/28/idINIndia-29765320070928.
Richter Consulting. 2004. 'The Canadian Apparel Industry: The Shape of the Future.' *Apparel Human Resources Council*. March 1. Available at: http://www.apparelconnexion.com/_Library/Labor_Market_Information_Study/2004_-_Labour_Market_Information_Study.pdf.
Riisgaard, Lone and Nikolaus Hammer. 2011. 'Prospects for Labor in Global Value Chains: Labor Standards in the Cut Flower and Banana Industries.' *British Journal of Industrial Relations* 49(1): 168–190.
Robbins, Allison. 2011. 'The Future of the Student Anti-sweatshop Movement: Providing Access to US Courts for Garment Workers Worldwide.' Available at: http://works.bepress.com/allie_robbins/1/.

Robinson, Joan. 1969. *The Economics of Imperfect Competition*. Macmillan.
Robinson, William I. 2001. 'Social Theory and Globalization: The Rise of a Transnational State.' *Theory and Society* 30(2): 157–200.
Rodriguez-Garavito, César A. 2005. 'Global Governance and Labour Rights: Codes of Conduct and Anti-sweatshop Struggles in Global Apparel Factories in Mexico and Guatemala.' *Politics & Society* 33(2): 203–333.
Rodrik, Dani. 1997. *Has Globalization Gone Too Far?* Peterson Institute.
Rogers, William. 2016. 'Vietnam Workers Strike Shoe Maker; Win Concessions.' *Left Labor Reporter*. Available at: https://leftlaborreporter.wordpress.com/2016/03/02/viet-nam-workers-strike-shoe-maker-win-concessions/.
Roman, Joseph. 2004. 'The Trade Union Solution or the NGO Problem? The Fight for Global Labour Rights.' *Development in Practice* 14(1–2): 100–109.
Roper, Matt. 2013. 'Zara Probed over Slave Labour Claims.' *Telegraph*. April 3. Available at: http://www.telegraph.co.uk/finance/newsbysector/retailandconsumer/9969494/Zara-probed-over-slave-labour-claims.html.
Ross, Robert J. S. 2004. *Slaves to Fashion*. University of Michigan Press.
———. 2006. 'No Sweat: Hard Lessons from Garment Industry History.' *Dissent* 53(4): 50–56.
Rotunna, Lorenzo, Pierre-Louis Vezina, and Zheng Wang. 2012. 'The Rise and Fall of (Chinese) African Apparel Exports.' CSAE Working Paper 2012-12.
Roy, Arundhati. 2004. *Public Power in the Age of Empire*. Seven Stories Press.
Rudra, Nita. 2002. 'Globalization and the Decline of the Welfare State in Less-Developed Countries.' *International Organization* 56(2): 411–445.
Rudrappa, Sharmila. 2012. 'India's Reproductive Assembly Line.' *Contexts* 11(2): 22–27.
———. 2015. *Discounted Life: The Price of Global Surrogacy in India*. NYU Press.
Russell, Beron. 2014. 'Opportunities and Challenges in Asia's Apparel and Textile Sector.' *Apparel*. February 12. Available at: http://apparel.edgl.com/news/opportunities-and-challenges-in-asia-s-apparel-and-textile-sector91123.
Sampler, Jeffrey and Sanjeev Sarkar. 2010. 'Surviving India: Case Study on Strategy.' *The Smart Manager* 9(6).
Sassen, Saskia. 1998. *Globalization and Its Discontents: Essays on the New Mobility of People and Money*. New York: New Press.
———. 1999. 'Globalization and Its Discontents: Essays on the New Mobility of People and Money.' Available at: http://www.citeulike.org/group/1128/article/631023.
Sawyer, Malcom C. 1988. 'Theories of Monopoly Capitalism.' *Journal of Economic Surveys* 2(1).
Schlesinger, Emil. 1951. *The Outside System of Production in the Women's Garment Industry in the New York Market*. New York: International Ladies' Garment Workers' Union.
Schling, Hannah. 2014. 'Gender, Temporality, and the Reproduction of Labour Power: Women Migrant Workers in South China.' *Sozial.Geschichte Online* 14: 41–61.
Schmalz, Stefan, Brandon Sommer, and Hui Xu. 2016. 'The Yue Yuen Strike: Industrial Transformation and Labour Unrest in the Pearl River Delta.' *Globalizations*.
Schmidt, Vivien A. 2002. *The Futures of European Capitalism*. Oxford University Press.

Schmitz, Hubert and Peter Knorringa. 2000. 'Learning from Global Buyers.' Working Paper, Institute for Development Studies, Sussex.

———. 2006. 'Learning and Earning in Global Garment and Footwear Chains.' *The European Journal of Development Research* 18(4): 546–571.

Schoenberger, Erica. 1994. 'Competition, Time, and Space in Industrial Change.' In *Commodity Chains and Global Capitalism*, edited by Gary Gereffi and Miguel Korzeniewicz, 51–66. Westport: Praeger Publishers.

Schumpeter, Joseph A. 2010. *Capitalism, Socialism and Democracy*. Abingdon: Routledge.

Scipes, Kim. 2000. 'It's Time to Come Clean: Open the AFL-CIO Archives on International Labor Operations.' *Labor Studies Journal* 25(2): 4–25.

———. 2005. 'Labor Imperialism Redux? The AFL-CIO's Foreign Policy Since 1995.' *Monthly Review* 57(1): 23–36.

———. 2011. *AFL-CIO's Secret War Against Developing Country Workers: Solidarity or Sabotage?* Lexington, VA: Lexington Books.

Scott, Allen. 2006. 'The Changing Global Geography of Low-Technology, Labor-Intensive Industry: Clothing, Footwear, and Furniture.' *World Development* 34(9): 1517–1536.

Seidman, Gay. 2009. *Beyond the Boycott*. Russell Sage.

Seigmann, Karin Astrid, Peter Knorringa, and J. J. S. Merk. 2014. *Voluntary Initiatives in Global Value Chains: Towards Labor-Led Social Upgrading?* No. 2014.

Selwyn, Ben. 2008. 'Bringing Social Relations Back in: (Re)conceptualising the "Bullwhip Effect" in Global Commodity Chains.' *International Journal of Management Concepts and Philosophy* 3(2): 156–175.

———. 2012. 'Beyond Firm-Centrism: Re-integrating Labour and Capitalism into Global Commodity Chain Analysis.' *Journal of Economic Geography* 12(1). DOI: 10.1093/jeg/lbr016.

———. 2013. 'Social Upgrading and Labor in Global Production Networks.' *Competition and Change* 17(1): 75–90.

Sethi, S. Prakash. 2002. 'Corporate Codes of Conduct and the Success of Globalization.' *Ethics & International Affairs* 16(1): 89–106.

Sexauer, Laura. 2007. 'Adidas, UW Keep Relationship Alive.' *Badger Herald*. October 10. Available at: http://badgerherald.com/news/2007/10/29/adidas-uw-keep-relat/. Accessed on 20 April 2014.

Shah, Minari. 2000. 'Country Roads II.' In *Marketing in India: Cases and Readings*, 173.

Shaikh, Anwar. 2016. *Capitalism: Competition, Conflict, Crises*. Oxford University Press.

Shaw, Randy. 2008. *Beyond the Fields: Cesar Chavez, the UFW, and the Struggle for Justice in the 21st Century*. University of California Press.

Sheng, Andrew and Xiao Geng. 2014. 'Piketty with Chinese Characteristics.' *Project Syndicate*. July 2.

Shukla, Madhukar. 1998. 'Strategising Research for Technological Innovation.' *Productivity* 39(2): 204–210.

Sideman, Gay. 2007. *Beyond the Boycott: Labour Rights, Human Rights, and Transnational Activism*. Russell Sage Foundation.

Silver, Beverly. 2003. *Forces of Labor*. Cambridge University Press.
Silver, Beverly and Lu Zhang. 2009. 'China as an Emerging Epicenter of World Labor Unrest.' In *China and the Transformation of Global Capitalism*, edited by Ho-fung Hung. The Johns Hopkins University Press.
Simpson, Peter. 2012. 'China's Urban Population Exceeds Rural for the First Time Ever.' *The Telegraph*, January 17.
Singh, N. K. 2012. *Eastern and Cross Cultural Management*. New Delhi: Springer.
Sivanandan, Ambalavaner. 2008. *Catching History on the Wings*. London: Pluto Press.
Skott, Peter. 1989. *Conflict and Effective Demand in Economic Growth*. Cambridge University Press.
Smith, Adam. 1776. *An Inquiry into the Nature and Causes of the Wealth of Nations: Volume 1*. London: Printed for W. Strahan and T. Cadell, 1776.
Smith, Adrian. 2015. 'The State, Institutional Frameworks and the Dynamics of Capital in Global Production Networks.' *Progress in Human Geography* 39(3): 290–315.
Smith, Adrian, Al Rainnie, Mick Dunford, Jane Hardy, Ray Hudson, and David Sadler. 2002. 'Networks of Value, Commodities and Regions.' *Progress in Human Geography* 26(1): 41–63.
Smith, Martin. 2008. 'Focus: A Critical Look at Global Strategic Campaigns.' International Centre for Trade Union Rights, International Union Rights: Focus on Strategic Corporate Campaigns, 15(3): 8–9.
Spence, Michael. 2011. 'Why the Old Jobs Aren't Coming Back.' *The Wall Street Journal*. June 24. Available at: https://www.wsj.com/articles/SB10001424052702303714704576385863720618134.
Starosta, Guido. 2010. 'Global Commodity Chains and the Marxian Law of Value.' *Antipode* 42(2): 433–465.
Steiner, Robert L. 2008. 'Vertical Competition, Horizontal Competition, and Market Power.' *Antitrust Bulletin* 53(2): 251.
Stevis, Dimitris and Terry Boswell. 2008. *Globalization and Labor: Democratizing Global Governance*. Rowman & Littlefield.
Stiglitz, Joseph. *Making Globalization Work*. London: Penguin Books.
———. 2006. 'China's Roadmap.' *Project Syndicate*.
Stockhammer, Engelbert. 2015. 'Determinants of Wage Share: A Panel Analysis of Advanced and Developing Economies.' *British Journal of Industrial Relations* 55(1): 1–33.
———. 2017. 'Determinants of the Wage Share: a Panel Analysis of Advanced and Developing Economies.' *Environment and Planning A* 48(9): 1804–1828.
Stockhammer, Engelbert, C. Durand, and L. Ludwig. 2016. 'European Growth Models and Working Class Restructuring: An International Post-Keynesian Political Economy Perspective.' *Environment and Planning A* 48(9): 1804–1828.
Stubbs, Richard. 1999. 'War and Economic Development: Export-Oriented Industrialization in East and Southeast Asia.' *Comparative Politics* 337–255.
Sturgeon, Timothy J. 2001. 'How Do We Define Value Chains and Production Networks?' *IDS Bulletin* 32(3): 9–18.

———. 2002. 'Modular Production Networks: A New American Model of Industrial Organization.' *Industrial and Corporate Change* 11(3). DOI: 10.1093/icc/11.3.451.

———. 2003. 'What Really Goes On in Silicon Valley? Spatial Clustering and Dispersal in Modular Production Networks.' *Journal of Economic Geography* 3(2): 199–225.

Sturgeon, T. and R. Florida. 2000. *'Globalization and Jobs in the Automotive Industry.'* Industrial Performance Centre Globalization Working Paper. MIT-IPC-00-012. Cambridge, MA.

Sum, Ngai-Ling and Pun Ngai. 2005. 'Globalization and Paradoxes of Ethical Transnational Production: Code of Conduct in a Chinese Workplace.' *Competition and Change* 9(2): 181–200.

Swank, Duane. 1998. 'Funding the Welfare State: Globalization and the Taxation of Business in Advanced Market Economies.' *Political Studies* 46(4): 671–692.

Sweezy, Paul A. and Paul Baran. 1966. *Monopoly Capital*. Monthly Review Press.

Tarrow, Sydney. 1998. 'Fishnets, Internets, and Catnets: Globalization and Transnational Collective Action.' In *Challenging Authority: The Historical Study of Contentious Politics*, edited by Michael P. Hanagan, Leslie P. Moch, and Wayne Te Brake, 228–244. Minneapolis: University of Minnesota Press.

Taylor, Lance. 2004. *Reconstructing Macroeconomics: Structuralist Proposals and Critiques of the Mainstream*. Harvard University Press.

Taylor, Philip and Peter Bain. 2001. 'Trade Unions, Workers' Rights and the Frontier of Control in UK Call Centres.' *Economic and Industrial Democracy* 22(1): 39–66.

Taylor, P., K. Newsome, and A. Rainnie. 2013. '"Putting Labor in Its Place": Global Value Chains and Labor Process Analysis.' *Competition & Change* 17(1): 1–5.

Teehan, Sean. 2014. 'Cambodia Garment Worker Strike Unravels.' *Al Jazeera*. January 8. Available at: http://www.aljazeera.com/indepth/features/2014/01/cambodia-garment-worker-strike-unravels-20141755530526443.html.

Teeple, Gary. 1995. *Globalization and the Decline of Social Reform*. Cambridge University Press.

Tewari, Manish. 2006. 'Adjustment in India's Textile and Apparel Industry: Reworking Historical Legacies in a Post-MFA World.' *Environment and Planning A* 38(12): 2325–2344.

———. 2008. 'Targeting Global Supply Chains: Innovations in Labour Organizing in the Indian Garment Industries.' Available at: http://stevphen.mahost.org/TewariGlobalSupplyChains.pd.

———. 2010. 'Footloose Capital, Intermediation, and the Search for the "High Road" in Low-Wage Industries.' In *Labor in Global Production Networks*, edited by Anne Posthuma and Dev Nathan, 146–165. Oxford University Press.

Tilly, Charles. 1995. 'Globalization Threatens Labour's Rights.' *International Labour and Working-Class History* 47: 1–23.

Ting-Fang, Cheng. 2015. 'Shoemaker Shifts Production to Vietnam Following TPP Deal.' *Nikkei Asian Review*.

Tokatli, Nebahat and Omar Kizilgun. 2004. 'Upgrading in the Global Clothing Industry: Mavi Jeans and the Transformations of a Turkish Firm from Full Package to Brand-Name Manufacturing and Retailing.' *Economic Geography* 80(3): 221–240.

Toscano, Alberto. 2011. 'Logistics and Opposition.' *Mute* 3(2): 30–41.
Traub-Merz, Rudolf and Jürgen Eckl. 2007. 'International Trade Union Movement: Mergers and Contradictions.' *Friedrich-Ebert Stiftung, International Trade Union Cooperation, Briefing Papers*. Available at: http://library.fes.de/pdf-files/iez/04589.pdf.
Tronti, Mario. 1966. *Operai E Capitale*. Turin: Einaudi.
UN. 2008. 'Protect, Respect and Remedy: A Framework for Business and Human Rights.' A/HRC/8/5.
———. 2011. Guiding Principles on Business and Human Rights: Implementing the United Nations 'Protect, Respect and Remedy' Framework, A/HRC/17/31.
———. 2015. *World Population Prospects*. New York: Department of Economic and Social Affairs. Available at: https://esa.un.org/unpd/wpp/publications/files/key_findings_wpp_2015.pdf.
UNCTAD. 2005. *TNCs and the Removal of Textiles and Clothing Quotas*. New York and Geneva: United Nations.
———. 2011. 'Non-equity modes of international production and development.' World Investment Report, United Nations, New York and Geneva.
UPI. 2013. 'Consumer debt soars in Asia.' April 22.
USAS. 2011. 'Victory at Jerzees Nuevo Dia!' Available at: http://usas.org/2011/05/23/victory-at-jerzees-nuevo-dia-groundbreaking-contract-signed-at-russell-plant-in-honduras/. Accessed on 27 June 2013.
———. 2012. *3 Years After Signing Historic Agreement, Honduran Workers and Fruit of the Loom Lead the Way*. Available at: http://usas.org/2012/10/10/3-years-after-signing-of-historic-agreement-honduran-workers-and-fruit-of-the-loom-lead-the-way/. Accessed on 27 June 2013.
———. 2013. *About USAS*. Available at: http://usas.org/about/. Accessed on 16 September 2013.
US Congress. 2009. *Letter Addressed to Mr John B. Holland Chairman and CEO, Russell Corporation, May 13*. Available at: http://hare.house.gov/uploads/Russell%20Letter.pdf. Accessed on 23 November 2013.
USJD. 2011. 'Justice Department Will Not Challenge Worker Rights Consortium's Designated Suppliers Program for Collegiate Apparel.' Available at: http://www.justice.gov/opa/pr/2011/December/11-at-1656.html. Accessed on 13 October 2013.
Valdmanis, Richard. 2014. 'Nike CEO Says Could Shift China Production over Labor Strife'. *Reuters*. May 1.
Van Voss, Lex Heerma. 1988. 'The International Federation of Trade Unions and the Attempt to Maintain the Eight-Hour Working Day (1919–1929).' *Internationalism in the Labour Movement 1830–1940*, 518–542.
Vijayabhaskar, M. 2002. 'Garment Industry in India.' In *Garment Industry in South Asia: Rags to Riches: Competitiveness, Productivity and Job Quality in Post MFA Environment*, edited by Gopal Joshi. New Delhi: International Labour Organisation, SAAT.
Vogel, David. 2005. *The Market for Virtue: The Potential and Limits of Corporate Social Responsibility*. Brookings Institution Press.

Voss, Kim and Rachel Sherman. 2000. 'Breaking the Iron Law of Oligarchy: Union Revitalization in the American Labor Movement.' *American Journal of Sociology* 106(2): 303–349.

Wahl, Asbjorn. 2004. 'European Labor: The Ideological Legacy of the Social Pact.' *Monthly Review-New York* 55(8): 37–49.

Waldinger, Roger D., Chris Erickson, Ruth Milkman, Daniel Mitchell, Abel Valenzuela, Kent Wong, and Maurice Zeitlan. 1996. 'Helots No More: A Case Study of the Justice for Janitors Campaign in Los Angeles.' Available at: http://escholarship.org/uc/item/15z8f64h.pdf.

Walsh, Declan and Steven Greenhouse. 2012. 'Certified Safe, a Factory in Karachi Still Quickly Burned.' *New York Times*, December 7. Available at: http://www.nytimes.com/2012/12/08/world/asia/pakistan-factory-fire-shows-flaws-in-monitoring.html?pagewanted=all.

Wang, Xiaobing and Nick Weaver. 2013. 'Surplus Labour and Lewis Turning Points in China.' *Journal of Chinese Economic and Business Studies* 11(1): 1–12.

Webb, Sidney and Beatrice Potter Webb. 2010. *Industrial Democracy*. BiblioBazaar.

Weil, David. 1992. 'Building Safety: The Role of Construction Unions in the Enforcement of OSHA.' *Journal of Labour Research* 13(1): 121–132.

Weinstone, William. 1946. *The Case Against David Dublinsky*. New Century Publishers. Available at: https://www.marxists.org/subject/jewish/case-dubinsky.pdf.

Weishaar, Bridget. 2018. 'Margin Gains in Store for Hanes.' *Morning Star*. March 21.

Welz, Christian. 2011. 'A Qualitative Analysis of International Framework Agreements: Implementation and Impact.' In *Shaping Global Industrial Relations: The Impact of International Framework Agreements*, edited by Konstantinos Papadakis, 38–60. Palgrave Macmillan.

Whalen, Charles J. 2008. *New Directions in the Study of Work and Employment: Revitalizing Industrial Relations as an Academic Enterprise*. Edward Elgar Publishing.

Whalley, John and Shunming Zhang. 2007. 'A Numerical Simulation Analysis of (Hukou) Labour Mobility Restrictions in China.' *Journal of Development Economics* 83(2): 392–410.

White, B. J. and B. R. Montgomery. 1980. 'Corporate Codes of Conduct.' *California Management Review* 23(2): 80–87.

Wible, Brad, Jeffrey Mervis, and Nicholas S. Wigginton. 2014. 'Rethinking the Global Supply Chain.' *Science* 344(6188): 1100–1103.

Wick, I. 2009. *The Social Impact of the Liberalised World Market for Textiles and Clothing: Strategies of Trade Unions and Women's Organisations*. Frankfurtam Main: Otto Brenner Foundation.

WikiLeaks. 2009. 'Contentious Closing of Jerzees De Honduras Maquila.' Available at: http://www.wikileaks.org/plusd/cables/09TEGUCIGALPA158_a.html. Accessed on 22 December 2013.

Wills, Jane. 2002. 'Bargaining for the Space to Organise in the Global Economy: A Review of the Accor-IUF Trade Union Rights Agreement.' *Review of International Political Economy* 9(4): 675–700.

Winefsky, Holly and Julie Tenney. 2002. 'Preserving the Garment Industry Proviso: Protecting Acceptable Working Conditions Within the Apparel and Accessories Industries.' *Hofstra Law Review* 31(2). Available at: http://scholarlycommons.law.hofstra.edu/hlr/vol31/iss2/8.

Wolensky, Kenneth C., Nicole H. Wolensky, and Robert P. Wolensky. 2002. *Fighting for the Union Label: The Women's Garment Industry and the ILGWU in Pennsylvania.* Penn State Press.

Wolfson, Theresa. 1950. 'Role of the ILGWU in Stabilizing the Women's Garment Industry.' *ILR Review* 4(1): 33–24.

Woo, Jung-en. 1991. *Race to the Swift.* New York: Columbia University Press.

Wood, Ellen Meiksins. 2005. *Empire of Capital.* Verso.

Wooldridge, Adrian. 2016. 'The Rise of the Superstars.' *Economist*, September 17.

WRC. 2007. *WRC Assessment Re Jerzees Choloma. Report of Findings and Recommendations.* Washington DC.

——. 2008. *WRC Assessment Jerzees de Honduras.* Washington DC. Available at: http://depts.washington.edu/brandrp/cases/Jerzees/Jerzees%20de%20Honduras%2011-07-08.pdf. Accessed on 28 June 2013.

——. 2009. 'WRC Analysis of "Collective Pacts".' Washington DC: Workers' Rights Consortium.

——. 2013a. 'Global Wage Trends for Apparel Workers, 2001–2011.' Center for American Progress. Available at: http://www.americanprogress.org/issues/labour/report/2013/07/11/69255/global-wage-trends-for-apparel-workers-2001-2011/.

——. 2013b. *Serious Labour Rights Violations at SAE-A Tecnotex and EINS (Nicaragua).* Workers' Rights Consortium. Available at: http://www.workersrights.org/freports/WRC%20Memo%20to%20SAE-A%20re%20Tecnotex%20and%20EINS%2003-08-2013.pdf.

Wright, Erik Olin. 2000. 'Working-Class Power, Capitalist-Class Interests, and Class Compromise.' *American Journal of Sociology* 105(4): 957–1002.

WSJ. 2018. 'Berkshire Hathaway's Annual "Woodstock for Capitalists".' *The Wall Street Journal.* May 5.

Yan, Sophia. 2017. '"Made in China" isn't So Cheap Anymore, and That Could Spell Headache for Beijing.' *CNBC.*

Yang, Jae-Jin. 2006. 'Corporate Unionism and Labor Market Flexibility in South Korea.' *Journal of East Asian Studies* 6(2): 205–231.

Yardley, Jim. 2013. 'The Most Hated Bangladeshi, Toppled from a Shady Empire.' *New York Times*, April 30.

Yeung, Henry Wai-Chung. 1998. 'Capital, State and Space: Contesting the Borderless World.' *Transactions of the Institute of British Geographers* 23(3): 291–309.

——. 2000. 'Local Politics and Foreign Ventures in China's Transitional Economy: The Political Economy of Singaporean Investments in China.' *Political Geography* 19: 809–840.

——. 2004. *Chinese Capitalism in a Global Era: Towards Hybrid Capitalism.* London and New York: Routledge.

———. 2007. 'From Followers to Market Leaders: Asian Electronics Firms in the Global Economy.' *Asia Pacific Viewpoint* 48(1): 1–25.

———. 2014. 'Governing the Market in a Globalizing Era.' *Review of International Political Economy* 21(1): 70–101.

Yeung, Henry Wai-Chung and Neil Coe. 2015. 'Towards a Dynamic Theory of Global Production Networks.' *Economic Geography* 91(1): 29–58.

———. 2015. *Global Production Networks: Theorizing Economic Development in an Interconnected World.* Oxford: Oxford University Press.

Yiping, Huang and Fang Cai. 2015. *Debating the Lewis Turning Point in China.* Routledge.

Zhu, Shengjun and John Pickles. 2014. 'Bring In, Go Up, Go West, Go Out.' *Journal of Contemporary Asia* 44(1): 36–63.

Index

activist, 7, 17, 23, 24n8, 36, 37, 40, 41, 44, 49, 70, 79, 80, 92, 97, 98, 104, 105, 107, 112n19, 114, 116, 117n27, 120, 124, 140, 144, 145, 154, 155, 158, 164, 168, 206n1, 228, 230, 231, 232
Adidas, 3, 19n1, 39, 48, 80, 81, 89–91, 102, 106, 107, 109, 110, 114, 115, 117n27, 118, 123, 155, 162–4, 189
AFL-CIO Solidarity Center, 59, 70, 164n29, 165n31
Africa, 3, 17, 47, 200, 201, 203
All-China Federation of Trade Unions (ACFTU), 92–4, 98, 106, 107, 115
Anner, Mark, 5, 24, 35, 57, 60, 63, 76, 91, 117n27, 144, 153, 156n17, 158n20, 164n28, 165, 166, 193, 195, 206, 210, 223
anti-sweatshop movement, 6, 7, 10, 17, 53, 60, 68, 70, 81, 85, 145, 156, 156n17, 232
Apple, 25, 97, 100, 101, 114
arbitration process, 60, 81, 94
assembly, 20, 44–7, 51, 54n4, 90, 103, 136, 140, 147, 157, 161, 201, 222n3, 229
asset, 29, 140, 180, 184, 204, 210
  competitive, 137
  jettison, 145
  scarce, 185
  strategic, 50
  values, 183
associational power, 67, 161, 168, 206n1, 207, 210, 217, 220, 225, 227
auditing regime, 18, 53n2, 61, 76, 155, 167, 228, 230–2

austerity, 22, 174n1
authoritarian state, 91, 112, 117n27
automation, 36, 70, 129, 184, 189, 224
automotive industry, 191, 216
autonomous, 44, 80, 92
Awami League, 1

backbone shop, 133n13, 215, 232, 235
balance of power, 56, 178, 200, 211, 225, 234, 235
Bangladesh, 1, 48, 49, 76, 80, 91, 128, 129, 142, 152, 155, 165, 167, 201, 202, 229–2
  garment sector, 35n15
  industrial job growth in, 45
Bangladesh Accord on Fire and Building Safety 2013, 81, 167
bargaining power, 5, 9–11, 13, 20, 30, 32–34, 44, 46, 51, 75, 85, 90–2, 94, 113, 113n20, 116n25, 117, 118, 128, 139, 149, 152, 164, 176, 178, 187, 193, 196, 202, 207–14, 218, 221, 225, 227, 228, 231–5
barriers to entry, 10, 11, 27, 47, 50, 68n11, 113, 114, 117, 136, 142, 148, 178, 180, 183–5, 189, 193, 225, 233
  high-, 26
  significance of, 30
Beijing, 173, 174
Benetton, 1
Berkshire Hathaway, 145, 150, 158
BJ&B, 82n32, 155, 155n14, 156
boomerang model, 74
borders, 24n8, 33, 36, 44, 49, 53, 54n4, 56, 57, 67, 70, 74, 86, 106, 154, 223

268 | Index

bottleneck, 31–4, 67
bottom up, 69n12, 163, 209, 232, 235
bourgeoisie, 14
  -constrained market growth, 214
  domestic, 22, 25, 143
boycotts, 37, 43, 54, 62, 70, 82, 83, 120, 145, 153, 153n12, 158, 232
branding, 19, 136
Braverman, Harry, 101, 207
brokerage, 210
Buffett, Warren, 145, 158
bulk purchasing order, in Western clothing brands, 175
bullwhip effect, 147n5, 226

California, 5, 66,
Calvin Klein, 54, 54n4, 62, 67, 125, 152
capital, 5n4, 8, 9, 13, 21
  accumulation, 42, 46
  -biased technology, 127
  -centric approach, 32
  collective, 42
  comprador, 121
  controls, 57
  domestic, 24
  fixed, 27
  flight, 4, 23, 36, 54, 67, 85, 176, 203
  globalized, 3, 14, 22, 40, 56
  -holding firms, 47
  hypermobile, 55
  intensity, 151
  -intensive automobile industry, 118
  -intensive manufacturing, 62
  -intensive producer-driven' industries, 75
  -intensive research, 35n15
  -intensive technology, 126
  -intensive textile mills, 146
  investment, 10, 27, 31, 36, 65, 68n11, 102, 191, 192
  land-owning, 94
  -light manufacturing sectors, 116
  manufacturing, 22

  mobility, 36, 60, 68
  outflows, 156
  territorial dialectics of, 22
  transnational, 17, 24, 34, 44, 92, 101, 112, 143
capitalism's gravedigger, 12
capital–labour relations, 89, 101, 113, 211, 213, 214
cascading effect, 121
caste, 129, 221, 223
Central America, 3, 5, 8n7, 46, 54, 80, 83n33, 145, 146n4, 151, 152, 161, 163, 163n27, 168, 195, 200
Central American Free Trade Agreement (CAFTA), 145, 149, 157
centralities, 212, 213
centralization, 66n8, 181, 182, 187, 216
Central General de Trabajadores (CGT), 80, 81, 82n30, 157, 162–6, 168
chase the work, 54, 66, 215
Chibber, Vivek, 14, 25, 48
child labour, 12, 38, 98
Chinese Communist Party, 98, 175
Chinese law, 96, 98, 103
chokepoint, 138, 138n25
Choloma, 156, 157
circulation, 8, 121, 123, 138n25, 188, 209
civil society, 60, 85, 91
clandestine organizing method, 53, 54
class
  capitalists, 42
  compromise, 55, 55n5, 211
  conflict, 55, 219
  consciousness, 59
  cooperation, 52
    divisions due to capitalism, 58
    managerial, 204
    organization, 118
    struggle, 14, 57, 118, 219, 223, 225
Clean Clothes Campaign (NGO), 78
closure, 8, 46, 49, 111, 131, 137, 140, 145, 146, 155, 162n26, 167, 229, 232

Coalition of Cambodia Apparel Workers Democratic Union (C.CAWDU), 77–9
codes of conduct, 18, 36–9, 69, 70, 72, 79, 110n16, 154, 228
codifiability, 29, 30
Coe, Neil, 26, 27n12, 30, 32, 147n5, 148, 180, 183, 208, 212, 219
collective bargaining agreement (CBA), 18, 35, 56, 58, 62, 63, 66, 69, 70, 72, 73, 76–83, 146n4, 152, 153, 155, 157, 159, 161, 162, 165, 210, 215, 217
collective bargaining by riot, 93, 115, 215, 231
collective power, 208, 210
colonial, 204
  neo, 38
  post-, 121, 143
commodity-producer, 146–52, 156, 164, 168, 169
Communist International, 59
Communist Party, 98
Communist Party of India (Marxists), 224
competition, 7, 18, 20, 42, 46n21, 47n22, 67, 83, 100, 101, 121, 149, 169, 182, 184, 189, 190, 193n16, 194, 197, 198, 208, 209, 213, 214, 216, 217, 233, 235
  atomistic, 185
  battle of, 187
  capitalistic, 176
  for contracts, 164
  domestic, 202
  foreign, 147
  globalized, 11, 178–81
  imperfect, 177
  industrial, 56
  international, 250
  limited, 26
  national, 24
  transnational, 2
  workers, 175

component supplier, 26, 28˙
comprador, 101, 123, 137, 193n16, 233
  bourgeoisie, 143
  capital, 121
concentration, 8, 45, 47, 51, 90, 99, 120, 161, 181, 182, 184–8, 191n13, 195–200, 215, 216, 226
concessions, 42, 84, 89, 108, 111, 112, 210, 220
conditions, 5, 11–13, 17–19, 24, 29–31, 36–39, 41–4, 52, 55, 59, 60, 62–4, 67, 70, 73, 77, 79, 83, 98, 100, 101, 104, 106, 110, 115, 124, 146, 154, 156, 158, 165, 167, 168, 188, 205, 207, 209, 210, 214, 215, 217, 220, 225, 230, 233, 235
consolidation, 13, 34, 34n15, 46–8, 50, 84, 99, 101, 113, 113n21, 117, 122, 124, 143, 176–8, 182–9, 193, 196–202, 220, 224–6
constant capital, 36, 170, 179, 183, 184
consumer market, 48, 137, 142, 198
consumption, 6, 10, 18–20, 27, 31, 33, 34n15, 40, 43, 47, 68, 69, 84, 90, 93, 115, 117n27, 121, 124, 125, 129, 133, 136, 138n25, 139, 140, 174, 199, 205, 209, 211, 235
containerization, 35
core labour standards, 24, 35
corporate campaign, 38, 40, 72, 141
corporate social responsibility (CSR), 38, 73, 77, 110n16, 111n16, 154, 210
cost-capability ratio, 148, 168, 183
cotton, 19, 20, 36, 45, 74, 120, 125–7, 129, 135, 145–52, 156, 168, 169, 184, 215, 234
countervailing power, 44, 72
crisis, 9, 21, 23, 31, 44, 50, 99, 137, 188, 189, 203, 204, 215, 234
  economic crisis of 1970s, 22, 55, 198, 233
  financial crisis of 2007-08, 14, 17, 48, 145, 186, 200

crisis (*continued*)
  garment workers' rights, 34–41
  of profitability, 176–7, 198
  of social reproduction in China, 111
crisis of profitability, 137, 176, 177, 195
cut-make-trim (CMT), 20, 51, 199, 201, 221, 224

debt, 126, 203
decentralization, 66n8, 92
degree of coordination, 208
degree of monopsony power (DMP), 10, 11, 13, 30, 68, 149, 176–8, 183, 185–9, 192–7, 199–201, 205, 206n1, 207, 214, 216, 233, 235
degree of spatial inflexibility, 214, 229
deindustrialization, 36, 57, 59
demand side, 95
Deng Xiaoping, 174
denim, 1, 47, 120, 123, 125–8, 135, 136, 142, 146–9, 170
design, 13, 19, 20, 64, 103, 114, 127, 129, 196, 199, 201, 224
Dhaka (*see* Bangladesh)
dialectical, 209
  struggle, 14
  synthesis, 12
discipline, 5, 10, 30, 48, 92, 183, 188, 191, 207, 233
Disney, 2
distribution, 8, 20, 26, 27n12, 29, 30, 33, 45, 47n22, 48, 50, 51, 103, 108, 123–5, 128, 129, 136, 138n25, 139, 169, 176, 180, 185, 188, 191, 193n16, 209, 216, 217–23, 226, 227
diversify, 48, 123, 126, 127, 227
division of labour, 33, 188, 221, 223
domestic market, 46, 124, 191, 198
Dominguez, Reyna, 80, 156, 157, 158n19, 160, 163, 164
Dominican Republic, 54n4, 67–9, 80, 82n32, 149, 155, 195

Dominican Republic–Central America–United States Free Trade Agreement (DR-CAFTA), 149, 157
Dongguan, 49, 89n2, 105, 109, 110, 112
downward pressure, 6, 10, 11, 23, 43, 45, 68, 119, 139, 144, 177, 179, 181, 187, 188, 200, 233
dragon multinational, 175, 200

economic rents, 113
economies of scale, 11, 50, 99, 100, 121, 126, 137, 142, 169, 180, 183
El Paso, 54n4, 67
entry barriers, 169, 180, 185, 193, 199, 214, 216, 233, 235
European Union (EU), 75n17, 76, 194, 201
exogenous, 23, 187, 193n16, 208
exploitation, 7, 13, 14, 22, 24, 32, 35, 36, 39, 42, 181, 207, 211, 219, 220, 222, 226
export processing zones (EPZs), 73, 192
export-oriented industrialization, 22
externalities, 177

fabric, 49, 62, 67, 68n11, 120, 122, 129, 149, 168, 224
factory fires, 43, 110
factory occupations, 56
Fair Labour Association (FLA), 38, 154, 155
fair trade, 36, 38, 39
fast-fashion, 18, 44
female, 35n15, 166, 222
feminized/feminization, 18, 35, 221–3
finance, 11, 27, 48, 93, 140, 177, 185, 235
financial institution, overseas, 126
financialization, 183, 218
first-tier, 46
fixed capital, 27, 36, 94, 183, 187, 191, 226
fixes, 9, 233
  brutal organizational, 119
  new, 176, 177

spatial, 99, 153, 188, 195, 197, 204, 216
technological, 99, 100, 189, 193n15, 198
flexible, 58, 99, 109, 130, 138, 147, 149, 212, 213
foreign direct investment (FDI), 24, 122–4, 126, 128, 137, 150, 174, 175, 200, 201, 211
formal, 225
  collaboration, 215
  hierarchy, 28
  sector, 35n15
  transnationalism, 44
  union bureaucracies, 56
Foxconn, 25, 97, 100, 101, 114, 169, 196
Fraction of capital, 182, 192, 193n16
fragmentation, 10, 27, 52, 221
free trade zone, 54, 67–9, 155, 159
freedom of association, 38, 41, 42, 71, 73, 83n34, 160, 167, 220
Friedman, Eli, 57, 89–92, 100, 112, 116
full-package supplier, 28, 201
Fung, Archon, 84, 95, 124, 196
furniture, 27

Gaobu, 89, 105–7, 116
Gap, 3, 7n6, 26, 28, 48, 78, 125, 128, 137, 138, 147, 148, 200
garment district, 1, 4, 44, 54n4, 205
GDP, 91, 93, 94, 175, 202n18, 203
gender, 31n14, 112, 221–3
General Agreement on Tariffs and Trade (GATT), 40, 68
Gereffi, Gary, 5, 10, 18, 20, 26–32, 44–7, 50, 51n27, 75, 85, 99, 101, 115, 135, 136, 147, 148, 180, 185, 188, 193, 195–201, 208, 219–21, 232
giant firm, 100
Gildan, 150–2, 155n14, 160, 168
global commodity chains (GVCs), 9, 11, 12, 17, 25–33, 44, 48, 50, 51, 62, 79, 83, 89, 90, 101, 113–15, 121, 145–9, 156, 175–200, 204, 206n1, 207–11, 213, 216, 218–21, 225–7, 230, 232–5
global financial crisis, 48, 186
global framework agreements (GFAs), 36, 52, 56, 60, 70–9, 81, 84, 232
Global Justice Movement, 17, 84, 124
global justice movement, 7, 17, 84, 124
global production network, 25, 32, 148, 212
Global Union Federation (GUF), 34n15, 52, 53, 56, 58, 71–4, 75n17, 77, 79, 84, 167, 230
Gokaldas, 48
Goodwin, Richard, 218, 219
Gorz, Andre, 84, 93
governance structure, 28–30, 181, 190, 194, 209
GPN 2.0, 30
growth model, 93, 217, 218
Guangdong, 25, 89, 91, 99, 100, 108, 111, 112, 115, 118, 122, 174
Guess Jeans, 6

H&M, 72n15, 75n17, 76n19, 78, 110n15, 138
handloom, 127
Hanes, 128, 149–51, 155n14, 160, 168
hartal, 1, 1n1
Harvey, David, 5n4, 9, 21, 38, 41, 66n8, 100, 195, 203, 204, 214, 216
haute couture, 19n1, 68
Hermanson, Jeff, 5n5, 37, 49n24, 64, 69n12, 102n9, 146n4, 148, 150, 153, 161, 168, 169, 215
Hermosa factory shutdown, El Salvador, 70, 155, 162
Herod, Andy, 32, 44, 53, 53n3, 219
high-value, 27, 115, 117n27, 127, 139
Honduras, 12, 25, 26n9, 37, 69, 69n12, 80, 82n30, 144, 146–52, 156, 159–63, 165, 168–70, 232

Hong Kong, 49, 90n4, 100, 106, 107, 114, 126, 142, 174, 175
hot cargo clause, 83
hot shop, 8, 59, 70, 140, 161
Hukou system, 96
human rights, 92, 156n17, 206n1
   workers self-organization as, 41–4

ideology
   GUF, 79
   working-class, 55
ILO Decent Work Agenda, 209
immigrant, 43, 54n4
imperialism, 58, 165n30, 205, 223
   anti-, 204
   labour, 164
   ultra-, 22
   US monetary, 173
import substitution industrialization, 22
independent union, 98, 115, 116n25
Inditex, 76–9
Indonesia, 39, 45n20, 48, 80, 81, 82n32, 97, 100, 102, 103, 123, 162, 203, 220, 221, 232
industrial
   action, 54, 62, 70, 72, 81n30, 98, 113n20, 117, 164
   cluster, 34n15, 46, 161
   geography, 46, 115
   relations, 55–8, 60, 62, 64, 70, 71, 82n31, 85, 86, 209, 227
IndustriALL, 34n15, 52n1, 59, 70, 72n15, 76, 77n21, 78–80
inequality, 93, 96
informal, 35, 73
in-house, 18, 19, 29, 126, 129, 133, 138, 139, 148, 168, 169
input-price, 19, 127, 181
inside model, 55, 58, 59, 71–6, 84, 86
insourcing, 114
institutional transnationalism, 56, 59
integrated retailer, 28
internalization, 149–51

International Labour Organization (ILO), 38, 41, 42, 44, 52, 57, 71–4, 76, 80, 209, 219, 220
International Ladies' Garments Workers Union (ILGWU), 5, 6, 43, 53, 54, 61–70, 80–3, 133n13, 146n4, 149, 153, 154, 155n14, 161, 205, 211, 215, 235
International Union League for Brand Responsibility (IULBR), 64, 78, 80, 82, 83, 83n35, 105, 146n4, 160, 162
internationalism, 24n8, 42, 44, 49, 57
interstate worker, 130
investigators, 10, 98, 155
investor, 73, 106, 110, 114
Item 807

Japan, 58, 93, 94, 175, 191, 217
JC Penney, 48, 122n2, 158
jeans, 6, 13, 45, 54n4, 121, 126, 127n4, 135, 145, 147, 148, 234
Jerzees de Honduras (JDH), 144, 145, 156–8, 162–4, 166, 169, 170
Jerzees Nuevo Dia (JND), 144, 159–61
jobbers agreement, 5, 64, 81n28, 205, 235
just-in-time, 17, 18, 35, 44, 115, 227

Kalecki, Michal, 176, 185, 186, 192, 218
Kannada, 8–11, 120n1, 131
Karnataka, 8, 48, 121, 133, 135, 225
Korea, 37, 47, 48, 49n24, 82, 102n9, 142
Kukdong, 37, 69n12

labour
   activists, 107, 114, 120n1
   agency, 18, 32, 33, 50, 195
   bargaining power, 208–10
   bureau, 104
   -capital compromise, 76
   child, 12, 98
   conditions, 62
   confrontation, 53
   cost, 5, 10

dead, 184
demographics, 111
discipline, 10
force, 111
geography, 53n3
global arbitrage, 175
imperialism, 164
innovations, 53
-inputs fall, 183
intensity, 5
-intensive sectors, 50, 91, 123
law, 98
living, 184
market, 17, 33, 35n15, 39, 58, 59, 63, 98, 95, 96, 101, 138, 139, 161, 162, 175, 185, 187, 192, 211, 218, 220, 225, 235
mobilization, 57
monitors, 120n1
movement, 59
networks, 140
power, 83–6
process, 31, 32, 101, 135, 179, 210, 227
-rich, 11, 33, 45, 47, 50, 197, 198, 200, 216
salve, 77
-saving technology, 11
shortage, 5, 33, 66, 90, 94, 97, 98, 100, 111, 113, 115, 117, 202
unions, 69
unrest, 117
violations, 139
lead firm, 19, 27, 27n12, 28–31, 50, 148, 162, 176–8, 180, 181, 183, 188, 190, 192–4, 198, 199, 208, 213, 233
lean production, 150, 227
Lefebvre, Henri, 203
legally binding, 85
leverage, 38, 43, 72, 75, 79, 81, 83n34, 103, 114, 117n27, 118, 121, 140, 141, 143, 152–4, 157, 167n33, 174, 190, 208, 210, 224, 232, 235
Lewis Turning Point, 95, 95n5

Li, Shi, 95, 96, 107, 124, 196
liberalism
  embedded, 11, 174n2, 214
  neo-, 41, 69, 70, 73, 84, 91, 174n2, 198
liberalization, 10, 11, 48, 96, 122, 124, 187, 198, 215
light electronics, 27, 169
liquidated damages, 83, 83n34
lock
  -in, 114, 117, 136, 142, 174n1, 220, 221
  -out, 89n2
logistics harmonization, 35
London, 4, 44, 107, 126, 205, 221
long-term contract, 62, 83, 136, 209
lower end, 27, 103

Maastricht Treaty, 41, 58
Mahutga, Matthew, 30, 31, 180
management, 4, 8, 9, 25, 47, 56, 58, 64, 71, 72, 74, 76, 99, 105, 123, 126, 129, 131–5, 138, 150, 157, 160, 161, 163, 164, 166, 178, 183, 191, 196, 206, 220, 222, 224, 225
Mango, 1
Mao, 174, 175
maquila system, 45, 46, 67, 69, 153, 157
marketing, 19, 20, 28, 37, 39, 62, 70, 81n30, 128, 129, 136, 178, 179, 183, 191, 206
market reform, 92
market share, 113, 127, 136, 151, 169, 178, 180, 181, 183, 186, 187, 190, 193, 197
market spatial inflexibility, 229
markup, 175, 179n7, 180, 186, 192, 218
Marx, Karl, 1, 13n8, 14, 20, 40, 42, 97, 118, 176n4, 180–4, 198, 204, 207, 216, 226, 233, 234
material conditions, 13, 24, 210, 214
maternity, 77, 104, 221
mature firm, 216
maximized profit, 43, 179

274 | Index

mega-supplier, 84, 121, 199, 201, 213, 214, 227, 228
mergers and acquisitions (M&A), 100, 183, 186, 199
Merk, Jeroen, 20, 47, 90, 102, 103, 114, 123, 125, 175, 189, 197, 200–2, 220, 221
Mexico, 5, 6, 37, 45, 46, 54, 54n4, 67, 69n12, 82, 151, 195, 203, 217
Middle East, 8, 125, 128, 129, 136, 137, 200
middlemen, 46, 124, 125
Milberg, William, 26n10, 48, 101, 180, 192n14, 193
militant, 49, 55, 58, 75, 116, 143, 164, 225, 227
minimum wage, 39, 48n23, 93, 99, 103, 110, 135, 159, 160, 231
mobilization, 57, 72, 219
modular, 29, 66
   manufacturing, 150
   network, 192
monopoly, 25, 50, 51n27, 68, 90, 100, 101, 119, 138, 143, 148, 177, 178, 181, 182, 184–7, 192, 193, 218, 219, 224
monopsony, 10, 30, 31, 121, 149, 169, 185, 193, 232
   capital, 50n27
   capitalism, 187n12
   definition, 192
   economic, 67
   in GVC, 177, 178
   power, 180
Moody, Kim, 184, 186, 187, 198, 225, 226
Multi-Fibre Agreement (MFA), 4n3, 6, 10, 17, 20, 32, 45–7, 68, 85, 92, 98, 102n9, 121, 127, 136, 145, 149, 182, 189, 190, 194–8, 200, 215, 216, 229, 234, 235
multi-stakeholder, 85, 86
mutual dependence, 85, 100
Mysore, 8, 132, 140, 141, 222

National Labour Relations Act, 63
nationalism, working-class, 57
Nazmul Huda, 2, 231
neoclassical, 26n10, 32, 180, 187, 217–19, 232
network, 7, 25, 26, 28, 30, 32, 33, 46, 50, 68, 79, 81n30, 106, 122n2, 124, 129, 136, 137, 139, 140, 147, 148, 160, 163, 175, 185, 188, 191, 192, 208, 209, 211–13, 219, 220, 223–5, 227
network theory, 212
neutrality agreement, 145
Nike, 3, 26, 37, 37n18, 39, 48, 89, 90, 91, 102, 102n9, 103, 107, 109, 110, 114, 115, 118, 155, 162–4, 189, 200
Nixon, 173, 174
North American Free Trade Agreement (NAFTA)

oligopolies, 11, 26, 27, 85, 100, 121, 148, 176, 177, 180, 181, 185, 186, 188–91, 193, 197, 204, 213, 216, 233, 235
oligopsony, 177, 180, 181, 190, 207, 213
one child policy, 94
organic composition of capital, 8, 84, 176n4, 183, 184, 235
organizational fix, 9, 50, 91, 119, 187, 193, 193n16, 198, 204
organizing model, 8, 59–61, 74
Original Design Manufacturer/Original Equipment Manufacturer (ODM/OEM), 103, 114
output price, 192
outside model, 55, 58, 59
overflow shop, 133n13, 215
overtime, 79, 104, 132, 135, 226

participatory transnationalism, 56, 60
paternalism, 167
Pearl River Delta (PRD), 90, 98, 102, 108, 112, 202
perfect competition, 180

Phillips Van Heusen (PVH), 9, 37n18, 125, 128, 129, 136, 137, 143, 152, 153, 168
pickets, 107, 131, 132, 153, 154
  retail, 66
  secondary, 43
piece-rate, 77, 130
planned economy, 92
point of consumption, 20, 31, 125, 140
point of production, 2, 26, 31, 34, 119, 125, 129, 138n25, 139, 140, 200, 221, 227, 235
police, 4, 9, 25, 92, 101, 104, 105, 107, 117, 118, 131, 135, 142, 205, 215, 226, 232
post-Keynesian, 179n7, 192n14, 217, 219
post-MFA, 10, 11, 47, 121, 127, 194, 196, 197
Pou Chen, 101, 102, 109, 110, 118
power loom, 126, 127
pressing warehouse, 129, 133, 138, 139, 225
price pressure, 148n7, 194
Primark, 1
privatization, 22, 70
producer-retailer, transnational, 127–9
production process, 7, 20, 26, 28, 40, 46, 50, 75, 85, 101, 108, 137, 139, 142, 145, 146, 150, 152, 168, 180, 208, 210, 211
profit/profitability, 5, 11, 18, 20, 21, 23n6, 27, 31, 32, 35, 36, 41, 43, 45–7, 49, 69, 73, 80, 81n30, 82, 89, 94–6, 100, 102, 113n21, 114–17, 121, 126, 128, 134, 136, 137, 139, 153, 158, 168, 169, 175–82, 183n10, 184, 185, 187, 189, 190, 195, 198, 199, 202, 206, 207, 210, 211, 214, 217–19, 223, 232
proletarianization, 22, 35, 47, 97
protectionism, 36, 57, 215
protest, 2, 17, 37, 40, 49, 72, 80, 97, 100, 104, 107, 110, 116, 154, 156n17, 160, 206n1, 231

PT Kizone, 162, 164
purchasing power, 39, 40, 115, 122, 140

race to the bottom, 5, 10, 23, 36, 41, 44, 54, 55, 60, 92, 117, 156, 197, 228, 232, 233
racial
  equality, 43
  exacerbations of, 58
Ramnagara, 8, 25, 125, 129–31, 133–7, 139, 141, 143
Rana Plaza, 1–4, 43, 167, 167n33, 230–2
rank-and-file, 60, 73, 222n5
raw materials, 19, 26, 36, 45, 67, 93, 99, 103, 121, 142, 175, 198
real competition, 179
real estate, 48, 93, 203
real wage, 18, 34, 35, 46, 46n21, 52, 90, 203, 218
Reebok, 37, 39, 102, 103, 155
regulatory framework, 73, 210
regulatory spatial inflexibility, 11, 67, 215, 235
relational rent, 27n12, 117
relocation, 5, 31, 49, 59, 66, 109–11, 140, 191, 194, 221
reproduction, 96, 96n6, 97, 111–13, 195, 216, 222n3
reserve army of labour, 5, 49, 95, 97, 192
returns warehouse, 133, 138, 139, 225
Ricardo, 180
right to organize, 5, 43, 66
right to work, 5, 66, 149
right-to-work states, 5, 66, 149
River Rich, 77, 78
Robinson, Joan, 24, 176, 185, 192
rural, 92, 95, 96, 112, 135
Russell athletic, 37n18, 145, 150, 155, 158n22, 169

SAE-A, 48, 82
Savar Upsala, 1
Schumpeter, Joseph A., 180

Sears, 2, 66
seasonality, 18, 19, 120, 139, 144, 145, 147, 149, 169, 234
Seattle, 7, 37, 49
self-organization, 41–4, 222, 233
Selwyn, Ben, 26, 32, 101, 181, 209, 210, 214, 219, 220, 226, 227
severance package, 130
sewing machines, 2, 4, 36, 36n17, 68n11, 159, 160, 169, 229, 233
Shahi Exports, 48, 138, 141, 224
Shaikh, Anwar, 24, 179, 180, 181, 210, 218, 226
shareholder, 73, 158
Shenzhen, 91, 99, 111, 174
skilling, 33
slavery, 59, 149
Smith, Adam, 176
social clause amendment, 40
social
   dialogue, 55, 55n5, 58, 72, 73, 79, 84
   insurance, 103–6, 108, 111, 112, 116
   model, 52, 55, 58, 79
   movements, 17, 33, 42, 43, 49, 84
   reforms, 104, 233
   upgrading, 101, 209, 219–21
Sohel Rana, 1, 1n1, 2, 231
solidarity, 8n7, 37, 43, 44, 57, 85, 110, 117n27, 118, 209, 211, 220, 225, 234, 235
Solidarity Centre, 69n12, 164n29, 165n31
sourcing price (or source price), 10, 20, 21, 187
South China, 14, 33, 44, 89, 90, 94, 99, 102, 111, 112, 118, 202
Spatial Fix, 9, 31, 50, 91, 99, 100, 149, 153, 176, 187, 188, 195, 197, 199, 202–4, 214, 216
spatiality, 112
special economic zone (SEZ), 174, 175
specialization, 19, 46, 47n22, 138, 170
Sri Lanka, 48, 129, 142, 168, 201, 224
standardization of production, 28

starter, 13, 234
state intervention, 34, 56, 182
strategic alliances, 27n12, 148, 186
strikes, 1, 3, 12, 37, 44, 59, 62, 66, 67, 72, 78, 89–2, 94, 98, 102, 104, 107–16, 133, 139, 153, 164, 202, 205, 215, 225–7, 232
   general, 56
   Honda, 116n25
   illegal, 234
   sympathy, 73n16
   wildcat, 97, 116, 132, 141, 142, 210
   Yue Yuen (China), 99, 100, 103, 116–19, 221
structural power, 10, 67, 138, 156n17, 161, 168, 207, 210, 211, 213, 214, 216, 220, 223, 225, 227
subcontracted, 17–19, 27n11, 56, 64, 74, 81, 111, 139
subjective agency, 13, 25, 101, 156, 168, 207, 214
subsistence, 207, 233
   production, 97
   wage, 95
sunk cost, 169
supply-chain city, 122
supply side, 95, 203
supranational, 40, 41, 52, 73, 214
surplus labour, 19, 92, 96
symbiosis, 11, 47n22, 50, 115, 121, 138, 141, 143, 177, 188, 189
symbiotic steady state, 177, 188, 233

Taft-Hartley Act (1947), 5, 66
Taiwan, 47, 103, 105n10, 107, 175
Tarzeen, 2
Tata, 123, 191, 196
technological
   fix, 99, 189, 193
   upgrading, 33, 93, 115, 117, 126, 136, 169
Tehuacan, 6, 7, 7n6
TEKSIF, 76, 77, 80

temporality, 112
Tendency of the rate of profit to fall, 176n4, 184
textile mill, 122, 125, 146
the South, 5, 8, 37, 48, 66, 99, 121, 149, 174
Tilly, Charles, 23n7, 40, 57, 214, 215
time-space compression, 47, 227
top down, 38, 52, 66, 74, 79, 84, 86,101, 166, 199, 209
toys, 27, 111, 202, 231
trade agreements, 18, 36, 38, 40–2, 69, 149, 150, 214
trade union movement, 49, 57, 215
Transatlantic Trade Partnership (TPP), 118
Trans-Pacific Partnership (TPP), 168
transnational collective bargaining, 55–7, 72, 79
Triangle Shirtwaist Factory, 4, 43
turnaround time, 76, 103, 115, 118, 123n2, 142
turn-key supplier, 28

underemployed, 96
underlying logics, 42, 216
unemployment, 33, 63, 96, 104, 175, 211, 215, 218, 219
union density, 5, 18, 24, 34n15, 53, 59, 62, 64, 66, 67, 70, 131, 161, 210, 217, 225, 229
UNITE, 6–7, 8n7, 68–9, 145n3, 154, 156
UNITE HERE, 6, 7, 68
United Nations (UN), 41, 94
United Nations Industrial Development, 34n15
United Students Against Sweatshops (USAS), 80, 82, 145n3, 154–9, 162, 167, 167n33
universality, 211
universities, 39, 40n19, 82, 113n20, 145, 154–8, 162, 166, 167, 169, 189
UN Global Compact, 43

UN Guiding Principles on Business and Human Rights, 43, 44
urban/urbanization, 22, 126
  centres, 7
  migrants, 96
  spaces, 135
  union, 140
  wages, 95
US Tariff Code, 54n4, 67

valorization, 12, 13, 50, 53n3, 128, 199
value, 19, 20, 180, 184
  -added, 54n4, 90n3, 188, 220
  capture, 50n26, 83, 85, 113–15, 117, 119, 135–9, 220, 235
  chain, 4, 5, 7, 10, 11, 13, 18, 27, 29, 32, 33, 44, 47, 50, 60, 86, 90, 100, 117, 128, 142, 143, 147, 149, 151, 169, 176, 177, 182n10, 185, 187, 189–92, 193n16, 194, 199, 208, 211–14, 219, 221, 229, 232, 235, 236
  creation, 135–8
  distribution, 176, 178, 179, 209, 216
  enhancement, 116
  -laden employers, 25, 34
  share, 183, 197, 227, 233
  surplus, 203, 217
variable(s), 2, 24, 39, 77, 83, 138, 142, 176, 186, 192, 204, 220
  capital, 32, 36, 179, 183, 184, 207
  -chief, 182
  commodities, 151
  in cost function, 208
  elastic, 5
  and garment sector, 35
  untested, 84
vertical, 45, 46
  competition, 185
  disintegration, 17, 43, 62, 212
  expansion, 91, 135
  growth, 114
  integration, 28, 119, 124, 135, 136, 147, 149–53, 168, 169, 177, 213, 224, 233

vertical (*continued*)
  market, 190
  power asymmetry, 190
  relationship between buyers and producers, 216
  tug-and-pull, 208
vertically, 11, 46, 48, 103
  dis-integrated, 4, 12, 19, 27, 28, 53, 74, 90, 145, 164, 176, 179, 205, 215, 216, 232
  integrated, 29, 46, 55, 75, 118, 128, 145, 147, 148, 151, 152, 156, 161, 166, 168, 187, 191, 201, 223, 235, 236
  outsourced areas, 6
Volcker, Paul, 173, 187

wage share, 217–19
Wallerstein, Immanuel, 204
Walmart, 1, 2, 28, 48, 82, 98, 124, 150, 160, 169, 186n11
warehousing, 11, 20, 85, 124, 197, 200, 232
  in-house, 129
welfare state, 55, 57, 58, 85
  of late industrial capitalism, 23
  post-war, 69
  retrenchment, 218
  series of militant labour conflicts during Great Depression, 227
wholesaler, 62, 102
wildcat strike in 2016, Bangalore, 89, 97, 116, 132, 141, 210
Winkler, Deborah, 26n10, 180, 192n14, 193
women, 2, 4, 35n15, 37, 111, 125, 129, 135, 141, 147, 156, 157, 166, 206n1, 221–3, 229, 233
Workers United-SEIU, 6, 64, 68, 146n4
Workers' Rights Consortium (WRC), 8–10, 38, 145n3, 154, 155, 157, 167n33
workers' strategies, 8n7, 47, 51, 116, 124, 125
working class identity, 57
workplace organizing, 92
work-to-rule, 104
World Bank, 17, 23, 52, 101
world systems theory, 26
World Trade Organization (WTO), 18, 37, 40, 49, 194
  establishment of, 68
  process of neoliberal globalisation, 41
  social clause, 41
World War II, 5, 11, 57, 58, 66, 76, 79

Yeung, Henri, 24, 25, 27n12, 30, 175, 199, 208, 212

Zhejiang, 89, 99